THE
Spiritual Exercises
RECLAIMED

THE Spiritual Exercises RECLAIMED

2ND EDITION

UNCOVERING *Liberating Possibilities* FOR WOMEN

Elizabeth Liebert, SNJM, AND
Annemarie Paulin-Campbell

FOREWORD BY
Agbonkhianmeghe Orobator, SJ

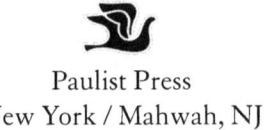

Paulist Press
New York / Mahwah, NJ

Prayer from Love: A Guide to Prayer by Jacqueline Syrup Bergen and Sr. Marie Schwan, CSJ, copyright © 2011, published by Loyola Press. Used with permission. Visit www.LoyolaPress.com for more information.

The Scripture quotations contained herein are from the New Revised Standard Version: Catholic Edition, Copyright © 1989 and 1993, by the Division of Christian Education of the National Council of the Churches of Christ in the United States of America. Used by permission. All rights reserved.

Cover and interior art created by Terry Mullen, S.N.J.M. Used by Permission of the artist. Cover and book design by Lynn Else

Copyright © 2022 by Elizabeth Liebert and Annemarie Paulin-Campbell

All rights reserved. No part of this publication may be reproduced, stored in a retrieval system, or transmitted in any form or by any means, electronic, mechanical, photocopying, recording, scanning, or otherwise, without either the prior written permission of the Publisher, or authorization through payment of the appropriate per-copy fee to the Copyright Clearance Center, Inc., www.copyright.com. Requests to the Publisher for permission should be addressed to the Permissions Department, Paulist Press, permissions @paulistpress.com.

Library of Congress Cataloging-in-Publication Data
Names: Liebert, Elizabeth, 1944- author. | Paulin-Campbell, Annemarie, author
Title: The spiritual exercises reclaimed : uncovering liberating possibilities for women / Elizabeth Liebert, SNJM, and Annemarie Paulin-Campbell ; foreword by Agbonkhianmeghe Orobator, SJ.
Other titles: Second edition.
Description: New York ; Mahwah, NJ : Paulist Press, [2022] | Includes bibliographical references and index. | Summary: "A companion to the Spiritual Exercises that does justice to women's experience across contexts and social locations while acknowledging obstacles that the Exercises hold for women in various contexts"—Provided by publisher.
Identifiers: LCCN 2021057249 (print) | LCCN 2021057250 (ebook) | ISBN 9780809155316 (paperback) | ISBN 9781587689277 (ebook)
Subjects: LCSH: Ignatius, of Loyola, Saint, 1491-1556. Exercitia spiritualia. | Catholic women—Religious life. | Spiritual exercises.
Classification: LCC BX2179.L8 L53 2022 (print) | LCC BX2179.L8 (ebook) | DDC 282.082—dc23/eng/20220128
LC record available at https://lccn.loc.gov/2021057249
LC ebook record available at https://lccn.loc.gov/2021057250

ISBN 978-0-8091-5531-6 (paperback)
ISBN 978-1-58768-927-7 (e-book)

Published by Paulist Press
997 Macarthur Boulevard
Mahwah, New Jersey 07430
www.paulistpress.com

Printed and bound in the
United States of America

To Katherine Marie Dyckman, SNJM, and Mary Garvin, SNJM, coauthors of the original edition, and to so many other women who pioneered giving the Spiritual Exercises in their diverse contexts

Contents

Foreword to the Second Edition ix
   Agbonkhianmeghe E. Orobator, SJ

Preface to the First Edition xiii

Preface to the Second Edition xix

PART I: CONTEXT 1

1. Reinterpreting the Spiritual Exercises: Problems
   and Possibilities 3

2. Remembering and Imagining: Wise Women
   Then and Now 19

PART II: MOVEMENT 39

3. Coming Together in Love: Processes and Relationships 41

4. Grounding in Truth: Principle and Foundation 68

5. Knowing Whose I Am: Prayer in the Spiritual Exercises 90

PART III: EXERCISES 123

6. Surrounded by Love: Exercises of the First Week 125

7. Who Do You Say That I Am? Exercises of the
   Second Week 148

8. Discovering the Depth of Commitment: Exercises of the
   Third Week 175

9. Mission and Mutuality: Exercises of the Fourth Week 189

PART IV: DECISION 205

10. Developing a Single Eye: Rules for Discernment of Spirits 207

11. Dancing toward the Light: Election 230

12. Black Appearing White: Rules for Thinking with the Church 255

APPENDIX—*AnyWoman*: An Imaginative Reappropriation of the
    Spiritual Exercises 277

NOTES 293

WORKS CITED 341

AUTHOR INDEX 353

Foreword to the Second Edition

The Spiritual Exercises of St. Ignatius of Loyola are a timeless gift to the church and a patrimony of Christian traditions of faith, and the wisdom, insights, and perspectives of women constitute an important key for unlocking their resources. The truth of this twin affirmation is evident in this revised edition of *The Spiritual Exercises Reclaimed: Uncovering Liberating Possibilities for Women*.

Like any literary or spiritual classic, the essence and value of the Spiritual Exercises appreciate with time. This aging process relies on creative and insightful curators, choreographers, interpreters, and midwives to uncover and nurture their timeless value. The authors of this revised volume can justly claim these designations for themselves. With profound insight and knowledge distilled from decades of experience as practitioners and scholars, they have made the Spiritual Exercises more widely accessible to a global, diverse, and inclusive demography.

Yet whether as a spiritual text, a prayer manual, or a personal diary, the Spiritual Exercises present particular and peculiar difficulties and challenges. Their historical, theological, and linguistic framework and preferences contain glaring evidence and offensive traces of sexism, patriarchy, and misogyny. For some people these are insurmountable problems. The genius of the original authors and the authors of this revised version lies in part in their ability to reclaim the Spiritual Exercises from the detritus of the antiquated, skewed, and distorted anthropology and terminology of the sixteenth-century European worldview and a cosmology propped up by an oppressive, militaristic, and domineering image of God.

The Spiritual Exercises have an end or a telos that neither manifests as a quietist piety nor exhausts itself in a self-referential devotion. The rich repertoire and combination of meditation and contemplation, reflection and pondering, aided by narratives of the gospel and carefully crafted images, help retreatants to achieve the end of the Spiritual Exercises in their particular context. This revised volume boldly underscores the centrality of a gendered experience and context of the Spiritual Exercises. In this sense, gender-sensitive perspectives rooted in social justice, equality, and a deep awareness of human dignity become critical junctures of (reinterpretation and discovery.

The preceding point should hardly surprise us. The Spiritual Exercises are about life. They are the outcome of the experience in life of spiritual pilgrim Íñigo. For this reason, the term *exercises* is inclusive of whatever activities, dispositions, or attitudes of a retreatant, each of which becomes a space of encounter between her and the Divine [1]. The desired transformation, conversion, and change occurs within, not outside of, the wide range or gamut of experiences and needs of those who enter into the path of the Spiritual Exercises. For this reason, integration, relationality, and connectedness become key guiding principles for making, giving, and interpreting the Spiritual Exercises. Due attention to the diversity and connectedness of the narratives, stories, contexts, and backgrounds of pilgrims makes for a richer experience of the Spiritual Exercises.

Honoring and integrating the situation-in-context of pilgrims of the Spiritual Exercises is a factor of their enduring and ongoing relevance. Rather than use the Spiritual Exercises as a blunt Neanderthal tool that neither changes nor adapts, irrespective of the context, this volume uncovers a wellspring of endless possibilities and opportunities, constantly renewed, refined, and adapted to meet the evolving needs of a contemporary generation. Over the years, the deepening of our understanding and application of the Spiritual Exercises has been enhanced by feminist epistemology, theology, psychology, and hermeneutics.

St. Ignatius of Loyola got away with what could have been a potentially fatal apocryphal redaction of the gospel when he created the plausible scenario of the risen Christ making a dawn visit to his grieving mother, Mary of Nazareth [219–20]. At the risk of sounding conspiratorial, I have often wondered about the hidden significance of this Ignatian pericope. The scene reveals the primary ministry of the risen Christ, who exercises the office of a consoler as friends do to one another [224]. Might there be a different way of seeing and reading this story? As I see it, this Ignatian apocrypha limns the unique capacity of women to contain mysteries interiorly beyond comprehension, like Mary who "treasured all these words and pondered them in her heart" (Luke 2:19), and the critical importance to listen to the insights that spring from such a depth of wisdom.

Foreword to the Second Edition

Over two decades ago, the original authors of this volume opened a path of new possibilities for women to encounter the Spiritual Exercises. Years later, the present authors draw upon a variety of hermeneutical and practical perspectives to widen, deepen, and extend this path. As newer monographs about women and the Spiritual Exercises of St. Ignatius of Loyola will show, they empower and embolden more women, from a variety of cultural backgrounds, faith traditions, and geographical locations to continue this enterprise of discovery to reclaim the gems of the Spiritual Exercises and create even more exciting, transformative, and liberating possibilities for women and men who study, make, or give the Spiritual Exercises.

Agbonkhianmeghe E. Orobator, SJ
President of the Jesuit Conference of Africa and Madagascar

Preface to the First Edition

Our work illuminates a centuries-old spiritual process that grew out of Ignatius of Loyola's spiritual experience and out of the pastoral experience he gleaned while working with women and men of his time. Over some years, Ignatius established a pattern of spiritual exercises that invited people into a profound experience of God and frequently evoked a deep conversion and a renewed sense of mission.

Eventually, Ignatius distilled this process into the text of the Spiritual Exercises so others might enter into their own dynamic spiritual transformation. As Ignatius intended, the Exercises have been adapted to a wide range of persons, time frames, theologies, and cultures. Insofar as these adaptations have addressed the spiritual situation of those entering into them, they have continued to speak deeply to human hearts and desires.

Our purpose, then, is to invite others into a direct experience of God, to create parameters within which radical transformation might occur through the action of the Holy Spirit. We examine this dynamic transformational process and illumine it in light of contemporary culture. The lens through which we focus our interpretation is the experience of women: women of the past, to understand their presence during the formative years of the Spiritual Exercises, but primarily women in the present, to invite their voices into the interpretive task. In so doing, we situate the Spiritual Exercises within our time so they might continue their transformative work in women and men engaged in today's world.

We write for various circles of people whose common bond is the Spiritual Exercises. We speak to those who are captured by the vision and spirit of the Spiritual Exercises and who seek to deepen their life and ministry in the midst of their everyday situations. We also write for those who passionately resist elements of the Spiritual Exercises or the ways they have been interpreted. We believe that in using women's experience as our hermeneutical key to understanding the dynamic of the Spiritual Exercises, we can address the situation of many contemporary women and men who seek radical spiritual transformation. Thus, while we begin with the text of the Spiritual Exercises, we continually try to illumine it in light of our experience as women and with women.

Even more significantly, we believe women are impoverished when their unique perspective remains invisible within some area of human discourse.[1] But men are also poorer when women's experience has been left out of the account. Indeed, the entire church is the poorer for losing the richness of women's experience and gifts, a poverty it can ill afford. Thus, while this work focuses attention on one of the significant renewal processes in the history of Christian spirituality, the implications of our work extend beyond the reinterpretation of this text to its underlying dynamic. This book is not primarily a textual criticism or a manual for giving the Spiritual Exercises. It springs from a desire to help redress an ancient imbalance and to open new perspectives on what it means to come "to the measure of the full stature of Christ" (Eph 4:13).

Three realities, then, continually interact in the work that follows: (1) the text of the Spiritual Exercises as we have received it, along with its history of interpretation; (2) our attempts to reconstruct the dynamic process evoked by the text, then and now, with all the challenges, frustrations, and "aha" experiences entailed in this hermeneutical endeavor; and (3) contemporary women's experience—that dynamic, ever-changing, and vast, yet largely untapped, reality. Contemporary women's experience provides the privileged perspective upon which we base our treatment of the text, but the text itself and its classical understanding ground and set limits on our interpretations. Fortunately, as we struggle to hold all these realities together, the text itself often opens up its meaning in surprising ways.

Organization and Conventions Employed in This Work

The discussion unfolds as follows. Chapter 1 lifts up the problems and possibilities that we find in the Spiritual Exercises and sets out the major interpretive perspectives we bring to the material. Some readers

Preface to the First Edition

may wish to skip this section and move directly to the next chapter or to part 2. Chapter 2 centers on the women surrounding Ignatius and the Spiritual Exercises during their early days. Here we attempt to address the problem expressed by so many women: "The Spiritual Exercises are so masculine in their origins and images." In fact, women have been present from the beginning, a perspective the standard histories have obscured. Because they were influential in the formulation of the Exercises, they can also influence contemporary interpretations.

Part 2 moves to the text of the Spiritual Exercises but focuses on the all-important processes by which one enters into them. Chapter 3 deals with the "who" of the Spiritual Exercises, the relationship of the persons involved and how they interact as the process unfolds. Scattered throughout the Spiritual Exercises we find various explanations, notes, and additional directives. Together these directives and explanations contain Ignatius's assumptions about the dispositions and conduct of both the person making the Exercises and the person guiding them. These process directions form the heart of the Spiritual Exercises. Chapter 4 deals with the "where," the Principle and Foundation. Here we examine the implications for interpreting the Spiritual Exercises from within a new cosmological paradigm, offering a liberating gesture to women. Chapter 5 lifts up the "how," the central activity of the Spiritual Exercises, prayer. It discusses the various forms of prayer that Ignatius recommends, some of which are embedded within the Exercises themselves and comprise an integral part of the experience (examen, meditation, contemplation, and Application of the Senses), as well as others Ignatius suggests as adaptations for various persons or situations (the Three Methods of Prayer and additional suggestions for prayer on the mysteries of the life of Christ).

With part 3, we shift the figure and ground, allowing the processes to recede to the background as we turn our attention to the content of the Spiritual Exercises. Chapters 6—9 treat material raised by each of the "Weeks," or dynamic movements of the Exercises. Each one builds upon the Week preceding it; in turn it is subsumed into the subsequent Week, forming an integrated process.

But the Spiritual Exercises is about more than inner conversion and personal holiness. Fruitfully entered into, the Spiritual Exercises issue in a spirituality actively engaged in the world. Part 4 treats those aspects of the Spiritual Exercises that undergird and enhance this outward direction toward mission. Chapter 10 addresses the wisdom Ignatius sets out for learning to distinguish the subtle inner clues about what leads to God and what does not; discernment of spirits provides us a "grammar" of personal and communal choices. Our choices intensify and focus our ordinary life in God, and chapter 11 explores Ignatius's method for carefully and prayerfully choosing in harmony with one's essential call. But Christian life is lived in community and particularly in that community called church. Chapter 12 addresses the often-painful issues raised by Ignatius's Rules for Thinking with the Church. Nothing less than a revisioned ecclesiology allows us to reclaim this final section of the Spiritual Exercises.

In the spirit of Ignatius's "repetition" and "Application of the Senses," we conclude by imaginatively reconstructing the dynamics of the Spiritual Exercises. The form, a contemporary morality play, *AnyWoman*, invites deeper reappropriation of the journey through the Spiritual Exercises and this book. It is best performed aloud by persons already immersed in the Exercises, utilizing the sensory images and objects elicited in the text. In our experience of exploring the possibilities in the Spiritual Exercises, this play has evoked new and creative ways of understanding and embodying them. Some readers may wish to begin with the drama as an imaginative introduction to the rest of the book. *AnyWoman* represents our constructive reimagining of the Spiritual Exercises.

The Spiritual Exercises make up the center of gravity of this work. Occasionally, when it helps us to illumine a point in the Exercises, we will range into other parts of Ignatius's corpus, usually his *Autobiography* and letters.[2] Ignatius wrote the text of Spiritual Exercises over a nineteen-year period. It was first published in Latin in 1548, twenty-six years after its inception.[3] We will generally follow George Ganss's translation (1991, 113–214, 387–432) based largely on the Autograph, the text Ignatius marked in his own hand.[4] It follows the paragraph numbering first employed by Marietti in the Spanish-Latin version of 1928; these citations will appear in square brackets. Thus, the reader may use any contemporary translation in tandem with this work.

Since the phrase "Spiritual Exercises" can refer both to a printed text and also to a process taking place over thirty days, more or less, some confusion may arise in differentiating the two. *Spiritual Exercises* will denote the text, "Spiritual Exercises" will denote the process or major dynamics within it, and "spiritual exercises" will denote a particular set of directions given by Ignatius. The distinctions, especially between the text and the process, frequently blur, making this convention somewhat arbitrary. When we mean to refer to both the text and the process at the same time, we will use the nonitalicized capitalized form, reserving the italicized form for references to Ignatius's book itself. Since we believe that the transformative process lies embedded within the text but is not simply coterminous with the content of the exercises, we generally refer to both the process and content with the term "Spiritual Exercises."

We employ two levels of citations throughout the volume. Those sources upon which we rely directly as we develop the discussion appear in parentheses within the text itself in the author-date-page style. The full bibliographical information for these citations appears in the works cited. Occasional digressions, elaborations, nuances, or caveats and further bibliographic resources appear in notes at the conclusion of the chapter. When these notes refer to sources that do not otherwise appear in the body of our text (and therefore not in the works cited at the conclusion of the book), we include full reference information in the note. These notes, therefore, serve as a kind of bibliographic essay that, together with the works cited, points to the various literatures undergirding this book.

The Spiritual Exercises are a rich and multilayered interpenetration of content and process. It proved impossible to treat all the options that opened up to us as we reflected, consulted, and discussed this spiritual classic. We have attempted to address those most salient to North American women. Our organization may appear somewhat arbitrary, but it emerged as we worked and prayed with the implications of the material. Therefore, we encourage you, our readers, to work systematically through the text with a copy of the Exercises in hand. We hope that at the conclusion of the volume you will have thought about the Spiritual Exercises in a new way and have posed many other questions to yourself and to the text.

Preface to the Second Edition

Since the publication of *The Spiritual Exercises Reclaimed: Uncovering Liberating Possibilities for Women* over twenty years ago, the situation of women engaged with the Spiritual Exercises has changed significantly. Two more generations of women have been exposed to the Spiritual Exercises in various forms. Each year, more women are engaged in directing the Exercises. Yet, surprisingly, our original work has not been replaced or even substantially expanded by newer treatments.

In a very real sense, the prophecy implied by the original title has been accomplished in many parts of the world. As the gains of the feminist movement have consolidated and as more women have been offered the Exercises in life-giving ways, many women have been able to claim the graces of the Exercises and make them their own. In many settings, a greater sensitivity to the importance of adaptation has largely addressed prior difficulties such as difficult wording, militaristic imagery, and the struggles some women felt in relating to Jesus as a man. For women with this kind of graced experience, the Spiritual Exercises have become a key tool for recognizing that the horizon can be expanded and that the Exercises, authentically made, are a source of liberating grace. Yet there is still more to do. Little has surfaced about how women in a variety of cultures might access the Exercises. In many contexts, it is still almost unheard of for women, and especially laywomen, to give the Exercises. On the other hand, in other contexts, more women than men now make and give the Exercises. How are the interpretations of Exercises changing in response to these realities? This new edition seeks to encourage these conversations and to invite women around the world into the process of reclaiming the Spiritual Exercises anew for this moment.[1]

Two of the original coauthors, Katherine Marie Dyckman, SNJM, and Mary Garvin, SNJM, are now engaged directly with their Creator and Lord. Were they still living, they would heartily endorse this revision; they would be the first to acknowledge that the world of women and the Exercises has significantly expanded beyond what the three original coauthors could imagine in the late 1990s when immersed in creating the original text. A new collaborator, Annemarie Paulin-Campbell, PhD, has joined Elizabeth Liebert, SNJM, to form the team responsible for this revision. In this new collaboration, we have sought to include greater breadth of experience from a much wider pool of women from various places in the world.

Paulin-Campbell is currently Head of School of Spirituality of the Jesuit Institute South Africa. In addition to her own experience of giving the Exercises primarily in South Africa, but also at St. Beuno's Spirituality Centre in North Wales, she has trained and supervised givers of the Spiritual Exercises in the South African context for more than twenty years.

Among those who saw the need for this revision from their European context and who engaged in valuable dialogue with us in the initial stages of the project are Carla Dias Rebelo and Isabel Diaz Nunez. Both women have worked extensively with the Spiritual Exercises in Christian Life Communities in Spain and Portugal, where there have also been significant shifts regarding women's involvement in the giving of the Exercises during the past twenty years.

Both authors of this edition regularly listen to the experience of women and the Exercises in their respective contexts. Their understandings and insights appear throughout the present edition. The voices of Paulin-Campbell's research subjects, twenty-two women from South Africa of various ages and life contexts, emerge vividly from the page as they speak about their experience of the Spiritual Exercises. Collectively, they demonstrate that shifts in image of self and image of God are facilitated by the imaginal and dialogical/relational processes in the Spiritual Exercises, with the women coming to see themselves as intrinsically valuable and unconditionally loved by God. Gospel contemplation (the use of the imagination to enter into gospel events), colloquy, and the relationship with the one who gave the Exercises proved to be the most salient factors in facilitating these key shifts, as was the dynamic of asking for what one desires. These women's experiences appear throughout this revision.

The expanded perspectives that guide this revision also include the key conclusions from the research conducted by Julia Dowd, whose research reports on experiences of the Spiritual Exercises by women faculty, staff, and administrators at Jesuit Universities in North America

(Dowd 2018). By applying a feminist hermeneutical lens to the narratives she collected, she discovered that many women through the Exercises had prayer experiences that challenged the traditional symbols and theology of their faith. Six theological themes emerged from Dowd's interviews: (1) Mary, (2) self-worth, (3) imago Dei, (4) the mystery of calling, (5) crucifixion, and (6) the beloved community. Through the Exercises, these women discovered Mary, Jesus, and God as liberating characters and forces that oppose and challenge traditional justifications of women's subordinate position in clerical and patriarchal systems. Dowd demonstrates that the Spiritual Exercises have the potential to open new pathways for partnership between Jesuits and women that can move Jesuit ministries into deeper engagement with social justice.

In the almost two decades since the original edition, numerous adaptations and applications[2] of the Spiritual Exercises have appeared.[3] Many of these insights, adaptations, and adjustments appear in the endnotes to this edition. We encourage you to check the notes frequently, because, as in the first edition, the notes form a (now updated and expanded) bibliography that covers the topics we treat in this work. Authors whose work we cited appear in the parenthetical references in the text, with complete information in the (likewise expanded) "Works Cited" at the conclusion of the volume.

At a more basic level, however, the current authors retain the hermeneutical lens of the original authors upon which the interpretation of the Exercises rests, with the addition of some more current insights. Chief among these new hermeneutic lenses is the notion of intersectionality. Intersectionality points to the interconnected nature of social categorizations such as race, class, gender, as they overlap and influence one another and result in complex and interdependent systems of discrimination and disadvantage. Depending on what the interlocutor sees as key, one might be looking at the interaction among race, education, sexuality, ability, age, class, language, culture, ethnicity, gender, religion, citizenship, and so on. Intersectional feminism tries to identify how different social and political discriminations overlap with gender (Liebert 2019a; Kim and Shaw 2018).[4]

Taking intersectionality seriously means that, just as the experiences of men cannot serve as the norm for experiences of women, neither can the experiences of North American, white, Roman Catholic women religious (the social location of the original authors) serve as the single lens on the experiences of women. Where we have access to the stories and experiences of women from a variety of backgrounds, we include their voices in this edition. Much of this data is still lacking, however, awaiting further research. We hope this new edition encourages such research by and about women's experiences of the Spiritual Exercises around the world.

It also seems useful to specify principles of adaptation to guide readers on their way through the variety of resources found today, even if few of these resources deal specifically with women's experiences of the Exercises. Erin M. Cline's recent study about the possibilities and limits of sharing the Spiritual Exercises across faith traditions offers a useful platform both for offering such guidelines and for beginning this current revision (Cline 2018, 74–111). Because of the delicacy and difficulty of her project, Cline carefully delineates both general principles of adaptation and then principles that can assist with retreatants coming from East Asian religious traditions. Cline's general principles of adaptation apply beyond working with interfaith retreatants and have provided us with general guidelines for adapting the Spiritual Exercises for contemporary Christian women. Chief among these general principles we find the following particularly useful for our purposes:

- Seek to remove any stumbling block that prevents the retreatant from entering into the retreat. Given Ignatius's initial directives for making the Exercises profitably (particularly Annotations 15, and 18–20), Ignatius clearly encourages the director to just this kind of commitment. Ignatius provides a very broad set of exercises that he regularly offered women and men who were not (at least not yet) ready to make the full Exercises in either the enclosed (Annotation 20) or nonenclosed (Annotation 19) versions. Indeed, this directive provides the single most relevant principle guiding this work.
- Update the historical and culturally anachronistic aspects of the Exercises. This task, particularly with respect to gendered communication and reception, pervades the revision. The delicate balancing act, however, comes both in the principle of selection (Is this point necessary in the dynamic of the Exercises?) and in the degree of adaptation (Does the proposed adaptation actually obliterate the intent or essential movement of this Exercise, or does it make it accessible in a way that the original text no longer does?) The line between appropriate adaptation and essential dynamics is frequently both highly subjective and subtle to discern.

- Adapt as lightly as possible for each individual, maintaining a mean between challenge and adaptation. It is not only possible but often tempting to adapt away a particular growth point. Just because a retreatant does not have any devotion to Mary, for example, does that mean that the Triple Colloquy should be rewritten to omit the colloquy with Mary? Is it better to support the retreatant in her attempt to form a relationship with Mary through the Exercises? How might a director assist?
- Use discernment about what and how much is adapted. Every adaptation, no matter its size, should flow from discernment: Does this shift assist this person to meet and deepen her relationship with her Creator and Lord? To deepen her discipleship? To desire spiritual freedom? To examine her deepest desires for how they might speak to her of God's desire for her? To choose a path of greater discipleship?
- Add supplemental resources as helpful for bridging from the experience of the one making the Exercises to the more foreign aspects of the Exercises. This principle, as the others, is highly subjective. What additional reading might make entering into a given part of the Exercises more possible or more productive? Finding these resources can be a mutual investigation.

Cline's final general principle applies directly to her project of adapting the Exercises across religious traditions. It requires a little more creativity to apply to our task of providing a gender-based application of the Exercises. She encourages her readers to engage in careful comparative work with the tradition of the retreatant to set the stage for any adaptation. Our "comparative" work will occur not across religions, but via immersion in current feminist scholarship and the experience of women from a variety of contexts. Such comparative immersion does, in fact, help us create appropriate bridges that women can use to cross fruitfully into the world of the Spiritual Exercises.

As we looked back at the variety of readers of the original version, three distinct but overlapping audiences emerge:

- Women who make the Exercises. You are the primary reason we write. Though you may not be the primary readers of this book, you are always our primary audience. How can we hear your experiences of the Exercises? How can we magnify your voices? How can the interpretation of the Exercises be influenced by the way God's grace works in you as you make the Exercises? You may find this book useful during your experience of the Exercises, but more likely it will be useful after you complete them and seek to deepen your experience of the graces you encountered.

- Women and men who give the Spiritual Exercises. We hope that you will be able to use this work to deepen your understanding of the perspectives, issues, and particular moments of grace for the women you direct through the Exercises, and so serve them better as you accompany them. We hope it challenges you at points to rethink your assumptions and your practices.
- Scholars studying Ignatian Spirituality, including Jesuits; lay and religious men and women and members of the Christian Life Communities. We have updated the notes throughout the text to aid you in expanding your knowledge of the Spiritual Exercises, and the dynamic tradition that has grown from them.

We welcome you, all of you, to this revised edition of *The Spiritual Exercises Reclaimed: Uncovering Liberating Possibilities for Women*.

Part I
CONTEXT

CHAPTER I

Reinterpreting the Spiritual Exercises

Problems and Possibilities

The *Spiritual Exercises* carry surprisingly liberating possibilities for women. The first persons to experience the Exercises were the women surrounding Ignatius, particularly at Manresa and Salamanca. The experience of these women guided Ignatius as he learned and developed the Exercises. The Spiritual Exercises continue to serve as a potent vehicle for numerous contemporary women to experience deep grace, spiritual freedom, and energy for ministry. Many contemporary women also give the Spiritual Exercises to both women and men and teach Ignatian spirituality alongside Jesuits. This book aims to uncover liberating possibilities, especially for women, throughout the text of the Exercises and its contemporary expressions. Our hope is that even more women can experience freedom and grace through the Spiritual Exercises.

This history, however, does not erase the difficulties many women have had with Ignatian spirituality and the Spiritual Exercises, either in their content or in the way they have been interpreted and presented. Ignatius was a person steeped in the culture of his time with its deep-seated patriarchy—how could he not be?—and it clings to his writings even today. To move past these difficulties, it will help to enumerate the chief ones.

Some are put off by the symbolism embedded in the text of the *Spiritual Exercises*, finding it at least uncongenial if not almost deadly to their spirits. Still others question Ignatius's unswerving obedience to the church, an institution that has been singularly destructive of women's full personhood at times in its history. The centrality of Christ in the *Spiritual Exercises* raises for others another cluster of reservations. These women wonder how they can ever become autonomous spiritual persons if they "access" God exclusively through a male savior.[1] The image of God and the image of self can be negatively impacted when what is considered normative is predominately male. How can the pivotal place of Christ in the Spiritual Exercises lead, not to further oppression of women, but to their liberation?

In the twenty years since this book was first published, and especially in the last few years, we have grown in our awareness about how Christian spirituality itself, in the way it is often practiced, can be oppressive to women. Given that the Exercises are at their heart about spiritual freedom, it is more critical than ever to attend to how they can be given in ways that are liberating for women.

We now live in a cultural climate in which, for example, the #MeToo movement has highlighted the widespread sexual abuse of women and has begun to publicly call it out as unacceptable. The Black Lives Matter movement underlines the double and triple jeopardy under which black and brown women in the United States labor, day in and day out. In some parts of the world women religious have been speaking out against sexual abuse by clergy, especially in India and in some African countries. How do such experiences impact the way these women come to the Spiritual Exercises?[2]

Possibilities for Women Today

Despite these significant difficulties, beneath the sometimes-repugnant symbolism, Ignatius's embeddedness in his culture, and women's struggles with an oppressive church structure, there lies a core of liberating possibilities for women in the *Spiritual Exercises* and in the spirituality flowing from them. Our experience suggests that spirituality based in the *Spiritual Exercises* can offer contemporary women numerous important values: (1) the value of the human experience of God shared with another or in a trusted small group; (2) the value of a spirituality of the whole person; (3) the value of a spirituality grounded in Scripture;

(4) the value of prayer in life, of contemplation in action; and (5) the value of adaptability and flexibility as signs of authentic spirituality.

The Experience of God Shared with Another

Each phrase, *experience of God* as well as *shared with another*, is important. Experience, says theologian Thomas Clarke, has to do with the *perception* of reality, with *receptiveness* toward the real in all its dimensions. Building up an authentic spiritual consciousness in any individual or community requires paying attention. Since spiritual consciousness is the raw material of spirituality, the first and most basic moment of spiritual accompaniment happens in the act of attending to the experience of God (Clarke 1983, 20, 22).

Yet women's unique spiritual experience has remained largely invisible, both to men and, more significantly, to women themselves. This invisibility has critical repercussions, as author Carol Christ notes:

> Women's stories have not been told. And without stories there is no articulation of experience. Without stories a woman is lost when she comes to make the important decisions of her life. She does not learn to value her struggles, to celebrate her strengths, to comprehend her pain. Without stories she cannot understand herself. Without stories she is alienated from those deeper experiences of self and world that have been called spiritual or religious. She is closed in silence. The expression of women's spiritual quest is integrally related to the telling of women's stories. If women's stories are not told, the depth of women's souls will not be known. (1980, 1)

Carol Christ uses the word *story* to include all articulations of experience that have a narrative element, including fiction, poetry, song, autobiography, biography, and even simple talk between friends. In this extended sense, story implicates *all* women to some degree. Stories shape lives. Without authentic stories, women lack imaginative possibilities to try out in their own lives. Certain religious stories provide orientation to sources of ultimate meaning, and many other seemingly mundane stories also have a sacred meaning that grounds one's existence in ultimates. Distancing women from their own experiences and from their history as women essentially denies them authentic spiritual consciousness. Thus, the basis for all spiritual care of women lies in effectively attending to women's experience through their stories (Christ 1980, 1–4). If this reality is true in North America, it is even more essential for attending to women's experience in communal cultures such as found in Africa and Asia.

Such attending forms the substance of the relationship between the one guiding the Spiritual Exercises and the one making them. In the context of the Spiritual Exercises, each person *listens* to her own experience in all its aspects, not just in areas she would name as religious. Attentive listening to one's experience is by no means automatic; many women must learn this skill.[3] Next, she *names* these experiences and gives them life outside herself. Simultaneously, she receives validation that her experiences are not idiosyncratic, but that she belongs to a community of shared experience and articulates one unique aspect of it.

This attending to experience applies both to the one giving the Exercises and the one making them. Both need to ground themselves in their own experiences to grow in authentic spiritual consciousness. The companion has the additional task of attending to the seeker's experience; indeed, the very quality of the companion's attending facilitates the seeker's attending. This mutual honoring of experience underlies the dynamic of the Spiritual Exercises. When it does occur, women's spiritual lives can flourish.

The Spiritual Exercises also provide a context where God deals directly with each person. If the one giving the Exercises is skilled enough to follow Ignatius's directives [2, 6, 15 and 18, for example], she or he will not dilute or distract from the relationship between God and the one making the Exercises. On the contrary, the one giving the Exercises will provide a safe and welcoming context in which the seeker can notice, name, clarify, appropriate, and act upon these direct experiences of God. This context and process can be extremely beneficial to women, estranged as many have been from their own spiritual experience; each one's experience is honored as a locus of God's action.

A Spirituality of the Whole Person

The Spiritual Exercises focus spiritual experiences and themes central to a Christian spiritual quest, allowing the seeker to find a way forward.[4] These themes are also basic to the *human* spiritual quest, pointing to issues that all spiritual seekers must address in some fashion. The Spiritual

Exercises, except when overly reified (and they have been, in many women's experience), provide wide latitude for individual women to come to grips with these issues in their own time and style. Furthermore, many women struggle with taking responsibility for their own lives;[5] the Spiritual Exercises encourage them to seek the healing and maturity they need to act as responsible agents in their dealings with God, others, and themselves. The Spiritual Exercises and the spirituality flowing from them provide one means to spiritual maturity, a means readily accessible to many women.

Although many commonly assume that the Spiritual Exercises are highly rational and "left brain," they evoke a far more holistic range of competencies. "Ignatian contemplation" involves rich use of the imagination, and a wide range of affects plays a crucial part in the experience of the Exercises. Memory undergirds the examen, a prayer form Ignatius thought so significant in the development of a continually discerning spirit that he never speaks of omitting it in favor of a greater good (Aschenbrenner 1972, 21; Liebert 2019b). Data gleaned through the senses grounds the repetitions Ignatius encourages, simplifying, focusing, and embodying material generated in meditations and contemplations. Repeated prayers, formal and spontaneous vocal prayer, spiritual reading, and reflections on the essentials of the Christian faith all find their place on the palette of spiritual exercises. Any and all may be used, their selection and timing based upon the needs of the individual. Ignatius states his goal explicitly: that persons "may become better able to profit from the exercises and to find their prayer a pleasing experience" [238]. Insisting on a single prayer style for all is definitely not Ignatian.

Furthermore, Ignatius directs the one giving the Exercises to pay great attention to the physical context in which they are received. Light and dark, eating and drinking, praying and sleeping, conversing and silence, standing, sitting, kneeling, lying down, the press of business or family affairs—all these should be adapted to the person's situation and the content of the Exercises. The Spiritual Exercises take embodiment with great seriousness. Ignatius understood the vital importance of a holistic approach hundreds of years before it became a popular concept.

A Spirituality Grounded in Scripture

The Christian Scriptures grew out of the spiritualities of the earliest Christian communities. Christians believe the Bible has a privileged position.

It contains the essential record of God's revelation to humankind and nourishes a rich variety of spiritualities. In turn, the continuous work of biblical interpretation occurs within a variety of spiritual contexts. Spirituality and biblical text, then, exist in a complex interrelationship.

Unfortunately, the Bible as it has been interpreted has not proven an altogether liberating text for women.[6] However, a growing body of feminist biblical interpretation has laid the groundwork for a biblical appropriation more friendly to women than that offered them throughout most of the church's history. Such woman-sensitive appropriation of Scripture opens to women the full power of this privileged avenue of God's revelation.

The genius of the Spiritual Exercises lies in bringing persons face-to-face with the biblical story, trusting that the Holy Spirit will reveal God through the contemplation of the biblical mysteries, primarily the person and work of Jesus Christ. The resulting encounters may not be particularly easy, yet the process respects each woman's attempt to live out of an authentic and liberating spirituality.

Prayer in Life, Contemplation in Action

In contrast to the notion that holiness requires a life of solitude, silence, and withdrawal from the world, Ignatian spirituality offers the possibility of experiencing God *in* one's daily life. Because of the complexity of modern life, women's situation today, regardless of lifestyle, differs radically from the sixteenth century. Many serve as the sole caregivers for spouse, children, and parents. An increasing number find themselves working double shifts, one at paid work outside the home, and another attending to a never-ending round of domestic duties. Many of these women feel like second-class Christians, with "the Christian life" reserved for professional religious persons who have a special call and the leisure to pursue holiness.

In fact, the spirituality that flows from the *Spiritual Exercises* suits Christians of any lifestyle, for it invites them to understand the call amid their own lives. Indeed, Ignatius conceived the *Spiritual Exercises* and completed most of the revisions as a layperson, prior to his ordination and the founding of the Society of Jesus. Ignatian spirituality can offer a viable spiritual path to contemporary women immersed in even the most repetitious or secular-appearing activities by encouraging each person to determine the pattern of life realistically possible given her actual circumstances.

Adaptability and Flexibility as Signs of Authentic Spirituality

Indispensable to the Spiritual Exercises is the principle of adaptation.[7] Individual persons and circumstances dictate a range of decisions about giving the Exercises. In the Eighteenth Annotation (preliminary consideration), Ignatius suggests choosing the basic form, length, and set of exercises to respect the "disposition of the persons who desire to make them, that is, to their age, education and ability." This preliminary consideration, together with the Nineteenth and Twentieth Annotations, spawned numerous versions of the Spiritual Exercises in the years following Ignatius. After studying the early Directories, or sets of directions on giving the Spiritual Exercises, Michael Ivens (1983, 4) concludes that virtually no age group, no social or religious category, no level of spiritual or educational attainment seems excluded on principle from the classifications in the Directories.

In addition to these large-scale adaptations, Ignatius sprinkles directions throughout the text for the one giving the Exercises to adjust the various exercises to situations and needs. For example, Ignatius instructs the Exercises guide to "adapt to the needs of the person," to do so "in accord with the person's greater or lesser progress," and that "the norm is the help found by the exercitant" [72]. When those giving the Exercises adapt them to each individual, women will find their unique personalities, desires, and competencies informing their experience of the Exercises. Such personal adaptation encourages women to take their own unique needs and desires seriously. The Spiritual Exercises can enable women to come home to themselves.

The Spiritual Exercises have always been adapted both to the persons making them and to the changes in the sociocultural context in which they are presented. For example, versions of the Exercises have taken root in inner-city Glasgow among persons with little formal education, as well as with Protestants, Jews, Buddhists, Confucians, and Taoists,[8] and inculturated to be offered in the townships of South Africa and in Latin America.[9] The rising self-consciousness of contemporary women makes up an entirely new cultural context, which, in turn, requires a fresh appropriation of the Spiritual Exercises.

So what does contemporary women's experience tell us about the usefulness of the Spiritual Exercises and about helpful ways to understand and interpret the Exercises? These are important questions, both for the women themselves and for those who direct others through the Spiritual Exercises.

Context

Meaning Making: Principles of Interpretation

Several interpretive strategies undergird our approach. We rely on a particular hermeneutical perspective in dealing with the text of the *Spiritual Exercises*, on feminist interpretation with respect to the seriousness with which we wish to take women's experience, and on certain epistemological perspectives in defining the nature of the questions asked and the possibility of arriving at some answers.

The Interpretation of the Text

An approach to a classic text[10] from the Christian spiritual tradition necessarily involves several levels of interpretation: the exegetical, the critical, and the hermeneutical. The most basic involves the exegetical task of determining the language, thought patterns, and intended meaning of the author within the culture of the time. The task of extensive reconstruction of the language patterns and thought world of Ignatius lies outside the scope of this work. Instead, this book relies on contemporary translations and extensive reconstructions of Ignatian thought published and critiqued in recent years. It is more than expediency that determines this strategy, however. This body of received interpretation informs the experience of the Spiritual Exercises as contemporary women meet them—the text comes to most women already translated.

The second level, the critical, involves the process of selecting a method for analyzing the text and assessing the quality of that analysis (Schneiders 1991b, 124).[11] This work falls within the class of criticism called ideology criticism. It lifts up liberating possibilities in the text and insists that these possibilities coexist with or supersede oppressive interpretations (Schneiders 1991b, 120). If this is the case, contemporary women may experience the *Spiritual Exercises* as a freeing and enlivening text. That some contemporary women find freeing dynamics in the *Spiritual Exercises* encourages this kind of ideology criticism.

The interpretive task also includes the reappropriation of a classic text by successive generations of readers who bring new questions to it. Four aspects of Paul Ricoeur's hermeneutical perspective allow contemporary persons to interpret a classic text through categories and experiences unavailable to its author: (1) Texts are partly the effect of an author's intentions, yet they also have meanings that the author did not envision. (2) The original readers do not have privileged status with respect to understanding or interpreting the text. (3) Texts have meaning both in the author's and original readers' life setting but also have meanings that transcend the immediate situation. (4) The hermeneutical process begins when the reader enters into the task of understanding the text (Capps 1984, 42–47). Thus, the *Spiritual Exercises* may legitimately extend beyond either the meaning Ignatius intended, or the meanings expounded in the history of its interpretation. One can read it anew from women's perspectives.

Not every possible interpretation, however, validly explicates a particular text. Valid interpretation must preserve the integrity of both the text and the context. In other words, the work itself determines the parameters of interpretation.

Feminism as a Hermeneutical Perspective

A work dealing extensively with women and their experience must take seriously the perspective of others who have focused on women; many of these works are self-consciously feminist in their orientation. Feminism refers to a movement to overcome the oppression of and discrimination against women deeply embedded in our social and cultural institutions. Feminism seeks, through imaginative immersion and active engagement, to develop and refine a critical consciousness based on women's experience of the asymmetries of power and opportunity and to develop alternative ways of living in which individuals of both sexes can flourish in diverse ways (King 1993, 4, 10, 19; Liebert 2019a). Theologically, the Gospels challenge us to align ourselves with the "reign of God." In this ideal social order, all persons and nature itself can flourish. To the extent that women, children, LGBTQ people, disabled or dependent adults, and persons of color have been excluded from this vision, they must be given priority.

Feminism does not seek to replace men's exclusive privilege with women's but seeks a vision giving advantage to both. Within a Christian theological context, it gives a lens with which to focus experience and sharpen attention to the ways the Spiritual Exercises function for women.[12]

Jesuits themselves have consciously moved in this direction. In March 1995, for example, the 34th General Congregation issued a document, "Jesuits and the Situation of Women," inviting all Jesuits to align themselves in solidarity with women and to take concrete steps to enhance the situation of women, not only in their individual relationships, but also in their institutions and in the cultures in which they live. They specifically note their appreciation for the contributions women have made to the Spiritual Exercises historically and currently: "They have enriched the Ignatian tradition and our own understanding of ourselves and of our ministry" (741).[13]

The fact that an increasingly large proportion of those giving the Exercises are women trained in the Ignatian tradition should feed into an expanded understanding for both women and men.

Contributions from Feminist Epistemology

Epistemology, the study of how knowledge is possible and of the origins, limits, and sources of knowing, can provide valuable benchmarks in searching for an interpretation that honors women's experience. Epistemology's first expression, says author Ellyn Kaschak, is not in the answers, but in the questions it generates. Beginning in the diverse experiences of women, feminist epistemology poses two basic questions: (1) How fully can the ordinary experience of this woman and of women in this society be understood? and (2) What are the *multiple* meanings of these experiences (1992, 10, 19, 32)?

Feminist epistemology asserts that knowing cannot be absolute. On the contrary, knowing is relative, contextual, and complex. One's understanding of truth, therefore, is not independent of its location, nor does it function without a social context (Farganis 1986, 24). Thus, feminist epistemology allows for interrelated and embedded aspects of the same experience and for the intersection of complex influences. Women's experience provides the starting point for analysis of women's spirituality. Women share certain experience by virtue of being women (e.g., the effects of a normative violence against women and economic disparity in earning power compared to men of the same education, job preparation, and race). At the same time, each woman is a unique individual, formed in a matrix of race, class, sexual orientation, family background, economic opportunity, age, and personal choices. Hunches about women as a group may arise from careful listening to many women recount their experiences, but these generalizations must not overshadow the particularities of each woman's spirituality. No woman speaks for all women.

Feminist epistemology also claims that no aspect of our experience escapes being engendered. Ellyn Kaschak (1992, 21) speaks of "woman" as a metaphor. As such, it is neither real nor independent, but a function of the viewer, the definer, the organizer of categories. In the case of "woman," or "the wife of a man,"[14] the organizer is male, and the category "woman" derives from his values, his needs, his experience. The very subject of discourse is a function of epistemology, one's manner of knowing, and what is defined as worth being known. It is inescapably gendered.[15]

Finally, feminist epistemology underscores the reality that culture, defined as a framework of values and beliefs and a means of organizing experience (Kaschak 1992, 30), dictates what is foreground and what is background, what is conscious and what must remain unconscious. Incest, an issue that has enormous implications for giving the Exercises, provides a clear example of culture defining our awareness. Until feminist consciousness provided a context for naming it, incest seemed a strange and horrible but relatively infrequent deviation from parental love. Indeed, many women who suffer incest "forget" about it; it becomes unconscious even to themselves. Culture, then, has defined the very nature of repression in women. Similarly, the determination of what constitutes "context" is an epistemological act, one of drawing boundaries. Whoever draws the line between the subject of focus and the background "context" controls the boundaries of the discussion.[16]

These insights of feminist epistemology have implications for a classic text such as the *Spiritual Exercises*. The Exercises have formed countless women and men in a way of holiness. They make up an epistemology, that is, a way of knowing and intimacy with God, with all things in God, and with self in relation to God. But the model of holiness assumed in the interpretation of the *Spiritual Exercises* has been gender marked and at points assumes a male norm for holiness. Both the *Spiritual Exercises* and their interpretation thereby merit a "negative hermeneutic" to uncover any complicity with a patriarchal ideology as well as a "positive hermeneutic" to uncover any liberating possibilities for women.

In line with feminist epistemology, then, this book employs both an "obedient" and a "disobedient" reading. As obedient readers, we try to grasp what Ignatius worked to communicate; as disobedient readers we look for the ways he reinforces social arrangements. Such an approach uncovers the values and loyalties with respect to women embedded in the *Spiritual Exercises*, not only what the text says explicitly about women (which is little enough), but how the process affects women, both positively and negatively (Miles 1992, 11). We will read the *Spiritual Exercises* as *women*, yet also from our social locations. The original authors were white, middle-aged, educated, Roman Catholic, celibate members of a religious congregation. Though the current team of authors and consultants now includes laywomen working in very different contexts, we are still white and relatively privileged socioeconomically. Our social location inevitably influences our perspectives on the situation of women and the interpretation of the *Spiritual Exercises*.

Contributions from Feminist Biblical Interpretation

Scripture, scriptural allusions, and biblically based prayer permeate the Spiritual Exercises. The approach to Scripture matters deeply. Feminist biblical interpretation has uncovered the androcentric bias of the canonical Scriptures. It has critiqued received interpretations institutionalizing women's marginal status in family, church, and society and lifted up for fresh consideration the women who do appear in the pages of Scripture. Without a critical feminist hermeneutic, the Scriptures themselves reinforce much that has crippled women.

Therefore, selecting and interpreting biblical texts—and extrabiblical texts as well—must flow from four hermeneutical moves: (1) a hermeneutic of suspicion (In what ways is this text an instrument of invisibility or domination for some groups of people or for this woman?); (2) a hermeneutics of proclamation (What portions of Scripture open toward greater interior and exterior freedom for this woman and for all women?); (3) a hermeneutic of historical reconstruction (How can we imagine women's presence in the biblical and historical record?); and (4) a hermeneutic of creative actualization (How will our lives be different now?) (Schüssler Fiorenza 1984, 15–22). Since biblical material constitutes such a significant aspect of the Spiritual Exercises, those who give the Exercises must alert those making them to how biblical texts function, both in their individual circumstances and in the psyche, as well as within the social situation of women in general.

These same feminist principles of biblical interpretation can apply to other texts, including the *Spiritual Exercises* themselves. This text faces the same four questions feminists apply to biblical texts: In what ways is this text an instrument of invisibility or domination for women? What portions of the *Exercises* facilitate greater interior and exterior freedom for all women and for this woman? Where are the women who influenced Ignatius and had an impact on the beginnings of the Exercises? How can we imagine the presence and influence of these women in the absence of a full record of their participation? One additional question is critical: What difference does this text make for contemporary women?

Contributions from Feminist Theology

Feminist theology, including its Christian forms, occurs within the praxis of life experience and is particularly grounded in women's experience of the Divine, themselves, community, world, and all of creation in an interacting dialectic (Ruether 1983, 12). A feminist perspective insists that theology is fundamentally relational and that speaking about God with integrity is inseparable from solicitude for all creatures, including—but not limited to—other human beings. This solicitude appears in the rightness of personal, interpersonal, social, and ecological relations (Johnson 1992, 21; 2018).[17]

Christian feminist theology bears witness to the dynamic character of religion and hence of theology itself. Those holding this perspective seek to correlate the central and liberating themes of biblical and Christian tradition with the experience of contemporary women. First, they critique the past, then recover the lost history of women in the Christian tradition and, finally, re-vision Christian categories in ways that take the integrity, equality, and experience of women seriously (Carr 1988, 7–9).

Feminist theological anthropology insists that women as well as men image Christ, not through replicating sexual features, but through participating in the life of Christ. Both women and men image God through their creativity, sociality, generativity, stewardship of the earth, intelligence, freedom, bodiliness, and destiny (Johnson 1993, 62, 70–75).

Finally, Christian feminist theologians share common commitments to shared theological reflection. They take issues of accountability seriously, asking whose interests theology serves, to whom theology is accountable, and for whom theologians speak. They work dialogically, asking with whom theological work converses, what truths emerge from it, and how various realities relate to one another. They proceed collaboratively, developing common purpose and processes.

Contributions from Feminist Historical Studies

Traditional research on the *Spiritual Exercises* often begins by documenting the four-hundred-year history of the Society of Jesus, chronicled in numerous languages, expertly interpreted from various cultural perspectives. The rich resources of church historians and Renaissance and Reformation scholars expand the data. The additional lens of the specialist in Ignatian spirituality refines and focuses the bounty. Yet even the combined fruit of these sources leaves much unsaid, particularly about the women present during this sweep of history. Because the experience of women has not been a major concern or emphasis in these historical studies, women have been largely excluded as subjects, authors, and interpreters of this history. A footnote, a few pages, or an exceptional chapter occasionally surfaces. Even these sources view women as objects of male study, not subjects of their own.[18]

The *Spiritual Exercises* face the same critique as spiritual classics in general; the elite and powerful dominate the subjects and sources of spiritual writing as in other historical writing. The "underside" of the history of spirituality, both theory and practice, reveals that persons on the margins of society are often ignored or trivialized. Men speak for and about women. Male biographers or chroniclers interpret women in terms of male perspectives and norms. When women are present in the history of spirituality, it is usually through the viewpoint of a male writer.[19]

Feminist theory provides the basic method for pursuing women's historical reality on its own terms. This perspective presumes that the interpretation of history involves a threefold movement: critiquing the patriarchal culture and androcentric mindset of the times; reclaiming women's participation and contributions according to their experience and perspective; and revisioning new and creative interpretations expanding the horizon of understanding. Allowing women's presence at the genesis of the Spiritual Exercises to emerge from the mists obscuring them requires that the tools for recovering women's history be applied to both the origin and to the contemporary reinterpretation of the Spiritual Exercises. This analysis frees women to claim their rightful place not only at the origins of the Spiritual Exercises, but also in their current reinterpretation.

Contributions from Feminist Psychology

Although Ignatius of Loyola lived prior to the rise of the modern discipline of psychology, he still employed a psychology implicit within the worldview of the time. Indeed, his attention to inner states and motions, and to human processes such as thinking, feeling, and choosing is remarkably sharp given the absence of a contemporary psychological mindset.

Three constructive contributions from feminist psychology are particularly illuminating for this project: relationality, embodiment, and particularity.

Women's primary experience of self is relational. In this culture, a woman, more so than a man, organizes herself in the context of interpersonal relationships. The researchers at the Stone Center describe women as "self-in-relation" (Jordan et al. 1991),[20] underlining the conclusion that connection with others makes up a key component in women's psychological growth. But this relationality, judged from the perspective of men's development of self, often appears diffuse, weak, and dependent. Only when theorist Carol Gilligan challenged the immense oversimplification that men's experience can be generalized to human experience was this judgment about women's development modified. The resulting conceptions of development recognize women's strength in affiliation as a human strength, something good for humankind, and not just a default setting for women.

Second, women's psychological self is grounded in their bodies. Women's bodies impinge regularly upon their lives; their endocrine systems can profoundly color their perception of reality; the rhythms of menstruation, gestation, birth, and lactation punctuate not only their biological but also their psychological reality, and the effects of menopause appear in their physical aging in overt and undeniable ways. Many women have experienced the indisputable connection between their bodies and their spirituality as a source of restriction within a system that tends to identify the body and nature with evil. But valuing the body-nature connection can contribute richly to healing the dualisms of body versus spirit and nature versus technology.

Third, women's development of self, voice, and mind, their ways of knowing and learning, do not match norms established exclusively with male subjects. Thus, what women need for their optimal intellectual development often varies from what men need (Belenky et al. 1986). Women's circles of storytelling, which serve to overcome the isolation that gendered, familial, and work relationships impose on them, offer many women a lifeline out of psychological stagnation.[21]

Despite the theoretical advances in allowing women a psychology of their own, however, the political, cultural, and economic structures within which the vast majority of the world's women live do not yet legitimate their development in ways that count, namely in the power arrangements between women and men. When women live in psychologically, physically, or sexually abusive situations, when exploitative images of their bodies bombard them, when their bodies and selves are bought and sold or taken as spoils of war, when professional and academic arrangements conspire to render them invisible, when economic structures enforce a perpetual economic dependence, women become psychologically constricted, if not deeply wounded. Such constriction or actual wounding of women's self-in-relation results in all manner of havoc in the psychological lives of women, including depression, loss of self-esteem, misplaced and destructive anger, inappropriate and paralyzing fear, inability to speak on one's own behalf, self-deprecation, and a high need for external validation.[22] These obstacles to women's full development as persons inevitably color their experience of the Spiritual Exercises.

Conclusion

Thus, again and again, women's experience grounds this exploration of the Spiritual Exercises. A person who enters the dynamic of the Spiritual Exercises and comes to understand and live out their fruit will manifest integrity in the interpersonal, social, and ecological relations. The Spiritual Exercises bear an examination according to the norms of feminist epistemology, biblical interpretation, theology, and psychology. The process of reinterpretation is precisely—and properly—the task of women.

This work, then, makes visible certain aspects of women's experience of the *Spiritual Exercises*. In so doing, it does not claim to describe the experience of all women, still less a normative experience that women ought to have. But many women over the course of the past four hundred years have experienced through the Spiritual Exercises a way of liberating intimacy with God. It is to these women, both historical and imaginative, that we now turn.

CHAPTER 2

Remembering and Imagining

Wise Women Then and Now

At that time there was at Manresa a woman of great age with a long record also as a servant of God, and known as such in many parts of Spain, so much so that the Catholic King had summoned her once to communicate something. One day this woman, speaking to the new soldier of Christ [Ignatius], said to him, "Oh! May my Lord Jesus Christ deign to appear to you someday." But he was startled at this, taking the matter quite literally, "How would Jesus Christ appear to me?"

—*Autobiography*, #21

While he was still in Barcelona before embarking, he sought out, as was his practice, all spiritual persons to converse with them, even though they lived in hermitages far from the city. But neither in Barcelona nor in Manresa during the whole time he was there did he find persons who could help him as much as he wished. He found in Manresa only that woman mentioned above, who told him she prayed God that Jesus Christ might appear to him. She alone seemed to him to enter more deeply into spiritual matters.

—*Autobiography*, #37

Context

Remembering

Who is this woman? Why is she nameless? The *Autobiography* singles her out for her significant spiritual influence on Ignatius. Today this prophetic yet nameless woman hovers on the edge of our contemporary consciousness as a symbol of invisible and forgotten women. When the history and interpretation of the *Spiritual Exercises* includes women's perspective, a whole new story emerges from the underside of the Ignatian tradition.

Although women were indeed present during the formation, reception, and transmission of the Spiritual Exercises, most people have heard little about their role in Ignatius's life or their impact on the theory and practice of the Spiritual Exercises in its early stages. Not acknowledging the presence of women during this foundational time, however, both denies women their history and gives many the sense that the Exercises are "too masculine" in source and substance. Both situations create problems for women's full appropriation of the Spiritual Exercises. This chapter aims to revive the memory of the women significant to Ignatius, highlighting their participation in and contributions toward the development of the Spiritual Exercises. In doing so, it invites contemporary women to see themselves as included in the dynamic development of the Spiritual Exercises and to claim with new energy the legacy left by Ignatius's female contemporaries.

Before discussing the women in the life of Ignatius, we need to recall the highlights of his own story. The life of Ignatius of Loyola provides ample material for writers, be they historians, devoted Jesuits, or storytellers searching for saints who make sense. Scholars from every century since Ignatius's birth have interpreted his life with a perspective drawn from their own historical and cultural realities.[1] Yet certain events stand out no matter what interpretive lens is used. Ignatius was a man who crossed the boundaries of the Middle Ages into the Renaissance. A Basque by heritage, Ignatius eventually received a classical education. Travels took him from Spain to the Holy Land, France, and finally to Italy, where he remained as founder and leader of a new order called the Company of Jesus.

Ignatius was probably born in 1491 just before the European "discovery" of America. He was baptized Íñigo López de Loyola and changed his name to Ignatius later in life. The youngest of thirteen children, his family network placed him in the house of the chief treasurer of Castile in his early teens. As a youthful soldier defending Pamplona against a French attack in 1521, his leg was shattered by a cannonball. He almost died during his lengthy convalescence at the Loyola castle. His recovery at Loyola marks one of the most famous conversion stories in the Christian tradition. As he was healing, he requested romance novels but received instead the only books available, the lives of Christ and the saints. He records in his autobiography that this turning point transformed him into a man who wanted to do great things for God.

Ignatius the soldier became Ignatius the pilgrim (as he called himself). In 1522 his spiritual journey took him first to Montserrat and then Manresa. These places provided the environment for the experience of God, and this year-long sojourn gave him the time to reflect and formulate what would become his spiritual classic: the *Spiritual Exercises*. In 1523, he followed his heart's desire to go to the Holy Land as a pilgrim. The religious authorities there refused him permission to remain, so he returned to Spain and continued to teach and preach the essentials of the *Spiritual Exercises*. At the same time, he became a student in Barcelona, Alcalá, and Salamanca. Under pressure from the Inquisition, he decided to pursue more serious studies in Paris from 1528 to 1534. At this time, Ignatius met those who would become his lifelong companions and grounded them in the Spiritual Exercises. Together they discerned their call to place themselves at the service of the pope and live by a common rule of life. Ignatius was ordained a priest in 1537, oversaw the approval of the Society of Jesus by Pope Paul III in 1540, and was elected first general superior in April 1541. In the years that followed, Ignatius provided the leadership that ensured the approval of the *Spiritual Exercises* and the Society, and he completed the *Constitutions of the Society*. He died on July 31, 1556.

The life experiences of Ignatius mediate the charism of the Spiritual Exercises. Consider the familiar images of his life: convalescing at Loyola, praying at Manresa, preaching at Alcalá and Barcelona, establishing apostolic projects in Rome. The multifaceted Ignatius—soldier, penitent, pilgrim, student, priest, and spiritual and religious leader—is frequently portrayed as a solitary figure, occasionally surrounded with like-minded men (popes, princes, and fellow Jesuits), and sometimes as a mystic absorbed in God or in conversation with the Virgin Mary and the saints. These powerful visual images form our sense of him: strong, singular, and often solitary.

Yet, Ignatius did not receive his spiritual enlightenment as an isolated individual set apart from history and culture. Rather he was a man of his times—and his times included women. Women were part of his world as he was part of theirs, and history records women exerting significant influence on his physical, psychological, spiritual, and apostolic life. Women, present in his childhood and youth, his convalescence, his conversion, his pilgrim travels, and his formulation of the Spiritual Exercises, often supplied the human resources necessary for his personal, spiritual, and apostolic success. They also practiced in their daily lives the principles of his Spiritual Exercises.

A more accurate picture reveals Ignatius not as a solitary figure but as one in relationships, and these relationships included specific women. Two groups stand out: influential women in Ignatius's early life, and women who were spiritual seekers, served by his ministry and who, in turn, desired to share in his mission. Some even asked to become Jesuits. Their desire for spiritual growth converged with Ignatius's spiritual vision and leadership, although history does not record how much these women influenced Ignatius or the formulation of his vision and practice. But their presence cannot be denied. Not just individuals, but a whole *company* of women emerge. God's transforming work in Ignatius the pilgrim, communicated to the women of his time, continues to be embodied in an increasing number of contemporary women on various continents searching for God and following a similar spiritual path. In places as far afield as Australia, Canada, the United Kingdom, and South Africa, many women now not only give the Exercises but also train others, both men and women, to give the Exercises. This company of women gathers as a "cloud of witnesses," expressing the wisdom and power the Spiritual Exercises offer to contemporary women.

Women of the Early Years

Although Ignatius says nothing in his *Autobiography* about his early years, three women provided him with life, sustenance, and healing. First comes Doña Marina Sanchez de Licona, Ignatius's mother. No records remain of her birth or death, but it is known that her father was a courtier and provided a valuable dowry for her marriage. Her memory is kept alive as visitors tour the restored Loyola house tower and walk through the room where Ignatius, the youngest of thirteen, was born. Various paintings of Mary and the infant Jesus on the walls evoke a sense of the holy associated with motherhood in that era.

Down the road from Loyola stands the house of the blacksmith. Here Ignatius spent many hours of his early years in the care of Maria Garin, the blacksmith's wife. As Ignatius's wet nurse, she is remembered for her physical role, "but no one ever speaks of the nurturing psychological role that she must have played in his early life" (Tellechea Idígoras 1994, 44).

When Ignatius was about seven, Magdalena de Araoz, the wife of Ignatius's second oldest brother, Martín García, who received the Loyola inheritance, became the lady of the house. Before her marriage she had served as a lady-in-waiting to Queen Isabella, who gave her as a wedding present the picture of the annunciation that still hangs in the Loyola chapel, another example of the prevailing Marian devotion of the times. Magdalena introduced Ignatius to Ludolph's *Life of Christ* and de Voragine's *Legends of the Saints* while he recuperated from wounds received at the battle of Pamplona, and played significant roles for Ignatius: sister-in-law, mother figure, healer, and educator. Historians describe her as one "who won his undying affection" (H. Rahner 1960, 115)[2] and was "ever sensitive to the marvels of God" (Tellechea Idígoras 1994, 143).

After Ignatius's conversion and recovery at Loyola, he set out in his new direction and encountered many women whose presence would influence the Ignatian story. They leave a valuable legacy for contemporary conversation. The first clues to the identity and behavior of these women appear in his *Autobiography*. Some women are specifically mentioned by name: Isabel Roser [*Autobiog.*, #54], Doña Teresa de Cárdenas [*Autobiog.*, #60], and Doña Leonor de Mascarenhas [*Autobiog.*, #80]. More frequently we encounter nameless women with generic titles: a woman of great age, a sister, prominent ladies, a mother and her daughter dressed in boys' clothing, a married woman of rank, the lady of the place, a woman well-versed, a mother and daughter, both widowed. Even more intriguing is the discovery that, hidden behind group references and impersonal pronouns ("the rest of the household," "they took care of him," "those who gave him alms," "many people came to visit him in jail," and "certain souls"), stood significant women with identities and lives of their own who influenced Ignatius and the early Society. For example, the simple words "with the help of the pilgrim and his companions some pious works were begun in Rome" [*Autobiog.*, #98] refer to the House of St. Martha, an important apostolic project built on the support and labor of specific and well-known women of the time.

Political, social, economic, legal, educational, and religious structures influenced women and men of Renaissance Spain and Italy.[3] Women associated with Ignatius and influenced by his spiritual teaching came from every class: royal, noble, middle, peasant, and lower. Many heard him preach and teach. Others had more individual and personal contact, giving financial and political support. In return, they expected access to the spiritual resources Ignatius and his Society offered.

Personal conversion, spiritual growth, and freedom were the primary goal of the Exercises. Women learned forms of prayer included in the Spiritual Exercises. Although it is not always clear what Ignatius meant when he used the term "Spiritual Exercises," the fruit in the lives of women is clear: they desired a deeper attachment to Christ expressed in deeds more than words. Women who associated with the Jesuits certainly found themselves filled with spiritual confidence and motivated by apostolic zeal. Ignatius's "objectified recording of his own religious journey for the help of others" and his desire "to induce in others a conversion and religious experience similar to his own during the early years of his religious quest" (O'Malley 1991, 3–4) characterized his ministry with women.

Ladies of Manresa

Women sensitive to the ways of God appeared regularly in Ignatius's life after his conversion. Particularly prominent are the women of Manresa, the most familiar one being the unnamed woman of the *Autobiography* described at the beginning of this chapter. Others are noted in general terms: "he still conversed occasionally with spiritual persons" [*Autobiog.*, #21], "helping in spiritual matters certain souls" [*Autobiog.*, #26], "some ladies who had come there to visit him" [*Autobiog.*, #32]. These ladies of Manresa received his spiritual counsel while he received food, shelter, nursing care, and financial support for his studies and for the projects of the early Society.

Testimonies for Ignatius's canonization process reveal more about the ladies of Manresa than his *Autobiography*.[4] Known for their laudable lives of prayer and service to the poor even before they met Ignatius, they welcomed him as he shared with them the fruits of his own spiritual experience. The chroniclers describe them as "very honorable women, good Christians, virtuous, and of good reputation" (Segarra Pijuan 1992, 96). One of the most influential was Inéz Pascual, who, with her friend Jerònima Claver, initially met a limping Ignatius on the way from Montserrat to Manresa. They first directed him to the hospice Jerònima ran and continued to provide him with food and shelter as needed. Later, Ignatius stayed at the homes of these and other women.

One of the more dramatic accounts of the life-saving interventions of these women occurred at the chapel of Our Lady of Viladordis just outside of Manresa. On that day, the women had discovered Ignatius missing from the Hospital of Santa Lucía and began searching for him. They found him in the chapel

> almost unconscious on the floor, so weakened by his prayers and abstinence that he could barely sample any of the things they had brought in their basket. Gradually he began recovering and when they saw that he was not strong enough to return to the city two of them decided to remain with him in the church while the others went back to Manresa in search of a steed, and they took him to the Amigant house as best they could and there he was well cared for. (Segarra Pijuan 1992, 96)

The women's care contributed to his recovery, and in turn, accounts tell how the people of Manresa profited from the pilgrim's Spiritual Exercises. Ignatius improved their lives by giving them a greater knowledge and desire for God.

Inéz Pascual

Inéz Pascual, one of the most significant of the Manresan women, emerged as a leader. The widow of a Barcelona merchant, she owned a house in Manresa and a "modest house and shop in Barcelona" (H. Rahner 1960, 174); she often went back and forth attending to her properties. She met Ignatius in Manresa, but on several occasions, he stayed with her and her son, Juan, with whom he shared a room. She sent funds to help support his studies in Paris and often collected money for him from friends in Manresa and Barcelona. According to later accounts, Inéz accompanied

Ignatius on his begging tours to homes of people of rank (Tellechea Idígoras 1994, 229).

Inéz received the earliest extant letter of Ignatius, dated 1524, encouraging her to practice virtue amid the criticism and gossip about her and other women associated with him (Ganss 1991, 326). This type of controversy occurred in both Manresa and Barcelona when women gathered around the pilgrim.

Women of Alcalá

Class differences and their implications showed up clearly in Alcalá, a town central to the formation of the Spiritual Exercises. In 1526 Ignatius arrived there as a pilgrim and layman. He intended to take up studies, but as he began sharing his spiritual exercises and teaching catechism, he became more focused on apostolic activities than on academics. People assembled to listen to him at dawn, midday, and late afternoon: the baker and his wife, the winemaker, caretakers of the hospice, married and unmarried persons, and widows appeared at the hospice where Ignatius had a room. Women gathered wherever he preached or taught, often giving him food, clothing, and supplies. Theologian Hugo Rahner describes twenty women of Alcalá as "widows, artisans' wives, servant-maids, so-called 'praying women' or *beatas*, women too of dubious occupation, a student's wench, young apprentice-girls—in short, life itself, ordinary, everyday, sinful and devout" (H. Rahner 1960, 11). However, the constant goings and comings of the women seeking Ignatius aroused suspicion, and the authorities brought him in for questioning.

Depositions taken during the subsequent investigation by the inquisitors suggest what went on at these various meetings:

> Ignatius taught his followers about "the commandments, capital sins, and the five senses and powers of the soul, and did so very well. He explained these by using the Gospels, the writings of Saint Paul, and the examples of other saints. And he told them that they should make an examination of conscience twice a day by calling to mind how they have sinned, and that they should perform this exercise before some religious image. He advised them further to confess every eighth day and to receive the Eucharist with the same frequency." (Tellechea Idígoras 1994, 251)

It is possible that Ignatius was giving the Spiritual Exercises he later described in his Eighteenth Annotation to these hearers, many of whom were women.

The *Autobiography* mentions several of these women, including one whose class was known, but not her name: "a married woman of rank came at dawn wearing a veil to his room" [*Autobiog.*, #59]. Her visit provoked an investigation of Ignatius and his activities. He also mentions a "mother and her daughter, both widowed. They had made great spiritual progress, especially the daughter." The unidentified women were María del Vado and her daughter, Luisa Velásquez, along with their maid Catalina.

These women had spoken to Ignatius on many prior occasions, listened to his lectures on the commandments and lives of the saints, and followed his recommendation for weekly communion.

> These two pious women had told Íñigo that they were determined to travel about the world, going from hospice to hospice in the service of the poor. He had always dissuaded them from such an undertaking because the daughter was so "young and so attractive." Íñigo said that he told them that they could visit the sick and poor without leaving Alcalá and they could even accompany the priest when he brought Viaticum to the dying. (Tellechea Idígoras 1994, 261)

The *Autobiography* [#60] also mentions Doña Teresa de Cárdenas, who visited Ignatius in jail in Alcalá. She took a great interest in him and worked hard to have him released. She was called "the fool of the blessed Sacrament" because of her great devotion (de Dalmases 1985, 99–100).

Another woman who played an important part in the Alcalá drama is María de la Flor, Mary of the Flower. She represents lower-class women whose lives were changed by Ignatius but who nevertheless caused suspicion and gossip among the townspeople. In her deposition for Ignatius's canonization, she describes herself as a "woman of ill repute, who went around with many of the enrolled students, and who was lost" (Tellechea Idígoras 1994, 253). She became intrigued with Ignatius as she observed him conversing with her aunt and friends. She gathered her courage and asked him to speak with her about serving God. Ignatius responded positively and told her she must meet with him "continuously for a whole month," to expect that she would experience joy and profound sadness, and that her advancement and "cure" would be found through this means. Ignatius, probably the first man who did not treat her as a sex object, introduced her to methods of prayer. In the enthusiasm of her conversion, she wanted to go to the desert and live like Mary of Egypt.[5]

Women Desiring Jesuit Affiliation

As the impact of the Spiritual Exercises on women expanded through Spain and Italy, and women experienced the spiritual and apostolic orientation and charism of early Jesuit leaders, many women desired a closer affiliation with the Jesuits. Some wanted to start a group of female Jesuits, while others wished to be incorporated into the existing Society. Women in convents undergoing reform also experienced a greater sense of spiritual conversion and developed apostolic desires like the early Jesuits. "Indeed, much of the appeal of the Jesuits for women was the opportunity to live a religious life in the world" (Blaisdell 1988, 238). Several women actually took vows. The Jesuit movement also appealed to women involved in the reform movement, who used their financial and personal resources to further the cause. As we shall see, Ignatius eventually resisted all forms of permanent affiliation with women although some Jesuits in Spain and women themselves did support the cause of female Jesuits.[6]

Isabel Roser

Isabel Roser was one of the women who did take vows in the Society. She belonged to the Catalonian nobility and was married to a wealthy merchant, situating her among the most influential families in Barcelona. Her relationship to Ignatius, a poor beggar desirous of traveling to Jerusalem, began when she encountered him teaching catechism to children in the street below her house. She and her husband invited him to dinner. "From that day on, Isabel became so fond of the pilgrim that she became his greatest benefactor in Barcelona, Paris and Venice" (de Dalmases 1985, 72). In an early letter from Ignatius to Isabel dated November 1532, he describes his gratitude to her: "For to you I owe more than to anyone I know in this life. As I am conscious of this, I hope in God our Lord that he will help me to cancel the debt of my gratitude to you." At the end of the letter, he closes with, "And to me may [God] grant no more than that which I desire for you" (H. Rahner 1960, 265–67).

After the death of Isabel's husband in 1541, she contemplated joining a convent but instead went to Rome to join Ignatius in his work. She and her companions, all friends of Ignatius, assisted in the finance, organization, and management of the House of St. Martha. In 1544, the ladies from Barcelona led by Isabel and including Vittoria Colonna (friend of Michelangelo) helped furnish the House of St. Martha.

While in Rome, Isabel applied to the pope for permission to take vows before Ignatius (H. Rahner 1960, 285). She and her two companions, Lucrezia di Bradine and Francisca Cruyllas, pronounced vows in the Society of Jesus before Ignatius on Christmas Day 1545, before the altar in the church of Santa Maria della Strada.

> I Isabel Roser, widow...promise and solemnly vow before God Our Almighty Lord, in the presence of the Holy Virgin Mary my mistress, St. Jerome and the heavenly court of Paradise and before all who are present—and before you most Reverend Father Ignatius, General of the Society of Jesus, our Lord, as the representative of God: perpetual poverty, according to the limits which are laid upon me by your Reverence, chastity, and obedience to the rule of life laid before me by your Reverence. (H. Rahner 1960, 286–87)

Rahner comments that this event laid out at least in principle the foundation of an order of female Jesuits, "a far from welcome Christmas present for Ignatius" (H. Rahner 1960, 287). This relationship proved stormy from the beginning and, in April 1546, due to a variety of economic, political, and personal reasons, Ignatius sought and received from Pope Paul III release from their vows for these women. Ignatius wrote a letter to his spiritual daughter renouncing her vows. After a complicated period of estrangement, Ignatius and Isabel eventually reconciled personally. Before returning to Spain, she made her confession to Ignatius, and they parted in peace. Upon her return to Barcelona, she adapted a small house as an orphanage and looked after children. Evidently, Ignatius later advised her to enter a convent that pleased him by its faithfulness to the rule (H. Rahner 1960, 288–91).[7]

Context

Juana of Spain

Another vowed woman member of the Society of Jesus was Juana, regent of Spain, the only known female who died a Jesuit.[8] Jesuit documents refer to her by her alias, Mateo Sánchez. She secretly took Jesuit vows as a scholastic although she remained active in the world.

Juana (1535–73) was the daughter of Charles V, king of Spain and Holy Roman Emperor; sister of Philip II of Spain; wife and later widow of the king of Portugal; and mother of Sebastian. In 1554, during the time her brother was married to Mary Tudor, her father appointed her regent of Spain for five years.

> In 1554…Juana of Austria, the talented and willful daughter of Charles V, sister of Philip II, and sometimes regent of Spain, managed to bring such strong pressure to bear that Ignatius took counsel with Nadal, Polanco, and several other Jesuits in Rome. This committee recommended the acceptance into the Society under certain carefully stated stipulations of "Mateo Sánchez," the code name for the Infanta. Juana therefore became a Jesuit and remained one until her death in 1573—a secret known only to herself and a few members of the Society. The discomfort those Jesuits, including Ignatius, felt with this anomalous situation and with the possibility of the recriminations it might provoke from Juana's brother should he learn the secret was balanced by the hope that she might provide the Society with help and protection. She in fact threw her support behind the Jesuits in some important matters, but she also caused them much anxiety. The experiment was never repeated. (O'Malley 1993, 75–76)

We know that after her mother died, Juana was brought up by Leonor de Mascarenhas, who knew Ignatius. Juana was educated in Latin and music and promised in an arranged matrimonial pact to the sickly heir to the throne of Portugal. Juana, a young widow at nineteen, emerges from the pens of those who wrote about her as a complex woman, but understandably so, as she was of royal lineage and by her nature involved herself in the familial and monarchical regime and intrigues of the day. Some have described her as one of the most beautiful women at the Spanish court and, more than that, as displaying "masculine intelligence" and strength of will. But we also know she lived a kind of monastic life and conversed with Francis Borgia, her director, "concerning the manner of ruling without forgetting to attend to the spiritual life" and the daily practice of the Rosary of the Holy Name (H. Rahner 1960, 54–55). One of the Jesuits writing to Ignatius described her as edifying the entire kingdom by her good example in her leadership position. "Besides dedicating herself to works of mercy and leading a secluded life in the privacy of her home, she dedicated herself with so much energy to the affairs of state that 'neither her age nor her sex seems to be a hindrance'" (de Dalmases 1991, 102–3). A great defender of the Society in controversies, she also supported the Roman College and others, and supported the reform of the Spanish convents (Meissner 1992, 250).

Teresa Rejadell

Teresa Rejadell was a noblewoman who belonged to the convent of Santa Clara in Barcelona. Teresa probably first met Ignatius during his student days in Barcelona while he was still searching for persons with whom to share his zeal for God. They sustained their relationship through correspondence. Their letters back and forth echo their earlier conversations and provide a "classic example of Ignatius's basic spiritual teaching, for [their correspondence] is like a commentary on the book of the Spiritual Exercises" (H. Rahner 1960, 330). Jesuit scholar de Dalmases (1985, 90) also recognizes the significance of their correspondence when he describes Teresa as "this fervent religious, rightly considered to be the best example of St. Ignatius's spiritual direction in the area of discernment of spirits." He recognized and confirmed her religious experience, her desire for God and to work for God's service: "Once more I confirm that you should chiefly dwell on God's love for you which is certain and think only of repaying him love for love" (H. Rahner 1960, 337). Ignatius's confirmation gave Teresa confidence in her experience and insights. The quality of empathy in these letters easily reveals the correspondence between Teresa's struggles, desires, and doubts and Ignatius's own, particularly in the areas of prayer and discernment.

Unfortunately, the passionate desire of Teresa and this small group of nuns wanting a deeper spiritual and religious life repeatedly met obstacles. Eventually Ignatius decided to step back from any involvement in the ongoing direction of reform convents. Although Ignatius had earlier encouraged Teresa and her sisters in their desires, he declined when they wanted to place themselves under obedience to him and put these desires into concrete action. During the painful correspondence back and forth between Barcelona and Rome, the women indicated they had support from the Jesuit provincial of Spain, Fr. Aroz, and had acquired the property on which to build a convent and funding from supportive family and friends. But Ignatius was immovable; he resisted providing any practical assistance for this foundation. Perhaps he could only see the disadvantages. Today, in retrospect, we can imagine the alternative had Ignatius seen in Teresa the potential for their partnership in establishing a place for women to live his vision, even in the manner allowed at that time. Teresa Rejadell represents a moment of sadness, a failure for the fulfillment of the Ignatian vision, a loss for all.[9]

Leonor de Mascarenhas

Leonor de Mascarenhas (1503–84) also expressed a desire to be a Jesuit. Her letter of February 1542 to Peter Faber states,

> I would with readiness choose the life of perfection, that is, follow you and Ignatius, if I were a man. But I am only a woman, a sinner making no progress in virtue, and so I may not join you in meditating and speaking about holy things, much less those that concern the Company of Ignatius. (H. Rahner 1960, 418–19)

This request culminates many years of contact with Ignatius and the Society.

Leonor was a noblewoman who served as the governess for the children of Charles V after their mother's death. She decided not to marry and lived a life of prayer and service to the poor. A close friend of Francis Borgia, she is called one of the most influential protectors of the Society. Ignatian scholar Tellechea Idígoras describes her as a "Portuguese Renaissance scholar and one of the most important ladies-in-waiting to Charles V's wife, the Empress Isabella and nurse to her newborn son Prince Philip" (1994, 299). Hugo Rahner refers to her as "the Mother of the Society of Jesus," for "she did all in her power to assist Ignatius in the founding of the Society of Jesus" (1960, 417).

Remembering and Imagining

Sebastiana Exarch

Sebastiana Exarch, wife of a rich citizen of Valencia, wanted to make a vow of obedience to her confessor and thus, in her mind, be admitted to the Society. After making the Spiritual Exercises, her desire to give herself wholly to God led her to write this imploring letter to Ignatius:

> Therefore, prostrate before God and Your Reverence, with all the reverence and humility I can, I beg you to grant me this permission for my Father so that he may be able to receive this poor offering which I make to God from my unworthy soul. For the love of our Lord I ask you not to consider the wretchedness of my state in being a woman but rather the mercy the Lord has shown me in willing to place desires for him in a vessel so wretched and of so little worth as mine. Consider that as the Lord makes no exception of persons, so he leads all, both single and married, straight to him. I hope, then, in God, my Lord and Father, that a soul so much God's servant as is that of Your Reverence, will not refuse this charity to mine, in which the Lord has placed so great a desire of serving him. (H. Rahner 1960, 302)

Because Ignatius continued to be adamant in his refusal, women never received a permanent place in the structure of the Society. In May 1547, Ignatius petitioned Pope Paul III "to free the Jesuits for all time from the spiritual direction of women who, living together as a community, wished to place themselves under the obedience of the priests of the Society of Jesus" (H. Rahner 1960, 290). Ignatius formulated his strong resistance to a women's branch of the Society on seeing the Franciscans and Dominicans "burdened and troubled by the constant complaints of their houses of nuns" (H. Rahner 1960, 308). "As far as we can judge in our Lord, what really matters is to keep the Society free to move unhampered in order to meet essential demands, and we must not tie ourselves down to unessential things. Moreover, we must, if we wish to progress along the way of the Lord, think first of ourselves and look after ourselves" (H. Rahner 1960, 308). This attitude appears in his letter to Isabel Roser releasing her from her vows: "According to my conscience, it is not fitting for this little

Society to have special charge of women bound to us by vows of obedience" (H. Rahner 1960, 289).

Mary Ward

The influence of Ignatius and the Society did not end with these women who knew him personally. A woman who carried forward the legacy of Ignatius and whose immense influence continues is Mary Ward. She was born thirty years after Ignatius, in 1585, into a devout Catholic family in Yorkshire, England, at a moment in history in which Catholics could be imprisoned or put to death for practicing their faith. She joined the Poor Clares in St. Omer, Flanders, but eventually realized that the Poor Clares was not where her vocation lay. Mary returned to London and began visiting Catholics in hiding and in prison. Her life of service to the poor and the sick drew other women to join her. It became too dangerous to remain in England, so they returned to St. Omer in 1609. Two years later, she had one of her most significant prayer experiences. She wrote of the experience: "Being alone in some extraordinary repose of mind, I heard distinctly, not by sound of voice, but intellectually understood, these words: TAKE THE SAME OF THE SOCIETY" (Orchard 1985, 29). She understood to mean that her community was to adopt the same "Constitutions" and therefore, the same kind of active apostolic life, as the Society of Jesus. She also heard in her prayer that she was to ask for permission from the General of the Society of Jesus for her group to do so but that it would not be given.

Mary Ward faced constant opposition even as her Institute's work in education flourished. Although there were some individual Jesuits who were supportive of what Mary and her companions were doing and who, as her apostolic work grew, saw the importance of it, she did not receive support at an official level. Furthermore, Jesuit Generals Aquaviva and later Vitelleschi firmly discouraged the Jesuits from involvement with the "Jesuitesses" (Orchard 1985, 56). A Jesuit, replying to the views of a well-known Catholic layman who was commending their fervor, said, "It is true—while they are in their first fervour, but fervour will decay and when all is done they are but women," suggesting that their efforts would not succeed (Orchard 1985, 56). She also met strong opposition from the broader church. These women's desire to live the apostolic spirituality of the Ignatian Exercises was seen as unacceptable because they were women. During her life, Mary suffered imprisonment by the Inquisition and her Institute was suppressed by the church in 1630.

One of her most-quoted phrases comes from a speech given at St. Omer in 1617: "There is no such difference between men and women; yet women, may they not do great matters, as we have seen by example of many saints who have done great things? And I hope in God it will be seen that women in time to come will do much" (Orchard 1985, 57).

According to Gemma Simmonds, Mary Ward "refused to accept a situation in which reality was defined and described through the dominance of male experience and perceptions. Then and now, such an approach not only excludes the concerns specific to women, but also fails to take seriously their experience as a category for interpreting reality itself" (Simmonds 2010, 2).[10] Although Mary Ward was greatly hampered by the societal and church restrictions of the time, yet she founded a congregation whose work has contributed much to a more inclusive way of approaching the Spiritual Exercises.[11]

Implications for Today

Expanding the horizon of the Spiritual Exercises to include women's experience reveals the participation and influence of a company of women imbued with an Ignatian vision, lived out through the world of women and influencing the larger milieu. Women provided for Ignatius's material well-being, food, shelter, and clothing, particularly during the critical time at Manresa. Women provided funds for Ignatius's theological education. Women attentive to his preaching of the Exercises allowed themselves to be formed by what they heard and thus deepened their prayer and service. Often this led them to activities not "suitable" for women at this time—missionary activities, radical convent reform, desire for equal membership in the new emerging Society. The presence and participation of strong, intelligent, and passionate women appear throughout Ignatius's life; they come from various classes, nations, and lifestyles, with names and identities, and influenced their culture through a variety of gifts. This network of women often knew one another and worked together in solidarity and service in Manresa, Barcelona, Alcalá, and Rome. Women were transformed by the Spiritual Exercises and inspired to live beyond words into deeds of service. These women fed the hungry, gave drink to the thirsty, comforted the sorrowful, healed the sick, visited those in prison, sheltered the homeless, and provided havens for women and children fleeing violence and abuse. They shared personal and financial resources for the works of the church and society. They were faithful witnesses to the church in turbulent times. They comprehended the significance of personal spiritual conversion and renewal as preliminary to institutional reform. They were present to the preaching and practice of the Spiritual Exercises and, like the men drawn to the early Society, claimed spiritual equality culminating in apostolic zeal. Yet they were also constrained by a culture that limited women's potential, and at times they even internalized these limitations.

When we acknowledge the women influenced by Ignatius and his spiritual vision by walking in their shoes, listening to their voices, and trying to capture at least a glimpse of their lives, hopes, and struggles, we must confront history's most formidable challenge for the future: to welcome knowledge, insight, and opportunity, and to creatively adapt the Spiritual Exercises to include women's perspective.

Four significant conclusions for the present emerge from this reflection on the past. First, the history of the Spiritual Exercises reveals the world of women as a place of revelation, further enabling us to discover God in all things. God is at work, now as then, in towns and cities, where women live in their homes with their families, or in convents and churches. Likewise, conversations of women with spiritual directors or confessors about their concerns centered on husband and children, family property and finances, faith development, service to the poor, and spiritual renewal become revelatory. Women carried on correspondence, searching for spiritual grounding amid the controversies in politics and church. Women desired more participation than allowed by culture, church, and the Society of Jesus, deeply sensing a call to "more." Nonetheless, women's relationships with Ignatius and the early members of the Society vividly revealed the presence and power of God laboring in the worlds of women through their spiritual conversation and apostolic action. Women today are still seeking this "more," and are still revealing the presence and power of God laboring in the world, the world not only of women, but also of society at large.

A second conclusion follows from the first. Since God's revelation can occur in the gendered experiences of women, inclusive discernment becomes essential in the inevitable struggle to make choices that lead to spiritual freedom. A scan through history reveals the enormous formative influence of social structures and the barriers created among people and between classes, races, genders, and religions. Such barriers create pockets of power and powerlessness, models of domination and subordination, situations of inclusion and exclusion, that must be eradicated. No longer can women's desires and actions be ignored in any movement toward social transformation for the reign of God.

Third, class is inevitably intertwined with power, and power partially determines the degree to which the fruits of the Spiritual Exercises can be actualized in the world. Women of various classes participated in diverse ways in the ministry of the Spiritual Exercises and early apostolates of the Jesuits. Class influenced the degree to which women participated in apostolic ministries, but it also influenced the mode of reception of certain texts and images of the Spiritual Exercises. Definite class assumptions occur in the imagery of the Exercises that addressed, perhaps unconsciously, upper-class women and men. For example, early in the Exercises Ignatius notes, "I ought not to seek...wealth rather than poverty, honor rather than dishonor" [23]. Obviously, one cannot be indifferent to such things unless one has access to riches and honor in the first place.

But while contemporary persons may be tempted to dismiss class distinctions as irrelevant, we still encounter ranking systems by ethnicity and race, education, professional expertise, gender, and socioeconomic status—the new and hidden class structure. The contemporary challenge facing the Spiritual Exercises might be stated thus: Can the current practice of the Spiritual Exercises accommodate and even welcome diversity in these areas? The Spiritual Exercises continue to have the potential to reinforce the status quo or to liberate for new possibilities.

Finally, this remembering raises the need for right relationships for mission. The tendency to limit women's potential by consciously or unconsciously accepting the cultural stereotypes for women is clearly visible in Ignatius's dealing with women. Ignatius and often even the women themselves are caught in assumptions about women's subordinate status and role. Women in relationship with Ignatius constantly grappled with the impact of his message in the reality of their lives; it caused conflict, challenge, ambiguity, struggle, liberation, desire for God, conversion, and suffering. How could women live out their spiritual vision, so identified with the context of their lives? The religious-cultural expectations restricting women to traditional roles in family and society prevented a free apostolic response to the Spiritual Exercises.

Yet historical data also provides examples of women helping Ignatius, and Ignatius facilitating the gifts of women for the common mission, so that all contributed as equals respecting the diversity of gifts. Nonetheless, it remains a mystery of history why, out of this pool of talented women, exceptional in their gifts of mind and heart—Inéz Pascual the businesswoman and fund raiser, Isabel Roser the activist, Isabel de Josa the philosopher, Vittoria Colonna the poet, Leonor de Mascarenhas the pastoral leader, Juana the politician, Teresa Rejadell the reformer, and Juana de Cardona the missionary—no one emerged as a leader comparable to Ignatius. None developed a partnership with Ignatius paralleling other great apostolic partnerships such as Jeanne de Chantal and Francis de Sales, Louise de Marrillac and Vincent de Paul, Teresa of Avila and John of the Cross. The loss of the energy and resources of these women who shared the passion of Ignatius and possessed the gifts to actualize this vision must confront us and cause us to reconsider how to form right relationships for mission today.[12]

What are the implications of the Spiritual Exercises for the mission of women today? Now, as then, women desire, receive, and benefit from the Spiritual Exercises, and they expect greater freedom and responsibility to pursue their own spiritual and apostolic desires. Conversion and readiness of heart continue to characterize those inspired and empowered by the Spiritual Exercises. When responding to the graces of the Spiritual Exercises, neither the culture nor the Society nor even the church can contain where or to what the Spirit is calling women—and chances are it encompasses more than the current reality.

Part II
MOVEMENT

CHAPTER 3

Coming Together in Love

Processes and Relationships

The one giving the Exercises should not urge the one receiving them toward poverty or any other promise more than toward their opposites, or to one state or way of life more than to another....During these Spiritual Exercises when a person is seeking God's will, it is more appropriate and far better that the Creator and Lord himself should communicate himself to the devout soul, embracing it with love, inciting it to praise of himself, and disposing it for the way which will most enable the soul to serve him in the future. Accordingly, the one giving the Exercises ought not to lean or incline in either direction but rather, while standing by like the pointer of a scale in equilibrium, to allow the Creator to deal immediately with the creature and the creature with its Creator and Lord.
—*Spiritual Exercises* [15]

My retreat this year was so interesting, and I use that waffle-word deliberately. I went to [a center with long experience in directed retreats] because retreat is such an important time to deepen my relationship with God, to give it full attention. The grounds were lovely, the meals superb, the liturgies actually helpful.

> But meeting with my director was very strange. It's like he never heard me. I'd describe my prayer, he'd latch onto a word, and treat it as if it were a code word for some universal experience. In would go the word and out would come the suggestion for prayer. Just in case there was something there for me, I'd dutifully begin my next day's prayer at that point, but soon be off to where my own experience took me. God was surely there in the retreat—I have no doubt about that—but I've always wondered what would have happened if the director had really listened to me and what was going on in my retreat. The whole experience was just a bit surreal.
>
> —A contemporary woman

Important aspects of the Spiritual Exercises take place prior to the first meeting of the companion and guide. The guide has already internalized the dynamic of the Spiritual Exercises at a deeply personal level and has listened carefully to the seeker, discerning the degree to which she manifests the gifts of openness, generosity, and readiness to embark on the Spiritual Exercises. The guide has also checked the external realities of setting, time, and context, recognizing that the final experience will be both freed and limited by these realities. Against this backdrop, specific suggestions aid the movement of the Exercises.

Annotations and Directions

The *Spiritual Exercises* is a book of directions, which Ignatius wrote for the guide rather than for the one making the Exercises. His recommendations occur in their most focused form in the first twenty points of the text, often called the preliminary annotations, and then periodically throughout the text of the *Spiritual Exercises*.[1] This material affects every aspect of the Spiritual Exercises. Thus, they truly begin at this level.

This chapter addresses virtually all the process notes internal to the *Spiritual Exercises*, treating them in several groups: overview and general notations, characteristics of the one making the Exercises, characteristics of the one who accompanies, and the role of the body in the Spiritual Exercises.

General Notations

Imagine trying to put down on paper the essential guidelines that will enable others to lead a retreat dynamic you yourself discovered through experience. Although no easy task, this is precisely Ignatius's challenge in composing the *Spiritual Exercises*.

He begins his text with some general considerations. Spiritual exercises, Ignatius observes, consist of any activities, including prayer, that assist in ordering one's life around God's priorities. Gradually one moves with greater and greater consistency and integrity toward this goal, letting go of any obstacles to one's wholehearted response to God [1]. In its entirety, the Spiritual Exercises is an intense experience of discipleship and God's service in ever deeper spiritual freedom. Ignatius's suggestions for particular exercises do not exhaust the possibilities. Both the seeker and the guide remain free to search for the spiritual exercises that best facilitate movement toward God, adapting to the pace and needs of each individual seeker [4].

Ignatius's Specialized Terminology

Ignatius uses terms in the introductory notes that he does not carefully define, including *motions, affections, disordered affections*, and *desires*. This technical language merits some discussion.

The term *motions* refers to interior experiences such as thoughts, reasonings, choices, moods, urges—any change in a person's inner climate (Ganss 1991, 338n4). The stimulus for this movement may be exterior—for example, one may be moved to tears by a film. Or it may be interior, as when one is moved to tears by the memory of her mother's death. Ignatius finds both inner and outer stimuli significant. For this reason, he directs the one making the Exercises to reason, remember, and imagine, but also to arrange the external environment so that it reflects the grace being sought [78–81, 213, 217, 229, etc.]. Ideally, both exterior and interior stimuli come together to foster a rich, internalized, direct, dynamic, and personal relationship with God.

Movement

Movement is the stuff of the Exercises; it indicates direction, marks progression or regression, and reveals true preferences. Since the Spiritual Exercises aim to promote movement, Ignatius encourages the guide to examine the experience and quality of the individual's participation if it is absent [6]. Movement, in fact, forms the primary matter for discernment.

Consistent with the anthropology of his time, Ignatius believed that interior movements are caused by personal beings. They may result from one's own activity, from God's action either directly or through an intermediary, or from malevolent forces intent on deflecting or destroying one's Godward direction. Interestingly, the phenomenon of interior movements and Ignatius's wisdom on how to notice and discriminate among them transcends his anthropology. A contemporary perspective that locates the origin of many interior movements in the dynamic unconscious, for example, can still employ the wisdom Ignatius discovered, though it obviously moves beyond his theological interpretation. Since Ignatius's wisdom about discernment transcends his time and place, it can be employed by those of widely differing perspectives.

Interior motions are heavily dependent on the social systems within which one lives. A biological substrate upon which an inner life develops clearly exists.[2] But the nature end of the nature-nurture continuum is relatively insignificant compared to the immense power of the systems within which one lives, particularly in early life. These systems internalized in one's early years can be largely unconscious. They seem to be just the way things are, because they govern reality as the person experiences it. For example, in contemporary U.S. society, there is a lot of talk about "white privilege," referring to the assumptions that white people can safely make about the way the world works to support them because of their race. African Americans—or any brown-skinned persons in the United States—learn very young that they cannot be unconscious of these realities. Their very lives may depend on their hypervigilance. But white people are largely oblivious to the reality that darker-skinned citizens, fellow church members, and neighbors experience, simply because white people don't have to be aware (Liebert 2019a).

This same dynamic exists in other cultures as well. In South Africa, people of all races are still struggling (in different ways) with the lingering effects of the systemic legal oppression of apartheid. One key aspect was triggered by the oppressive system of so-called Bantu education, which was designed to inculcate a sense of inferiority in Black learners and to silence their stories and their history. Twenty-five years after the end of apartheid, this experience still has a profound and often unconscious negative impact on image of self and image of God for many who make the Spiritual Exercises.[3]

The term *affections* also begs explication. *Feelings*, or the subjective sensations in response to internal or external stimuli, and *affections* are often used interchangeably. Here *affections* will function as a more inclusive term. Affections include, beside subjective sensations arising from stimuli, reflecting about these sensations and choosing to follow some but not others. Affections indicate the direction of one's heart in a way that feelings, as subjective response to stimuli, cannot. Affections both move one and result from movement, which explains why Ignatius says affections lead to greater reverence than merely thinking [3].

Affections can be in harmony or disharmony with one's personal integrity. For Ignatius, "ordered affections" align one with God's purpose for one's life. "Disordered affections," on the other hand, conflict with one's deepest humanity, unfolding spirituality, and growth in spiritual freedom. Ignatius uses this term to designate a tendency or attachment lying outside the scope of the Principle and Foundation [23], the "plumb line" anchoring the Spiritual Exercises (Ganss 1991, 388n2).

The term *desire* surfaces in the preliminary notes and reappears as a refrain throughout the Exercises: "Ask for what you desire; here it will be" [e.g., 5, 16, 20, 48, 91, 104]. Ignatius is clarifying the grace of the particular meditation or contemplation and inviting the one making the Exercises to ask God to grant that favor during prayer.

But there is another potential fruit of focusing on desire throughout the Exercises. Desire refers to an interior movement toward what one perceives as good. Desire stands at the heart of the person, the source of all one's striving (McGrath 1993, 27; Ursúa 2020, 98). A superficial reading of the text might lead one to believe that the one making the Exercises controls his or her own desires. However, a closer reading reveals that Ignatius clearly understands that God both implants our Godward desires and brings them to completion [5, 16, 20]. Hence, Ignatius's constant exhortation to ask for what we desire, trusting that God will implant those desires that will lead us Godward, becomes a way of actively cooperating with God's gracious initiative in one's life.[4]

As many have noted, the Holy Spirit rarely appears in the Spiritual Exercises. Perhaps Ignatius simply mirrored the general paucity of systematic treatments of pneumatology in his time (Dreyer 1996, 49, 88). But perhaps desires express the role of the Holy Spirit in the Exercises.[5] That the Holy Spirit works directly through desires was not a novel teaching, even in Ignatius's day.[6] One cannot even *desire* God, or any good, without the Holy Spirit first igniting that desire. The Holy Spirit reveals the true condition of the heart by allowing one to see desires for what they really are and what they really move one toward. If desires express the role of the Holy Spirit in the Spiritual Exercises, the centrality of desire within the Spiritual Exercises is then rooted directly in a trinitarian spirituality.

Those Who Will Profit from the Exercises

According to Ignatius, a particular disposition should characterize the one who embarks on the Spiritual Exercises, namely, a spirit of generosity and self-donation [5]. Ignatius willingly spent considerable time and effort developing this disposition in persons he was preparing for the complete Spiritual Exercises, especially when he sensed that they had great potential for influencing the renewal of the church (Clancy 1978).[7]

Who will profit from the Exercises also has to do with other internal developmental criteria and with external circumstances. Additional Directives 18 through 20 address these various circumstances. Ignatius clearly believed that some people were not suitable candidates for the fullest form of the Exercises as described in the Twentieth Annotation. His general principle—that the Exercises must be adapted to each person's circumstances—led him to judge carefully the seeker's ability to bear the exercises and profit from them without fatigue. When he found the developmental prerequisites lacking, or circumstances that would not easily allow the fullest form of the Exercises, Ignatius offered an adaptation suited to each one's present desires, circumstances, and abilities.[8] Ignatius constantly encouraged a shorter, foundational form for most people as more suitable to their present spiritual condition and abilities. For those whose circumstances prevented them from withdrawing from daily life for the entire thirty days, Ignatius suggests spreading the Exercises over some months, and provides in the Nineteenth Annotation one example of how to do this.[9] Today most women encounter the Spiritual Exercises in this form.

Ignatius's insistence on adapting the Exercises to the person receiving them reveals a positive pedagogical principle as useful now as it was then: give those making the Exercises as much as they are willing to receive or as much as their circumstances will allow; give them, likewise, whatever will provide them greater help and progress.

The third criterion for determining who should make the Exercises is pastorally pragmatic. As the fruit of the Spiritual Exercises became evident, Ignatius received numerous requests to lead others in the Exercises or to send one of the company to do so. Such requests poured in from the monied, titled, the politically influential, and those interested in church and convent reform so crucial at the time. He had to set priorities in this evangelical explosion. His solution: offer the intensive labor of companioning the full Exercises to those who would achieve greater results as "time is insufficient to do everything" [18]. This pragmatism has led some to charge that the Spiritual Exercises are elitist.[10]

The One Making the Exercises

The most developed treatment in Ignatius's introductory notes addresses the dispositions and actions of the one making the Exercises. She should relish a few points deeply rather than try to cover many points [2], enter the Exercises with a spirit of generosity [5], work diligently at the exercise at hand rather than desiring to know the exercises further along the process [11, 127], spend a full hour on each of the exercises [12], work actively against any temptation to cut short difficult or apparently unprofitable exercises [13], strive to develop the virtue opposing any disordered affection [16], and share the various movements during the Exercises with the one giving them [17]. As the Exercises progress, she should focus her whole day, not just the times explicitly set aside for formal prayer, on her purpose [74]. She should use her whole body in prayer [75–76], arrange her exterior environment to match the feeling tone of the exercise [78–79, 130, 229], and bring her whole demeanor into harmony with the tenor of the exercise in which she is engaged [80, 81, 82–87, 89, 210–17]. She should use penances to dispose her to receive the graces she desires [82–87, 130, 229]. Whatever reading she does should enrich her contemplation [100]. These dispositions and characteristics, which encourage considerable self-assertion and autonomy, are good news for the many women making the full Spiritual Exercises today.

The One Giving the Exercises

The third cluster of material in the preliminary notes centers around the qualities, attitudes, and actions of the one giving the Exercises. Ignatius presumes that the person entrusted with giving the Exercises should himself or herself have made the Exercises. Once that experiential foundation has been established, he expects the guide to adapt the length of the Weeks, the length and placement of prayer, the particular exercises given, and the amount and kind of penance suggested to fit the needs of the one receiving the Exercises [4, 8–9, 18, as well as 72, 89, and others].

The one guiding the Exercises must have extraordinary self-knowledge and the self-discipline to refrain from inserting him- or herself into the relationship between God and the one making the Exercises. Such insertions may be quite subtle or even unconscious: telling the one making the Exercises more than what her current experience indicates is necessary [8, 10], preaching or lecturing at length about the subjects for the seeker's prayer [2], and expressing undue curiosity about the seeker's thoughts or sins [17].

Ignatius also urges the giver of the Exercises to act with either gentleness or assertiveness according to the needs of the seeker [7], to adapt the dynamics of the Exercises according to the needs of each one [4, 6, 8, 9, 10, 18–20], and to refrain from any overt or covert persuasion toward particular vocational choices on the part of the seeker, even if the object of choice is desirable in itself [14, 15]. For Ignatius, the guide occupies a crucial role in the dynamic, but a role always in service and subject to the relationship between God and the seeker and to the needs of the seeker in fostering this relationship.

Mutuality and Generosity between Seeker and Companion

Following the explanatory notes and just prior to the beginning of the Spiritual Exercises themselves, Ignatius speaks of how the guide and seeker—indeed "every good Christian"—should relate:

> It should be presupposed that every good Christian ought to be more eager to put a good interpretation on a neighbor's statement than to condemn it. Further, if one cannot interpret it favorably, one should ask how the other means it. If that meaning is wrong, one should correct the person with love; and if this is not enough, one should search out every appropriate means through which, by understanding the statement in a good way, it may be saved. [22]

The mutuality of this admonition is striking. Ignatius asks of each party this respect and willingness to put as generous an interpretation on another's words as possible, and, if necessary, to expend considerable energy searching out possible mutually acceptable positions. This admonition does not apply more strongly to the one making the Exercises, nor is the assumption of correctness limited to the one giving the Exercises.

Contemporary feminist epistemology corroborates Ignatius's insight by recognizing the relativity of all knowledge. It therefore implies that there may be multiple valid interpretations depending upon the unique and varied horizons of the interpreters (Farganis 1986, 30). Thus, all parties in the discussion need to "search out every appropriate means through which, by understanding the statement in a good way, it may be saved." Even similarly situated women will not necessarily hold the same views.

Ignatius's presupposition will have particular relevance for those who accompany women in the Spiritual Exercises. These companions, especially if they are male, need to convey implicitly and explicitly their willingness to learn from and, at times, be challenged by these women. The primary interpreters of the Spiritual Exercises, then, are those in the midst of them. This experience forms the basis for any generalizations about women's experience of the Spiritual Exercises. Furthermore, this presupposition calls into question any notion of an elite director and a subservient directee.[11]

Ignatius's presupposition asks, then, for a deep and sincere attempt to struggle with both sides of a question. At times this will mean entertaining uncomfortable perspectives, but at other times, it will call for reliance on another's generosity to hear out our cherished point of view.[12]

This presupposition taken to its logical extreme, however, seems to legitimate the conclusion that all interpretations are equally good and that, finally, one has no way to judge between them—a position Ignatius did not hold. He insisted on two external criteria with which to adjudicate truth claims: the orthodoxy of the position as determined by the hierarchical church and "the greater glory of God." Each of these norms causes some problem for contemporary persons, who tend to have more suspicions about orthodoxy as a basis for assessing the truth of an assertion than Ignatius did. Furthermore, many of those currently making the Exercises do so from traditions outside of the Roman Catholic Church, which would have different criteria for "orthodoxy." Contemporary persons also tend to believe that orthodoxy is itself inescapably a social construction bound by the same constraints as other shared social realities. Uncovering the discriminatory treatment women have received at the hands of the hierarchical church, the worldwide sexual abuse crisis, and the abuse of women religious by clergy only heightens suspicion. Pope Francis's warning against clericalism also requires that we make every effort to bar its effects in the dynamic between the giver and the receiver of the Exercises.

The criterion "the greater glory of God" presupposes that one knows what the greater glory of God might be, and therein lies the difficulty. The possibility of arriving at a consensus about God's desires in any fine detail is not self-evident to contemporary persons. Whatever violates or diminishes human beings also diminishes God's glory (Johnson 1992, 14). That, at least, can be said. After that, careful discernment is key to recognizing what constitutes "the greater glory of God" in a specific instance.

Fortunately, Ignatius also proposed processes for assessing the validity of certain choices, in the *Spiritual Exercises*, particularly election and the Rules for Discernment of Spirits. These processes provide women with powerful tools for assessing their inner data and will be especially helpful for women who feel they have been liberated from an unthinking obedience to external authority but lack a way to sift the data of their own inner experience. Furthermore, many contemporary persons no longer look to organizations, hierarchies, and experts to point out the better way forward and look more to their own experience and that of others they know, or what feels good at a more superficial level. Having a method for assessing and weighing becomes even more vital when people find themselves adrift on a sea of their own subjective interpretations. But since, as we shall see, election and the Rules for Discernment of Spirits do not provide absolute certainty about the way forward, it remains necessary to rely on the community to help us discern adequately and to rely on God to lead, correct, and forgive in the inevitable instances when we do not discern adequately.

The Role of the Body

Contrary to the frequent perception of the Spiritual Exercises as overly heady and superrational, they contain many encouragements toward an embodied spirituality. Because of the important implications for women,[13] this discussion includes not only the Annotations and Directives but other body references within the Exercises. Some references are overt, as when Ignatius suggests bodily preparation before entering into each spiritual exercise [75, 239, 244, 246], during it [76], and upon its conclusion [77]; or when he discusses how physical arrangements form an important backdrop to the Exercises and should be focused toward the particular mysteries the seeker is engaging [79, 130, 229]; or indicates that the timing, frequency, and intensity of individual exercises be adjusted to the age, physical condition, and disposition of each person making the Exercises [72, 129, 205].

Encouragements toward embodied spirituality also occur indirectly, but they are nonetheless significant in their subtlety. For example, Ignatius directs the guide to observe whether the seeker experiences any interior motions, and, if not, to investigate how the seeker enters the exercise, including the way the body is used [6]. He expects that adding or changing the embodied expressions of a spiritual exercise will prompt deeper engagement and, conversely, that disembodied prayer may prevent or hinder engagement with the mystery. He urges the seeker to engage various exercises with the whole self, understood as a composite of body and soul [47]. Finally, Ignatius suggests forms of prayer grounded in embodiment, a topic treated in the following chapter.

Clearly, Ignatius thinks of the body as an important part of any spiritual exercise. Its use is to be governed by a "right mean" [84, 213]; that is, the body becomes a rightfully proportioned facet of the whole person. He develops this latter point extensively in the additional Directives dealing with penances [82–90] and in the Rules for Taking Food [210–17]. In sum, positive aspects of Ignatius's treatment of embodiment harmonize with the Principle and Foundation, which encourages the use and enjoyment of any aspect of creation insofar as it assists one's divine vocation. Such relationship to creatures, including the body, is "ordered" in Ignatian terminology.[14]

Yet Ignatius's treatment of the body evokes ambiguity today. For example, in the First Week, he asks the seeker to contemplate her soul imprisoned in her corruptible body [47] and the corruption and foulness of her body [58].[15] Such suggestions, when used today, seem to objectify the body, splitting it off from other aspects of personality. Contemporary seekers find the objectification untenable. Such images, even when contextualized within the overall direction of the particular exercise and understood as a product of Ignatius's time, must today be reappropriated within a more unified conception of the human subject. Ignatius's positive sense of the body emerges when he assumes that the seeker is an embodied and unified subject.

Women, often more strongly than men, are still socialized in ways that result in an ambivalent or negative relationship with their bodies.[16]

Movement

For women who already have body-image struggles, it is particularly important to ensure that they do not reflect on themselves using language or imagery that describes the body in negative ways. At the extreme, this can result in eating disorders or self-mutilation. At a less extreme level, it may result in a lack of self-acceptance and an understanding of the body as a gift of God in and through which God may be encountered.

Ignatius intended his treatment of penance [82–90] to reinforce a balanced relationship to one's body, but it too appears ambiguous to many contemporary persons. To the extent that penance is perceived to be or interpreted as yet another form of hating the body, it reinforces the worst in women's relationship to their bodies. By closely examining what Ignatius does say, one can explore the possibility of reclaiming this aspect of the Exercises for contemporary women.

He begins by distinguishing between "interior" penance, the fruit of the grace of God acting within to bring forth contrition and sorrow for sins, and "exterior" penance, self-inflicted responses to our sinful condition. Ignatius assumes that exterior penance is the *effect* of interior penance and not the other way around. In other words, without God first acting to bring one to a new freedom, one's self-chosen actions are as liable to reinforce an inordinate attachment as to liberate. Without recognizing this priority of God's freeing grace, a point so easily unnoticed, one misinterprets Ignatius's comments on penance.

Ignatius next devotes two points to the distinction between temperance and penance, temperance being the moderate use of eating and sleeping, and penance being the deprivation of even that which is deemed essential. Interestingly, what Ignatius calls "temperance" in bodily matters has been elevated to such importance today that it can border on a new intemperance. In pursuit of the healthy lifestyle, some will go to inordinate lengths to achieve a toned body, buy and prepare food devoid of pesticides and additives, protect their skin, and take preventive health measures of all kinds. Simultaneously, they avoid "penance" as Ignatius defines it at all costs. A toned and healthy body is a "good"; even so, one can become addicted to a "good." This example highlights the need to discern an appropriate asceticism for today. It necessarily includes the appropriate self-care with which many women struggle, but which may be the *agere contra* movement counteracting many women's self-neglect.

Ignatius divides exterior penance into three kinds: eating, sleeping, and chastising the body—with the last [85] being the one contemporary people most resoundingly reject. Ignatius is more moderate here than might be expected in his culture. He permits rather than promotes penance, and for a specific reason: to help persons find the right mean with their own bodies [84]. He sets clear parameters about the limits of penance. Finally, Ignatius suggests three reasons for doing it: to make satisfaction for sins, to obtain a new kind of freedom that includes the body with the spirit, and to obtain a particular grace. Notice that all the examples that he lists are graces of inner conversion and freedom.

Problems and Possibilities for Women

The preliminary Annotations and Directives sprinkled throughout the text of the *Spiritual Exercises* offer a vision of relationship, a whole way of being that undergirds the culture of the Spiritual Exercises.[17] They set forth a rich variety of material significant to women, both negatively and positively. Seven aspects of the material emerge as significant: the potential elitism of the Exercises, overrigid or overliteral application of the text, and issues around gender arrangements, embodiment, penance, and desire. When these issues are understood in a context of right relationship, the positive potential of the Exercises for contemporary women emerges.

Are the Exercises Elitist?

Many still think of the Spiritual Exercises as thoroughly elitist. This arises from a perceived preference for men over women and for educated, leisured, and monied classes over common people, for those who can withdraw for an enclosed experience of the Spiritual Exercises over those who must continue to carry on their ordinary life in the world, and for "professional religious" over laypersons.

Ignatius and the first members of the Company did give the Spiritual Exercises to women in all the forms sketched out in Annotations 18, 19, and 20 (O'Malley 1993, 75, 132–33), but access to the Exercises increasingly favored men over women. While a wide variety of men, women, and children from all classes experienced some form of the Exercises through the preaching and catechesis of the early Companions, propriety around gender arrangements eventually resulted in increasingly stricter separation between the Jesuits giving the Exercises and the women desiring to receive them. Ignatian scholar John O'Malley (1993, 129) tellingly observes that women made up the only group of persons whose participation in the Exercises decreased after Ignatius's lifetime.

One of the characteristics of contemporary North American, European, and Australian spiritual culture, however, is its feminization. Anecdotal evidence suggests that far more women than men seriously explore their relationship with God, engage in retreats, or approach a serious vocational choice through discernment (Ursúa 2020, 95). With respect to the Spiritual Exercises, such anecdotal evidence also suggests that, in many parts of the world, more women than men now make the Spiritual Exercises,[18] that increasing numbers of women give the Exercises to both women and men, and that there tends to be more ecumenical engagement with people from a variety of Christian denominations engaged with the ministry of the Spiritual Exercises.

However, such an analysis depends to a large degree on the country and to some extent on how many Jesuits there are in that place. In countries where there are still large numbers of Jesuits, such as India and in many African countries, more men than women still make the Exercises and, in some places, it is almost unheard of for a woman to give the Exercises, apart from some religious.

What implications will this difference by culture and Jesuit ethos have for the Spiritual Exercises? In places where the presence of Jesuits is decreasing, the culture of the Exercises will gradually become influenced by the presence of women as both receivers and givers of the Exercises. Ways of relating and of ordering the environment and schedule, ways of praying, and the range of symbols and images evoked will become more compatible to women. As the number of women involved in the Spiritual Exercises increases, men will have the opportunity to choose the Exercises within this gendered context. It remains to be seen if men will abdicate the Exercises to women, as so frequently happens when women become present in higher ratios. In places where Jesuits still serve as the exclusive gateway to the Exercises, however, gendered assumptions and communications may go unchallenged for the near future because there is little cultural support for such challenges at present.

But what about the charges of elitism centering around privilege, money, leisure, and education as doorways to the Exercises? These issues continue to plague contemporary people as they did those of Ignatius's time. It takes considerable money to free oneself and to compensate a director for thirty days. Unless they belong to religious congregations that offer, support, or require the Spiritual Exercises, women's lives scarcely ever allow such disengagement. The Nineteenth Annotation format may well emerge as the premier form of the Spiritual Exercises simply because it allows access by a greater number of persons, particularly laypersons. Indeed, over the years since this book was first published, Nineteenth and Eighteenth Annotation exercises[19] have grown steadily as numbers of religious have declined and fewer and fewer people can afford to make the fullest expression of the Exercises described in Annotation 20.

Two other questions underlie the issue of elitism in its various forms: What are the "real" Exercises, and what are the second-best or "watered down" Exercises? Although there is some debate about what constitutes the "real Exercises," we maintain that Ignatius considered all forms of the Exercises "real." We challenge a hierarchical ordering that favors the Twentieth Annotation, then the Nineteenth as second best, and only grudgingly includes the Eighteenth Annotation as legitimate expressions of the Exercises. The appropriate form of the Exercises is the one possible for and desired by the seeker and tested by its fruits.[20]

Overliteral Experience of Ignatius's Text

The second problem area centers around the danger of overrigid or overliteral application of Ignatius's directives. Should the one making the Exercises *always* remain for a full hour in each of the prescribed Exercises [15]? *Ought* women look at the corruption and foulness of their bodies, and upon themselves as a sore or abscess from which has issued great sins [58]? Should one *always* act against a temptation, and might not a less direct approach sometimes lessen the power of a compulsion? That most women find such images less than helpful and that more helpful symbols should replace them raises little controversy within the community of practitioners.

More significantly, should the one giving the Exercises follow Ignatius's text precisely, or should he or she introduce the dynamic of the Exercises by moving freely from within the seeker's needs, images, language, and desires? Working with this tension requires adapting to the seeker's needs and experience, as well as the way God works with the person. The Exercises should never be imposed upon the seeker (Gray 1993, 75–77). If the dynamic of the Exercises somehow does violence to the one making the Exercises, it must be sacrificed to the needs of the seeker's relationship with God. At the same time, inviting an individual seeker to try new forms of prayer, bodily postures, arrangements for eating, or ascetic practices invites her to find her own "right mean" [84, 213]. All external aspects of the Exercises, that is, all the dynamics suggested by another and therefore coming from "without," exist in a delicate relationship with internal call and relationship with God.

The one facilitating the Exercises has the primary responsibility for adapting them. This person assumes the responsibility to reverence the culture of the Exercises from deep personal experience and love, to reverence the reality of the one desiring to make the Exercises, and to bring these two "cultures" together in a way that respects both. The rest of the task basically requires that they stay out of the way of the direct relationship between God and the seeker.

Gendered Communications

The third problem area clusters around gendered communications and arrangements between the guide and the seeker. The hierarchical arrangement of power connoted in the long-standing language of director-directee symbolizes these relationships, especially when the one giving the Exercises is a man and the one making them is a woman. A male director may unconsciously express his expert status, and a female directee just as unconsciously receive his expert advice. Women may more easily abdicate their personal autonomy in spiritual matters and succumb to overdependence on a guru, especially if male and even more so if a cleric. All these forms of hierarchical power must yield to a new and deeper understanding of the integrity, autonomy, and subjectivity of the seeker. Coming to this stance may require radical conversion in worldview, attitude, and actions in both the giver and maker of the Exercises.[21]

Even the arrangement that one person "gives" the Exercises, and one person "receives" them, Ignatius's language, suggests an imbalance of expertise. This imbalance must be understood as strictly functional and temporary. Just as God, the only "director" of the Exercises, accommodates to the needs of humankind and individual seekers, so too the guide accommodates the seeker's needs. When the guide cannot fulfill this commitment, he or she must withdraw from the role.

The role of gender in communication also raises the issue of matching guides and seekers. How does one handle the situation where one party adamantly insists on working with a person of a given sex? Persons may express such strong sentiments—for or against—that they refuse to consider the alternative. Whether such rigid gender preferences stem from unconscious resistance or from consciously chosen ideology, a predetermined decision about the gender mix can foreclose surprising graces. In line with the presupposition [22] that both parties presume a generous interpretation of the words and motives of the other, we propose an openness in principle to working with a person of either sex, discerning in each circumstance if the guide and seeker are helpfully matched.[22]

Embodiment in the Exercises

Ignatius encourages the use of the body in the Spiritual Exercises in several ways. This support is helpful to women, who tend to have negative issues about their bodies. Thus, ironically, women may find authentic embodiment as difficult as men, though women's path to integration may differ significantly from men's. Studies show that a surprisingly high percentage of women are dissatisfied with or even hate some aspect of their bodies. For example, dieting is endemic among preteen girls, and eating disorders have reached epidemic proportions among North American women. The cultural overvaluation of youth leads women to expend inordinate time and expense delaying or covering the natural effects of aging on their bodies. Since body images subtly but profoundly influence self-perception, this body loathing negatively impacts women's health. Clearly, in this area all is not well for women.

The body is a primary locus of differentiation: one's body makes one always and irretrievably oneself. The surrounding world, whether nature, interpersonal relationships, or culture, is mediated through this body and no other. The store of data to which memory returns, which imagination recombines and creates, and that intellect ponders all comes to oneself through this body. The body stores and remembers every experience. In the body-self, each person is, therefore, totally unique. And God loves and personally relates to this unrepeatable body-self. Therefore, body is, in a very real sense, a sacrament of God. From this perspective, embodiment is a precious gift, never to be numbed, squandered, or denigrated. Instead, embodiment is to be relished, honored, enjoyed, and celebrated for its wisdom and revelation.

As the silence around gender arrangements breaks down, the pervasive reality of the physical and sexual abuse of women, children, and dependent adults appears in all its ugliness.[23] Women who have suffered these forms of abuse will need particularly sensitive accompaniment in order to experience their embodied selves as loved by God and as a healed, positive, sacramental aspect of their persons. Here the gender of the one giving the Exercises may prove crucial, and women's desires in this regard must be honored scrupulously. Women who have survived abuse may react strongly to aspects of the Exercises, including the centrality of Christ; the relationship to church as hierarchical and clerical; issues of sin, guilt, and penance in the First Week; and even to God, whose "laboring for me" did not protect her from such deep wounding. Issues of the physical arrangement of space, inclusive language, and touch will, at minimum, need careful attention—and may sometimes require delicate negotiation—to establish a climate of trust and healing.[24] But at a far more significant level, the one who gives the Exercises must offer a safe space for the appearance of *any* feeling at *any time* the woman decides to share it. Any unconscious censorship from the one who gives the Exercises can profoundly derail the work of God with the seeker in this area.

Sexuality is an intrinsic aspect of embodiment and is thus inherent in all human responses. Understood as the gendered response of the human being moving toward generativity, sexuality includes but extends far beyond genital activity (Ursúa 2020, 90). Because of its centrality to personhood, issues of sexuality often emerge within the context of the Spiritual Exercises; indeed the absence of any allusions to sexuality might profitably be noted. An individual woman may need to reclaim her sexuality as a gift from God. Another may need to experience healing from using her sexuality to manipulate others, another from denying her sexuality. Yet another may need to move toward a new freedom in relating to one or the other sex.

Issues of sexuality also hold importance for the one giving the Exercises. His or her sexual integration is perhaps the single most significant factor in establishing right relationship between the guide and the companion and in preventing sexual acting out in the relationship. Furthermore, the one giving the Exercises must exercise caution about sexual stereotypes and avoid value judgments about diverse lifestyles. In short, the giver of the Exercises provides the safe relational space that will enable the seeker to bring such sensitive material before God.

The body is too significant a facet of the human person to denigrate, ignore, or allow to "rule the roost" like a spoiled child. Denigrating the body has been the legacy of too much of the spirituality inherited from the past. Ignoring or numbing the body—through illness, trauma, or simply through internalizing the skewed understanding of body endemic in contemporary culture—is the legacy of the body's betrayal. Indulging the body remains perhaps the particular problem of the affluent, who not only have everything but far more than what their bodies need. Ignatius's comments on penance, as strange as they may sound to contemporary ears, have relevance here.

Penances and Contemporary Women

Ignatius's treatment of penance has a focused and limited purpose. He simply sets out a series of practices that aim to help the individual become at home in her body. He wants it to receive neither too little nor too much attention, so that the body may become part of the ordered response of the whole person within the structure of the Exercises and beyond.[25] Because the issue of penance is difficult for the entire culture, and not only for many women, this topic merits a more extended treatment.

Author Kathleen Norris (1993, 23) helps contemporary women begin to reconstruct penance. Asceticism, she notes, can offer a radical way of knowing exactly who one is in the face of the powerful societal forces that aim to make us forget. The antidotes she suggests include awareness, intentionality, and moderation. An evening without television can become an invitation to nourish the inner world through a novel or poetry; an understanding of the body's use of antigens can remind us to diversify our foods naturally before the body must do so through allergic reactions. The possibilities are endless, the freedom welcome.

Historian and theologian Margaret Miles (1981, 149–54) provides a context in which to place a contemporary asceticism. She begins where Ignatius did—with the approach that changes in the condition of the body can open the soul to greater insight. This belief also makes sense within an anthropology that understands that body and soul together comprise one person. Today's seeker, just as in Ignatius's time, often comes to the Spiritual Exercises inattentive to habits of food, sleep, and practical daily concerns. Various exercises and directives, including penances, help focus attention on these aspects of self and facilitate a reintegration marked by conscious awareness and a more productive synthesis in service of others. The discernment question follows: To what am I attached and therefore unconsciously substitute for the source of life?

Three more points complement a contemporary approach to penances (Miles 1981, 160). First, an asceticism for today must consist of practices as fully good for the body as for the soul. The body is an essential element of our humanness and must be cared for and honored *as spiritual practice*.²⁶ Second, ascetic practices must be temporary and individually designed to locate and correct a particular debilitating addiction. They must confront those aspects of contemporary life that destroy both body and soul. Third, some ascetic practices remain perennially useful because they address essential human needs. Fasts, not only from food, but also from frenetic activity, stimulants, deadening amusements, superfluous possessions, and domination of others can have a deeply liberating effect. Disciplines of prayer, silence, and solitude address the contemporary situation just as surely as they did in earlier times.

Ignatius himself provides a final point. Paying close attention to his insight about inner conversion leading to outer asceticism can help keep penances in their rightful place as useful means to a significant goal: assuming one's rightful freedom as called, graced, and missioned.

Ignatius's treatment of penance centers on the individual person. Expanding his perspective to include cultural and social systems and the natural environment within which each individual dwells as an interdependent member uncovers new possibilities for reclaiming asceticism. For example, the rising and falling prices of produce at the grocers can become an invitation to bioregional food consumption, that is, eating only locally produced seasonal fruits and vegetables. Such a practice discourages devastating cash crop economies in developing countries and saves the expensive fossil fuels used to transport perishables huge distances to affluent markets. One's body—its needs and how one satisfies them—literally become an embodiment of one's place in the community of creatures. On the other hand, taking the notion of intersectionality seriously, women in very poor communities may struggle to provide basic subsistence for themselves and their families. In this case, suggesting penances around food could be unhelpful and needs to be reimagined in light of this structural reality.

At their deepest, then, the Spiritual Exercises invite women to use every aspect of their embodied selves to foster their openness to God. This embodiment is not simply offered for the duration of the Exercises, but as habitual practice.²⁷ As they come to love, comfort, and responsibly use their bodies, women will take immense steps toward becoming most deeply their unique body-selves. Subsequent action on behalf of others will flow from this unified, healed, transformed self.

Desires and Contemporary Women

Finally, what implications does the treatment of desires in the Spiritual Exercises have for women?

Desires can be freighted with meaning for women. Women may often feel that paying attention to their desires is somehow selfish and that they should not honor them if they are being truly generous with God. Or they may experience a pervasive hopelessness with respect to their own desires: "I can't have it anyhow, so what is the purpose in saying what I desire?" Or they may well be able to articulate their desires but unsure about trusting them at all or distinguishing which they can safely trust to lead them toward God. In these situations, it would not serve women well to dictate to them—or have Ignatius dictate to them—what they should desire, Ignatius's suggestions on the desired grace to ask for in each Exercises notwithstanding. This procedure, while faithful to the text of the Exercises, would distance women from their own sense of themselves as expressed through their desires. The primary goal here remains helping each woman get in touch with her own deepest desires and feel free to place them before God without first having to compare them with those Ignatius suggests. Only after women have noticed and named these desires can they be discerned in dialogue with the desires Ignatius names. The woman who resists paying attention to her desires may require some encouragement to ask for what she desires, albeit tentatively, by understanding that the Holy Spirit works precisely through her desiring.

Relationship provides the interpretive frame. Desires initiate relationship because they move one toward that which is desired. Ignatius certainly understood that the heart is often "plagued by a plurality of desires," as author Thomas McGrath (1993, 30) puts it, but for Ignatius the issue centers around the most fundamental and appropriate desire, which in turn orients other desires. Assuming, as Ignatius did, that desires indicate the state of our heart and that not all are benign and growth producing, how might one discern desires?

Once women can notice, name, and own their desires, they can begin to look at the fruit of them. "Is what I desire an object to be possessed or a subject with which to be in communion?" The desiring feels different in each case. "Do my desires close me in on myself or open me out to others?" These questions pointedly raise issues of "selfishness" and appropriate care of self. "Do my desires activate my deep generosity toward all

God might reveal?" This last question can serve as a principle with which to test desires. Desires may activate an anxious striving or nonproductive self-castigation. Or they could issue in a peaceful sense that one cannot move oneself toward God, but that God can and does hold oneself lovingly no matter what. These vastly different outcomes suggest different responses, yet all of them illustrate the significance of desires as an aspect of women's personhood.

What if a woman's desire at a point in the Exercises doesn't match Ignatius's? She can go with her own desire and see where it leads her, or she might "try on" Ignatius's suggestion and see where that takes her. What happens interiorly in each case? Perhaps each avenue might be appropriate at various times, or even within various repetitions on the same exercise.

Wisdom for the One Giving the Exercises

Exploring the processes and relationships within the Spiritual Exercises highlights the person and preparation of the guide. As women swell the ranks of those guiding the Exercises, what is the ideal preparation for this ministry?

Certain basic knowledge characterizes competent spiritual guides. They know Scripture. They need not be professional biblical scholars, but they do need the facility to adapt the biblical material in the Spiritual Exercises appropriately, simultaneously faithful to the Scriptures, to the dynamic of the Spiritual Exercises, and to those they guide. They also need to know the broader themes of Ignatian spirituality so that they can faithfully adapt the Spiritual Exercises to the time, place, and the circumstances of those making the Exercises today. In addition, they should have a basic grasp of contemporary theology and psychology, two disciplines that explore the inner life of human beings and their relationship to God.

Psychologically, spiritual guides serve as important affective mentors for those they accompany. The more they themselves live a rich affective life, the more readily they will help those they accompany to develop their own affectivity in their relationship with God. The personal maturity of these guides is essential to forming and maintaining an appropriate, trustworthy, and helpful relationship. They understand and maintain appropriate ethical boundaries at all times,[28] meeting their own needs for intimacy and support outside the spiritual guidance relationship.

Spiritual guides also take their own continual growth in the spiritual life seriously, and they employ appropriate means such as prayer, spiritual direction, retreat, study, and supervision. They will themselves have made the Spiritual Exercises before they agree to guide another. Knowing that the issues of those they accompany will inevitably raise their own unrecognized or undealt-with issues, they will regularly deal with these upwellings in their own spiritual direction and supervision.

There are many routes to such preparation, formal and informal, but no shortcuts. Women, who have until relatively recently been excluded from theological and pastoral formation, will need effective programs, mentoring, and even financial support to ensure their access to such preparation, especially where it is still rare for women to guide others in the Exercises. Paradoxically, women's presence in programs to prepare for guiding the Spiritual Exercises has proven an instrument of profound renewal not only of the women themselves, but of the very ways of guiding the Exercises.

With these key generalizations in hand, what practical attitudes and behaviors can assist those who guide others as they prepare to accompany women through the Exercises? The following suggestions apply to both women and men who guide others.

- Know yourself. Actively work on self-knowledge. Know the things and persons that matter to you. Know your strengths and weaknesses. Ask for the grace to become aware of your blind spots. Own your besetting sins. Be aware of how God works with you. Ask also for the grace to see yourself as a deeply loved sinner, the key grace of the First Week of the Exercises. The more you know yourself and your own interior motions, the less likely you will be to project yourself onto the one you are accompanying.
- Act out of humility. Take each woman (and man) as unique in God's eyes. Start with the assumption that you do not, and cannot, know what *this* woman senses, feels, thinks, and values, nor can you know how God and she interact, what God desires for her, her unique vocation, and so on. All these things are to be discovered in the dynamic of the

relationship between each woman and her Creator and between her and her guide.
- Take the Fifteenth Annotation with absolute seriousness: to allow the Creator and Lord to deal directly with this woman, "do not lean or incline in any particular direction, but rather, standing by, like the pointer of a scale in equilibrium, allow the Creator to deal immediately with the creature and the creature with its Creator and Lord."
- Allow the Eighteenth Annotation to take root. Adapt the Spiritual Exercises to the disposition of the person who desires to make them, that is, to her "age, education, and ability." But be especially alert to your assumptions about the values attached to age, education, and ability, as well as to gender. Exercises other than those that Ignatius offers in the full (Twentieth Annotation) Exercises are not less good. The Exercises that "work" for this woman are her Spiritual Exercises. This flexibility of attitude and practice takes constant monitoring, lest we promote one version of the Exercises over the Exercises that meet this person where she is. Ignatius offers a very pragmatic principle here: Give those making the Exercises as much as their circumstances will allow; likewise, give them whatever will provide them with greater help and progress.
- Listen contemplatively, giving deep attention to the singular person you are engaged with, trying to see that person as God sees her. It means using all that you are to try to make an empathic connection while at the same time bracketing all that you are so that it does not obscure the unique person in front of you, a delicate dance that takes constant monitoring. Contemplative listening is itself a deep spiritual practice, and one that those who guide the Exercises need to internalize and practice assiduously.
- Check what you think you hear and see if the speaker verifies or nuances or contradicts your perception. Let her lead you into a greater and clearer sense of who she is and how God is working uniquely with her.
- Attribute the best intentions to your seeker as illumined in the Presupposition [22]. Ask what she means, stay alongside

her even in her critiques, her anger, her sadness. Try to "save" her comments, her perspective as deeply as possible.

Clearly, these attitudes and commitments apply just as surely to any person who assists others through the Exercises and any person making the Exercises; they are not at all unique to women, either as guides or as seekers.

In determining if the Spiritual Exercises are appropriate (or which version of the Exercises are best suited) for this woman, some strategies include the following:

- Ask her what she desires of the Exercises. If these desires include a deeper relationship with God, a willingness and attraction to deepen her following of Christ, a hunger for growth in contemplation in action, a sense that she is being invited to spend this time in the Exercises, she is likely a candidate for the full Exercises in the enclosed or daily life forms. Conversely, ask her what she fears or resists as she contemplates making the Exercises; this too helps clarify her existential context, and sometimes illumines some of those intersecting dynamics addressed above.
- See how deeply she can access her interior motions. If she can do so readily and with some nuance, it is a key indicator that the full Exercises could be beneficial, since the ability to be self-reflexive is a prerequisite for the full Exercises. If she does not reveal or cannot name her interior motions with any specificity or accuracy, she may be a candidate for some of the creativity invited by the Eighteenth Annotation. It may also be useful to engage her in spiritual conversation for some time of preparation during which the guide must be particularly alert to tracking her interior motions or lack thereof. (Note that she may simply not have language for her inner life, yet she might still have an inner life that is deep and rich, in which case the issue is lack of language rather than lack of awareness.) Indeed, growth in self-awareness, especially of one's inner motions and their direction and meaning, may be one of the deepest fruits from

a woman's foray into the Exercises. Either strategy could honor her unique person before God.

- Pay as close attention to the physical arrangements and bodily context as Ignatius does throughout the Exercises. Assume that this woman is embodied, and it is as an embodied self that she will relate to God. Indeed, body is the substrate of all interior motions, so begin the support of her interior motions right at this point. Head off the body-denigrating images that Ignatius occasionally throws into the Exercises, such as "soul imprisoned in corruptible body" [47] and "corruptibleness of her body" [58]. You will likely have to search for alternative nondualistic language to help convey the deeper dynamic that Ignatius is trying to convey in such passages as these.

Conclusion

Ignatius's introductory and process material sets up the psychological space and the interpretive world in which the Spiritual Exercises occur. So central are these processes and relationships that from them emerge some provisional conclusions about the Spiritual Exercises.

First, movement is a central reality in the dynamic nature of the Spiritual Exercises. Desires function both as indicator and activator of movement and are discerned within each individual's human development and motivation and God's free action of grace. Rather than any externally determined priority of "higher and lesser," internal and contextual parameters determined by the individual herself should be used to judge desires. Desires can be "read" through affections, the "tracks" inner movements leave in the psyche. While an individual does not totally control these inner movements, one's participation in her own movement does matter. She collaborates through her attitude of generosity toward God; through her openness to movement, change, transformation; through her active hope for God's action in her life, personally, corporately, structurally; and through her willingness to discern the direction of her inner movements, even when they uncover disappointing or destructive tendencies.

This perspective leads to a stress on adaptability. Nothing in the Spiritual Exercises is so sacred that it must be done one and only one way.

The needs of each seeker guide adaptation. All persons should be met where they are and encouraged to move where they can, as far as they can, in the style that most suits them. The Spiritual Exercises are a means, not an end.

Considering the preceding, this reading of the Spiritual Exercises is nonhierarchical, dynamic, cyclic, fluid, and process oriented. It makes room for many persons—while still acknowledging the Spiritual Exercises may not be for all. It also acknowledges the complexity of both the Spiritual Exercises and the relationships between the persons giving and making the Exercises, the relationship between the Exercises and the many cultures into which it is received, including the gendered culture of contemporary women. It is impossible to generalize for any group, including women, perhaps even more so at this juncture in history when women's roles are changing so profoundly, if unevenly, in various contexts. Thus, conclusions and suggestions must remain provisional and tentative. At the same time, and perhaps because of this process-oriented and tentative stance, the Spiritual Exercises contain a freshness that continually invites one to probe their depth.

CHAPTER 4

Grounding in Truth

Principle and Foundation

> Human beings are created to praise, reverence, and serve God our Lord, and by means of this to save their souls.
> The other things on the face of the earth are created for the human beings, to help them in working toward the end for which they are created.
> From this it follows that I should use these things to the extent that they help me toward my end, and rid myself of them to the extent that they hinder me.
> —*Spiritual Exercises* [23]

I am drawn outside any time the weather permits. Here I come alive in an unaccountable way. Energy rises gently inside me even as I become still.

A student has just given me a book on chaos theory. I am strangely moved and excited by the photographs. Suddenly unlikely things are related: an aerial view of the coastline of Great Britain and a mushrooming cumulus cloud. An oak tree reproduces the same pattern as the cloud—down to the smallest vein in the smallest leaf. Fractals, they call them. Invisible to us until computers could graph the countless points of non-linear equations. Funny, what finally lets us see what has been there all along. Hmmm.

My eyes range over the saltwater marsh at my feet and up the side of the forested mountain which the Native peoples believed to be a sleeping princess. I can see her hair streaming out behind her. Where I am now sitting is just about in her ear. Today she is clothed in muted grey-green velvet, trimmed in browns around her neck. She has straw hair at her crown. The colors of the marsh upon which she lies are likewise muted. The morning fog lingers over the damp turf. Two brilliant white egrets move in and out of my line of sight as they fish in the waterways. A gull wheels. My attention is caught by a hummingbird in the oak just over my shoulder. For a while, my eye traces the delicate angular etching of the oak tree against the sky.

The marsh edge is also a people place, a space caught between hills, where animals and humans alike share the corridor. Once I saw a fox in the yard, napping. School sounds waft out over the marsh from the playground next door.

I sigh deeply, exhaling all the air out of my lungs. Again. The air smells damp and cool and clean.

Suddenly everything comes together. I know why I am here. I know the purpose of human life. There are moments when we—and I—manipulate, destroy, create, cure. But our true place in all this is so simple. To notice. To appreciate. That's all.

—A contemporary woman

Juxtaposing Ignatius's seemingly didactic statement and one woman's narration of her religious experience raises the question of appropriate starting points for the Spiritual Exercises. Both are human responses to the meaning of life.

Human beings are formed within a matrix of stories of family, culture, religion. One's very life is story. Every human person tells and lives within many stories throughout a lifetime. Periodically, we all need to ask,

Who am I? Who is God? How do I fit in this world? What is my heart's desire? Is God leading? Am I? Or are we walking together?

Entering into the Spiritual Exercises joins us more deeply with individual and cosmic senses of story. The Exercises concern personal stories as well as the stories of faith communities, the community of the universe, and ultimately God's story-in-Jesus. This chapter will explore the Principle and Foundation both for its distillation of Ignatius's story and for its invitation to consider one's own relationship to others, the world, and God. Considering both the problems and possibilities inherent in its articulation will involve contrasting sixteenth- and twenty-first-century worldviews, or cultural stories about "the way things are," and their implications for women, and for theology and spirituality generally. In light of women's ever-expanding consciousness and experience, this chapter concludes with wisdom for one giving the Exercises and a contemporary reframing of the Principle and Foundation.

Different Ways of Telling the Story

The Principle and Foundation tightly articulates the basic principles of Ignatian spirituality (Ganss 1991, 393n18) and expresses the prevailing sixteenth-century European worldview. A worldview situates humans with respect to earth and its events, other persons and companion creatures, and God. As a document of the sixteenth century read in the twenty-first, however, the Principle and Foundation often raises strong resistances. The history of interpretation also reveals a certain hesitation and ambiguity about the real purpose of the Principle and Foundation and how the one making the Exercises can best deal with it.

Contemporary persons often react negatively to the anachronistic and privatized notion of "saving their souls," the objectification of nature, and the preoccupation with the well-being of humans. The very language of "using" or "ridding" self of things in working toward one's end sounds more like either Pelagianism or an outgrowth of an individualistic consumer society than a lofty ideal toward which to strive. To "make oneself indifferent" to all created things could suggest a coolly detached, almost antiseptic stance toward creation, in contrast to the positive view of creation that figures so prominently in the Contemplation to Attain Love at the close of the Exercises. The admonition not to seek certain life situations rather than others in a dualistic, patriarchically oriented hierarchy[1] seems presumptuous, especially considering desires one "ought" to have. It is startling to confront the possibility that health, wealth, and good reputation may not be the "goods" that one supposes.

For women, probably the most offensive portion in the original text has usually been translated, "Man is to use [other things on the face of the earth] as much as they help him on to his end." Although "man" presumably refers to humankind, as Ganss renders it, women's growing consciousness that for thousands of years both they and nature itself have been used as means to an end can trigger a painful reaction. How can we reclaim this key section of the Exercises in ways that are fruitful for women?

Principle and Foundation in the Structure of the Exercises

Structurally, the Principle and Foundation [23] and the Contemplation to Attain Love [230–37] act as bookends to the four weeks of the Spiritual Exercises (Cusson 1988, 52n21; Tetlow 1989, 13). The Principle and Foundation distills the fruit of Ignatius's mystical experiences in the period from his recuperation at Loyola to his most treasured experience along the river Cardoner at Manresa about two years later, when he received an intellectual vision of great depth and intensity. Yet it reads much like a rational philosophical statement. The Contemplation to Attain Love, on the other hand, is an impassioned outpouring of gratitude and mutuality of love by and for a God who lavishes gifts of all kinds, seeks to assure every form of presence, and labors in and with humans in all of creation. The Contemplation to Attain Love may well be, like the Song of Songs, a reciprocal pledge of love and deeds between God and each person completing the Exercises.

The Spiritual Exercises unfold like a symphony in which the opening movement (the Principle and Foundation) presents various themes. Subsequent movements then develop them through repetition and variation, with everything culminating in a final grand movement that unites all in a sweep of sound and passion. In essence, the Principle and Foundation establishes the basis and contains, in highly compressed form, the themes and dynamics of the entire Exercises.

Movement

History of the Principle and Foundation

Ignatius's early mystical experience moved him to begin composing the *Spiritual Exercises*, originally known only as "the book." His profound awareness of being loved and taught by God set free his desire for the Holy Mystery. His subsequent education in classical theism, which stressed the transcendence of God, was balanced by his own mystical experiences, which gave him a heart knowledge no book could impart. Regardless of how he phrased the Principle and Foundation, this mystical experience reoriented his life. While the theologically proper terminology of the Principle and Foundation could not adequately express his subjective experience, it could and did withstand the inquiring probe of the Inquisition.

Historically, Ignatius began giving a simpler version of what became the Exercises as we know them to pious persons of good will, especially women, at Manresa, Barcelona, and Alcalá (Cusson 1988, 46). These first Exercises lasted about a month and included several instructions that presumably incorporated the material of the later Principle and Foundation. In Paris, he further modified his presentation, allowing a preparatory stage to create the necessary dispositions.

Apparently, from the time Ignatius wrote the Eighteenth, Nineteenth, and Twentieth Annotations until the publication of the *Official Directory* in 1599, the Principle and Foundation was considered part of the matter connected with the election and consequently not utilized with persons making the Exercises according to the Eighteenth Annotation. In other words, Ignatius connected the Principle and Foundation with making the whole of the Exercises according to the Twentieth Annotation (Tetlow 1989, 19).

Ignatius's purpose for the Principle and Foundation seems to have been twofold. He wanted to situate the one making the Exercises within God's plan of creation, but he also hoped that reflecting on the wonder of creation might elicit a deeper affectivity, a great desire for this God who so desires each person. Like any good director, he "felt out" each person's religious depth, and only if the individual evinced a certain maturity of experience did he speak of his own awareness or move the person into the full Exercises. In this sense, the experience of the Principle and Foundation served as a kind of screening process.[2]

Several commentators have helpfully illumined the core of the Principle and Foundation. Joseph Tetlow (1989) employs the Latin term *Fundamentum* for Principle and Foundation, a term found in all the sixteenth-century directories of the Exercises. William Barry (1994, 9) speaks of the *affective* Principle and Foundation. Both understand the essence of the Principle and Foundation as a profound felt awareness of "being created *momently* by our God and Lord in all concrete particulars" (Tetlow 1989, 7). Tetlow's choice of the word *momently* conveys the radical awareness that creation of each person consists of a continual outpouring of gifts and a luring by God through the individual's deepest desires. This luring leads to transformation and to the service of others, including the universe. Distilling Ignatius's terse prose, our response is threefold: to praise, to love, and to serve. In light of this love, we hold all things reverently and gratefully, but also lightly, so that we can embrace them or let them go depending on how they help us to praise, love, and serve in our everyday lives.[3] To paraphrase John's Gospel, "The Father/Mother goes on working and so do I" (John 5:18). Placing that insight within the context of an emerging scientific paradigm gives an expansiveness and awesomeness to Ignatius's inspired genius that has hitherto been unavailable.

Humans have always struggled to find meaning, to locate their place in relation to others, the world, and God, considering their understandings or perceptions of the world. The recognition that God creates humans moment by moment expands to include the sense that God creates everything moment by moment—suffuses the very evolutionary process—and that humans can and indeed must collaborate in that process.

The Exercises provide symbols that mediate a dynamic deeper than antiquated terminology or images. The Principle and Foundation evokes a religious experience in the one making the Exercises, a sense of awe and wonder at this God-in-Christ who cherishes and creates each one moment by moment through the different eras of our lives. Such a relationship fosters liberation and a growing desire to become God's word for others.

Worldview and Cosmology

A brief survey of the cosmology and general worldview of the sixteenth century will provide significant clues to the formulation of Ignatius's Principle and Foundation.

At the level of the individual person, worldview functions like a pattern, a thread that draws apparently disparate pieces together and joins them into a coherent whole, a tapestry of that person's story. A given person's personal, functional worldview, that is, the background myth within which she lives, has been radically shaped by the totality of life experiences: location and situation of birth, family of origin, illnesses, religious background, opportunities for travel and education, interrelationships, physical makeup, and condition, as well as cultural circumstances. The effectiveness of her personal worldview, or the birth of a new one where the old has failed, rests ultimately with the individual and the extent to which she is in touch with her experience, deepest intuitions, and longings as part of a larger moment in time (Zohar 1990, 232–33). Ignatius described his worldview; each woman needs to bring her own to consciousness.

Cosmology, or the story of the universe at large, has an enormous impact on one's worldview even though one may not be conscious of it. This includes its origins, development, and destiny, as well as humans' place in the dynamics of the solar system. Traditional cosmology operated as a kind of wisdom tradition, drawing upon philosophy, religion, art, and natural science. In the last three centuries, cosmology has become increasingly mathematical, seeking concrete answers to physical facts of the universe, its size, composition, age, structure, and so on.[4] Social and political structures, philosophy, theology, as well as anthropology, ecclesiology, and spirituality—literally every aspect of life—mirror one's perception of the universe.[5]

Ptolemaic Cosmology

Ignatius lived between 1491 and 1556, at the cusp of the late Middle Ages and the European Renaissance, and just before the Scientific Revolution—an enormously unsettling process that began with the publication of Copernicus's theory of astronomy, "On the Revolutions of the Celestial Spheres," in 1543. Prior to Copernicus (1473–1543), Western scholarly thought about the universe had been largely dominated by the work of Plato and Aristotle and the ensuing cosmology of Ptolemy (2nd c. CE). Thomas Aquinas (1224–74) embraced the thought of Aristotle, assuming the inferiority and subordination of women, along with a Ptolemaic and Aristotelian geocentric, or earth-centered, cosmology. Christendom subsequently came to accept this cosmology because it seemed compatible with Christian Scripture and provided a perfectly balanced whole.

Ptolemy envisioned the planets as a series of nested or concentric spheres in which lower layers were moved by the next higher ones. Each layer was embedded in a single ethereal sphere or "shell" and carried around by it. The sphere of the stars, which did not move but remained fixed to spheres and carried about by them, surrounded all. Ptolemy adopted Aristotle's notion of the four elements—earth, water, air, and fire, which extended as far as the moon in an area of change, generation, and corruption. During patristic and medieval times, including the period in which Ignatius lived, people thought the airy realm between earth and the moon was filled with demonic spirits, with the devil ruling over the nonhuman and non-Christian world (Ruether 1983, 81). In contrast, the supralunar world of Ptolemy's cosmology, a magic region composed of ether reaching from the moon's orb outward to the stars, was changeless and imperishable. Later theology saw this as the dwelling place of God and the angels and saints.

A metaphor, the "Great Chain of Being," referred to a presumed hierarchy of existences beneath this incorruptible substance of the heavenly world, each imparting form and change to the one below it. The farther one was from the pinnacle, the Unmoved Mover, the more inferior the being. Women ranked toward the bottom of the chain, but above children, animals, and lifeless matter. The hierarchical dualism of mind over body was duplicated in the hierarchy of male over female and human over animals and nature.

Patriarchy, a system of oppression of women that has existed in Western civilization for the past five thousand years, also affects social structures as well as cosmological, scriptural, and theological formulations. In patriarchal cultures, domination of women provides a social and symbolic link to the domination of the earth, which is seen as feminine.[6]

As one commentator explains, "Medieval theology as a whole can be characterized as an all-embracing Christian interpretation of the world, but at the same time, as an interpretation of Christianity from a geocentric cosmology" (Wildiers 1982, 77). This total enmeshment of physics and religion reflected a cosmological worldview that was static, ordered, hierarchical, dualistic, and anthropocentric, or human centered (McFague 1993, 136). It was also clearly androcentric, or male centered. As historian and philosopher Carolyn Merchant points out, any potential advantage women might have accrued from their association with earth as the center of the universe in a geocentric Ptolemaic cosmology was obliterated in the next scientific shift when the sun, associated with man, became the center (1983, 128).

In 1543, Copernicus published his thesis postulating a heliocentric, or sun-centered universe. This thesis threatened not only the Ptolemaic model of the universe, which Christians had adopted, but also the status of theology and women. Challenging the reigning cosmology's claims about the physical universe repudiated the preceding religious outlook as well as the antiquated science.

While the medieval cosmology of Ignatius's time was flawed, the mechanistic worldview that ultimately followed proved even more harmful to nature and to women. While the birth of Newtonian physics did away with the Great Chain of Being, the popular association of women with earth persisted. The living cosmos of Greek and medieval times was now understood as a nonliving machine. The rational mind was seen as the essential self, while matter, nature, and the universe became objects for exploration and mastery. With the universe now understood as mere matter, lifeless and dead, nature could rightly be probed, subjugated, and manipulated (Johnson 1993, 14). Women, still identified literally and symbolically with the natural world, could be probed, subjugated, and manipulated as well. Both were identified—and treated—as objects.

This analysis does not imply that Ignatius himself intended to disparage women or that he demeaned the beauty of the earth; persons of the Middle Ages reverenced nature as a reflection of God. Rather, it attempts to make clear that cultural consciousness and prevailing scientific paradigms affect the way one articulates human experience and responds to questions of human meaning. Ignatius reflected his times in his views of heaven and earth, the human person, the origins of evil, even images of God.[7]

Toward a Paradigm Shift

Science is often perceived as objective "hard" data that unambiguously defines reality. The way the universe has been investigated and interpreted for the past four hundred years has gained its credibility from this understanding of science. But philosophers of science recognize that, by itself, science cannot resolve the questions of meaning and purpose that lie behind the increasing mass of data and the theories developed to account for it. Science provides but one story among many elucidating the meaning of the universe.

Over the last century and a half, changes in science, especially quantum and information physics, thermodynamics, and the physics of chaos and flow have turned medieval cosmology upside down and inside out, not only in the West, but also the form of mechanistic determinism that succeeded it. The rise of women's liberation and ecological movements also highlight the fact that divergent perspectives have replaced the worldviews of Bacon, Descartes, and Newton.

Humans are latecomers on the scene of an evolutionary process that began some fifteen billion years ago with the birth of the universe in the Big Bang.[8] An unfolding cosmology reveals an expanding universe that has evolved through several eras of expansion, cooling, and condensation. Eventually gravity condensed matter into galaxies and stars, and earth's sun ignited into being some five billion years ago. Several bands of stardust revolving around the sun became the planets, moons, asteroids, and other objects of our solar system. Earth is but one planet moving around one star, which itself is one of three hundred billion stars of the Milky Way galaxy, which in turn is one of a trillion galaxies in a breathtaking universe (Swimme 1996, 80).

Through a dynamic evolutionary process combining both chance and stability, the earth's molecular structures became more and more complex. Life was awakened at primitive levels, fostering the eventual development of everything from cells to plants to animals and humans. This highly complex process, is, in a very real sense, one process.

Most atoms that make up the bodies of all living things were created by supernovas. The Big Bang produced hydrogen and much of the helium in the universe while all other elements were forged in the furnace of the stars. Human genetic structure closely parallels the DNA of other creatures. Humans are literally made of stardust and, therefore, in one sense, no different from a stately rose or a sleek jaguar. From the unity of an incredibly tiny bit of energy/matter has evolved lavish, organically connected, and radically interdependent diversity.

This brief evolutionary story highlights an enormous paradigm shift in the way that we relate to ourselves, to others, to the cosmos, and to God. However, Western culture has only begun to move from a static, ordered, dualistic, anthropocentric view of the universe to a process, evolutionary, dynamic, organic, interdependent, and relational one. Indeed, scientists now have sufficient understanding of the laws of physics to connect the physical and biological aspects of creation through the same laws, bridging what has, to date, seemed an unbridgeable chasm between "living" and "non-living" (Bejan and Zane 2012, 1–76).

This era marks the beginning of a new revolution, a new narrative about the universe, humankind's place in it, and in relation to the Creator. No longer can a human story be told apart from a universe story; the two are inextricably bound together. Because of the remarkable advances of science and technology, scholars are not at a loss for data, but it has not yet been sufficiently assimilated to bring about a wholly new awareness of the relationship between ourselves and the universe. As theologian Thomas Berry wisely surmises, we are between stories.

Implications for Theology and Spirituality

In the Principle and Foundation, Ignatius presented his view of God, world, and self. An emerging new cosmology shifts the perspective on theological questions pertaining to that opening consideration.[9] At least seven implications flow from the new cosmology in reference to the Principle and Foundation.

- Classical dualisms of humans over earth, men over women, and spirit over matter are obsolete. Yet, current metaphors such as "the rape of the earth" and "virgin forests" highlight the continued tendency to identify women and nature as objects in relation to men's experience. "Sexism…has an ecological face" (Johnson 1996, 12; Johnson 2007, 108–9).
- Human beings are radically interconnected with all other creatures. Quantum physics insists on the fundamental interrelationship of the world of matter. "Every living being of Earth is cousin to every other living being. Even beyond the realm of living we have a common origin in the primordial flaring forth of the energies from which the universe in all its aspects is derived" (Berry and Swimme 1992, 5; Bejan and Zane 2012, 126–47).
- God is not distant from the universe but a sustaining presence in all of creation. God's presence is not inseparable

from creatures (pantheistic) but present and involved with the universe while still being independent of it (panentheistic) (O'Murchu 1997, 50). The universe is pregnant with the presence of God, whose creative action is at the heart of the evolutionary process. God acts as compassionate partner, as lure toward the future and as co-Creator. Indeed, God labors on humans' behalf [236].

- A human-centered norm of progress must give way to a universe-centric focus. Humans are within the cosmos, not apart from or above it. Earth can flourish in the absence of humans, but humans cannot flourish in the absence of earth. Humankind is dependent on earth, its larger body (McFague 1993), for existence. The poet, novelist, and essayist Wendell Berry somewhere reflects that humans rely on creatures and survive by their deaths. In sustaining life, humans break the body and shed the blood of creation. When done respectfully and reverently, it is sacrament; when done destructively or greedily, it is desecration. The arrogance of human beings is destroying plant and animal species, which each took millions of years to evolve and are necessary for planetary ecology.[10]
- Cultivating a renewed sacramental vision is the richest way of recovering both a sense of reverence for and companionship with all of creation. "Sacrament" has a much broader context than usually imagined.[11] An earlier genius of humankind saw nature as the primary source of revelation. The work of poets, artists, and mystics has always drawn attention to the numinous quality of the ordinary, calling us to poet Gerard Manley Hopkins's realization that "the world is charged with the grandeur of God."[12]
- Salvation is planetary and global as well as personal. A shift from other-worldly to this-worldly redemptive hope flows from this new paradigm. Persons no longer seek simply their own redemption but that of all creation, including the earth itself. The life and death of Jesus must be lived out salvifically by all Christians. The universe, the sacred body of God, also needs salvation (Rom 8:18–23).[13]
- Humans are called not to dominate nature, but to be cocreators within the evolutionary process. Humankind is not

the center by means of which all is dominated, but the center through which all enter into kinship and communion. Women and men are called to become partners in mutuality and respectful companions of all creation.

The current paradigm shift invites us to recapitulate the wisdom of the previous epistemological shift from Ptolemaic to Copernican cosmology even as another takes place. The task calls for a return to nature with a second naiveté, reimagining and reparticipating in the mythical, poetic, and religious, even as the struggle with the political, ecological, economic, and technological realities continues.

Many persons' worldviews remain largely unexamined, unconscious frames of reference for living and relating to God, self, and creation. Each person making the Spiritual Exercises needs to answer the implicit questions in the Principle and Foundation: How would you describe your world and how it influences you? How do you imagine God? What is your relationship to others and all of God's creation? What is your part in creation? What are the dominant influences on your sense of God, humans, heaven, and earth? What does it mean to exist in this vast unfolding universe?[14]

In Ignatius's era, people in the West making the Exercises operated out of a universally accepted cosmology. Today, the cosmology of the one guiding the Exercises can conflict with the one making them, or both can be operating out of an irreconcilable hybrid. It is incumbent on those giving the Exercises to ascertain what cultural, philosophical, theological, and scientific assumptions they bring to the text. These presuppositions will affect how guides "hear into speech," the one making the Exercises, to borrow author Nelle Morton's (1985, 74) felicitous phrase.

Reframing the Principle and Foundation

In its essence, the opening line of the Principle and Foundation, "Human beings are created to praise, reverence, and serve God our Lord," seeks to uncover both who God is and our relationship to this Creative One. Paradoxically, many women may need to pay attention to self as a prelude to paying attention to God, to discover for the first time—or all over again—the God present within the mystery of oneself. To turn away from self is to turn away from God, despite inner voices chanting "Don't be selfish." As one woman said, "It was easier to use my gifts in an outward way, to share what I could with family and faith community than to try to look inside myself and cherish, nurture, and enjoy myself as a gift from God to me." Seeing oneself and all of creation as continually loved and desired into being by a passionate and solicitous God prompts an awe and still deeper reverence for God, self, and the sacrament of creation. Such was the case with Ignatius at the river Cardoner. A sense of the diaphanous presence of God in everything undergirds the awareness of gift.

The second part of that goal, "by means of this to save their souls," has been well discussed by Ganss (1991, 392) and others. Ignatius understood "soul" as the Hebrew equivalent of the "total self." But the new cosmology puts a different spin on soteriology, for now salvation includes the universe. Furthermore, feminist theologians stress the relational, communitarian nature of salvation, seeing salvation as not only a single past event, but an ongoing reality in which humans participate. Like Jesus, women must call for responsibility—for themselves, for the powerless, for the earth, the greater body of God. It makes a great deal of difference if the one making the Exercises seeks life for self and others "beyond this world" or precisely in the messiness and beauty of ordinary experience.[15]

The traditional "means" of the Principle and Foundation, "other things on the face of the earth created for human beings...use these things to the extent that they help," seems singularly anthropocentric in light of our dependence on the earth and the need for a compassionate relationship with it. As interdependent companions of all that exists, we must place much more focus on the welfare of all species, not just the human, as Pope Francis has so strongly stated. The global pandemic caused by COVID-19 brought home for all to see the interconnection of every system in the world and in the broader cosmos and has revealed just how far we need to go in strengthening our interconnections with all creation.[16]

A closely related issue concerns the objectification and dismissal of other human beings as "means," particularly women and children. Statistics fluctuate, but the continuing reality that a very small percentage of people use the vast amount of the world's resources while millions die from starvation, water pollution, or the loss of arable farmland is morally reprehensible. The U.S. Catholic bishops' pastoral on the economy, "Economic Justice for All" (1986), admonished all to reflect not only on how purchases affect the poor but on a broader definition of the poor. The "poor," they are clear, must also include the earth itself—a more radical idea then than it is now. More recently, Pope Francis extends an urgent appeal for a "new dialogue about how we are shaping the future of our planet," a dialogue that must include everyone (*Laudato Si'* 14). The increasing gap between the rich and the poor around the world, combined with a growing realization that humans are fast approaching the limits that human behavior can exert on planetary resources, means that the more fortunate among us are being called with increasing urgency to simplify and to use less that all may have a sustainable future.

In this light, however, *nonuse* may have significant negative as well as positive meanings. One can ignore gifts of nature, of the arts and sciences, or of the person, such as self-expression through poetry, dance, journaling, painting, and other visual arts. Everyone should have access to these gifts of God, not just the affluent. All things beautiful are important resources for spirituality and should be treasured as such.

Many women stumble on Ignatius's phrase "make myself indifferent." In contemporary English, *indifference* usually means "lack of interest, concern, or sympathy." Unfortunately, this definition completely mistakes Ignatius's meaning. It leads people to believe that strong feelings cannot coexist with the indifference Ignatius calls for at the beginning of the Exercises. A second definition of *indifference* comes closer to Ignatius's usage: "absence of compulsion to do or toward one thing or another." By "make oneself indifferent," Ignatius clearly means holding all created things as less important than God and God's call. Freedom from compulsion can indeed exist alongside strong feelings, and Ignatian indifference asks that we allow these strong feelings to fuel our move toward God. For some, "freedom" or "spiritual freedom" serves as a helpful reframing.[17]

One woman, engaging in discernment about her future professional direction, was delighted to report that her anxieties and frustrations were gradually stilling to a lovely peace. She assumed that this delightful feeling of peacefulness, so unusual to her normal "monkey mind," must be indifference. But then, to her dismay, little bits of energy started to appear nudging her toward a possibility she had not seriously considered. Frustration returned: "I lost my indifference. Now what?" When her Exercises guide noticed the energy in the new feeling, she gently asked, "How do you think God will call you, if not through your feelings and desires? Could this energy be just that?" This exchange allowed her to move from the common understanding of indifference as passionless, and experience herself living the second meaning, passion without compulsion; once she made that shift, she could freely and enthusiastically choose this new direction as God's call. Over the course of her retreat, she was able to confirm a new sense of direction for which these little inklings of energy were the first sign.

Nor can "making myself indifferent to all created things" be dealt with as simply a question of will power. Indifference presumes passion. Women cannot act with indifference in any positive sense until they have identified their desires and passions. Indifference demands liberation. Detachment follows from attachment to Someone whose love empowers with blessed freedom.

Ignatius suggests that we understand the phrase "make myself indifferent" in a wider context, since moving toward something gives fullness of life in the service of the world, while avoiding something ties down the spirit. Indifference does not so much seek this rather than that—health rather than sickness, wealth rather than poverty—but rather, entails a more receptive looking for, with, and in God at whatever life circumstances are present, precisely because of a grounding relationship with God. "Making myself indifferent" means finding God who sustains, supports, and lures toward the future in the process of life. While few people genuinely enjoy this degree of freedom, the *desire* for it remains essential.

Putting the notions of indifference and ordering one's life into a wider intersectional perspective vastly expands their meaning. One woman's life is intrinsically intertwined with all women's, and indeed all other created beings. To adequately understand the depth of the Principle and Foundation, it is necessary to grasp this wider intersectional flow of power and disempowerment. Each woman's immediate and intergenerational family, her community, her educational level and experiences, her occupation, her socioeconomic status, her ethnic roots, and her culture's norms all contribute to her strength and her call. That is the grace-filled ideal. But the intersectional reality of structural sin works its woe as well. Can a woman working in a sweat shop in Bangladesh give energy to anything except surviving and feeding her children (Liebert 2019a)?

After the named things one "ought not to seek" (health, wealth, honor) comes a fascinating phrase, "and so on in other matters." What might the "and so ons" be for women in contemporary society? Cultural myths, certainly, including beauty, body shape, youthful appearance, dependence on external validation—especially from men—stylish dress, security, and doing it "right." Having the one making the Exercises list her own "and so ons" could prove helpful.

Desires also intimately relate to the Principle and Foundation because desires flow from a worldview and reveal how one wishes to be in relationship. Those guiding the Exercises do important work when they assist those making them to discover what they really want—their functional Principle and Foundation. Some women have little sense of the choices or options existing even within impossible situations. The difficulty might stem from a lack of imagination, but also, all too frequently, from fear. "I can't say what I think to my boss. I'll lose my job and then where will we be?" or "I know my husband isn't good for our children, but what can I do? If I kick him out, he will take it out on them." For a woman growing up in oppressive systems, desires are actively discouraged; during apartheid, for example, a woman would have had her horizons of desire and her sense of possibilities severely curtailed by an educational system designed to do so. At another more internal level: "It's risky to discover my own needs and desires because it leads me into the unknown. It will be my fault if I fail."

Women may listen to exterior voices saying they are inferior, not "good enough," or "different," rather than listen to God speaking through their own deepest desires. In some contexts, the community culture dictates. For example, a woman may not desire to marry or have children, but a strong communal expectation may limit her interior freedom to listen deeply to God's desires for her. Women generally put the needs and desires of families, parents, and coworkers first, leaving little room for self. In not a few cases, they face enormous conflict from spouses or partners when seeking to fulfill their God-given desires. Church may also program women to see themselves as inferior or "not enough" that they may not allow themselves the luxury of desires for fear of yet another disappointment.[18] Internalizing the core of the Principle and Foundation will give a sense of their dignity and uniqueness and elicit authentic desires and genuine indifference. One woman imaged the movement into healthy autonomy as "coming out of a coma."

Psychological and sociological studies of women have indicated that many lack "voice," a metaphor for growth in autonomy and maturity. Even a community of two, the one guiding and the one making the Exercises, can facilitate and encourage a woman's movement toward greater freedom and delight in self and a healthy desire to serve others when affirmed or lovingly challenged. Those giving the Exercises cannot presume capacity for self-reflection, for tapping into and articulating one's experience, feelings, desires, and thoughts.

Strong and powerful women can also get caught in desires evoked by their very success, such as the desire to make more money, to associate oneself with what one earns, to look down on those less powerful or successful, to "do it myself." Feminism itself can set up conflicting desires. For those women who have "found their voice," how do they choose to use it?

The Principle and Foundation is intended to evoke a present or remembered experience, an awareness of how God continues to create and to cherish each individual moment by moment throughout life. This realization must precede any consideration of sin, or else the First Week becomes painfully introspective. The Principle and Foundation "grounds" a person in graced self-awareness and God-awareness, food for the journey of life and ministry. The God of the Principle and Foundation loves women compassionately and asks them to trust themselves and act out of this deep, true sense of who they really are.[19]

Wisdom for the One Giving the Exercises

An inductive, intuitive approach to the Principle and Foundation enables the guide to feel out where each woman enters the process in terms of cosmology and worldview. Moving from a macro to a micro level, a new paradigm generates not only cosmic but also personal questions for the one making the Exercises: What is my world? What is the center of my universe? What is my cosmology?

Discussing a faith autobiography or asking a series of informal questions offers clues to a woman's desires and relationship to the Creative One. For example, the one giving the Exercises might ask potentially revealing questions such as, Who are you? If you had a photo album of important people and events in your life, what would it look like? Who would be in it? What in your life do you feel most strongly and passionately about? What is the goal of your life? How do you experience God? How do you and God communicate? How do you image Jesus? Why are you choosing to make the Exercises?

Movement

Since each woman experiences the call to make the Exercises uniquely, the guide needs to begin with each individual's experience, her story. Each person is, in effect, a living, breathing Principle and Foundation. It is perhaps more important to let the one making the Exercises articulate her own Principle and Foundation rather than reflecting on that of Ignatius. Articulating the end or goal of one's life in relationship to God is a "luxury" some women have not had the opportunity to explore or have resisted because of the responsibility it might entail. Asking a woman what her "passions" are might elicit a variety of responses: "to raise my children to be good Christians," "to seek intimacy with God in Jesus," "to live a good life of service to others," "to be a person of integrity and authenticity," "to use my education," "to satisfy my husband, parent, or employer" and so on.

Probing these passions and not simply taking them at face value will yield a variety of rationales for making the Exercises: to meet others' expectations, to be worthy of God, to be a vital contributing member of the faith community or world, to grow in faith, to find one's life direction, to discover and use gifts for leadership, or to discern a call to ordained ministry. The guide must listen carefully to the self-expression, worldview, and theology of the woman making the Exercises. This dialogue over days, weeks, or even months, such as Ignatius encouraged, will also reveal obstacles that need additional work or may prohibit moving beyond the Principle and Foundation at this time.

Humans develop and order experience through images. Granted that no image of God is adequate, it is important to discover how one relates to God. Naming God implies a corresponding self-image. If God is a tyrant, I am oppressed; if God is beneficent, I am gifted.

The two-tiered universe of an earlier cosmology easily lent itself to a theologically dualistic perspective. Western classical theology's understanding of God, almost exclusively shaped by men, presented God as male, as power and might. It experienced God predominantly "as noun, as transcendence, as order, as structure, as law, as rationality" (Nelson 1983, 13). This form of patriarchy physically and emotionally distances women, but also men, from God; it makes God wholly other, above and beyond, and relegates Divine Love to being measured through conformity to law and order—or at least conformity to church and society.

Images of God as judge, tyrant, beyond caring, oppressive, and domineering are common among women, particularly those who have experienced psychological, physical, or sexual abuse. On the other hand,

and equally unhelpful, God can also be experienced only as comforting, allowing a sort of pseudodependent, immature relationship that never challenges one to assume responsibility. Unhelpful, incomplete, or even destructive extremes need to be recognized and challenged. The heart of the matter is God image.

A growing body of work by developmental theorists highlights the fact that many women have been socialized to forget their own needs, desires, or passions.[20] One highly intelligent woman remarked, "I can see that I arrived at the age of legal adulthood with only the barest acquaintance with my inner being. I knew myself as someone who existed to please, to serve, and especially to accommodate to others." Another woman remarked, "I hide from myself by not listening to what I want and need, but by clinging to my dependencies on others, by blaming my family of origin. I live my fear as I crave things I don't want and need and believe the cravings. I fear that I am not enough. There is anxiety that my not-enoughness will be discovered."

In denying one's essential self, one denies the very image in which one is made. Failing to love self, one's inmost being expressed in embodied spirit, means failing to love God. The guide can help by asking for clarification. What is it that makes you genuinely happy, that gives you joy? Who are you when you are most fully alive, most fully your true self? What gives you energy?

Other women find the traditional language of "surrender to God" both offensive and threatening. They equate surrender with obliterating themselves and relinquishing their lifetime of struggle for basic existence, much less for appropriate political power.[21] Many women react to the subliminal message associated with military surrender, realizing the horrible ramifications for them and their children. To surrender to this God would be seen as an act of fear. As one woman declared, "I will have no God, if the only way to God is through the demise of the self that I have worked so hard to form." On the other hand, to surrender the depressed and empty self that women so often experience, as well as a false image of God, provides the way forward (Carr 1988, 212).

The most basic image necessary to the process of the Exercises consists of God as loving Creator who calls us to full humanity, to identity, and to collaboration (Sheldrake 1983, 95). Seeing oneself as a unique and precious creative act of God gives a joy that does not come from success or external validation. Freely and willingly handing oneself over to this God, to a relationship of mutuality that transforms and transcends what one knows about oneself, removes probably the single most difficult psychological obstacle to spiritual growth.

Conclusion

Ignatius added the Principle and Foundation to the Exercises after his initial work with both women and men. Although we cannot tell from the text of the Principle and Foundation how women influenced its formulation, its impact on women today is of great concern.

Because of the complexity of our era, reflecting on the assumptions inherent in the Principle and Foundation as articulated by Ignatius is as important now as it was for sixteenth-century Christians. At the core of the stated Principle and Foundation exists a way of perceiving reality that needs to resonate with Ignatius's mystical experience, not by replicating his experience, but in one's affective awareness and life direction. Ignatius's experience of God as loving Creator allowed him to see others and the known world as an expression of that love and worthy of his own. The affective Principle and Foundation or *Fundamentum* constitutes the sine qua non, the lens, the central theme that runs throughout and grounds each movement of the Exercises. This relationship with God both expresses and opens one to the continuing dynamic of the Exercises.

A new scientific paradigm that relocates humans in their relationships to God, others, and the cosmos puts the Exercises and all of life into a whole new perspective, providing a liberating movement for women and nature and an expansiveness and numinous quality to all of creation. Theology and spirituality are deeply affected by a new scientific paradigm. A new understanding of cosmology radically shifts meanings of sin, salvation, and sanctity from an individualistic soteriology to one of interrelationship, not just with God and others, but also with the planetary systems. Incarnation is no longer seen as an isolated event. The embodiment of God takes place in all of creation as it moves toward greater complexity and communion.

Two contemporary women offer a rendering of the Principle and Foundation that comes close to summarizing these rich insights:

Gounding in Truth

Gracious God, when Your love spilled over
into creation
You thought of me.
I am
from love   of love   for love.
Let my heart, O God, always
recognize,
cherish,
and enjoy Your goodness in all of creation.
Direct all that is me toward Your praise.
Teach me reverence for every person, all things.
Energize me in your service.
O God
may nothing ever distract me from Your
love…
neither health nor sickness
wealth nor poverty
honor nor dishonor
long life nor short life.
May I never seek nor choose to be other
than You intend or wish.
Amen.

(Bergan and Schwan 1985, 11, alt.)[22]

CHAPTER 5

Knowing Whose I Am

Prayer in the Spiritual Exercises

God sees and knows what is best for each one and, as he knows all, he shows each the road to take. On our part we can with his grace seek and test the way forward in many different fashions, so that a person goes forward by that way which for them is the clearest and happiest and most blessed in this life.
—Letter from Ignatius to Francis Borgia, 1548 (Veale, 1995)

You know, this prayer thing has me stumped. I really do want to pray. But when I sit down, my mind seems to go blank. I talk to God, but God never seems to talk back. After doing this for a while, I get discouraged and quit. Pretty soon, the nagging is back: "You should be praying." So I make a resolution, start again, and pretty soon, I stop. What I really like to do is walk in the wild, so on Sunday afternoon, I give myself a treat and go out to the headlands and hike. Sometimes there I really feel like I am praying. But it doesn't seem to carry over to Monday through Saturday. Anyhow, when my friend told me about the Spiritual Exercises, my heart

Knowing Whose I Am

jumped a little. Maybe I can really learn how to pray. So here I am.

—A contemporary woman

From the General and Particular Examinations opening the First Week to the Contemplation to Attain Love closing the Fourth Week and beyond,[1] prayer permeates the Spiritual Exercises. This rich variety of responses to God may be one of the best-kept secrets of the Spiritual Exercises.[2] Any woman can find here a form of prayer that not only works for her but also actually delights her. Yet, lacking awareness of the possibilities, how can one choose the richest and most pleasurable [238]? The following survey describes the feast of prayer forms found in the Exercises as well as raises problems and suggests possibilities for contemporary women.

Repertoire of Prayer Forms

All manner of techniques for prayer exist, but prayer happens in the graced moment when desire for God initiates an awareness of and response to this One who has first loved us. Desire draws us, but the desire is placed there by the Spirit of God. And where the spirit of the Lord is, there is freedom (2 Cor 3:17) and delight. Not at every moment, of course, for relationship with God, like any other relationship, has moments of mystery, frustration, emptiness, challenge, dread, boredom, and fear. At these times, a technique or structure may help. Yet too much structure or the wrong technique can deflect from one's desire. Discerning the form, style, and timing of prayer is essential.

Particular and General Examinations

Although Ignatius presents two forms of examination, namely, the daily Particular Examination of Conscience [24–31] and a General Examination of Conscience intended to lead to a general confession [32–44], practice over the years has tended to collapse the two into one process of regular reflection.

The Particular Examination, often called the examen, sets out a regular, structured way of attending to daily life. Upon rising, one recalls the subject of examination and resolves to attend carefully to that issue [24].

After the noon meal comes a formal prayer time [25]. It begins with awareness of one's desires, the indicator of the condition of the heart. Ignatius suggests that appropriate desires for this prayer focus on consciousness of how one has maintained or ruptured the connection with God and on the desire to prevent any future rupture. The body of the prayer consists of an examination of the morning hours. This prayer is repeated after supper, reviewing the afternoon hours [26].

In several additional directives [27–32], Ignatius seems to have three positive strategies in mind. First, one cannot attend to a habit until conscious of it. Second, involving oneself as much as possible will speed the process. Third, the effects of one's attempts to become conscious grow cumulatively over time. As one continues into the Exercises, this examination can become a powerful means of deepening the effects of the other exercises [160].

The goal of the Particular Examination—refined consciousness of God's presence and action—remains as valid today as in Ignatius's time. Along with these positive strategies, however, comes the risk that the external process, especially because of its regular focus on sinfulness, will remain only an external process or will simply reinforce a sense of habitual failure. The close attention to faults and failings and the system of keeping account suggested by the text can create a huge burden for most contemporary women. The form of the practice clearly needs reclaiming.

Ignatius intended the second or General Examination of Conscience [32–42] to help persons prepare for confession. In Ignatius's time, the faithful usually confessed once a year, and the preparation for this confession could take several days (Ganss 1991, 395n22). Seen in this context, Ignatius's detailed instructions provide a method for such preparation. Although his points in this section raise many questions today, his comments about the value of confession [44] still have merit, perhaps more so in a contemporary climate in which both Roman Catholics and Protestants have tended to underplay its worth.[3] Confession or the sacrament of reconciliation can have beneficial spiritual effects as long as it is entered into freely and arises out of a genuine movement of the Holy Spirit.

In fact, the fivefold method of the General Examination lends itself to contemporary adaptation. It deals with thanksgiving, desire, review, and assessment, asking pardon and commitment to renewed growth. This simple progression has generally superseded the Particular Examination and forms the foundation of most contemporary adaptations, including George Aschenbrenner's now classic adaptation in "Consciousness

Examen" (1972).[4] This form takes its name from Ignatius's term *consciencia*, which can mean conscience or consciousness (Ganss 1991, 396n26). The contemporary shift from using "conscience" to using "consciousness" acknowledges a watershed in understanding the role of examination in the spiritual life.[5] It signifies a shift in emphasis from individual acts to the fundamental orientation of one's whole life.

Contemporary spiritual writers on examen tend to work extensively with this form of examen. For example, Tim Muldoon speaks of two forms of examen: the first when we come to a pause point or an inflection point, where we ponder where we've been or what the previous days, weeks, and months might have been like for us, and the second, which looks more specifically at our consciousness of our past day (32–33). Gone is the distinction between General and Particular Examen that Ignatius draws so clearly. Mark Thibodeaux expands the daily examen prayer, which he calls "the most amazing prayer you've never heard of" (2015, vii), into a way of praying without ceasing that can ground a systematic reflection on all parts of life.[6]

A practice of daily reflection such as that proposed in the reclaimed examination of consciousness both depends on and fosters the skills of noticing, naming, and acting on one's awareness of God's presence in daily life. Noticing interior movements will be key all through the Weeks to follow. It is a prerequisite for implementing the Rules for Discernment of Spirits and therefore essential to making carefully discerned decisions. It is truly a foundational spiritual discipline, with significance far beyond the Spiritual Exercises themselves.

Meditation, with Repetition and Résumé

The next kind of prayer presented in the Spiritual Exercises is meditation, which consists primarily in thinking, reasoning, and considering, though imagination and affections also play significant supportive roles. The context for meditation, as for all prayer in the Exercises, consists in disciplined time, specific place and posture, exterior and interior awareness of the environment, and attention to one's desires. Ignatius's structure for meditation [46–49, 54] includes a preparatory prayer, two or three preludes (or considerations framing the experience to follow), several points providing the body of the consideration, and colloquy or personal response. He closes each meditation period with a vocal prayer that all could recite by heart.

Movement

The preparatory prayer can be as simple as a single sentence based on the Principle and Foundation, in which one asks that everything one does be ordered and directed to the service and praise of God, which Ignatius uses consistently throughout the Exercises [46]. Or it can be something that the individual herself brings. The point of the preparatory prayer is to set all that follows into the wider context of the greater glory of God. Sometimes two, but usually three, preludes follow. Through them one gathers or "composes" all parts of one's mind. Memory is directed to place the topic accurately in its context, the history of God's dealings with humankind. The imagination is invited to create the place. The will is activated through asking for what one desires. The final prelude always concerns desire, and it changes with the focus of the prayer. When Ignatius mentions a specific desire, it signals the most significant grace of the prayer as he understands it. Through the preparatory prayer and preludes, one says to God, "Here I am, every bit of me, ready to pray."

The next part of meditation develops the subject matter. Ignatius breaks the material into "points," usually three, each suggesting a slightly different aspect for consideration.

Then one talks, "as one friend to another," to God, Christ, or Mary, as suggested by the particular meditation. This conversation, or colloquy as Ignatius calls it, can happen at any point, but Ignatius specifically recommends it for the end of the prayer. Colloquy is so important that Ignatius sometimes treats it as a new dimension of prayer. The colloquies themselves add to the material for the next pondering and conversation. In effect one says to God, as to a friend, "As I was saying yesterday…now, as I think about it today, I wonder…." Finally, Ignatius suggests a definite conclusion to the meditation, reciting a familiar prayer such as the Lord's Prayer.

But Ignatius does not stop here. To derive the most from each prayer period, he suggests spending some time after its conclusion noting how it went [77]. Were there consolations and desolations? Where? How did one cooperate with the consolation and work against the desolation? The review brings discernment of spirits into play, exercise by exercise, prayer by prayer, helping bring about greater consciousness of how God works and how one responds.

Then the prayer is repeated. The word Ignatius uses, *discurrir*, means something like "range over" or "wander about," but not aimlessly. Instead, Ignatius wants the one making the Exercises to "turn over" the preceding prayer and its review (Peters 1967, 35), to return to both the consolations and the desolations. Repetition [62–63] and résumé [64] serve to distill the prayer into greater focus, allowing one to go progressively deeper into the mystery of God. The prayer may also become simpler and quieter with each repetition. Active prayer may become more passive; the seeker may do less and less, and God may do more and more. Repetition and résumé allow these possibilities.

Ignatius has created a process that can be used by anyone. A person quite practiced in prayer and its many manifestations might minimize this structure almost to the vanishing point, but another person will find the structure liberating, allowing her to hear in entirely new ways what God desires to communicate. The structure given by Ignatius encourages such freedom. The one giving the Exercises has the challenge of facilitating it.

Imaginative Contemplation

In the Second Week, Ignatius introduces contemplation [101], by which he means attending to persons and events largely by means of imagination. Its form parallels that of meditation: preparatory prayer, preludes, points, and colloquy. The contrasts between these two forms of prayer, however, are particularly instructive.

Meditation employs reasoning, supported by memory and imagination, while contemplation employs imagination, supported by memory and reasoning. The preludes to a contemplation ask the seeker not only to recall but to actually re-create the event, both by situating oneself imaginatively within it and by desiring interior knowledge of it. Seeking to be so intimately present to the events and persons truly brings a new knowledge of them. Each of the three points entails imagining the event from a somewhat different perspective and employing a different aspect of the imagination. The colloquy, still "friend to friend," now specifically mentions affections that "I feel in my heart" [109]. Finally, the seeker repeats the contemplations, noting the presence of consolation and desolation. This repetition moves from the surface of events and personalities into the very mystery these persons and events reveal.

The desired outcome of imaginative contemplation—affective knowing—brings about different fruit than does meditation. Engaging the affections ignites prayer, giving it movement, texture, passion. Feeling deeply about someone or something not only moves one to action but also sustains these actions in the face of opposition. Affections form the primary subject matter considered in discernment of spirits. They are so significant to the dynamic of the Spiritual Exercises that when absent, the one giving the Exercises should probe for possible obstacles.

Ignatius introduces contemplation in the Second Week of the Exercises. This Week requires sensibilities and capabilities not necessarily conscious or developed in the First Week. The dispositions and abilities upon which both the Second Week and imaginative contemplation rest include the ability to recognize one's motives, to plan for long-term goals, and to "notice key interior facts," as authors William Barry and William Connolly (1982) put it. These same prerequisites make affective prayer and discernment of spirits possible. As one's breadth of prayer experience and degree of self-reflectivity grows, so does one's authority and initiative.

Colloquy: Substantial Prayer in Its Own Right

The Spiritual Exercises present colloquy within Meditation and Contemplation. For example, see Ex. 53, 61, and 63 for Ignatius's instructions on colloquy in the First Week, and Ex. 109 and 147 for the Second Week. Because of Ignatius's pedagogy, namely, teaching colloquy within the progression of the Exercises, it is easily overlooked as an integral form of prayer in its own right.

Every exercise throughout the Spiritual Exercises is meant to end in a colloquy, or, as Adrien Demoustier (2002, 16–17) says, "to make contact with the Word." That is, no matter what the subject of the Exercises, the one making the retreat is encouraged to make personal and even intimate contact with God, directly (Christ, the Father, or the Trinity) or through the mediation of Our Lady. We respond to the One who has already met us in the grace of the exercise. We address our response to God, but at the same time, we attend to the reality beyond the words, namely, the mystery we call God.

At the beginning of the Exercises, this conversation may seem stilted or a little contrived, but gradually, as the one making the retreat experiences the Christ of the Exercises, the conversation becomes more and more intimate and simple. Over time, it may contain more silence than speech as union with God becomes more and more habitual. It becomes like a river running continuously through us. In fact, by the end of the

Exercises, it is clear that colloquy is meant to escape the boundaries of the Exercises.

The first hint of this progress appears in a surprising place: the description of the Third Degree of Humility [166, 168]. Here Ignatius invites the one making the retreat to mull over the degrees and make colloquies throughout the entire day. But the most obvious indication that continual direct conversation is a fruit of the Exercises appears in the Third Week, as the one making the retreat accompanies Christ in his passion. Here colloquy can be the single action that takes up the entire prayer. By the time the retreatant arrives at the Contemplation to Attain Love, the long process of Ignatian contemplations becomes something received directly, without intentional work. This kind of experience is marked by silence as words give way to immediate presence.

Application of the Five Senses

The Second Week explicitly introduces the Application of the Five Senses, perhaps Ignatius's finest example of holistic, embodied prayer. His understanding of this form of prayer cuts across the whole array of prayer forms, illustrating the basic truth that faith is as much rooted in one's body as in one's mind.

Ignatius does not use the term *Application of Senses* in the First Week. He does ask those making the Exercises to use all their senses explicitly and graphically in the meditation on hell [65–72], "to see the huge fires, hear the wailing and so on." But this exercise is quite different from Application of the Senses introduced in the Second Week. While the senses are employed in both, Application of the Senses engages the interior senses in a way that is more receptive than active.

In the fifth contemplation of the Second Week [121], Ignatius finally speaks of "Application of the Five Senses." From then on, he specifies this method for the final period of prayer each day. The first point highlights seeing; the second, hearing; and the fourth, touch. But the third point, stressing fragrance and taste, forms the heart of this experience of prayer: "I will smell the fragrance and taste the infinite sweetness and charm of the Divinity, of the soul, of its virtues, and of everything there, appropriately for each of the persons who is being contemplated. Then I will reflect upon myself and draw profit from this" [124].

Ambiguity abounds in the interpretation of this form of prayer. Ignatius's brevity may indicate either a presumed familiarity with it, at least at one level, or a deliberate vagueness that allows for diversity of God's action without raising a red flag for the Inquisition. At any rate, the debate about what Ignatius meant is far from over.[7]

David Fleming, however, offers an interpretation that respects the dynamic progression of the prayer of each day, which moves from active engagement to deepening reflection on the points where one has been touched, to our "full body and soul involvement—our being actively passive—in the final prayer of the day." Application of the Senses is another level of reflecting and deepening within oneself as one closes out the day: "It is like having all the prayer highlights of the day cascade over us in a drenching shower; it is akin to what we call an 'overload of sensible experiences'" (Fleming 2004, 19). "It is a way of getting out of our heads and going deeper into the perceptions, feelings and promptings that have taken place over a day, especially at day's end, when tiredness can make other kinds of prayer burdensome" (Simmonds 2018, 1).

Three Methods of Praying

Ignatius introduces this section [238–60] with a surprising assertion: prayer should be both one's own and it should be pleasing. To foster these fruits, he sets out a variety of methods from which to choose.

The first method consists in pondering, after suitable bodily recollection and preparation, a doctrine or an aspect of the person in order to enter more fully and personally into it [238–48]. Ignatius's belief that all prayer is supported by the body appears in his direction [247–48] to pray on each of the five senses. His third method introduces praying "according to rhythmic measures," that is, measured by one's breath [258–260].

Most of the Three Ways of Praying have already made an appearance in the Eighteenth preliminary Annotation. Yet the *Directory* of 1599 states that these exercises also have value for the spiritual progress of those who have made the Exercises (Palmer 1996, 343), contradicting a common conclusion that relegates these methods to "beginners."

The placement of these points suggests their usefulness amid everyday life, either after completing the Spiritual Exercises in an enclosed situation or as a shortened, Eighteenth Annotation form. The three separate yet overlapping methods of prayer are to be used according to circumstances, and, indeed, are to become as natural as breathing itself (Barnes

1989, 270), and as simple. Indeed, George Aschenbrenner (2004, 150) has a lovely metaphor for the third method: "Your breathing person is a praying person. Prayer has so deeply watered and sanctified your person that it easily spills over into words."

Problems and Possibilities for Women

Each prayer form of the Spiritual Exercises suggests areas of opportunity and concern for women: imagination itself, women's consciousness, using one's mind as prayer, cultivating the imagination, the possibilities and pitfalls of desire as central to prayer, embodiment in prayer, and, once again, what it means to take adaptation seriously, this time in the matter of appropriate prayer forms.

Imagination

Modern Western culture, in so lauding the intellect, often allows it to overshadow the rational power of imagination that makes knowledge possible. Imagination, long equated with "the feminine," and therefore irrational, became a burden borne unequally by women. Many still feel burdened by the Cartesian "divorce" of the intellect and imagination, whereas in truth they are intimately connected. Comprehending the complexity of their interaction means understanding imagination as a kind of transformer or scanner that collects images from the outer world. Juxtaposing them with images in one's memories provides raw material for reflection and abstraction. Imagination literally feeds inner reality. Reclaiming imagination's possibilities for prayer is good news for women, who have long been stereotyped and trivialized for being imaginative; women can call on this strength in their prayer.

Philosopher Ray Hart (1968, 242) notes that "in the scale of cognitive acts, imagination remains nearest the event, elaborating its feeling-tone in a universe of non-discursive discourse." The imagination knows things in their concreteness, in their uniqueness within an ambiance of affectivity, while reason takes from reality, drawing deductions and abstractions.[8] For example, one may not be aware of the essence of blue herons, but be thrilled by the beauty and dignity of *this* blue heron on a misty morning. Cognition through the imaginative system complements the conceptual, intellectual approach to truth. Without replacing reason, imagination brings together all the faculties into equilibrium or simultaneity.

Imaging makes up the first level of the imagination. It becomes multivalent as it moves into symbol, suggesting one or more meanings. Those symbols with wide human application are called archetypes (Bryant 1984, 83). Whatever the level of imagination, its language is indirect, using images, symbol, story, metaphor, myth. These modalities engage the whole person, not just the mind, demanding response. The language of knowing God is primarily the language of images. In Cardinal Newman's famous analysis, belief begins and grows, not through a notion or concept, but in the image or symbol. Imagination therefore is central to both faith and prayer. As the locus of God's initiative, it also ultimately sustains all forms of prayer, preceding even apparently imageless prayer.

Imagination not only discloses the outer world, it also gives glimpses into the inner world of the psyche using the symbolic language of feeling-charged images. Most persons think they control their reality; they fail to see how the unconscious influences them. Only when experiencing unexplained or unusual surges of emotion, feeling out of sorts for no apparent reason, or making slips of the tongue does one intuit the presence of an unseen force that contains enormous energy, forms of intelligence, and even distinct personalities.

Carl Jung spoke of individuation, a lifelong process of coming to conscious awareness of the totality of one's person—becoming an *imago Dei* in light of who God calls one to become. Individuation, achieved largely by bringing both our conscious and unconscious life into harmony and collaboration, remains much more easily said than done.

The symbols of the unconscious life present themselves to the level of consciousness primarily by two routes, dreams and imagination, but also by prayer fully entered into. Many women have dream experiences during the Spiritual Exercises every bit as revelatory as conscious prayer or ritual.[9] Assuming that the guide has some skill at helping the one making the Exercises unpack the dream, might not the guide pay attention to these as well? This strategy does not mean that the Spiritual Exercises assume a therapeutic tone, but that the guide chooses to listen to, and to help the retreatant listen to, the totality of God's work in the person at both the conscious and unconscious level.

A Jungian technique called active imagination provides another way of using the imagination to constructively approach the unconscious.[10] Ignatius and others utilized aspects of this process long before researchers in neurology, psychology, and philosophy "discovered" the giftedness of right-brained functions. Many writers have pointed to similarities between active imagination and imaginative contemplation. Both use dialogue with images or symbols that arise during the course of attentiveness. In prayer, this may mean dialoguing with persons within the scriptural scene. It may also mean conversing with aspects of the personality or dream figures.

Some women feel they have no imagination, at least no visual imagination, hesitating to employ it in relation to prayer. Yet their imagination may be much more active than they realize. They might be invited to notice such commonplace life situations as planning what they will wear to their friend's wedding, organizing their day to make sure that the children get picked up, or preparing what they will say at an important meeting. These simple exercises can expand their understanding of imagination and help them claim the kinds they do have. Nonthreatening guided exercises and symbolic fantasies, such as those offered by Anthony de Mello (1978), can prove both helpful and revealing, preparatory to scriptural prayer.

One guide relates a provocative example that occurred during a workshop on imaginative prayer. A woman was asked to imagine that a sculptor had created a statue of her. In her imagination, she was to walk into a room where the covered statue waited and remove the sheet. She did so and was at first delighted by the likeness, but subsequently repulsed when she saw the statue portrayed her standing with her hands over her eyes, covering her face. Still following directions, she watched incredulously as workmen came in, lifted the statue, and loaded it into the back of a pickup truck. She followed the pickup to a familiar location—in actual life, her therapist's office. The workmen placed the statue in the waiting room and there, merging with the statue, she stood with her hands over her face. Children coming into the waiting room begged her to remove her hands, but she couldn't. Finally, she was told that Jesus had entered the room and was standing in front of her. She couldn't see him. Suddenly she heard Jesus say words to her that she had often heard from her spiritual director: "Ann, look at me." He gently touched her immobile hands and took them away from her face. At that moment she began to feel differently about herself and God. This imaginative encounter triggered an awareness in her in a way that many other efforts had not succeeded in doing (Kelly 1991, 12).

There is nothing magical about this or several other helpful techniques such as "image guidance" or focusing.[11] When prayer seems blocked, it helps to explore whether images are the culprit. If one's images of the holy mystery of God are static or worse, destructive, then chances are this inner state directly affects one's spiritual life.[12]

Examen: Prayer of Women's Consciousness

The particular examination, suitably adapted in form and focus, has the potential to become truly a prayer of women's experience. The seeker begins by acknowledging her own gifts and exploring the implications of her gifts. In this process, she also discovers the negative consequences of her choices. Rather than emphasizing areas of failure, however, women generally profit more from reflecting on areas of giftedness, graces, breakthroughs, and successes, recognizing how God has brought fruit into all dimensions of life. Women often need time to acknowledge their gifts and to take responsibility for their own lives, since they may not habitually do so. They may need to get in touch with their own initiative and responsibility in response to an initiating, enlivening, and loving God. The dailiness of the particular examination fosters this internalization.

The examen also fosters the realization that the present moment, ordinary as it may be, is the fruit of one's past choices and leads to future ones. It moves from a superficial survey of what happened in a day to a deeper sense of patterns in one's life. This first step, noticing, needs to be followed by analysis, judgment, and choosing, for as one sees, one judges and acts. The practice of examen can evolve from exterior norms to interior movements, from individualistic assessment to communal and social responsibility, from a specific list of daily practices to a discerning way of life, from externally imposed norms to a sense of personal coresponsibility with God.

Self-knowledge plays a role in every great religious tradition, yet one can never become totally aware of everything about oneself. Sooner or later, the particular examen leads to the unconscious. The process of integration requires bringing to light aspects of the self kept out of consciousness, in order to use them in service of one's goal.

By definition, one has no awareness of what is unconscious. How does one notice what one does not notice? Clues do exist: in dreams, slips of the tongue, resistances and desires, and projections, both positive and negative. Pertinent questions reveal pivotal insights. What are the "musts" in my life? Where do they come from? What if I disregard one of them? What do I really dislike in others? How is this quality present in me?

What do I really desire, and how does it differ from what I have deemed an "acceptable" desire? What is going on when my response is out of proportion to the situation? When examen reaches this depth, it becomes a prayer of ongoing conversion par excellence.[13]

Examen can raise particular difficulties for women. They may come to this prayer with a stronger sense of being sinned against than of sinning. The important move then becomes the transition from being a victim to being a self-directed agent of one's own life, a shift that may take months or years. "Why is this taking so long? Why can't I just forgive and get on with my life?" they may say. Sensitive accompaniment will help them continue patiently through the process, rejoicing at each new degree of freedom.

Women can also notice too much and be blinded by detail. Learning to sift the wheat from the chaff and letting the less important go in service of the central can sometimes prove a difficult struggle. They may need an outside perspective, someone who helps them evaluate their experiences and choices in light of their deepest desires. The guide must exercise vigilance here by focusing on such questions as the following: Where does the deepest integrity of this person really lie? Am I reflecting the desire I want her to have, or is it really her desire, flowing from her integrity?

Practiced over time, examen can truly be a prayer of women's experience. As such, it becomes a source of revelation, not only for the individual woman, but ultimately, all persons.[14]

Meditation: Using One's Mind as Prayer

Ignatius's presentation on discursive meditation [45–54] explicates more of a specific method than any kind of teaching on this form of prayer. Many women report disliking his outline of meditation. Some find it too heady or the structure cumbersome and artificial. Contemporary women may not need all the accompanying suggestions, preferring to prepare themselves for prayer by listening to appropriate music, utilizing body movement, yoga, fantasy, or a simple breath prayer.

Having the colloquy at the end seems to separate the affective element from intellectual activity, thus maintaining a dualism of head or heart prayer. On the contrary, one should view this necessary form of reflection from an affective perspective. Using one's mind is not an isolated endeavor any more than prayer of presence or of the heart is divorced from intellect. One brings the fullness of one's being to whatever form of prayer is employed.

Bringing her mind to bear on affective states can be a revealing exercise, particularly when dealing with "negative" emotions. For example, spending a period of meditation "standing in one's anger" or journaling about it in the presence of Jesus can facilitate an enlightening and healing meditation, as can praying over Jesus's own anger in the temple (John 2:13–17). Body movement can also provide an expressive and prayerful medium (Fischer 1988, 190–92).

The rich tradition of discursive prayer prior to Ignatius began to deteriorate in the fourteenth century when reflection on religious or mystical experience was separated from the rest of theology. Prior to this time, theology implicitly contained the fruit of a profoundly prayerful life, as seen in the writings of Bernard of Clairvaux, Gregory of Nyssa, Bonaventure, and others (W. Johnston 1995, 60–73). This separation greatly diminished the "base" of meditation, resulting in the contemporary need to broaden the human experience grounding this form. One effective way to do this is by reading widely: devotional classics or "spiritual reading," theology, and literature, including novels and poetry. Drama, film, art, and dance also add immeasurably to the depth and meaning of this or any form of prayer.

A second historical reality affecting prayer, still very much alive for many, is the perception of progressing in stages of prayer. In this model, meditation lies near the bottom of the ladder, implying a "second-class" status. Yet, real life does not bear out this approach to growth in prayer. Most of the great mystics or persons writing about prayer today report frequently using discursive prayer. Like any relationship, there are times of greater intellectual intensity as well as quiet and "being with."

Another antimeditation bias emerges from the more recent Eastern influence on contemporary prayer. Non-Christian and even Orthodox techniques generally focus on less activity by the pray-er and a gradual elimination of thought, image, and symbol from consciousness. But both active and passive prayer have a place; the seasons and conditions of life change, calling forth a variety of prayer styles (Houdek 1995, 32).[15]

"Asking for What I Want and Desire"[16]

The second prelude in Ignatian meditation remains significant for women: "asking for what I want and desire" as it is phrased in the First

Week [48] or "ask for the grace that I desire" in the Second Week [91]. This directive spills over into the third prelude of the Ignatian Contemplations throughout the remainder of the Exercises. Because desire appears so consistently throughout the Exercises, it bears further comments beyond those in chapter 3 unpacking Ignatius's specialized terminology.

When we know our deepest desires, we know something important, not only about ourselves but also about God, as our deepest desires come from and point to that same God. Desires are also powerful expressions of our passions, and these passions are what move us to action. Knowing our desires also points to the potential for our most powerful actions—for good or ill. Desires, however, are ambiguous. They can be both signs of and distractions from our true direction. They can be an authentic expression of who God has created us to be, or they can represent impulses that are not central to our God-given identity. Which desires are worthy? How does one tell the difference? For Ignatius, noticing the shifting of desires becomes the stuff of discernment of spirits.

Before we can get that far, however, we must believe that our individual desires are, in fact, significant enough to give them our attention—and here is the rub for some women. If they believe that what they desire doesn't matter, that someone else will tell them what is important, or that any desire that they have will likely be contrary to what God desires, they are unlikely to trust their desires. They may even find it difficult to identify and name their desires. Nor will they be able to know who *they* really are—identity is expressed in those things they commit to as revealed by what they most deeply desire. But the deepest loss will be that they are unable to discover the true core of their longing that could lead more deeply into God. This self-estrangement is not in an individual's power to fix. Though it has indeed been overcome once and for all, we all still live with its effects. Nothing can heal this inner division except to lean back into God's saving mercy, depending upon God to reveal our dividedness and help us choose to let our desires be purified, and then to act with greater integrity, however small the step forward. Sometimes all one can do is desire to desire to be close to Jesus.

Honest prayer affects our desires. As we continually bring our desires to God, flawed, partial, and conflicted though they may be, we find that they begin to get sorted out. Ann and Barry Ulanov agree: "Prayer enlarges our desire until it receives God's desire for us. In prayer we grow big enough to house God's desire for us, which is the Holy Spirit" (Ulanov and Ulanov 1982, 20).[17] Our prayer focuses our desire. Our desire inhabits our prayer. This conclusion allows us to look at desire beyond its function at the level of the individual meditations and contemplations, and recognize desire as a key dynamic that threads throughout the four Weeks, linking them together in each individual's experience of the graces of the Exercises.

William Barry (2001, 26–43) helpfully illuminates how the shifting of desires marks the transition from one Week to the next. The essential desire, the desire that indicates that a person is affectively prepared to engage in the Spiritual Exercises, is a real trust in God and an experienced-based belief in God's loving care and providence. Such desire will allow the one making the retreat to trust that anything in one's heart can be open to God. This desire may come easily or it may come after days of prayer, but its appearance signifies the grace of the First Week. The desire to know Jesus and to love and follow him more deeply ushers in and grounds the Second Week. The desire that signals the transition to the Third Week is the desire to accompany the loved one into the place of that loved one's suffering. Barry suggests that a key contemplation at the beginning of every retreat would be to focus on Jesus as he turns and says, "What are you looking for?" (see John 1:38). As these words penetrate the heart of the one making the Exercises, she will know better who she is at this moment in relationship to God inviting her to the Exercises.

Desires also play an important part in other aspects of the Exercises. Continual prayerful reflection on desires reveals that they point to vocation. As Frederick Buechner observed, "The place where God calls you to is the place where your deep gladness and the world's deep hunger meet" (Buechner 1973, 95). Buechner has qualified "desires" as "deep gladness" because not just any desire is worth a vocational commitment. Ignatius recognized similarly that our deep desires need to be cultivated. He directs those making the Exercises to learn about their desires by means of the Examen, and then he instructs them to reflect on their vocational choice in light of the person of Christ. For Ignatius, there is no better context in which to bring our purified desires to the world's deep need than the presence of Christ.

Contemplation: Cultivating the Imagination

Drawing on a tradition of the late Middle Ages,[18] Ignatius invites the seeker to envision a particular scene in Jesus's life as a kind of icon through which she moves and to become involved in Jesus's own life experience as a participant. The one making the Exercises consciously creates the scene and the persons involved, and allows the story to unfold, prompted by the reading of Scripture and the action of the Spirit.

One woman related the following. She had been praying with the story of the risen Christ appearing to Mary Magdalene (John 20:11–18). After listening to her describe her prayer, her Exercises guide remarked, "You know, I think you are looking *at* the story. You are not inside it. Why don't you let yourself *into* it?" With that encouragement, she returned to her prayer. The next day she reported, "I allowed myself to feel what I imagined Mary must have been feeling as she walked in the garden. Then Jesus turned around, and I recognized him, and he gave me the warmest, most loving hug!" She later observed, "I always thought I had no imagination. But it's not true—I have a great deal of imagination. I never knew Scripture could be so alive." The difference imagination can make in the feeling-tone of prayer may be life-changing.

Scripture, as noted, has a symbolic character. A Scripture text does not just provide a revelatory glimpse into the past, but a way of looking at oneself and others in the present. The events are mysteries that become alive and operative in the present. The story enters into one's own journey.

One author relates the experience of a woman asked to pray over the incident of Peter walking on the water (Matt 14:23–33). She had no difficulty getting into the boat, recognizing the presence of both Jesus and Peter, with whom she identified in her desire to be with the Master. Things went well for a time, but prayer seemed to "break down" when she attempted to get out of the boat. She told Jesus she could not do it and admitted to him she was scared because she could not swim. She then "felt" that Jesus was asking her if she thought he was making her do something beyond her capacity. She immediately replied, "Yes, you are...you often have." The deepest encounter took place as she realized she really did not trust Jesus because she did not know him well enough (Sheldrake 1987, 106). Her prayer did not really "break down," however, as the Spirit moved her in a direction she needed to go.

Imaginative contemplation does not mean slavishly sticking to the script, much less spending inordinate time on unnecessary details of the scene. Visualizing Jesus clearly is not important; a sense of presence is enough. Often communication is "felt" or intuited, rather than heard as ordinary conversation.[19]

Yet, because many people equate the imagination with the ability to visualize, they feel they cannot do this type of prayer. But imagination does not rely only on sight. People can get in touch with their own imaginative process by focusing on the sound of car tires crunching on a gravel driveway or of rain pelting the roof, by smelling the odor of a bakery or a loved one's perfume, by feeling the soft, wobbly head of an infant or the lushness of velvet, or by tasting a favorite dish or a cold beer on a hot day. A simple fantasy may unloose the imagination: "You are on a beach…a hillside…sitting by a river.…Briefly describe the scene using different senses.…In the distance you see someone approaching.…Let the imagination take over." Success in such imaginative exercises gives courage to move beyond fear and anxiety and opens us up for imaginative scriptural prayer.

Some women begin prayer by reflecting on their immediate life experience rather than on Scripture, but this procedure does not preclude imaginative contemplation. Jesus can be invited into the scene, to participate in the mystery of an individual's life, perhaps consoling, healing, challenging, or drawing attention to a new perspective. The risen Jesus makes a past or present event the word of God. More often, the seeker's lived experience, when probed with the guide, calls to mind a specific Scripture passage that can take on a whole new perspective in light of a daily happening. The seeker "backs into" Scripture, so to speak.

Some persons find themselves drawn to a quieter, nondiscursive, imageless form of prayer, the classic notion of contemplation.[20] Persons drawn into this manner of prayer by way of solid discernment need not be excluded from the dynamic of the Exercises, which encourages the seeker to enter as she can and not according to rigid definitions or forms of prayer. Ignatius insists that the guide allow God to deal directly with the seeker [15].

The imaginative aspect of prayer may last for most of the time or be a relatively brief experience, possibly a threshold to something quieter and more reflective. Imagination is not an end, but a powerful way of disposing one for an encounter with the living Christ, who often speaks directly to a present situation or condition. Believing that God alone controls prayer gives one the freedom to follow wherever the Spirit leads.

Application of the Senses: Embodiment in Prayer

Ignatius's terse description of Application of the Five Senses has opened a multidimensional approach to the senses, exterior and interior.

Knowing Whose I Am

The reflection on the five external senses within the First Method of Prayer [247–48] could well serve as a "priming" experience for most persons beginning the Spiritual Exercises.

The first and most immediate dimension of the Application of the Senses presumes an aliveness of the exterior bodily senses at the service of a faith perspective. The second dimension employs sense imagery by way of imagination and memory. The third dimension implies the activation of the interior senses by a Presence beyond human capacities to initiate.

The first dimension, awareness by the external physical senses, leads one beyond simple apprehension: "When we become present to and respectful of our bodily knowing and sensing, we become available for relationship with everything that is, including God" (Ruffing 1995, 105). This kind of openness may sound simple, but the fast pace of contemporary life carries with it a sensory numbing as one of its unhappy by-products. The deeper implications of a good part of experience get lost; life is not lived contemplatively.

Gemma Simmonds emphasizes the holistic nature of the prayer of the Application of the Senses, noting that the use of the Spanish word *sentir* has resonances that include mental and bodily processes as well as intuition and feeling. "Our imitation of Christ becomes more exact as we feel each sensation with and in him" (2018, 1). She points out how often we see women in the gospel connecting to Jesus through their bodies and their senses and argues that "the application of the senses confirms the body and its senses as a trustworthy conduit for intuiting and understanding the things of God" (2018, 2). Many women may resonate strongly with this way of praying and find their instinctive way of sensing and knowing validated.

One woman's recollection exemplifies how simple sensory awareness can lead to God and how all three dimensions coalesce:

> I recall when I was spending some time along the Icicle River. Whenever I have been in this picturesque area, surrounded by age-worn pines, the roar of the turbulent river in my ears, the scents of the season sharp in my nostrils—sun-toasted needles, naturally ripened blackberry vines—I have felt in my heart a great longing for God. As I contemplated the beauty of countless mountains surrounding the little valley through which the Icicle River flowed, I became aware that I had the privilege of seeing this beauty and of praising God for it. In a

flash of insight, I knew that God did not make all that wondrous scenery to get praised for it. I realized that God is so lavish as to make the beauty whether anyone ever even sees it! It was a momentary insight into the total meaning of things. I felt at-one with the earth and with my fellow inhabitants. The experience tapped into my interior creative sense, making me aware of my surroundings and, as my senses seemed to come alive, of my body's relationship with them. I saw for this moment the magnanimous nature of God, with plenty of room for inserting my gifts into life-with-God. I relinquished my need to be a "something," knowing that just to be, as the mountains just "are," was enough for this God.

Another woman making the Exercises was encouraged to express grief in body movement. She was surprised to realize an enormous unresolved anger emerging instead. The body registers and remembers every experience, even if the mind is not conscious of it. Thus, Application of the Senses becomes a way of honoring a memory and either deepening and savoring it or bringing it consciously to God for healing.

This first dimension also includes an awareness that goes beyond mere sensation. Imagination gives entry to the deepest realities because it approaches life in its wholeness: matter *and* spirit, not matter *or* spirit. Imagination establishes a relationship between the two, eliminating dualism and hierarchy. Rather, they fuse together in a kind of double vision or overlay of transparencies, allowing one to intuit the presence of mystery in the most ordinary things. The exterior senses become a portal to a deeper reality grasped only by faith. Imagination is integral to the living out of contemplation in action (Fischer 1989, 23).

One woman's experience exemplifies this "double vision." She was literally confronted by her psychological "shadow" on a busy street in Chicago's South Side. A young woman approached and asked her "to take her home and give her something to eat." The immediacy of the request stung her at several levels: she felt compassion for the woman, overwhelmed by the intensity of the brief exchange, and haunted by the "more" of the experience. Subsequent prayer helped her see God asking her to take care of herself instead of continually "pushing beyond" physical limitations. This first dimension of Application of the Senses, then, allows a person to enter fully into the present moment and be open to the deeper significance of immediate experience.

Knowing Whose I Am

The second dimension moves inward, relying on the imaginative use of the senses along with memory, either reliving an experience such as the above or inserting oneself into a gospel scene, an event in one's life or some artistic endeavor. Seasoned pray-ers will recognize moving into a mystery of Jesus's life as a participant—or even as Jesus—interacting with specific characters. Time demarcations blur and Jesus becomes present now, consoling, challenging, teaching, supporting, or healing. A distinct affective quality usually marks this level of Application of the Senses.

Another woman contemplated the same scene in Matthew 14:23–33, where Jesus invites Peter to walk on water:

> I was sitting in the open boat, feeling myself tossed from side to side, wet with the spray of crashing waves. I could not hear what my companions were yelling because of the noise of the storm. We were all terrified. I saw Jesus in the distance, coming across the water from the right, but I wasn't afraid of him at all. I wanted to get out of the boat to walk toward him, but I was so exhausted I wasn't sure I could make it. I had waited so long for his coming! Suddenly, he seemed to be right beside me, calming both the water and the rapid palpitations of my heart. He didn't speak of any lack of faith but told me not to worry….I had been walking on water for the last eight or nine years. But he assured me he had repeatedly kept me from "going under" both when I begged for help and when I simply needed it. I felt the blessed tears which for me are always a sign of God's presence. His words were so reassuring and vindicating amid a storm of confusion, ambiguity, and diminishment. I spent the remainder of prayer in deep gratitude and peace.

Previous dimensions, external sensation, or internal imagery may move to a still deeper dimension beyond the active capability of the pray-er. The interior or "spiritual" sense metaphorically describes an ineffable immediate experience of the Divine. The Exercises themselves give only an extremely brief description of this dimension, but Ignatius's letter to Teresa Rejadell, a cloistered nun from Barcelona, sheds further light on it:

> For it frequently happens that our Lord moves and urges the soul to this or that activity. He begins by enlightening the soul;

that is to say, by speaking interiorly to it without the din of words, lifting it up wholly to His divine love and ourselves to His meaning without any possibility of resistance on our part, even should we wish to resist. (Young 1959, 22)

Ignatius's deepest dimension taps into a long tradition originating with Origen and later adopted by Augustine (K. Rahner 1979a, 1979b). Augustine's immortal passage illustrates well the interior senses (although it leaves some ambiguity about his understanding of the body). It seems clear, however, that God's use of the interior senses leads toward an appreciation of the concrete world, not away from it:

> But what do I love when I love my God? Not material beauty or beauty of a temporal order; not the brilliance of earthy light, so welcome to our eyes; not the sweet melody of harmony and song; not the fragrance of flowers, perfumes, and spices; not manna or honey; not limbs such as the body delights to embrace. It is not these that I love when I love my God. And yet, when I love him, it is true that I love a light of a certain kind, a voice, a perfume, a food, an embrace; but they are of the kind that I love in my inner self, when my soul is bathed in light that is not bound by space; when it listens to sound that never dies away; when it breathes fragrance that is not borne on the wind; when it tastes food that is never consumed by the eating; when it clings to an embrace from which it is not severed by fulfillment of desire. This is what I love when I love my God. (Augustine 1961, 211–12)

Ignatius says simply, "Smell the fragrance and taste the infinite sweetness and charm of the Divinity" [124]. What he speaks of cannot be taught, only received in gratefulness and awe. This gift of God obliterates any notion of dualism, consecrating once again the embodied spirit and the preciousness of the entire being. For Ignatius, "this form of the Application of the Senses was the very essence of *sentir*—the feeling for the things of God" (H. Rahner 1968, 2). Mystics characteristically use sensory imagery in describing their experience of God. For example, Teresa of Avila, a contemporary of Ignatius, is more explicit than he in describing one of her intense religious experiences:

> But when this most wealthy Spouse desires to enrich and comfort the bride still more, He draws her so closely to him that she is like one who swoons from excess of pleasure and joy and seems suspended in those Divine arms and drawn near to that sacred side and to those Divine breasts. Sustained by that Divine milk with which her Spouse continually nourishes her and growing in grace so that she may be enabled to receive His comfort, she can do nothing but rejoice....With what to compare this the soul knows not, save to the caresses of a mother who so dearly loves her child and feeds and caresses it. (Teresa of Jesus 1950, 384–85)

If Teresa were to make the Exercises today, how might the one guiding the Exercises respond? Experiences that defy gender and role stereotypes, that come clothed in a baroque mix of metaphors, could prove daunting to someone unacquainted with the classic mystics and the possibilities of divine initiative very much present in our era. Granted, no one today would use this type of language, yet the experience could be equally profound.[21]

A contemporary woman speaks simply of her experience, implicitly pointing to a common obstacle for many persons—intellectualizing:

> I have been hearing the music again. I mean, quite literally, I hear music, like I did as a child....When I play it, I am likely to burst into tears, for its source is the Mystery, and I am playing something sacred that vibrates in places that are once again receiving light after many long years of darkness. I know that intellectualism has lost its grip on my being. What I do or what I become are not important so long as I listen to the music and dance.

Intellectualizing does not pose a trap just for men. Women too often interiorize cultural myths that honor only rational thinking and scientific proof. Persons who dismiss intuition and imagination approach life with an enormous handicap.

Application of the Senses, at whatever dimension, addresses a fully embodied way of knowing, not only through the intellect, but also the heart, feelings, intuition, and imagination. The mind wants to know, to analyze and abstract, but the embodied spirit wants to be surprised and willingly risks encounter with the fullness of one's being. Knowing God in this way points not just to God in all of creation, but also to God within. The external senses are a threshold to awareness of how God touches, embraces, and intimately creates each person, moment by moment, even if one does not feel it.

Colloquies and Women's Experience

The original writing group's three consultations with experienced directors of the Exercises—more than twenty years ago—yielded a piece of data that we didn't stop and question because it matched our own experience, namely that many of the religious in the congregations they worked with had developed a strong reaction against the Exercises and wouldn't take the initiative to make an Ignatian retreat of even eight days, let alone the full Exercises. It seemed that many resisted the Exercises—not a surprise after a pre–Vatican II mandatory regimen of Ignatian eight-day preached retreats year after year, which is what would have characterized the rule under which these religious lived. Once they could choose for themselves, many of these religious headed for individually directed and often non-Ignatian retreats, and lately, many have abandoned even individually directed retreats. Some phrased their objection as "I really don't pray that way"; and many of these women seemed to have gravitated toward prayer of silence, Centering Prayer, or Christian Meditation, or they incorporated Eastern practices into their prayer. At the time, it almost seemed as if many women religious outgrew the Exercises.

In hindsight, using the reflection of Franz Jalics (2002, 26), we can now see that the issue was not necessarily the Exercises themselves, but the way they were interpreted and presented. We readily spot one kind of progression in the Exercises: taken as a whole, they move from considerations of the generous love of God to the retreatant, a sinner, through increasing depth of relationship with Christ in the Second Week, to coming alongside the suffering Christ in such a way as to suffer alongside him in the Third Week, to—if the grace of the Exercises blossoms fully—simple contemplative presence with the risen Christ at the conclusion of the Fourth Week. From this contemplative presence, the one making the retreat joins in Christ's work in the world as the retreat concludes. Most givers of the Exercises see this cycle as making up the reality of the

Exercises. If a retreatant comes back in a successive year, the same process repeats—starting from the beginning of the First Week, exactly what happened to the religious who, year after year, listened to different retreat masters preach their version of the Exercises, often heavy on First Week points for prayer.

This progression describes how the focus of the four Weeks shifts. But another development trajectory can be traced by looking at the progression of the colloquies. When we follow this trajectory, we can see how to interpret the Exercises to allow an organic progression into deeper contemplative prayer: After each period of imaginative contemplation in the Second, Third, and first half of the Fourth Week, Ignatius asks the retreatant to set the Scripture aside and speak freely and spontaneously and confidently to Mary, Jesus, or the Father. With beginners, this part of the prayer is quite brief, engaged as the retreatant is with the memories, thoughts, and reflections from the individual gospel scenes. But over time, the preparatory work with Scripture becomes less and less detailed. The conversation grows easier and more comfortable and makes up an increasing amount of the time given to prayer. Once one comes to the Contemplation to Attain Love, the entire time of the prayer is taken up with immediate presence to God. At this point, Scripture-based prayer fades away—one dwells in what the Scripture-based prayer was meant to facilitate. The retreatant now contemplates God at work in creation and meets God by gazing at the works God is doing. This shift prepares the retreatant for everyday living, now characterized by God's constant presence and simple prayer.

This progression suggests that, over time, the presentation of Exercises must shift according to the way an individual's prayer has shifted. The second and subsequent times that retreatants come to the Exercises, they do not need to start at the beginning of this progression when it comes to prayer. They can come back to the Exercises with the way they now pray. The First Week will feel entirely different and fresh from the perspective of simple contemplative prayer than from that of step-by-step meditation. Had the earlier presentation of the Exercises considered the progression from meditation to imaginative Scripture-based prayer to simple direct gazing on God and God's works, from wordy prayers to the prayer of silence, perhaps those women religious discussed by our early consultants would not have resisted the Exercises so strongly later in life.

Movement

Taking Adaptation Seriously
The Three Methods of Prayer

The literature on the Spiritual Exercises contains considerable discussion about whether the methods Ignatius offers [238–60] best suit "beginners" or those "advanced" in the spiritual life. The terms of the discussion come across as another form of hierarchy that makes value judgments about the rich diversity of prayer. Those who do not find their experience represented among the "valuable" prayer forms feel once again disenfranchised from their birthright. The guide has a responsibility to help the seeker find the most useful, indeed pleasurable, method of prayer, establish a faithful practice, and adjust this practice in the face of the inevitable shifts that will occur as her relationship with God deepens.[22] A double-faceted corollary suggests itself: whatever prayer form facilitates the dynamic movement of the Exercises may be used, whether or not Ignatius specifically suggests it, and the best kind of prayer is that which supports living one's everyday life with intentionality and integrity.[23] Guides face a subtle temptation here: to impose prayer forms they either like or know while subtly discouraging prayer forms they do not find helpful themselves.

Franz Jalics (2002, 32) makes a further point, one that connects the colloquies directly to the Three Methods of Praying. He begins with the position that the Three Methods of Praying are an integral part of the Fourth Week, not simply an appendage to be used by those who are not, for some reason, able to do the full Exercises. Jalics calls attention to a phrase in the Fourth Preliminary Annotation in which Ignatius is describing each of the Weeks: "…and the Fourth, to the Resurrection and Ascension. To this week are appended the Three Methods of Praying." Assuming, then, that the Three Methods of Praying are integral to the Fourth Week, and noting that, as with other places of importance in the Exercises, Ignatius provides a numbered progression (e.g., three classes of persons and three ways of being humble), Jalics suggests that each method is most useful at different stages of readiness for and progression through the Exercises, culminating in the Third Method.

The First Method, which focuses on the Commandments, is especially suited for those who are at First Week readiness, and who still have sinful habits; this method's fruit is the letting go of the world's noise [239]. The Second Method [249–57] serves superbly for the person who habitually engages in the kinds of contemplations of the Second, Third, and the first part of the Fourth Week, during which the one making the Exercises looks for significance, makes comparisons, and attends to feelings of consolation and relish—exactly how Ignatius describes the fruit of this Second Method of praying. The Third Method makes sense for the person who has already interiorized the full Exercises, including and especially the Contemplation to Attain Love, and who is able to be immersed somewhat regularly in direct gazing at the person of Jesus. Here, there is no consideration to be done, simply the immediate presence to the word that is being said and the reality behind it. One looks directly at the person addressed, not at images, icons, memories, recollections, or comparisons. Since this wordless gazing is notoriously difficult to attain and maintain, Ignatius suggest breathing as the anchor, but other traditional ways of preparation may also assist such as a chime, a posture, or a sacred word.

The implications for the Exercises are significant. First, how each person prays should help focus the way the Exercises are presented. Would those disaffected women religious who appeared in the original consultations have responded more positively to a presentation of the Exercises that took their increasingly simple prayer into consideration? The second implication connects to the larger contemplative tradition: the Exercises are not a rigid form of meditation heavy on sin and hell as many assume, but they also draw from and contribute to the larger contemplative tradition, and gradually introduce contemplative prayer. Once such contemplative prayer has taken root, it becomes one's normal spiritual nourishment; once tasted, retreatants never want to leave it. Third, such simple prayer founded in the Contemplation to Attain Love and the Third Additional Method of prayer makes great sense for life after the Exercises. As Jalics says, "Experience richly shows that it is precisely the busiest people who are most grateful for this contemplative way of praying" (2002, 40).

Some modifications can make the Additional Methods of Prayer more appropriate for contemporary women. Today ruminating on wisdom teachings such as the Beatitudes and prophetic calls issued by the church might replace an exclusive focus on the Ten Commandments. For example, the Barmen Declaration[24] or the Roman Catholic bishops' pastoral *Economic Justice for All* (1986) or Pope Francis's encyclical *Fratelli Tutti* (2020) can yield rich and fruitful prayer in relationship to issues of justice. Instead of reflecting on the capital sins, a focus on the virtues necessary for living in harmony with the entire planet may make more sense. Once again, Ignatius's focus on the individual can expand to include all the systems in which the seeker lives.

In contrast to a culture that fosters numbness, the prayers on the Three Powers of the Soul and on the Five Senses of the Body stir up and "befriend" all these aspects of the person. Sensory stimuli bombard the contemporary world. Traffic roars constantly in the background; even in rural areas, the night sky rarely becomes black because of the artificial light of cities; "Muzak" assaults our ears in every elevator, waiting room, and even over the telephone; the text messages and social media notifications beep constantly; and stimulants and other chemicals enter the body through overly processed food, to say nothing of the chemicals sought to counter the deadness felt inside. No wonder our senses shut down. They never rest. A sabbath from overstimulation may prepare one to experience the senses anew; a simple fast from ordinary foods evokes a fresh, vivid taste of the first foods consumed.

In like manner, becoming aware of one's powers of memory, reasoning, and choosing will prepare all these aspects of oneself to profit from the Exercises. These additional methods are not simply preparation for prayer, they *are* prayer in their own right.

Additional Prayer Material on the Life of Christ

A long section entitled "The Mysteries of the Life of Christ Our Lord" [261–312] immediately follows the Three Methods of Prayer. It consists of fifty-one additional Contemplations for use during the Second, Third, and Fourth Weeks [162] or after the Exercises are completed. Each Contemplation centers on an event in the life of Christ and gives only the three central points, presuming the preparatory prayer, preludes, and colloquy. The Spanish translations from the Latin Vulgate are Ignatius's own, and thus do not correspond exactly to contemporary versions (Ganss 1991, 421–22). This section does not contain a new method of prayer but raises the issue of adaptation once again. It gives valuable insight into the biblical material in the Exercises, how Ignatius uses Scripture, and how it can inform prayer today.

What Ignatius includes and omits has engendered much interest. He bases all but two Contemplations on Scripture: the appearances of the risen Christ to his mother [299], which he justifies with the statement that Jesus appeared to many others, and to Joseph of Arimathea [310], which he takes from the lives of the saints. The first eleven cover the infancy narratives. The final twenty-four cover passion and resurrection narratives, with two unexpected changes: he adds a "Thirteenth Apparition" based on 1 Corinthians 15:8 and excludes Pentecost (Egan 1987, 83).

Omissions from the sixteen remaining passages covering the public life of Christ are likewise glaring. There are no healings of the sick, blind, or lame, no exorcisms, no forgiveness of sins, and no parables (Peters 1967, 114). The passages in which Jesus interacts with women are few (the wedding feast at Cana [276], the conversion of Magdalene [282], the raising of Lazarus [285], in which Mary and Martha are only supporting characters, and the supper in Bethany [286]). Ignatius, like many others, equates Mary Magdalen with the unknown sinner.

Ignatius's biblical scholarship reflects his time. For example, he selects from several Gospels to construct the points for one contemplation, creating a kind of harmony. This procedure, usual in his day, has been eclipsed since the rise of modern form criticism. Clearly, a contemporary approach to the Spiritual Exercises must be undergirded by advances in biblical scholarship.

Ideally, the one making the Exercises will have internalized the fruits of modern biblical scholarship and make such shifts easily, but it is equally possible that a woman approaches the Scriptures without the benefit of modern Scripture scholarship. She may find great consolation in a literal interpretation of Scripture, for example. She may have difficulty with Ignatian contemplation until she can resolve the theological issue of "correct" interpretation of Scripture. "That's not the word of God, that's my imagination," she may insist. Yet, if not forced to identify Ignatian contemplation too facilely with her understanding of a biblical word of God, she may still desire to experience what Jesus might want to say to her today. She may then willingly explore through active imagination how he might address her immediate needs. The biblical event simply frames this conversation. Once she experiences the immediate presence of the living Christ, her resistance to imaginative contemplation of Scripture may well lessen. Gentle and suitably framed suggestions about the ongoing and personal nature of God's revelation and the place of Scripture within this revelation will also help.

Even biblically literate women may be startled to uncover the patriarchy embedded in Scripture. If this discovery occurs during the Exercises, the strong feelings evoked become important material for prayer. They may wish to abandon the biblical text as a source for prayer. They may need encouragement to stay with this unpleasant discovery rather than abandon the biblical text.

In accord with the principle that the Exercises should be adapted to each person, women may need a selection of mysteries adapted to their predilections and preferences in prayer. If they so desire, they should receive encouragement to pray with passages involving women or having particular relevance to women. Some likely pericopes include the woman taken in adultery (John 7:53—8:11), Jesus weeping over Jerusalem (Luke 13:34), the woman who causes Jesus to change his mind (Mark 7:24–30), the first resurrection appearance to Mary Magdalene (John 20:11–18), the cure of the bent-over woman (Luke 13:10–17), the cure of the woman with the hemorrhage and the raising of the little girl (Luke 8:40–56), and the women who follow Jesus (Luke 8:1–3). Other alternatives include inviting women to put themselves in the place of male characters, such as Zacchaeus, Lazarus, or Peter, or encouraging them to pray with a single Gospel and allowing the figure of Jesus to develop within its theology and spirituality.

Since the individuals making the Exercises will vary widely in their experiences, desires, biblical interpretation, and theology, one cannot possibly propose a single list of texts women might find useful. The one giving the Exercises must have an ease with Scripture and knowledge of contemporary scholarship in order to move seamlessly between the biblical text and the needs of each person. There is no shortcut to this intimate acquaintance with the Scriptures.

Wisdom for the One Giving the Exercises

Unlike many mystics, Ignatius does not elaborate a mystical theology or an extended teaching on prayer to undergird his work. He does not describe stages of prayer or nights of the senses and spirit as do his contemporaries Teresa of Avila or John of the Cross. He simply outlines forms of prayer, offering several possibilities that might appeal and lead one to God.

Within the Exercises, he assembles a rich fare of prayer practices and techniques borrowed from the living tradition, adding his own particular emphasis on service as fruit of prayer. His stress on concreteness, the beauty of creation, embodied prayer, use of the imaginative faculty and openness to affectivity generally appeal to women, even if certain images are repugnant or outdated.

Ignatius's emphasis on disposing oneself for prayer should encompass music, yoga, body movement, fantasy and breath prayer, whatever techniques tend to move the seeker toward centeredness and focus. A respectful use of indigenous and Eastern practices has helped many persons. Those women out of touch with the gift of the senses or who tend to intellectualize might find Ignatius's Prayer on the Five Senses of the Body [247] or adaptations thereof helpful. Often women use artwork, poetry, or even body movement to report back to their guide. These media are significant because by their very nature they operate at a heart level.

In moving into the dynamic of the Exercises, some women are so intent on praying "correctly" that they violate their own spirituality. Anyone making the Exercises must be in tune with where God leads and seems to be present rather than rigidly adhere to the specific form of prayer suggested. For example, in Jesus's healing of blind Bartimaeus (Mark 10:46–52) one can move into prayer with a word or phrase that becomes a mantra. Alternately, one can simply be present to the God-in-Jesus who heals or recall an event in life where one was healed of a form of blindness or perhaps assisted another in this way. Whatever prayer form facilitates the dynamic movement of the Exercises should be used [2, 15, 76]. This flexibility seems to reflect the mind of Ignatius: prayer forms are not sacred—the relationship with God is. Ignatius's chief concern lies in assisting others to experience God and subsequently to go out in service to others.[25]

Finding ways that are "pleasurable" [238] does not simply mean experiencing comfort and warmth. It may mean confronting the need to take care of the earth, to probe questionable policies in church or government, or to go to that person with whom one violently disagrees. Perhaps "pleasurable" really means "deeply satisfying" with respect to one's integrity and call. The one making the Exercises should remain open to these new possibilities. Unfortunately, prayer itself can be an idol, substituting for the living God. The way God desires to be found *now* may be different than in the past.

A related issue is the imposition of a hierarchy that judges some prayer as better than others. Theologian Karl Rahner maintained that mystical experience does not mark a higher stage of the Christian life, but rather expresses the *psychology* of the individual person. Extraordinary mystical phenomena may reveal God's intimate presence but may use the language of the pray-er's psychosomatic structure. Theologically, the experience of God in meditation or in classical infused contemplation is the same gift of God (K. Rahner 1986, 75–77). God dwells in any form of prayer.

Thus, persons who apprehend life in Ruth Burrows's "lights on" modality consciously experience God's presence and action at least some of the time (1980). Others grow through the darkness and nakedness of pure faith in what Burrows calls "lights off" or Karl Rahner terms "winter grace." Neither journey is better: it simply is what it is by the grace and gift of God. Many experience a combination of both.

The body of Ignatius's writing does not seem to advocate any one form of prayer. He was not concerned whether a prayer form was more "advanced" but whether it was authentic for an individual and a wellspring of integrity and service. The ultimate criteria of any prayer or religious experience or lack thereof lies in the quality of one's life and the ability to go out in love and compassion to others, oneself, and the earth itself. Fidelity to prayer and a desire for God mark any authentic relationship with God. It matters not whether the prayer is characterized by parapsychological phenomena, rich affect, or complete blankness. Outward indications of authentic prayer, however described, are recognizable over time: interior freedom and trust of God, self, and others; greater flexibility and less judgmentalism; lessening of various kinds of fear; a mellowing-out or gentleness; absence of defensiveness; and, of course, peace and joy.

The guide, too, needs to be a person of deep prayer who grants others the freedom to pray as they can. He or she needs to be able to intuit when God invites the one making the Exercises to a different prayer form, which may elicit some initial fear and hesitancy. This sensitivity by the guide to God's action presumes an awareness of the subtleties of the Rules for the Discernment of Spirits, as well as a knowledge of the broader tradition of prayer. It is a knowledge born of personal experience and study, coupled with total reliance on the Spirit.

Part III
EXERCISES

CHAPTER 6

Surrounded by Love

Exercises of the First Week

...that I may feel an interior knowledge of my sins and also an abhorrence of them;
...that I may perceive the disorder of my actions in order to detest them, amend myself, and put myself in order;
...that I may have knowledge of the world, in order to detest it and rid myself of all that is worldly and vain.
—*Spiritual Exercises* [63]

Mortal and venial sin, compounded by stories of the fires of hell, are the antithesis of my belief about a loving and compassionate God. The content of the first week of the Exercises as well as its reasoned and rigid structures is repugnant to me.
—A contemporary woman

The loved sinner stands at the center of the First Week of the Spiritual Exercises. Although sin provides the focus, the First Week really dwells on love, God's love, which is greater than human sin. This Week moves from awareness of and responsibility for sin to awareness of God's gracious love, a love that forgives sin and welcomes the sinner, like the forgiving and prodigal parent who embraces and welcomes home erring offspring. Stories provide an avenue for this discovery.

Material and Dynamics of the First Week

The subject matter for the first meditation is the First, Second, and Third Sins (the angels, Adam and Eve, and the unnamed sinner in hell for one mortal sin, or for fewer sins than the retreatant may have committed [45–54]). The second meditation focuses on one's own sins [55–61], the third, a repetition [62–63], the fourth, a résumé [64], and the fifth, a meditation on hell [65–72]. This content and the corresponding additional notes help anchor the retreatant in surprisingly powerful ways that may not appear immediately obvious; they bear a closer look.

The first exercise concentrates on the cosmic scope of sin in three stories about choice involving the angels, Adam and Eve, and an anonymous sinner. The second exercise invites the one making the Exercises to move from observer to participant. She takes center stage in her own dramatic struggle to choose the direction of her life through memories of her personal "sin stories." She ponders her personal environment, her relationships, and her work. Where has she lived? Who has she lived with? What has she been doing with her life? In the third and fourth exercises, utilizing repetition, she returns to the subject of her prior meditations, specifically her experiences of inner movements, both positive and negative, that potentially lead to greater insight and affection. The First Week concludes with the fifth exercise, a meditation on hell that draws upon the symbolic memory of all the senses (seeing, hearing, tasting, touching, and smelling), graphically dramatizing the ultimate human evil imaginable—hell and whatever that suggests to the individual. There, in stark contrast, she realizes the unfathomable love of God. The graces of the First Week evolve from a more objective awareness and understanding of sin and its effect, to a deep personal realization that she is a loved and forgiven sinner. The pain of truth leads to the process of healing and the response of gratitude.

The content of the Week includes a substantial number of additional directives "for making the Exercises better and finding more readily what one desires" [73]. They begin in the material for the particular examen, where Ignatius suggests actual practices to embody the examen and gather increasing fruit from its practice [27–31]. They continue with some detailed instructions on how to prepare for sleep and pray upon awakening [74], how to use one's body to assist in meditation [75], encouragement to change postures to find the best posture for that prayer time [76], how to review after the prayer time [77]), how to focus one's thoughts and emotions on the larger dynamic of the Week [78], suggestions on shifting the ambiance in which one prays in order to enhance participation in the Week's dynamics [79], how to respond with one's demeanor and eyes [80–81], and a substantial treatment of penances [82–90]. With these directives, Ignatius is filling in the process that brings alive the content.[1]

However, by itself the content does not fully reveal the subject matter of the First Week. Besides Ignatius's extensive directions for how to do meditation, he also gives explicit directions for what to pray about as one enters the subject matter, and, in one case, the emotion that one might ask for during the meditation (an exclamation of wonder and surging emotion in light of how the angels and saints have protected and prayed for us [60]). The preparatory prayer, in which the one making the Exercises asks that all be ordered to God's greater glory, begins, ever so subtly, to point to the ultimate grace of the Week. In the second prelude of each meditation, Ignatius suggests the deeply personal and positive graces that reveal the ideal fruit of the exercise: in the first exercise, one asks for the grace of shame and confusion at one's sins in comparison to God's goodness; in the second, for growing and intense sorrow; and in the meditation on hell, for sufficient understanding of the seriousness of hell that it might serve to deter if nothing else does—I could actually choose to squander the love that God has so graciously extended no matter who I have been or what I have done, a love I have been internalizing throughout the First Week exercises.

Finally, the suggestions for the colloquies further frame the content. In the first exercise one engages directly and personally with Christ from a position at the foot of his cross, in wonder that he has done all this for her, pondering what she is invited to do for him. In the second exercise one is invited to a "colloquy of mercy," evoking gratitude and a resolution to amend her life. The repetition expands both the time and the subjects with whom one is invited to converse to include Our Lady, her Son, and the Father. In the meditation on hell, the colloquy points back to Christ, conversing gratefully with him that the one making the Exercises is not included among those in hell—how much pity and mercy he has shown me.[2]

Exercises

In the First Week, such cosmic and personal stories of conflict, alienation, and destruction tend to disturb and disorient. Thus, the one making the Exercises immediately must decide whether to trust the storytelling mode that grounds the Exercises and thus enter the narrative herself or to remain an observer. To continue implies confidence that the insight and self-understanding flowing from this reflection can move one toward the goal of personal freedom and not toward irrelevance, self-negation, or unhealthy guilt. A decision to probe these stories in faith-filled attentiveness can reveal a new understanding of God's mystery present in the power of narrative. Difficult stories also have potential for revelation and transformation. An attentive ear, listening to the truth in both the cosmic and personal stories, combined with a confident voice willing to engage in spiritual conversation, can uncover deeper levels of meaning and direction.

Two questions may quickly arise in the one making the Exercises. What are the First Week exercises about? What is going to happen? These questions touch on context and process. Answering them requires that one remember that God's gifts and hopes for humanity depend on one's free response to a personal call. Biblically based and imaginative stories reveal the cosmic struggle between good and evil, leading the one making the Exercises to the liberating discovery of God as compassionate Creator. In other words, the seeker experiences the story of sin and grace.

This awareness marks the major consciousness evoked in the First Week. As the one praying the Exercises notices multiple inner movements, she gains a clearer sense of what is of God and what is not of God. The God who creates and cares, divine majesty and infinite goodness, grounds one's deepest desires and deserves one's trust. Christ on the cross labors and saves. Each person, created in God's image and gifted in the mutuality of creation, is bound both by personal sin and, in some mysterious way, by the power of sin in the world. Such a realization can evoke tears, sorrow, confusion, helplessness, and repentance. The God of love and mercy calls to conversion.

Frequently, those making the Exercises struggle between opposites; they feel tempted to trivialize and deny sin or to become overwhelmed at its enormity. Yet the movement of the Exercises continues: from avoiding to encountering and finally to accepting and understanding sin as a reality of faith. Paradoxically, in confronting sin, the presence of goodness becomes more visible, bringing in its wake an aversion to everything not of God. In the First Week, a person's prayer moves from awareness, confusion, and sorrow to a response of deep gratitude and love. The grace of the First Week emerges when personal desires come gradually into greater harmony with God's will and desire.

Human finitude and its redemption make up the content of the First Week meditations. Meditation calls upon memory, imagination, reason, and will in considering the reality of cosmic and personal sin. Repetition provides an opportunity to circle the material, allowing feelings of attraction or resistance to lead toward deeper insight and affectivity. The meditation on hell activates sensory awareness as a prayer of the whole person.

Since the First Week text offers five exercises, be they meditations, repetitions, or résumé, the question immediately arises: Is all this material to be given on one day? How could anyone internalize that much material? What about the other days given to the First Week? This question arose in the first decades of the Society. Although various directories propose assorted options, in the early decades, the dominant interpretation was to give all the material at once over one day, beginning with the evening prior, adding some additional materials each day as the First Week meditations were again repeated. The repetition facilitated depth; the new material facilitated variety, which might also lead to greater interiorization. This cyclical manner of giving the Exercises of the First Week also highlights the internal logic of the Week. A minor early voice, captured in the Directory of Vitoria (1555), spread the First Week materials out over successive days in much the same manner as for a retreat following the Nineteenth Annotation. This linear interpretation was clearly not the generally accepted procedure at the time, but it has now become the favored way of moving through the First Week (Steinke 2013).

Problems and Possibilities for Women

The First Week seems clear and the dynamic consistent. Yet women's realities raise probing questions and troubling issues. Some of the factors women identify as blocks to entering into the First Week include the negative tone of the material, dissatisfaction in praying with the Bible, and perceived lack of imagination. Some women regress to a more negative image of God when they begin to confront sin, perhaps because Ignatius says so little explicitly about mercy in conjunction with sin. They react to the idea of the mortal sin of one person. Some complain that the material is anachronistic. One might say, "I want to get out of my head," another,

"I don't know what I want or desire." The one making the Exercises may also find the subject matter of sin and hell distasteful, the desired emotions of shame and confusion fearful, and some prayer forms artificial.

Some difficulties flow from an overly rigid sense of structure ("How do I do it right?"), fueling the impression even prior to the Exercises that a person must fit into a pattern and perform according to a script, and she will be evaluated on successfully accomplishing the tasks. Acting on this assumption distorts the Spiritual Exercises, making them into a grueling regimen with predetermined tasks to accomplish, obstacles to overcome, and goals to reach.

Reexamining the process and content of the First Week, however, will provide women with alternative perspectives. A contemporary worldview can open up a deeper realization about the interdependence of all creation and foster the basic recognition that she is not God. This assent leads to a growing sense of truth about self and God in light of the creation and fall. The actual meditations provide starting points for an affective response arising from prayer; they are not necessarily ends in themselves. Additional biblical stories, personal experiences, images, and insights beyond those suggested by the text can emerge as fruitful material for prayer of the First Week.

Images of Self and God

Those giving the Exercises know that the texts of the Spiritual Exercises, particularly those passages describing the self envisioned by the Exercises, require critiquing. This critique is particularly important when the "self" is a woman, because meditating on this material can create hazards for both self-concept and God-image. Women especially react to the self-deprecation underlying the suggestion "to consider my soul as imprisoned in this corruptible body, and my whole compound self as an exile in this valley (of tears) among brute animals" [47]. Another text raises similar problems:

> I will reflect upon myself, by using examples which humble me: First what am I when compared with all other human beings?...I will look at all the corruption and foulness of my body....I will look upon myself as a sore or abscess from which have issued great sins and iniquities and such foul poison. [58]

While this dramatic statement of mortality may have merely startled Ignatius's audience or echoed experiences of the early companions,[3] it seems to offer little of positive value for contemporary women, and may, in fact, be counterproductive.

Entering the Spiritual Exercises with a positive self-image and a holistic understanding of the human person engenders the possibility of a deeper positive valuation of oneself as a whole being with a body, mind, spirit, emotions, and relationships. In this way, relationship and connection replace dualism and polarization. When the one making the Exercises discovers and appreciates her own story and uses her own voice to tell it, she contributes powerfully to the larger story of faith.

Listening becomes an essential skill for the one making the Exercises. She must first learn to discern and honor her own authentic inner voice. This awareness and acceptance can prove difficult, as the most familiar voices she may hear are the loud, dominating voices of external authority or the strident voice of her own inner critic. This dynamic has particular complexity in some cultures. For example, in an African context, wisdom traditionally resides in the community and especially with the elders. Claiming the authority of her own voice becomes a prerequisite for personal authenticity and for contributing to the wisdom of the faith community. How does a woman from this kind of context listen for and honor both her own voice and the wisdom of the community? How, in sifting both, can she discover God's invitation to her?

Each woman's self-identity questions relate to concepts of self-image and God-image and make up an essential dynamic of this First Week. She is encouraged to reflect on her self-image: self as personal and as public, but always as relational. The Exercises assume the importance of self-definition leading to self-understanding. Each of the Weeks move toward a greater self-reflexivity and therefore relate to the dynamic direction of human development.

The actual dynamics of the First Week demonstrate how Ignatius starts with the "big picture," a cosmic perspective, and gradually moves toward the personal and specific. Personal responsibility, or lack of it, is also viewed according to its impact on the greater reality. The more self-reflexive one becomes, the more one sees one's personal role in the dynamics of creation. For Ignatius, relating to God is the precondition to reflecting on one's self-image.

The harmful effects of negative imagery extend beyond self-concept to God-concept, particularly in relationship to sin. When the woman making the Exercises perceives God primarily as patriarchal king, lord, or judge, she may base her sense of sin largely on submission and judgment. Classifying sin as mortal and venial assesses responsibility according to an exterior moral hierarchy. "Contemplating my many sins" may be exactly what a given woman should *not* do until she broadens her sense of sin and interprets it within the context of a loving God. An inner experience of knowing oneself as loved by God and rejecting any internalized self-hatred reveals an authentic First Week conversion. Conversion may also relate to ordinary events of daily life and its missed possibilities for growth.[4]

Ignatius uses a limited range of names for God in the Exercises, but these need not limit the possibilities for contemporary women. Images of God depend on one's experience of God, and how God acts in human history. Who am I? Who is God? remain constant underlying questions. The Principle and Foundation invited the seeker to consider the God of love and mercy as integral to her personal worldview. The subsequent movement of the Exercises, namely, awareness of the self as loved by God and the corresponding opportunity to respond in grateful loving service of others, invites one to love with greater and greater freedom. Even when employing Ignatius's names for God, contemporary women can reappropriate them. For example, naming the relationship of creature and Creator does not necessarily imply that the one making the Exercises should find herself near the bottom of the pyramid model of creation, reflecting an outdated cosmology (i.e., angels and men below God, but above children, animals, and inanimate creation). In fact, she participates in a network of interconnected life and creation where God constantly creates and initiates. Many metaphors point to this holy mystery of God: friend, lover, healer, father, mother, teacher, source of life and energy. As one's awareness grows, one responds in praise and thanksgiving, recognizing the God of mercy and forgiveness.

Christ is mentioned several times in the First Week. One powerful image encourages talking to him as friend to friend. Another suggests God's relationship to humankind in Jesus, a God of love and forgiveness. If one's sense of God flows from the experience of Jesus, who called God "Abba" and who compared God to a shepherd searching for a lost sheep or to a woman searching for a lost coin, then a more recent understanding of sin in terms of a fundamental option makes sense.[5] In this instance, the pattern of choices reveals a person's life direction more than isolated and individual acts. Those in touch with the cosmic Christ sense that Christ implicitly continues to act in creation. The First Week also refers explicitly to Christ on the cross, the traditional symbol of sin and salvation, but even more, of gratuitous love.

However diverse the words or images used by the one making the Exercises, the grace of the First Week remains clear: to know God, source of merciful forgiveness and compassionate love, and to know oneself in relation to God. Praise, service, wonder, and gratitude well up when encountering the God who knows each person more intimately than she knows herself.

Sin, Personal and Social

Ignatius's understanding of sin grew from his own conversion story. For him sin was "iniquity, disorder, ingratitude and slavery to Satan," and he wished to integrate all the "biblical ways of expressing what is evil into one dynamic consideration of the history of sin" (Cusson 1988, 141).

One's understanding of sin depends on one's worldview, sense of God and human relationships, and degree of freedom and responsibility. Because an understanding of sin implies a wide range of culpability, conscience formation and education likewise exert significant influence. Some equate sin with disobedience to laws and transgressions of rules. This lack of nuance in the categories of sin has taken its toll. One woman said tellingly, "I grew up thinking and feeling that almost everything was a sin, venial or mortal, especially mortal if it looked, sounded, smelled, or felt good. Now I realize that this belief was the sin I committed against myself." Others understand sin as infidelity to or breaking a covenant relationship of love. As Fischer and Hart (1995, 118) express it, "Sin or moral evil is the use of this capacity for free decision in ways that destroy our relationship with self, others and God—in fact with all of creation."

By pondering her culpability rather than exclusively contemplating her "many sins," the seeker can more productively reflect upon the First Week. Such consciousness asks each person to develop a true sense of sin and self in the context of a living, loving, relational God. Each woman needs to let God reveal where she refuses love. Since the First Week deals with sin and salvation, it also touches on God's love and forgiveness. Only persons of faith can comprehend the depth of the reality of sin. Indeed, saints seem to be the experts on sin, as Julian of Norwich illustrates: "It is God's will that we recognize sin, and pray busily and labour willingly and seek meekly for teaching, so that we do not fall blindly into it, and if we fall, so that we quickly rise. For the greatest pain that the soul can have is at any time to turn from God through sin" (Colledge and Walsh 1978, 328).

In the process of the First Week, the person living the Exercises moves from the more objective meditations on sin as a cosmic and historical reality to its personal reality. At the same time, the perspective shifts from observer to participant, eliciting a greater sense of responsibility for exercising personal freedom. Women can be encouraged to take responsibility for personal sin in ways that have meaning for their lives. For example, a woman may understand sin as whatever lessens humanity, decreases the capacity to love, or gets in the way of developing her potential as an image of God. Sin ultimately goes against her own being, for its roots are relational. Thus, sin includes both individual and social responsibility.

Traditionally, specific acts such as lying, cheating, stealing, or inflicting bodily harm on another were termed sinful. Yet sinful situations, such as sexism, racism, or the voracious consumption of the planet's limited natural resources, also constitute sin. Middle- and upper-class women face several particular challenges from the First Week as they reflect on sin. They can unconsciously maintain a situation of privilege while avoiding awareness of the interrelationship of oppression, racism, classism, and sexism, and of their complicity in such social sin. Clues to this complicity can be as subtle as assuming that "flesh"-colored bandages will match one's own skin color and that local newspapers and television will reflect mainly people of one's own race.[6] A growing grasp of the personal and collective nature of sin initiates conversion and the desire, with God's grace, to right the wrongs in one's personal life and in the larger society.

Again, the Spiritual Exercises invite the seeker to engage prayerfully in the graced and sinful moments of the larger human story. The dialogue between the past cosmic story and personal stories of sin and grace has implications for the larger human and earth community. Personal sin has social and planetary repercussions.

This expanding awareness of human sin fosters a greater sensitivity to global realities. Where before one might have reflected only on individual acts of commission and omission, a contemporary examination of consciousness moves one toward an awareness of the transcendent and of the intimate connection to all created reality. Theologian Marjorie Suchocki describes sin as violence acted out in the variety of ways of inflicting "ill-being" on oneself, one another, and the earth: "Feminist scholars see the sin of pride as describing the sins of the powerful who refuse to recognize the rightful boundaries of others, and the sin of hiding as the refusal of the responsibility to become a self that is so often the plight of women and men who are not in positions of power" (1995, 32). Interestingly, the way to transcendence, which Suchocki equates with well-being as opposed to ill-being, consists of the threefold use of memory, empathy, and imagination, a complement to an Ignatian perspective (1995, 36).

Sin, therefore, extends beyond the personal to the structures that maintain sin patterns. Although one may not be a conscious agent, one still participates at a level that perpetuates social and global sin. The challenge of the First Week includes becoming aware of the inadvertent, unconscious, and inevitable collusion in structural sin. The question becomes crucial: How am I benefiting from the oppression of others or my desire to maintain a privileged status quo? Sins against creation and the destruction of the earth exemplify the universal participation in sin. "The tendency to violence that persists in human nature is the ground of sin....Through organic solidarity of the race, we are affected by the sins of others, and our own sins likewise have an effect upon all others" (Suchocki 1995, 101).

Reflecting on the double and triple disadvantages revealed by intersectionality further complicates reflection on sin. What might be an appropriate response to racism, for example, if one is a white, economically and educationally advantaged professional woman? Or a white disenfranchised ex-felon who can no longer access public housing or a decent job? Or a black hospital worker who is afraid to return home lest she bring an infectious disease home to her children? What complex combination of sinner and sinned against accurately reflects each woman's sense of sin and herself as a loved sinner?

Since the Second Vatican Council, sin cannot be considered without simultaneously understanding the universal call to holiness.[7] Holiness today means living love—love of God expressed by love of neighbor, contributing to the world here and now. Sin disrupts love, bringing disorder and disharmony to relationships.

Relating the call to holiness and the disorder of sin in the First Week of the Exercises makes the prayer experience more immediate and contemporary. Conversion, healing, and transformation are all part of the process of the First Week's movement toward freedom. As a woman moves from a privatized sense of sin to a more relational, structural perspective, she increasingly understands sin, not just as individual isolated actions, but as choices that affect many. Like throwing a rock into a pool of water, her decisions ripple outward to touch others. Her actions and decisions matter.

Understanding Personal Sin from a Feminist Perspective

Studies in feminist theology and psychology suggest an evolution in understanding women's experience of sin and its effects on their lives. The pioneering work of Valerie Saiving in 1960 recognized that the experience of men and women differs in significant ways. She noted that establishing male experience as normative is inadequate for women's self-understanding and that the traditional categories of sin do not address the situation of women. She challenged the notion of "pride and the will-to-power" as the primary offense (Saiving 1992).[8]

Following the work of Saiving, feminist thinker Judith Plaskow challenges the assumption that equates sin with pride and egoistic self-assertion, suggesting that this norm better describes the experience of men. She notes the impact of cultural expectations in defining "the feminine": "The 'sin' which the feminine role in modern society creates and encourages in women, is not illegitimate self-centeredness but failure to center the self, the failure to take responsibility for one's own life" (Plaskow 1980, 92).

Theologian Anne Carr (1996, 186) points out the need to reinterpret Christian categories of sin in light of the experience of women. From a feminist perspective, sin occurs in "the breaking of relationship with both God and with human beings that can take the form of weakness as well as pride in its denial of the importance of human responsibility in both the personal and the political realms." A male theological perspective has dominated the definition of sin as pride and rebellion, she notes, and has failed to pay attention to the sin "of those who are powerless, who lack agency, selfhood, and responsibility, and who have suffered violence and abuse." Women's sin, then, frequently manifests itself in a lack of self-assertion in the face of society and culture's expectations. It may consist not so much in what she does, but in what she fails to do, such as not assuming responsibility for choices or for naming her own values and gifts (1996, 8).[9] She recognizes, however, that as contemporary women assume more "masculine" roles in society, they will also take on the "sin" of the masculine culture.

Mary Potter Engel (1990, 152–54) extends the notion of sin by drawing attention to women whose primary experience of sin has been as victims of violence, particularly as survivors of domestic and sexual abuse. In naming the evil present in systems of domination and oppression, she also identifies the pervasive reality of sin as those choices causing violence to both victim and perpetrator: "those free, discrete acts of responsible individuals that create or reinforce these structures of oppression" (155). While not blaming the victim, Potter Engel raises awareness that some victims unwittingly contribute to oppression in their own situations and invites serious consideration about ways of responsible action.[10] These four authors trace an evolution of thought regarding the interplay between sin and women's issues and the implications for foundational theology and pastoral practice.

Growth in feminist consciousness brings on awareness of situations always present in society but only now coming to public attention.[11] In this climate, women often identify themselves, not first as sinners, but as victims of sin and oppression. This self-identification can lead to lament as a personal form of prayer. In lament, one names the suffering caused by injustice, evil, and pain and cries out for God's help. Naming the trouble begins the healing; turning to God in faith and hope opens one to grace. Through the prayer of lament, the seeker shifts her understanding of sin from her own experience of being sinned against to important new questions: What is sin for me? How do I understand myself as good? How do I avoid taking responsibility for my life? How is God an integral partner in all this? In light of these realities, a prayer of lament may prove a more appropriate starting point for the First Week of the Exercises than a prayer of contrition.

Contemporary women's frequent experience of violence and victimization calls forth the memory of biblical women, also victims. Some of them, such as Susanna, were vindicated. Others remained forgotten until a later generation cried "Enough!" The Levite's concubine, already raped by angry men and then cut into twelve pieces by her own master (Judg 19:1–30) and the violent revenge done to the women of the tribe of Benjamin tell tales of horror either too often forgotten or repeated unreflectively throughout history.[12]

Today's suffering women more typically cry out against the evil that has touched their lives, acknowledging and naming their grief, sorrow, pain, and oppression. From here, they can move to a freer, deeper, and more authentic awareness of personal sin.

Exercises

Biblical Passages and Interpretation

Persons of faith reverence "God's word" as a source of revelation, yet they rarely probe how the process of personal formation ties into biblically based religious imagery. If a person making the Exercises asked herself, "What are the sources of my knowledge and feelings about the Bible?" she would realize both the strengths and the limits of her biblical understanding. This realization will surely assist her engagement with the material of the First Week.

For some, emphasis on selective biblical references and personal stories of sin have precipitated a negative self-preoccupation and a legalistic or privatistic spirituality. For others, the biblical images and stories of the First Week fall into the category of fantasy rather than revelation.[13] Another potential pitfall lies in traditional interpretation, such as the example of Adam and Eve's story, which isolates women as a source of sin and temptation and reveals an image deeply imbedded in the recesses of the religious imagination of both women and men. Persons come to these First Week meditations with unconscious assumptions and attitudes about the biblical material. However, they often fail to examine their degree of familiarity with the stories and the way they have interpreted them. For example, they may reflect on a familiar and long-remembered story and, in praying over the actual biblical text, discover something new and surprising.

The earlier discussion of biblical hermeneutics highlighted the fact that biblical stories in the Exercises must first be critiqued before being retrieved; critical consciousness and constructive recovery can coexist in the experiences of the Exercises. Mining Scripture uncovers valuable sources of Christian imagery and a rich vein of possibility for women.

Artists' interpretations of the biblical characters and events with their recurring depictions of the great questions of life, death, and destiny have deeply formed religious imagination. For example, cathedrals serve as repositories of art and culture and form spirituality. Stained glass windows, carved and colorful statues, and painted walls and ceilings chronicle the biblical stories of God and humankind. Artists and preachers function as influential interpreters of the Bible for most of the faithful, just as they did in Ignatius's time.

Today, few persons making the Spiritual Exercises come to the meditation topics of angels, Adam and Eve, and sin without preconceived ideas derived from either the tradition or today's popular culture. Popular culture presents images that probe life's meaning and open new possibilities for understanding old ideas. The recent popularity of angels, for example, reveals a deep human desire to touch the divine and to stretch the limits of humanity.[14] Many are still fascinated by relationships between the sexes and the struggle of good against evil, reflected in modern communications. Anyone can access religious information at a popular level in religion columns in newspapers and magazines, the Internet, books and television, educational programs, or even office jokes. Any conversation between the guide and the one making the Exercises needs to raise consciousness about these less obvious aspects of biblical formation.

In light of this realization, consider again the creation story. Humans are created in God's image, male and female (Gen 1:26–28), but the religious imagery for Eve is much more ambiguous than for Adam. Artistic representations reinforce two diverse interpretations of Eve, which have implications for the image of women: Eve as temptress and source of man's sin, often pictured as naked and talking to a snake or, more positively, as "a power equal to man" (Freedman 1983, 56).

An important strand of the ancient tradition offers a favorable image of Eve, placing her in continuity with Mary. The crypt of the Church of the Dormition in Jerusalem stresses the continuity, where a brilliant ceiling mosaic depicts heroic biblical women surrounding the central image of Mary. Mary's significance cannot be separated from her foremothers, including the first mother. Despite this positive tradition, however, Mary and Eve are often opposed to one another. Mary became elevated to the most holy woman while Eve represented the most sinful. Eve personified everything evil in women, especially sexual sin, lust, and temptation; she reflected cultural stereotypes that identified women as less rational than men and therefore as "the weaker sex."[15]

References to this negative understanding of Eve abound in the apocryphal literature and in patristic sermons and writings, as well as in the New Testament itself. In giving directives about women's dress and demeanor, the First Letter of Timothy states, "I permit no woman to teach or to have authority over a man; she is to keep silent. For Adam was formed first, then Eve; and Adam was not deceived, but the woman was deceived and became a transgressor" (1 Tim 2:12–14). Tertullian furthers this line of interpretation as he addresses a third-century female audience in *On the Dress of Women*. "She would carry herself around like Eve, mourning and penitent, that she might more fully expiate by each garment of penitence that which she acquired from Eve—I mean the degradation of the first sin and the hatefulness of human perdition" (Clark 1983, 39).

Because Eve's many faces in art, literature, and theology frequently reinforce a negative image,[16] a stereotype of Eve as the cause of "man's downfall" has been projected onto women. Yet the more positive image of Eve, also based in the tradition, suggests that the "original sin" was the rupture of right relationship between women and men. The loss of this insight about original sin reinforced patriarchy as a model for systems of domination and oppression. A way forward lies in recognizing universal human dignity lived out in right relationships.

Hell

The theological issue of hell in the First Week can provoke continuing dialogue, and the fifth and final meditation on hell often causes much resistance and consternation. For some, the idea of hell belongs to an unreal world unrelated to life today.[17] Unfortunately, this meditation has too often become an exercise in literalism, where the residue of traditional preaching of fire and brimstone distorts and limits conscious reflection on its reality. Despite these negative aspects, hell often reappears in the imaginations of artists and the debates of theologians.

Author Alice K. Turner (1993), who has explored the history of hell, maintains that no world religions equal Christianity in giving such importance to hell: a "fantastic underground kingdom of cruelty, surrounded by dense strata of legend, myth, religious creed, and what, from a distance, we might call dubious psychology." She notes that poets and artists have taken an "immoderate interest in Hell" (1993, 3) while theologically, hell fades in and out of favor. Two factors remain constant: the desire for cosmic justice where evil is punished and fear as a fallback motivator for virtuous living when love is not enough—as Ignatius suggests in the second prelude to the meditation on hell [65]. A serious question remains for the interpretation of the First Week: How can praying about hell be a grace-filled experience for contemporary women?

Hell means different things to different people. Ignatius suggests one approach to hell, but other ways may prove more profitable. One person might try to imagine the opposite of God or might imagine her own personal hell. Another might prefer to reflect on the iconic representation of Jesus's descent into hell, echoed in the Creed, which suggests the divine confrontation of evil, sin, and death and the ultimate triumph of love. Some might choose to sidestep Ignatius's imagery for biblical reflections leading to the same dynamic movement. Or another might profit from returning to the writings of traditional wisdom figures who themselves reflected on this mystery.

For example, Teresa of Avila recounts what she calls a "copy of hell," noting prayer brought anguish and torment without knowing why. Later in the same work, she narrates in more detail her vision and understanding of hell. She uses descriptions full of sensory images: a long and narrow alleyway like an oven "low and dark," the floor consisting of "dirty muddy water emitting a foul stench and swarming with putrid vermin," followed by her sense of being placed in a small cupboard in a cramped position. This was combined with an interior fire and "despairing and tormenting unhappiness." She calls this experience of prayer one of the greatest favors God gave her "because it helped me very much to lose fear of the tribulations and contradictions of this life as well as to grow strong enough to suffer these and give thanks to the Lord who freed me." As a result, she had a great desire to "help souls, to free them from such torment" (Teresa of Avila 1976, 199, 213–15).

A middle-aged religious who ministers to street children describes her modern version of hell: "Sometimes when I am on the street with the kids of Brazil, I feel like I'm in hell." Today, the meditation on hell invites each person making the Exercises to enter into the worst possible scenario not for its own sake or to induce guilt, but to assure oneself that one does not experience hell alone. Paradoxically, Ignatius wanted to facilitate an experience of God's profound depth of love through internalizing the truth of personal experience with the meditation.

Women's stories may reveal hell as an experience or situation or even an interior awareness. Some contemporary women name the violence done to themselves or others as hell on earth: sexual abuse, domestic violence, a degrading life below the poverty level, homelessness while raising children, genocide, starvation, poisoned air and water, disabling physical or mental conditions. Images and stories about sin and hell cluster around broken relationships, past and present. Such an approach may open up further profitable reflection, always in the context of the grace of the Week.

Exercises

Wisdom for Those Giving the Exercises

Various themes appear in the First Week in story, symbol, and religious imagination. Three areas that touch specifically on the one giving the Exercises include refining the relationship between the persons giving and making the Exercises, affective and intellectual transformation, and discerning areas of confirmation and challenge.

Refining Relationships

The relationship between the one giving and the one receiving the Exercises develops in depth during the First Week, when each grows in ease, trust, openness to God, and desire for the graces of the Week. As each recognizes the mutuality of gifts and limitations, a trusting relationship provides for effective communication and feedback. As they need to pay less attention to clarifying their relationship, they can pay more attention to the seeker's growing relationship with God.

Hospitality in spiritual conversation assumes that words will bring greater understanding. A wise companion will ask herself, "How do my words and language welcome the presence and the experience of the other?" Women making the Exercises need to trust their own stories and to probe their deeper meaning, but this trust can only grow when women claim their voices and tell their stories. The guide's role in dismantling the stone wall that excludes women's stories and in creating stepping-stones toward women's empowerment cannot be underestimated. Only then can women's stories liberate personal power, inner strength, and sense of self expressed in relationships of freedom and purposeful action.

Sensitivity to the cultural context and its many manifestations is key in refining relationships between the guide and the one making the Exercises. Does the culture of the one making the Exercises lean toward individualism or collectivity? Does it expect and encourage docility or assertion? Does it honor youth or old age? Is it high or low impact on the environment? Missing such cultural cues conveys that the one giving the Exercises doesn't really "hear" the one making the Exercises. For example, in an African context, there is a very strong emphasis on the interconnectedness of all of life and on the importance of harmony in the community. As Agbonkhianmeghe Orobator expresses it, "When we recall that sin is a shared reality and event in Africa it makes sense to think of sin as poisoning the community's life blood."[18] Therefore, the understanding of sin leans toward its communal effects, and it may be important to offer the possibility of a communal ritual of reconciliation rather than simply offering the sacrament of reconciliation. In some indigenous contexts, a ritual of exile and restoration to the community may powerfully convey the mercy of God to the one making the Exercises and to the community.

The First Week, which deals with difficult stories from Scripture and life, requires receptive and nonjudgmental listening from the guide to create a trusting relationship. A woman who discloses sinful experiences may fear rejection. Therefore, sensitive listening by the person giving the Exercises may manifest the love and forgiveness of God.

Affective and Intellectual Transformation

Also crucial to the transformative dynamic of the First Week is attentiveness to any deceleration of forward movement. The deepening of the First Week may be marked by hesitation, fear of a rigid and imposed structure, uncertainty, and even doubt about the value of personal experience. The one making the Exercises needs to understand that "doing" certain actions suggested in the Exercises does not matter; experiencing the underlying dynamic does.

The guide needs to attend to any content of the First Week that proves difficult for a woman. In such cases, the guide needs to notice how she experiences problems. Does she have difficulty with the biblically based stories or their interpretation, her personal sin story, or the anticipation of the meditations on sin and hell? Alert to the temptation to either dismiss or overemphasize, a wise guide will respond sensitively, preferring to say, "How can we use this material profitably?" rather than an unequivocal, "We can't use this." The conversation thus can lead to further exploration: "What can you learn from these stories? Can you allow yourself to be open to discover a threshold of insight?"

One giving the Exercises might find particular manifestations of sin surprising. Ironically, these sins may be the very things for which women have been lauded: passivity or indirect influence; staying in the background ("behind every great man is a woman"); silence, dependence, self-effacement, feeling rather than thinking; sacrificing to the detriment of self; or denial of one's gifts. At times, gifts waiting to be developed will be understood as sinful: for example, justified and liberating anger, assertiveness, leadership, or independence. Other times, women may avoid naming some things as sin, especially inaction or fear of failure. "That which I have failed to do" is as important as "that which I have done."

Although the guide should pay attention to gender's influence on interpreting sin, it is not the only important factor to consider. Often the sin and conversion experiences of those who belong to the dominant culture and those outside it differ. When the Exercises call attention to "pride, riches and honor" [142] as leading to sinful ways, a contemporary reading might highlight classism, racism, and sexism. Conversations among women professionals in business, law, and medicine, and women who constitute their support staff—secretaries, receptionists, nurses—reveal oppressive relationships among women in the workplace, sometimes subtle and other times blatant. Women's workplaces also include the home and those who serve there. The topic of women and sin has significant implications for the lives and self-perception of women and deserves continued reflection and discussion.[19]

The dynamics of the First Week may evoke deep feelings, including sorrow, confusion, helplessness, and repentance as well as a deep-felt knowledge of God's loving presence. Their expression is necessary. The guide also needs to pay attention to feelings of liberation that women themselves may hesitate to acknowledge and receive. An experience of being a loved sinner, for example, can liberate one for a qualitatively new level of responsibility for one's own life.

Discerning Areas of Confirmation and Challenge

Another responsibility of the person guiding the Exercises lies in the ongoing discernment of when to encourage, affirm, and challenge in response to the movement of the First Week. Those making the First Week exercises will often need to struggle before things become clear. Struggle by itself does not indicate the absence of the Holy Spirit. It simply may surround coming to terms with what truly constitutes good and evil, heaven and hell, freedom and bondage, acceptance and rejection, gratitude and fear.

Sometimes, however, the struggle manifests itself in deadening silence, getting "stuck," or staying in superficial or heady responses. Usually, the guide can pick up enough material through intuition and careful listening to ascertain whether this is the case. When the situation is ambiguous and the guide needs clarification, one or two open-ended questions can aid discernment: What is your favorite image of God? Why? Tell me what you know and feel about angels? What do you have to say about Adam and Eve? Where did you learn about hell, and how have your ideas changed? How much do you reflect on sin? What difference do any of these topics—angels, Adam and Eve, sin, hell—make in your spiritual life? Conversing about these or similar questions makes conscious the formative power of these stories and themes in spirituality and gives an opportunity to assess their present value. The way people read sacred stories in Ignatius's time and today may differ. Yet the search for a living, empowering word remains the same.

The companion giving the Exercises can make a significant contribution by providing alternative stories from the tradition or from film, television, novels, drama, daily newspapers, and magazines to expand possibilities for prayer in the First Week. Some find meditating on the stories of Sarah and Hagar valuable. Others have fruitfully pondered the stories of the women in Matthew's genealogy—Tamar, Rahab, Ruth, Bathsheba—women who transcend their sin and witness to the power and plan of God. At other times, women have found solace and courage in various psalms that voice their experience of sin and salvation as well as God's loving mercy and forgiveness.[20] Others find that art and literature stimulate their imagination and open their hearts to new possibilities for prayer and insight. Whatever means are used, they should never present sin in order to break the spirit or evoke guilt, but only to help in truthfully portraying oneself in the world.

If listening to the stories of others is so significant, paying attention to one's own story should prove even more so. Thus, the importance of language magnifies as the person becomes engaged as the subject of her own sacred story. The power to name oneself and God forms the basis of self-identity. The person giving the Exercises may need to invite the woman living the Exercises to expand her concept of God beyond a traditional understanding of "God-He" by suggesting other metaphors for God beyond male imagery. The vocabulary of prayer can also provide alternatives. For example, the person making the Exercises might pay attention to the words of the Jesus prayer or the liturgical penitential rite or biblical phrases of the fraction rite "Lamb of God," or Psalm 51, or she might reflect on the familiar words of the prayer that Jesus taught, "Forgive us our trespasses as we forgive those who trespass against us." Each phrase or prayer gives a different nuance about who God is and who she is. In naming oneself and God, the choice of words matters. While such a personal perspective provides the starting point for reflection, it may not be the ending point. Wise guides can suggest various ideas for reflection considering their retreatants' experience, and then encourage them to let go enough to share another's experience without crossing personal boundaries.

The last issue for the one giving the Exercises moves from depth of the personal reflection to the breadth of the theological foundations inherent in the First Week, which can paralyze even the most experienced companion. Accompanying someone through sin and sinfulness in a constructive way can be daunting. Women can put false guilt on themselves instead of cultivating a mature and authentic conscience. Distinguishing authentic anger that energizes and directs action for good from self-destructive anger that leads to depletion and despair demands serious discernment. In-depth spiritual conversation around topics of God's reality, God's will, human realities of freedom, sin, salvation, and the person and the role of Christ can prove invaluable. For all these issues, those giving the Exercises can profit from a commitment to their own continuing education and supervision.

Conclusion

The First Week centers on God's graciousness and the seeker's lack of gratitude. The dynamic of the First Week leads to gratitude, the result of a deep and personal understanding of one's place in the cosmic order, as well as to a realization of one's use or misuse of God's gifts. This entire process leads to a deep experience of God's unconditional, passionate, and personal love.

As the First Week concludes, the guide may again recall the various motivations that women bring to the Spiritual Exercises. Whether a sixteenth-century woman of Alcalá or a twenty-first-century woman of Seattle or Lesotho, questions of meaning emerge from life changes, transition experiences, or a sense of one's own mortality. Situations arise in family life, work, economic circumstances, or church participation that disrupt the familiar sense of identity and relationships and call for a response. A desire for a deeper spirituality results from an initial or renewed discovery of God. Whatever the reason propelling them toward the Spiritual Exercises across the centuries, women acknowledge both rich resources and ambiguity in them. Contemporary women's significant interest and participation in the Spiritual Exercises may reveal important insights about the Spirit's call to the church in modern times.

CHAPTER 7

Who Do You Say That I Am?

Exercises of the Second Week

...to ask for an interior knowledge of our Lord, who became human for me, that I may love him more intensely and follow him more closely.
—*Spiritual Exercises* [104]

I read about the call of the disciples and they are all men. The women who follow Jesus seem to come to him because they have something wrong with them that he has to fix.

—A contemporary woman

"Now we will begin the Second Week." These words often elicit a sigh of relief both from the one receiving and the one giving the Spiritual Exercises. For some, the First Week seems like a qualifying exam or probation, "Whew, the hard part is over; I've made it through." Others struggle and learn about faithful presence: "I know God's faithful love in a way I'd never realized before." Whatever the First Week experience, the transition from the First to the Second Week and the anticipation of praying over the life of Christ opens a new set of feelings and expectations. Most persons who make the Exercises are searching for opportunities to reflect more closely on the person of Jesus and to deepen their personal relationship with him. Indeed, the grace of the Second Week is in finding

Who Do You Say That I Am?

"an interior knowledge of our Lord" so as to "love him more intensely and follow him more closely" [104].

Material and Dynamics of the Second Week

How does one enter into the Second Week? The meditations and contemplations strategically placed throughout the week help to refine one's ability to make freer choices in following Christ. The Second Week exercises directed toward this process include the Call of the King [91–100], the Two Standards [136–48], Three Classes of Persons [149–57], and Three Ways of Being Humble [165–68]. First, the Call of the King considers discipleship and invites the seeker to cast her lot with Jesus. Yet life includes struggle and, sooner or later, all must answer the questions raised by the meditation on the Two Standards: "Whose side are you on? and How do you know this? How might that relationship grow over time?" The two additional exercises offer nuances to this invitation to discipleship. Even when not making life-changing decisions, for which Ignatius will provide assistance through ways for making an election, one finds that daily choices ultimately form the pattern of ongoing fidelity to Jesus.

The Ignatian contemplations in the Second Week focus attention on the mysteries of Christ [101–34, 158–64], moving the seeker from self-preoccupation to the mystery of a God who shares in our humanity. The Gospel Contemplations proceed from Jesus's birth to his death, linking the mysteries of the life of Christ with the mystery of God's presence in our own life. Imaginatively entering the gospel scenes brings one into contact with Jesus in Nazareth, now by the Sea of Galilee, now in Jerusalem. One imagines his actions, his words, and how he touches people's lives. Contemplative awareness makes it possible to really see people, listen to their voices, share in their experiences, and respond in faith to the myriad ways of God-with-us. Consciousness of one's life before God gives a momentary glimpse into the mystery of God at unexpected times: walking, working, eating, resting. Paradoxically, even distractions and busy thoughts may also provide graced insight.

At the beginning of the Second Week, prayer focuses around hearing God's call and listening attentively and lovingly to God's revelation of love incarnate, Jesus. Imagining the Trinity's perspective of a sinful yet loved world leading God to "dwell with us" situates the Second Week within the mystery of the incarnation. Traveling the road from Nazareth to Bethlehem engages one with the reality of Jesus's birth and the vulnerability of God who chooses to enter human history. The seeker accompanies Jesus as he journeys through "cities and villages, proclaiming and bringing the good news of the kingdom of God" (Luke 8:1).

The grace of the Second Week, a deepening relationship with Jesus, offers new ways of knowing, loving, and following. For some, a new experience of intimacy may be experienced as a lover-beloved relationship. Rob Marsh (2006, 11) suggests that "Second Week knowing leads to loving because in it we feel desire, feel attraction, feel knowledge in the flesh. And through desire knowing moves into action—not just any action, but the action that emerges from loving and from loving what the lover loves. To know and to love move us to follow: not just doing but doing *with*, doing what he is doing." What may have begun as an individual "Jesus and me" piety can develop into an intimate relationship of love overflowing into service; the Second Week is about words and actions. The first question, "Who do you say that I am?," leads to the next: "Where do you stand and with whom will you walk?" Both questions require a response.

To Know, Love, and Serve Christ Our Lord

Christ is central to both Ignatius and the Spiritual Exercises, yet persons receiving the Exercises today don't always know how to answer the question, "Who do you say that I am?" Their dilemma raises the question, "Which Christ?" Some stress the divinity of Christ and tend to emphasize a Christology from "above"; others stress the humanity of Jesus, a Christology from "below." Many names and images present themselves to the contemporary believer, both as inheritance from the Christian past and fruit of the current christological debates. How can Ignatius's understanding and experience of Christ in his historical and cultural context illuminate contemporary experience without confining the Spirit of God?[1] What will help contemporary seekers discover the identity of "Christ our Lord" for today?

Ignatius blends together the Gospel accounts and the writings of Paul, displaying a quite different sensibility than that of the modern Scripture scholar who differentiates the distinct understandings of Jesus presented in the New Testament. For today's seeker, any of the following could provide an entry point: Scripture, worship, liturgy, any of the arts. Each forms one's image of Jesus, resulting in a variety of Christologies. Doctrine, debated or professed, along with conscious or unconscious belief patterns, influences personal and public understanding. Questions continue to challenge and enrich the believer today.

The specific images of Jesus the Christ in the contemplations of the Second Week differ according to their placement in the hidden life or the public life. The retreatant first considers the pregnant Mary, the infant Jesus, the Lord born in poverty, the eternal Word, Christ our Lord, and the child Jesus. The Meditation on the Two Standards presents "Christ our Supreme Commander and Lord," and the remaining contemplations name him as "Christ our Lord." Ignatius uses this title most frequently even when referring to the historical Jesus. Regardless of the name, the grace remains the same: attaining an "interior knowledge of Our Lord, who became human for me" [104].

Today's believers, conscious of the distinctions between the Jesus of history and the Christ of faith, may more often assume the perspective of a postresurrection Christian in the presence of the Spirit of Christ the Lord. They wish to move beyond the limitations of an exclusive emphasis on the physical maleness of Jesus and its patriarchal association with male domination. Consequently, some women continue to raise fundamental issues concerning the relationship of women to "Christ our Lord."

Problems and Possibilities Raised by Christology

Individual women's critiques of Christology usually begins tentatively, as both church and culture tend to resist such critique. Some find themselves unable to relate to Jesus of the distant past; biblical stories seem irrelevant to their lives. Others struggle with the temptation to settle for a private, idiosyncratic relationship with Jesus and hesitate to make a deeper public commitment, given its attendant conflict. Others find the language associated with Christ so irritating that it blocks them: for example, the Nicene Creed's English translation reads, "I believe in Jesus Christ, who for us *men* and for our salvation…was made *man*." The first reference to *men* emphasizes exclusive male language and the subsequent *man* emphasizes the maleness of Jesus rather than his humanity.

Many reject the image of Jesus as a blue-eyed, light-haired, white European male. Others react similarly to the stern Pantocrator overseeing the worshiping community from an ancient apse. They perceive images that idealize men, distance the divine, and often portray Jesus Christ in the image of men in the dominant culture. Other images go to the opposite extreme and place Jesus in domestic scenes emphasizing the gentleness and meekness associated with women; "feminizing" Christ also elicits a negative reaction. Few images of Jesus interacting in the historical, cultural, religious events of his times include women. Whatever the sources of their intellectual and spiritual formation in Christology, many contemporary women admit that their experience of Jesus the Christ simultaneously oppresses and liberates.

Theologian Elizabeth Johnson (1991) explores the problems raised by the maleness of Christ in her article of the same name. If Jesus is the revelation of God, then when "the Christ symbol points to maleness as an essential characteristic of divine being itself," the exclusive use of Father-Son imagery to describe the relationship reinforces these exclusive symbols (108). Because the "Word made flesh" dwelt among us as male, men more closely identify with Christ than women because of their natural physical resemblance. If male human beings represent Christ more fully than female, then reconciling the theological dictum, "What is not assumed is not healed," with women's experience becomes impossible (109).[2]

Although the emphasis on the maleness of Jesus has proven problematic for some, Johnson rejects a "naive physicalism which collapses the totality of the Christ into the human man Jesus" (113). She underscores the importance of sexuality in all human experience. "The fact that Jesus of Nazareth was a male human being is not in question. His sex was a constitutive element of his historical person along with other particularities such as his Jewish racial identity, his location in the world of first-century Galilee" (108).

Johnson further states that appreciating Jesus's maleness as a historical reality does not determine his identity theologically as the Christ nor does it establish his maleness as normative in any way for members of the Christian community (115). Both Scripture and baptism remind the believing Christian community that baptism into Christ obliterates all distinction based on sex, race, or class, for all are one in Christ Jesus (Gal 3:28). Both seeker and guide need to develop this consciousness so that the "maleness" of Jesus does not become an obstacle to a woman's ability to grow in the knowledge of Christ, loving more deeply and following more closely in discipleship.[3]

Other feminist theologians of various countries and cultures, of different races and economic classes, and from various Christian churches bring additional responses to the question, Who do you say that I am? Jacquelyn Grant speaks of the experience of African American women noting the marginalization of women by sex and race and class. Oppressed women identify with Jesus as cosufferer:

> The pervasiveness and interconnectedness of racism, sexism, classism and other forms of oppression which define a good portion of the lives of black women make "trouble" inescapable. Jesus, for many black women, has been the consistent force which has enabled them not only to survive the troubles of the world, but to move beyond them. (Grant 1993, 56)

For them, Jesus becomes not only cosufferer but also equalizer and liberator.

Virginia Fabella (1989, 113), reflecting an Asian woman's perspective, notes that the question is not "Who is Jesus?" but "Where is Jesus found?" Her answer: Jesus dwells in solidarity with suffering people. Jesus must be "not only healer, exorciser, consoler, friend; he will also be transformer." Jesus stands as a liberating figure for those women and men who do not take issue with "the maleness of Jesus," who understand the gender of Jesus as accidental to the liberation process.

From an African feminist perspective, Mercy Oduyoye (2001, 55, 58) speaks of the role of Christ as the one "who liberates from the burden of disease and from taboos that restrict women's participation in their communities. The triple burdens of racism, poverty and marginalization are countered by claims that Christ liberates from oppressive cultures." She names another key way in which African women experience liberation by Jesus as being "freed to choose," suggesting that "Jesus is the antidote to their ascribed positions in church and society, the cultural contexts in which they experience the Christ in their lives."

Still other feminist theologians have taken seriously women's response to classical formulations of Christology. They have directed their scholarly work toward naming the sexist and androcentric bias of doctrine and symbols of Christology; at the same time they search for other expressions more liberating for women, frequently emphasizing Jesus's relational qualities as their common theme rather than gender and cultural images.[4]

Still, for Ignatius, "Christ the Lord," the central focus of Christian faith, is the Christ of the Second Week revealed through the mystery of God, Divine Majesty, and Trinity. Jesus of Nazareth is revealed in his life, message, ministry, suffering, death, and resurrection, and the proclamation by the community of faithful believers. As contemporary women critically reflect on the Christ images in the Exercises, they need to bring to conscious awareness their assumptions about Jesus Christ and the ways they experience convergence or conflict with the Christ images of the Exercises. As they do this critical inner work, they frequently name themselves as resurrection Christians, believers recognizing the risen Christ in their midst today.

Specific aspects of the Second Week attractive to women include prayerful exploration of the "hidden life" of Jesus. For some, this begins far earlier than the contemplations of Jesus's early childhood. For example, connecting with Jesus in the womb along with the contemplations of the annunciation and nativity can be extremely powerful. Pondering simple daily acts such as being able to bathe and hold the newborn Jesus, both for those who have physically experienced motherhood and for those who long for that experience, can likewise carry enormous significance. Many of the early contemplations involve domestic scenes, giving glimpses into Jesus's human formation: experiences of dependency, nurturing, and learning. The daily world of Jesus's family lifts up the importance of mothers and parental and postnatal care of vulnerable children. Community and familial relationships across generations, occasional travel, and everyday religious and cultural norms provide a familiar and reassuring context for prayer.

Other women feel drawn to Jesus's public life and his inclusive call to discipleship, issued to both women and men and lived out through deepening knowledge and loving commitment. They identify with his strong and focused relationships and the sense of mission he developed as he discovered his own "Principle and Foundation." His relationship with the land, the people, and the events of his life in the desert, towns, mountaintops, or at table all formed his own sense of identity and shaped the way he related with others.

In addition to Scripture, the writing of the mystics and religious and liturgical practice offer further rich images. Jesus as prophet, teacher, and healer appeal to those who desire more holistic interpretations. The ancient but relatively unknown image of Jesus as Mother[5] opens up a new perspective on Jesus the Christ, beginning with Matthew, who compares Jesus to a mother hen crying out his anguished desire to gather the children to his protective care (Matt 23:37). Julian of Norwich calls Jesus "Mother": "So Jesus Christ, who opposes good to evil, is our true Mother. We have our being from him, where the foundation of motherhood begins, with all the sweet protection of love which endlessly follows" (Colledge and Walsh 1978, 295). Some women discover great profit in following the liturgical seasons in companionship with Christ, while some have had the opportunity to visit the actual sites of Jerusalem and Galilee, as did Ignatius.

The grace of the Second Week invites one to know, love, and follow Jesus. Many who receive this grace find the experience suffused with various images and experiences as revelatory. Regardless of the image, the grace of the Second Week remains constant. As a transition from the First Week into the Second Week, the seeker is invited to pause and ponder what captures her passion, her heart, and invites her to go beyond what she can imagine in order to discover her deepest desires.

Call of the King

The Call of the King acts as a bridge between the First and Second Weeks, "functioning both as a conclusion to the First Week of experiencing God's merciful justice and as a foundation of the Second Week and beyond for all the contemplations of Jesus' life" (Fleming 2004, 37).

Steeped in medieval metaphor, Ignatius remembered his former life and the romance novels that motivated his fantasy and directed his desires. The Call of the King draws on this experience. It begins with a parable of a temporal king, then shifts attention to the eternal King. "King" and "kingdom," however, suggest a reality deeper than their literal meaning. Beneath the images lies the truth of commitment, single-heartedness, sacrifice, and freedom. Ignatius knew the magnetism of a powerful and appealing leader. Just as a temporal king could capture one's heart, energy, and commitment, so the call of Christ the eternal King would elicit great desires to follow the way of discipleship and be transformed by entering a deeper and more intimate relationship. Thus, the grace of the week, to know, love, and serve the eternal King depends on the seeker's desire to hear the personal call of Christ and to respond generously.

While the call of "Christ our Lord" suggests a global image of the "world assembled," it is also intimately personal. As one moves more deeply into prayer, Christ shares his desire to bring about the reign of God while the seeker considers her free response to this invitation to participate in God's project. Fleming uses the word *beckon* to convey the sense of a strong invitation. "He puts his whole self into the call; his voice is strong, his eyes invite, his arm and hand reaches out and draws us in," and yet, "what beckons does not include is any sense of duress" (Fleming 2004, 108).

Ignatius's own life clarifies the intent of this consideration. Monarchy pervaded the spirituality of the times, touching rich and poor.[6] The metaphors of monarchy and politics also formed an intrinsic aspect of Ignatius's life, as they did for noblewomen such as Juana of Spain, sister of King Philip. The parable associating a temporal king with Christ the King expressed a natural link for Ignatius. Since his daily life included kings and battles, victories and defeats, as well as courage, loyalty, and commitment, comparing an earthly king with Christ as King was not a question of opposites, but of transference. Ignatius assumed that, if a subject has an experience or memory of a good and powerful king to whom she owes loyalty and service, she can transfer that energy and desire to her commitment to the eternal King. Although the image of a king may at best be irrelevant and at worst anathema for many women making the Exercises today, the underlying psychological and spiritual dynamic of transferring desire and energy evoked by an admired human to one whose call and love is so much greater remains a powerfully transformative dynamic that can be entered into in a multitude of ways.

Problems and Possibilities in the Call of the King

The inherent issues and problems in the language and imagery of the Call of the King become increasingly marked as the monarchy becomes more and more anachronistic. Structures of contemporary life champion democracy, not monarchy. Although the language of God's kingship has a strong biblical base, its usage in the context of this exercise tends to emphasize God as male conqueror. A God associated with violence and domination claims victory and defeats enemies, thus implying the holiness of war. Many women reject the militaristic language and the underlying concepts: obeying a temporal king, conquering infidels, participating in the victory, being a good subject or an unworthy knight for an eternal King who wishes "to conquer the whole world and all my enemies" [95]. This triumphalist language and images of kings and knights seem far removed from the experience of the modern world. The metaphors suggest that women should be in relationship with a powerful male and with a hierarchical and impersonal system that expects unquestioning allegiance and self-surrender.

Not only may the metaphor of the king be problematic, the expression *kingdom of God* further alienates those resistant to militaristic language. When a person finds the metaphor so distasteful, she may also find that its use blocks a positive affective or relational response. When this blockage occurs, it eliminates the possibility of encountering the deeper meaning of the image.

Reclaiming this notion of king and kingdom means expanding one's biblical perspective. Some who search more deeply note that Jesus himself resisted the title of king; others gave him that name, but he did not use it to define himself. Some emphasize Jesus's continuity with the Old Testament kingly tradition, alluded to in the angel's message to Mary, "the Lord God will give to him the throne of his ancestor David. He will reign over the house of Jacob forever, and of his kingdom there will be no end" (Luke 1:32–33). The Fourth Gospel's account of Jesus's death on the cross includes the inscription, "Jesus of Nazareth, the King of the Jews" (John 19:19), an image kept alive through the apocalyptic vision of Revelation:

> The kingdom of the world has become the kingdom of our Lord
> and of his Messiah,
> and he will reign forever and ever. (Rev 11:15)

Thus, two images of "king" emerge: one problematic in its militarism and one potent with possibilities suggesting God's ability to achieve a reign of peace and justice. Each image illustrates an understanding of Jesus as King in "historical variations and permutations" (Pelikan 1985, 47).[7]

The Call of the King, then, can elicit two quite different responses. Some might perceive this meditation as an irrelevant, meaningless, perhaps even contradictory example, detrimental for women's spiritual growth. Or, by confronting the historical limitations, it is possible to discover a parable that today, as yesterday, has possibilities for transformation by posing these questions: Does this image free us to find God? Could it help us to find God in the future? Story and myth provide an avenue for interpreting the Call of the King, not as literal history, but as entry into truths that lie deep within the human spirit. Kings and queens, gods and goddesses, magicians, shamans, healers, heroes, and villains dwell in the depths of the human psyche. The magnetism of special leaders continues to capture the human imagination as they touch the deep human desire for good to triumph over evil.

John Veltri helpfully calls attention to this idea of story and myth in relation to the Call of the King. He suggests that an extraordinarily strong personal myth of the king existed in Ignatius's psyche, which makes sense if one looks at the worldview and experiences that shaped him. We, however, do not need to appropriate this myth that was so powerful for Ignatius, which impelled him to greater love and service. Rather, we need to discover our own myth embedded in the stories and myths that have shaped our own psyches, necessarily different from that which was so profound for Ignatius. Veltri suggests that such myths "draw upon unconscious energies, fed by our own history, whether personal or collective," and that "myths can express the direction of our lives and help us express what is ultimately ineffable—the world of ultimate meaning" (Veltri 1998, 350, 351).

Spiritual writer Edwina Gateley (1990, 47–48) grappled with this struggle to claim her own myth in her Exercises retreat. She writes, "I followed Christ as King, I was the soldier, the fighter. Now I see Christ as Shepherd, shedding the image of Christ as King" and realizes, "it is the compassionate woman who will feed the sheep—not the soldier in you. You have fought a good fight. Give birth to the compassionate woman….I have been a soldier for such a long time. But it is the compassionate woman who will feed the sheep. From soldier, strong, unyielding, to woman, life-giver, nurturer." Eventually, masculine images no longer held for Gateley, even though she had been deeply formed and shaped by them. She had to discover and give birth to new images and metaphors that resonated with her own evolving experience. Likewise, as part of the journey to freedom, each woman must discover and live from the depth of personally meaningful metaphor and myth.[8]

Finding and following a charismatic leader reveals qualities associated with discipleship. What if, like Ignatius, a retreatant recalled a person who unleashed her admiration and loyalty in a relationship that elicited personal greatness? Such a relationship could become a catalyst of great desires—sharing vision, hopes, struggles, resources, sacrifices, risks, work, commitment, and success. Could not this personal motivation and relationship be understood as the necessary disposition for entering into the Call of the King today? Zeal, loyalty, active engagement in a life project, living for a goal bigger than one's personal gain, making sacrifices for the common good—all these values still merit admiration in contemporary life, even in their finitude. Opening up and out to Someone beyond oneself, yielding in love, can be a contemporary and equally compelling Call of the King.

Barbara Bedolla (1984, 28) suggests inviting retreatants to consider those who have been prophets in their own lives, claiming that these personal prophets have already evoked in their own hearts a vision beyond themselves. That vision can act as a bridge to the invitation of Jesus.

Framing this consideration as "Jesus's dream" may also be helpful: "Jesus has a dream. God has a dream" (Fleming 2004, 109). It is a dream about the reign of God and each person is invited to "bring our life dreams into the dream of Jesus." This idea of claiming our dreams within the bigger dream of God is very appealing. Too many women have given up their dreams, and yet the generous yes to this call is not about giving up our dreams but letting God help shape them.

Many models in our religious traditions pertinent to the relationship between God and the world emphasize God's transcendence and minimize God's palpable presence in concrete reality. In light of this dynamic, reconstructing the Call of the King might involve reflecting on the actions of this King as the one who sustains life, defends the poor, and is present to and engaged directly in the life of the people. Why not deemphasize the image of "king" as powerful but self-serving and emphasize a powerful king ruling for the benefit of the people?

The parables provide an avenue to make this shift. Parables raise awareness of God's desires for inclusion, peace, and justice for the people and the land. They highlight the reality that God's reign exists as a way of living and being, not as a physical place, geographical location, or political system. Jesus spoke of the kingdom of God as like a mustard seed, or yeast, and even a banquet.

An ecological awareness presents an additional possibility for reclaiming the concept of God's reign. Naming the earth as God's body expands the reign of God to include the care of the earth, as well as its people. This image may capture the imagination of those who find it hard to relate to God because they do not have any lively imaginative picture of how God and the world *as they know it* are connected. Using this ancient image of the earth as God's body stresses the incarnational, sacramental understanding of our world. It also underscores our human responsibility for the care and reverence of that body, not as dominators but as members of a common community.[9]

After reconstructing images of king and kingdom to assume God's reign of peace and justice, battle images become more fitting. War must indeed be waged against injustice and oppression of people and the earth. All people, but especially those most oppressed, find themselves forced to struggle, even mightily, for dignity and human rights, often giving their lives in the process. Today's interest in political and ecological theology illuminates this meditation in new ways, for it requires that Christian faith permeate the projects of those who desire to establish a more just society.

Two Standards

The meditation on the Two Standards marks the transition from the contemplations on the hidden life to those on the public life of Jesus. This meditation reminds the one making the Exercises that the call usually entails struggle. At this point, it is not a matter of making a choice for Christ—that has already happened—but rather, the one making the Exercises is invited to become more aware of the likely ways in which various spirits seek to influence her.

The meditation on the Two Standards extends the invitation to follow the pathway of discipleship, focusing not so much on choice as on the discernment essential to making choices. Ignatius points to this discernment in the third prelude [139], where the one making the Exercises is directed to ask for what she needs. In this instance, the desire consists of "insight into the deceits of the evil leader, and for help to guard myself against them; and further, for insight into the genuine life which the supreme and truthful commander sets forth and grace to imitate him."

The one making the Exercises must carefully discern what reinforces and sustains her call to discipleship and what hinders deeper commitment. The standard or banner is not always easy to see in the heat of the day. Ascertaining what is life giving or death dealing to self and others remains a continual challenge. The underlying touchstone, of course, is always the life, death, and resurrection of Jesus and openness to his Spirit.

But discernment in the Two Standards acts like a tuning fork for discerning the realities of life, indicating resonance or dissonance with the God who dwells within.

This meditation draws on the deep power of myth, vividly contrasting the characters of Christ and Lucifer in cosmic confrontation. The text describes a concrete place, complete with graphic imagery and imaginative design. Yet this cosmic struggle echoes within each person and a world marked by the continuing struggle between truth and deception.

Whether clothed in the imagery of the Two Standards or not, struggle pervades all conflict between nations, in families, churches, societies, or one's own self. Paul recognized this reality when he acknowledged, "I do not understand my own actions. For I do not do what I want, but I do the very thing I hate" (Rom 7:15). The Two Standards unmasks every person's need for God and the cost of choosing to follow Jesus. This discernment leads to greater commitment, which Ignatius recognizes by the presence of three virtues: poverty rather than riches, reproaches or contempt rather than honor, and humility rather than pride [146]. According to Ignatius, all other virtues flow from these three.

Problems and Possibilities in the Two Standards

"I want to scream every time I hear the phrase 'Two Standards,'" reported one woman who rejects the graphic imagery of this Exercise. Indeed, many women struggle with language that appears to affirm war and valorize virtues they equate with oppression. For some women it may not be possible to give the meditation as it stands. Other creative ways may need to be found to help her to enter into the underlying dynamic and grace of the meditation.

Yet for others, the battle imagery is not an obstacle, and allowing the imagination freedom may prove valuable. One woman said of her experience,

> When I got to the field I turned to Christ's army and Jesus was waiting for me on the border....Once inside I walked with Jesus and was amazed at all the people all busy doing different things, all races, from all times in history. As we came to the centre of the army there was a glowing light, also amoeba shaped and I just knew that God was there and with Jesus I went into the centre and became one with God and as that

happened I felt the army/amoeba move outwards and I knew that we had gained ground in the battle. This prayer was a turning point and most subsequent prayers carried the same theme of going into the centre of God. This is where I found my personal vocation and this prayer continues to sustain me. (Paulin-Campbell 2008, 146)

Those affiliated with Christ are also invited to choose spiritual and material poverty as well as reproaches and contempt leading to humility. Such emphasis on the traditional categories of pride and capital sins, besides presenting reproach and contempt as desirable, raises negative responses in some contemporary women. Imagine a single mother who has recently earned a college degree and found a full-time job after being dependent on food stamps, living in her car, and placing her children in a school for the homeless. The idea of her asking for reproach, contempt, and material poverty as a desirable path to spiritual growth is inconceivable. She will say, "There is nothing here relevant to my life, nor does this type of language or imagery contribute anything positive to my spiritual path and desire."

Humility, too, is an ambiguous virtue, especially if presented as the desirable result of reproaches and contempt. Often the expectations for humility reflect a gender bias with differing written and unwritten norms for women and men. Some women associate humility with patriarchal obedience and submission to father, husband, or priest. Humility has frequently been equated with passivity, hiding, and low self-esteem, all of which have been detrimental to women's responsible adult development.

Women themselves note the contradictions that arise interiorly when they sense an authentic call to find voice, speak truth, claim and honor their good name and person, and assert themselves, particularly in situations of oppression and injustice. Often women do not see the call to humility as in their own best interest but realize how it has been used in the name of religion to silence and subordinate them. In addition, humility can show a false face for women, hiding the truth of their own giftedness and contributions. A deeper understanding of "true" as opposed to "false" humility is necessary, as our culture itself is ambiguous on the topic.[10]

Yet humility carefully understood can open possibilities for women and remind them of their power of choice. Humility means truth, both of one's strengths and gifts of God, as well as one's weaknesses and limitations: one's reality before God. This truth provides a strong foundation for authentic discernment. Ignatius's famous letter to Teresa Rejadell recognizes the temptation to false humility. He describes how the enemy tries to get the person not to talk about the good things she has received from God so that fruit will not be produced in others, "for to cultivate awareness of what one has already received is always a help toward even greater things" (Ganss 1991, 334). Women themselves attest to the power and encouragement to do greater things that emerge out of an awareness of their gifts. For example, in her *Dialogue*, Catherine of Siena has God say,

> No virtue can have life in it except from charity, and charity is nursed and mothered by humility. You will find humility in the knowledge of yourself when you see that even your own existence comes not from yourself but from me, for I loved you before you came into being. (Noffke 1980, 29)

A woman cannot have true humility unless she has a strong sense of self. Only then is she capable of self-transcendence.

In some cases, though, women find that their oppressive life situation gives them few options. Humiliations, poverty, insults, and contempt are their daily lot. They have little choice and few opportunities to change their condition. Other women, from Ignatius's time to the present, receive insults and contempt as a result of a freely chosen strong and faithful commitment. This poverty and humiliation differs from that imposed by culture, class, or economic situation; it arises from freely identifying with the poor out of love for Christ. It also emerges out of simplifying one's life to sustainable proportions for the sake of all. In this sense, words such as *riches, honor,* and *pride* may reveal meaning and challenge for contemporary women by uncovering deeper questions: "Where does my treasure really lie? Do I accumulate and hoard? Do I worry what people will think of me? What are the sources of my security? How much do I equate self-worth with possessions, status, and power?"

The Two Standards may also reveal new and personal standards and standard bearers, drawing attention to women's gifts and leadership in the community. For example, Marge Piercy's novel about the French Revolution, *City of Darkness, City of Light* (1996), captures the struggle for liberation by the people, especially the women, and links it to the contemporary passion for human dignity and global freedom. The character of Claire, actress and revolutionary, who cries out for food for the children and elderly, could help a retreatant reexamine the Two Standards. Like

Claire, women and men today gather others of like mind to work for a common task and values. Standards still give identity and direction to expressions of community, whether the opening pageantry of the Olympics or civic parades, religious processions or political rallies. Standards still have meaning; to raise a standard and follow it means publicly claiming identity and commitment.

The deeper reality of the Two Standards raises issues about when and how women take a stand and when and for what reasons they may risk alienating those standing somewhere else. Taking a stand raises an inherent question: "If it results in rupturing a relationship, is it worth it?" Likewise, pondering the Two Standards leads to other questions: "Where and with whom do I stand? What communities of resistance and solidarity am I aligned with?" Women may discover not only new ways of following but new ways of leading. Finding the courage to anchor oneself clearly may be a deeply liberating experience. The Standard of Christ is a sign of inclusion, equality, and freedom, a vision for a new humanity.

Meditating on the Two Standards may also open new areas of self-knowledge, understanding the divided places within. The struggles for "standing" may move from exterior causes to interior realities: "Who or what represents Lucifer and Christ in my particular struggle?" Delving into issues of truth and power touches people deeply, for this meditation focuses on conflict within themselves as well as outside. It concerns doubt and fear and denial. It means exploring what pulls people apart.

This meditation not only touches individual struggles and stands, but it can also lead to forming communities of solidarity and commitment where persons and groups live dedicated lives. God's reign of peace and justice, community and responsible relationships is a dream to which many women willingly commit themselves even through a long and taxing struggle.

Three Classes of Persons

This meditation follows the notes on the Two Standards in the text and precedes the section on the public life of Jesus. The subtitle gives a clue about its purpose: "An aid toward embracing what is better" [149]. Where the meditation on the Call of the King elicited commitment and the section on the Two Standards clarified the strategies of movement toward and away from God, this meditation and the exercise following, Three Degrees of Humility, illuminate the degree of potential response to Christ's call. The issue here concerns detachment from anything impeding movement toward God. The seeker desires a depth of indifference to ensure that nothing deafens her to the authentic voice of God.

Ganss's translation uses the familiar word *attachment* in this meditation about good persons who have received a sum of money and are considering how best to dispense of it [153–55]. Attachment comes from the old French *attaché*, which means "nailed to." *Addiction*, a more contemporary term, attaches desire to certain specific behaviors, things, or people and enslaves its energy. One can be addicted to ideas, relationships, substances, being liked, work, power or powerlessness, self-image, or anything. Even "small" addictions stand in the way of freedom and love by sapping the energy of our desires. Psychiatrist Gerald May calls addiction "the most powerful psychic enemy of humanity's desire for God" (May 1988, 3). Ignatius's Three Classes of Persons pinpoints one of the most difficult tendencies to uproot in the human heart: nailing desires to something less than God.

Ignatius's case study presents "the postponers, the compromisers and the wholeheartedly indifferent" (Ganss 1991, 407). All three "desire to get rid of the attachment," that is, the addiction. The first type talks and talks, substituting multiple words for action, and wishful thinking surfaces frequently as "if only" dreaming. The second person tries to "have it all," to persuade or manipulate in order to have the best of both worlds. This person will go to great lengths to do many things, except the one thing necessary. Finally, the third type of person roots her decision in love and her desire for true freedom, choosing that which God most desires—that is, choosing with indifference.[11]

Problems and Possibilities for Three Classes

Emphasizing indifference achieved by will power alone downplays the seeker's need to cooperate with God's Spirit. Too much stress on diffidence can imply that the self-surrender is equated with loss of identity, choice, and even oneself. However, this meditation can provide real possibilities for gaining clarity about both desires and addictions. It poses the questions, "What is the one thing I refuse to turn over to God's care? What is my 'no' point? What do I find myself playing mind games around rather than letting go and trusting in God's love?"

Grappling with these questions can help the one making the Exercises learn an interior way of love integrated with greater intentionality and freedom. In consciously giving over her life to God, she receives life in surprising ways. The writings of Teresa of Avila illustrate that conscious self-surrender provides the only true antidote to attachment or addiction:

> One day while I was anxiously desiring to help the [O]rder, the Lord told me: "Do what lies in your power; surrender yourself to me, and do not be disturbed about anything; rejoice in the good that has been given you, for it is very great; my Father takes His delight in you, and the Holy Spirit loves you." (Kavanaugh and Rodriguez 1976, 324)

Both Teresa and Ignatius realized that self-knowledge and awareness, coupled with prayer and waiting on God, provided the only means of moving beyond attachment or addiction and into greater interior freedom.

Paradoxically, detachment also deals with finding oneself. Not only must an individual possess a self in order to give it away, but the gospel also insists that she must lose herself to find herself. Authentic self-donation, prompted by the Spirit of God, can be recognized by the fruits of strength, the building up of oneself and others rather than depletion and depression. Teresa became more herself, stronger, and more effective for mission as she gave herself over to God.

The contemporary phenomenon of burnout often reveals addiction and drivenness: earning God's or others' approval, a warped self-image, or doing things "my way." An addicted person needs to uncover the addiction and deal with it in a balanced manner. She must learn to create boundaries of self-care that lead to reflection and renewal. Only with these boundaries in place will renewal occur and yield an energized self for mission. Discernment provides the crucial direction to any choice: one puts trust in God's creative power at work.

Three Ways of Being Humble

This exercise is not presented as a formal meditation but as a subject to ponder prior to engaging in the exercises related to making a major vocational choice. Ganss calls this exercise neither a meditation nor a contemplation, but a "consideration" permeating the days devoted to election (1991, 410). It presents three ways a person decides a course of action. The first, and most fundamental, uses sin as a criterion for choosing, employing the "mortal/venial" language typical of the time. It assumes obedience to God's law as the basic choice for salvation. The second way stresses indifference when faced with equally desirable options. The third and "most perfect" way imitates Christ by preferring poverty and contempt. This last way only makes sense when it emerges freely from solidarity with the poor Jesus and his friends. George Aschenbrenner (2004, 107–11) offers another way of describing this consideration. He calls it "The Three Ways of Loving." This language may be more helpful where the words *humility* or *humble* might be misinterpreted.

Problems and Possibilities for Humility

The major problem facing a seeker as she ponders this exercise lies in paralysis by her "I." "*I* don't have or even want this kind of humility. *I* can't do this. *I* can't reach this high level three," she says to her guide. "*I'm* not good enough to go the whole way of discipleship. *I'm* not as generous as others. *I* guess *I* don't have what it takes to really do the Exercises." This woman interprets this exercise in terms of levels of perfection, and she grades herself low, believing only the elite can ascend to the highest, or third, level. In this instance, the emphasis subtly shifts and attention transfers to oneself. Personal achievement and competition or their opposites, defeat and driving willpower, become the dominant motivations. Rigid self-consciousness and determination can replace the desired freedom of spirit and spontaneity before God.

This contemplation can be especially problematic for women in situations of poverty and oppression where it may all too easily further oppress rather than liberate. The final section of the exercise could be misinterpreted as exalting poverty when its actual purpose is to free the one making the exercise to draw even closer to Jesus and to share his way as fully as possible. For a woman to ask for poverty when she is already living in a soul-destroying situation of actual poverty is masochism and not liberation. For many women who are struggling to break the cycle of poverty for themselves and their families, this meditation must be appropriately adapted if it is not to be deeply problematic. Jesus himself did not live in the kind of poverty that many women experience. He lived a life of *simplicity*, which may be more helpful language. In such situations it may be more helpful to look at the solidarity of Jesus with a woman in a situation of poverty, rather than to give the sense that this is something Jesus desires for her. We need to remember that Ignatius was coming out of a situation of relative wealth and influence from which he desired to be detached. Many women are coming out of vastly different situations and lack of freedom.

Despite these potential pitfalls, this consideration can open to humility, greater generosity, deeper self-knowledge. Prayer over each section leads to an integration and recognition that humility, understood as gift of God and God's work, does not ultimately depend on personal effort but on openness to God's power. This consideration invites persons of good will and those who desire God to be more like Christ.

From the beginning of the Exercises, indifference—the second way of humility—invites the seeker to follow God's ways, wherever they lead. The third way of humility, transcending even indifference, is a radical choice to give over all of one's life to be with Jesus no matter the consequences. Jesus is the model of humility, who washes the feet of his disciples and ultimately empties himself (Phil 2:6–8). From the beginning, Christian tradition has recognized the humility of Jesus as model for believers:

> The value of humility as a willing dependence on and obedience to the saving mysterious God, taught by Jesus and embodied in the "way" that led to his death on the cross, was so deeply ingrained in the Scriptures that early Christian writers could not help but see it as close to the heart of the Church's spirituality. (Daley 1995, 9)

Unfortunately, humility became distorted and distanced from its original biblical basis, but the three ways of being humble retrieve this basic meaning. They speak to a growing capacity for love, freedom, and magnanimity rather than subservience. As long as the seeker desires to develop a healthy, balanced sense of self, this consideration can challenge her to become "more." The seeker who prays for the "desire to desire" the fullness of humility realizes that its achievement is gift, not the fruit of her striving.

Who Do You Say That I Am?

The Contemplations and Scripture

To know, love, and follow Jesus Christ presumes both a call to discipleship and a personal response. The Contemplations on the life of Christ invite the one making the Exercises to enter into the gospel events and grow as a more mature and committed disciple. The material for the Contemplations introduces the Trinity's view of the world and the annunciation of the angel Gabriel to Mary [101–9], the major events of the hidden life, the nativity [110–17], the presentation and flight into Egypt [132–33], and Jesus's obedience at Nazareth and his encounter in the Jerusalem temple [134]. Ganss notes that these initial contemplations intend to create "affective attachment to Christ in his poverty and humility" (1991, 403).

After the interlude of the Two Standards and Three Classes of Persons, the seeker moves into the events of the public life. At the same time, the seeker becomes more aware of the disposition needed for an election, an aspect treated extensively in chapter 11. The contemplations about the public life of Christ include the journey from Nazareth to the Jordan and the baptism of Christ [158–60], the desert temptations, the following of Christ by Andrew and others, the Sermon on the Mount, Jesus walking on the water, his preaching in the temple, and the raising of Lazarus to the events of Palm Sunday [161]. Ignatius encouraged blending the contemplations of the life of Christ with the Key Meditations. The formative process of the Exercises depends on their reciprocal interaction.

Besides the biblical events mentioned above, Ignatius suggests additional mysteries in the life of our Lord as further resources for prayer. Eleven options exist for the section on the "hidden life." The "public life" includes sixteen additional mysteries, some mentioned earlier in the Second Week section. The use of these "mysteries" of the life of Christ suggests that the events or episodes in his life include theological themes worth pondering more deeply, such as mysteries of trinitarian life, incarnation, and redemption. The seeker reflects not only on what happened to Jesus but also on why and what it means for discipleship today.

The fact that Ignatius allows for additional mysteries in [261–312] suggests that one might also draw on materials beyond the ones he offered that might connect more readily to individual women's experience. Indeed, Ignatius himself hints at such freedom in [18], where he encourages the director to adapt to each retreatant and in [162], where he suggests ways to lengthen or shorten the Second Week. For example, an invitation to spend time with the visitation can be a powerful experience of connection with the nascent Jesus, while praying the story of the woman at the well can open up space for real, honest, and liberating encounter with Jesus.

Ignatius expected that the movement of God, so real in his own life, would be replicated uniquely in each person's life. Contemplating the action of God in the sweep of human history and concretely in the life, death, and resurrection of Jesus brings a deeper awareness of God active and present in one's personal history today.

Problems and Possibilities for Second Week Contemplations

Did Jesus call any women? The "Call" events begin exclusively with men who then tell other men. Even the "come and see" passages in the Fourth Gospel involve only men. Most of the selections suggested in the text of the *Spiritual Exercises* include no women except Mary Magdalene. Ignatius's description of her as a public sinner, however, reflects a common characterization now repudiated by Scripture scholars. As with Second Week contemplations, women are often hard to find, frequently nameless and marginal.

Yet the Spiritual Exercises also provide a welcome opportunity to recover the long-neglected stories of Jesus and women. The discovery of numerous hidden women helps answer the lingering question, "What was it like for a woman to follow Jesus?" Strong and courageous women take center stage during Jesus's hidden life: Elizabeth, Mary, and Anna. The women of the public life provide many and diverse encounters with Jesus. In addition, many scriptural examples show Jesus as free from patriarchal standards of male behavior, sometimes scandalizing his male disciples. Even a cursory examination reveals that Jesus related to women in a human way, demonstrating empathy with their plight as poor and marginalized.

As Jesus called women to discipleship, he invited them too into a deepening knowledge and commitment. Women often served as the catalyst for Jesus breaking boundaries and stereotypes. Jesus associated with the oppressed, the poor, and the most destitute; he interacted with those most despised, the prostitutes, and he broke taboos involving women. He included among his closest friends Martha and Mary, sisters of Lazarus.

Who Do You Say That I Am?

Jesus included and empowered women. He noticed women in their world and in his. He saw, heard, felt their various emotions, and he was moved and acted in response to his own "contemplative awareness." Women witnessed both the birth and death of Jesus and found themselves sent to evangelize and be recipients of the Spirit's transforming power.

These biblical women model a process that is valid and fruitful for women today. Women's narratives in response to the Second Week prayer experiences often reflect the common human experience of getting to know somebody more and more deeply. Friendship begins through simple conversation: "Tell me about yourself." All stories are important: stories of growing-up years, family life, neighborhood, school and church, and the larger social and cultural milieu. Women are naturally associated with the childhood of Jesus, but they also appear in his public life as active and caring disciples. He had an amazing ability to create and sustain relationships, exhibiting mutual care with a variety of persons. Perhaps the traditional expectations about knowing, loving, and serving Christ the Lord has been based on experience more typical of men moving toward autonomy and achievement. Women's development, on the other hand, usually flourishes in attachment, intimacy, and relationships. Jesus serves as a model of integrated humanity, exhibiting the values of care and connection more typical of women, as much as those traditionally associated with him—autonomy, justice, and independence.

Wisdom for the One Giving the Exercises

At this point, the one giving the Exercises needs to pay attention to how one living the Exercises responds. The dynamic of the Second Week leads to a gradual personalizing of commitment, moving from an objective sense of a "Call of the King" to a profound personal commitment to know, love, and follow Christ and to accept the concrete implications for her life. A wise companion will emphasize the grace desired, namely, openness to really hear the call of Christ even more than the content of the story. The deeper issue for the meditation is crucial: "Do I really want to hear God's voice, knowing I will be changed by what I hear? Can I trust that God may speak even in ancient and unfamiliar ways, as well as in those more compatible with contemporary idiom?"

In guiding another through this Week, certain signs indicate how one's personal story and the story of Jesus converge. The process need not be linear, with each exercise following on the other, step by step. It may just as readily be cyclic, with themes appearing and disappearing, then surfacing again later. Various responses, such as thinking about, pondering, and feeling, may surface at unexpected times. Biblical stories may raise reflections on theological themes, such as Jesus's humanity or divinity, or one's personal degree of freedom.

The guide needs to be aware of the various movements that particular gospel stories may suggest. Some women may be attracted to and familiar with the Jesus of the Gospels, preferring consoling passages that deepen the relationship, but avoiding conflict or hard sayings. These difficult sayings might provide opportunities to probe more deeply the call to discipleship. Yet the guide should note what disturbs or does not ring true, such as militarism, male-stereotyped characters and events in gospel passages, and simplistic or stereotyped understandings of humility and pride. Both attraction and resistance need attentive discernment.

The one giving the Exercises occasionally needs to stand back and examine the selection of material. The giver must remain faithful to the dynamic of the Exercises and the seeking of the graces. But the "how" can and must be adapted to this person, this woman. This adaptation, including the selection of material, must be done with discernment and intention. First, notice why one text is included and another left out. Why select this material? Is it congruent with the grace of the week? Is it consistent with the seeker's own dynamic movement through the Week? When is changing direction necessary? The material of prayer will influence how one responds to the Christ who calls.

Each person needs to articulate a personal Christology as a means of greater self-knowledge about her relationship to Jesus Christ, though she may do so without traditional christological language. Some leading questions may prove helpful: "What have been your most significant sources of knowledge about Jesus? How have your images of or relationship with Jesus changed through the years? Who is the Jesus you are looking for? What draws you into the mystery of Jesus and what characteristics do you most admire and desire to emulate?" Christology is an important component of the Second Week—as it will be in the Weeks following. The call to imitate Christ moves beyond gender stereotypes; Christ is—and invites all to be—faith-filled, strong, gentle, compassionate, confrontative, wise, loving, peaceful, and relational.

The guide will often find specific issues arising in relationship to prayer and decision-making, whether related to the Two Standards, Three Kinds of Persons, or Three Degrees of Humility. One main responsibility, then, consists of assisting the persons to a deeper level of insight by providing helpful questions: "Where do you stand? With whom will you work? What are you willing to struggle for, to die/live for?" Thus, a discerning guide identifies issues associated with significant choices along with the inner movements they raise.

What if God asks one to do the hardest thing possible? Facing choices and making priorities and commitments can create fear and anxiety. One question focuses the guide's work—How is generosity manifested or blocked? The guide looks for clues, listens attentively to what holds the seeker back or impedes a fuller donation of self. Guiding the Exercises includes being with the person in discernment. The guide uses intuition and experience to reflect on how the seeker may be invited to greater generosity. A helpful guide will listen for how she makes decisions and what motivates her, carefully noting responses that seem too heady or emphasize willpower alone, such as "I should be able to do this" or "I feel guilty because I can't do better." Discernment remains critical during this struggle, clarifying what attracts her and whether the attraction is of God.

Often the lives and commitments of others provide inspiration and encouragement during this Second Week. Ignatius suggested reading lives of the saints, as they had been influential in his conversion process [100]. Today there is renewed interest in the Communion of Saints, and those engaged in the Second Week can benefit from multiple resources currently available in books, articles, and videos. Insights emerging from historical theology and women's history and spirituality also provide a rich source of reflection.[12] Suggesting biographies of contemporary women living radically committed lives of faith can also be extremely powerful.

Conclusion

The grace of the Second Week consists in knowing, loving, and following in the path of discipleship with renewed life and commitment, a discovery of being called by God to follow "the Way." The engagement

Exercises

demanded from those who walk this way is nothing less than the whole person—body, senses, imagination, intellect, will, memories, hopes—immersed in life here and now. Ignatius saw no difference between the Jesus of history and the Christ of faith, and the Second Week fosters an encounter with the Jesus of history through the mystery of the resurrected Christ living among us today.

Experienced guides, also disciples on the way, can profit from their own learning. By gradually becoming freer from the text, yet understanding the dynamics of each Week, they develop greater freedom to follow the movement of the Spirit in the seeker. Together, guide and seeker search for and verify the fruits of the Exercises, knowing there is a "call waiting" that requires clear and open reception. The Exercises do not aim to replicate the God experience of Ignatius but to encounter the living God who communicates in many and diverse ways through the central mystery of the life, death, and resurrection of Jesus.

CHAPTER 8

Discovering the Depth of Commitment

Exercises of the Third Week

...to ask for heartfelt sorrow and confusion, because the Lord is going to his Passion for my sins.
—*Spiritual Exercises* [193]

I cannot accept that the suffering and criminal death of Jesus was "God's will." What kind of God would desire such torture for a beloved son? I feel God must weep for the atrocities humans do to each other, most of all what happened to Jesus.
—A contemporary woman

The Third and Fourth Weeks of the Exercises together form a single movement. George Aschenbrenner emphasizes, "Though the whole revelation of the mysteries of Jesus has an overarching integrity, his suffering and death into resurrection have a special coherence and unity" (2004, 118). As the seeker begins this part of the Exercises, there is a clear movement toward a closer identification with the experience of Jesus, first in his suffering, and then in his glory.

In the Third (or Passion) Week, the one making the Spiritual Exercises hears anew the invitation to walk the way of discipleship, now accompanying Jesus through his passion. To know, love, and follow Jesus gains new meaning as well; it now includes the call to compassion with Jesus's suffering. Following Jesus draws the seeker into the drama of the cross, for she goes up to Jerusalem and engages in the conflict that leads to death. Being with Jesus means entering into *his* perspective, focusing not on her own personal experience of the passion, but willingly sharing his experience, his choices, his anguish, his truth, his desires, his aloneness, his sense of the absence of God. The attentive guide will notice the readiness of the seeker to enter into this Week as her prayer becomes simpler, and she moves toward a forgetfulness of self in growing union with Jesus.

Like those who accompanied Jesus in his ministry, the seekers have experienced his deeds of power and heard his words of life during the first two Weeks of the Exercises. They are now confronted, however, with the fearful choice of whether to follow him into the depths of powerlessness. In this experience of suffering, Ignatius says, "divinity hides itself" [196].

Material and Dynamics of the Third Week

Who is the Christ of the Third Week? One commentator notes, "With Ignatius we are always before the Christ of majesty, the Creator and Lord, the eternal King who fulfills his mission here on earth by passing through the painful death from which he delivers us" (Cusson 1988, 299). Third Week prayer, however, stresses the invitation to connect with the vulnerability of Jesus in his ultimate humanity: pain, suffering, betrayal, and death. The one making the Exercises is invited to share Jesus's sense of failure, grief, loss, and betrayal by his friends.

The contemplations of the Third Week [190–209] feature Jesus in mortal conflict with powerful religious and political institutions of his time and culture. They begin with the Last Supper, harmonizing the paschal meal of the Synoptic Gospels with the foot washing and last discourse of the Fourth Gospel. The second contemplation considers "how Christ our Lord descended with his eleven disciples from Mt. Sion where the supper had been eaten into the valley" [201] and entered the garden of Gethsemane. The subsequent contemplations lead to the house of Annas, the house of Caiaphas, the house of Pilate, and to Herod, as well as Simon of Cyrene, the presence of two thieves, and his followers Joseph and Nicodemus. These scenes trace Jesus going from house to house, encountering strong and powerful men and being betrayed by the very friends he had gathered around him. Ignatius briefly mentions Our Lady in her loneliness, grief, and fatigue [208] as sorrowful mother [298].

In what may seem a strange placement, Ignatius also offers Rules for Eating at the end of the Third Week. Eating is often problematic for many women, especially those with body image issues. But thinking about eating mindfully as appropriate and discerned self-care can be an important aspect for many women making the Exercises and may entail a kind of asceticism proper to the Third Week and beyond.

Given the inevitable end of this journey with Jesus, why would anyone choose to enter the passion week? The answer lies in the mysterious and compelling call to the depths of discipleship and in the experience of having fallen in love. "A long week later, as Jesus goes to his cross, what dies is not just a dream or a project. It is my beloved. I'm not mourning my shattered hopes, my doomed calling. I'm mourning a man, a man I have come to love. At the start he was all abstraction and hope and activity; but by the end he is *this man*, a man I have come to know intimately" (Marsh 2006, 8). For some, the Third Week confirms the decisions made during the Second Week. For others, the call to share the totality of Jesus's human limits and abandonment becomes a time of transformation.

Prayer during this week may be unpredictable. Some experience the dryness and distance of God so concretely that this state itself becomes an experience of the passion. For others, the prayer of the Third Week offers an experience of great consolation. The entire paschal mystery grounds the Third Week. Followers, then and now, must choose their response to this encounter with mystery, an encounter that can lead to new depths of compassion, friendship, and love. Whether one meets the suffering servant or the glorious Messiah in prayer, the invitation to plumb the depths of God's saving love remains the same.

Problems and Possibilities for the Third Week

Some women feel reluctance as they anticipate the Third Week. Pain and powerlessness feel too familiar and a suffering God seems a contradiction. On the other hand, some women who have struggled with this may find they can more easily identify with Jesus in his powerlessness and suffering. As always, careful discernment will help to determine whether hesitancy is a warning that proceeding will either be harmful or an opportunity for conversion, grace, and greater intimacy. Several problem areas as well as possibilities may emerge during the Week.

Christ Image

While Jesus is the central figure in all the passion narratives, each portrays him differently.[1] It is therefore important to give careful thought to which version of the Gospel texts to use with a particular retreatant. In addition to these biblical portrayals, the tradition has emphasized, in both doctrine and devotion, images of the suffering Christ that have become stumbling blocks for some contemporary women. Some of these images are connected with a theology of atonement and satisfaction that is particularly unhelpful for most women. The image of Christ as sacrificial lamb and victim, for example, caused one woman to respond in this way: "The all-knowing, all-powerful, and all-good Father God sent his Son to earth to be killed. The Son went meekly as a lamb to the slaughter without complaint. This sounds to me like cosmic child abuse is the way of salvation." These suggestions of abuse and passivity seem to glorify suffering in silence as a holy victim prevails; women today reject this "victim" image as detrimental to their own self-development.

The servant image can likewise prove problematic for some women who see Christ as servant, reinforcing the idea that servitude—even slavery—is preferred for followers of Christ. Womanist theologians cite this servant image as an example of how some use Jesus to reinforce white male supremacy. Holding up Jesus as a model servant, directly or indirectly, can subtly encourage toleration of slavery or keeping marginalized persons "in their place" as servants, helpers, caretakers. The image often reinforces a romanticized concept of servanthood suggested by those with no firsthand knowledge of its realities. Systems of domination and subordination reflected in relationships between lords and servants do not provide appropriate models for contemporary emulation.

How, then, can the image of Christ as model "servant" open up new possibilities for contemporary women? As Ruether comments, "The essence of servanthood is that it is possible only for liberated persons, not people in servitude. Also, it exercises power and leadership, but in a new way, not to reduce others to dependency, but to empower and liberate others" (1990, 54). In this model, persons choose the model of servanthood initiated by Jesus and flowing from his free and independent choice—they are not coerced by another. Finally, gospel servanthood transforms disciples into friends: "I do not call you servants any longer, because the servant does not know what the master is doing; but I have called you friends, because I have made known to you everything that I have heard from my Father" (John 15:15). Turning these Christ images around provides an opportunity to explore whether they still have meaning for women. Theologian Anne Carr, for example, reinterprets the image of "victim": Jesus was neither a passive victim nor did he acquiesce to a sacrificial death. Rather, Jesus died because of the way he lived, because of the fidelity and commitment of his life and his liberating message (Carr 1996, 174).

The Cross

Just as some Christ images can become obstacles to entering the Third Week, the cross as sign and symbol of Christian discipleship can block some women's progress. "If any want to become my followers, let them deny themselves and take up their cross daily and follow me" (Luke 9:23). Walking the way of discipleship in the footsteps of Jesus is one thing, but uncritically accepting the sign of the cross as a devotional symbol when it has historically also been a sign of domination and violence on battlegrounds and in Jewish ghettos is another. Today many women feel increasingly sensitive to the interrelationship of all systems of domination and resist association with symbols and language that perpetuate any kind of oppression.

Yet the cross symbolizes not only domination and death but also life and liberation. Contemporary women theologians and artists provide new interpretations. For example, the sculpture *Crucified Woman* has both shocked and inspired. It has stimulated theological reflection about the relationship of art, the female body, and the needless suffering of women. Themes of relationship, healing, and justice emerge as life-and-death questions. Who is on the cross today? One woman on seeing the sculpture responded,

> The usual image of a man hung on a tree really imprisoned me to the idea of a male God. The image of a woman liberates me into the idea that my being a woman allows me to identify with God's act. Beautiful, powerful, a challenge to take up the cross and not be a passive bystander. (Dyke 1991, 26)

The cross can also represent significant relationships. At a symposium exploring the Christ symbol and women, those in attendance were invited to bring a cross that belonged to them and tell the stories associated with it.[2] Whether jewelry, symbols of covenant commitment, artistic representations, mementos of someone or something special, each cross and story represented a personal and meaningful relationship.

The sign of the cross remains a sign of contradiction for some women today. Seeker and guide will need to ponder its power for liberation and life in the contemporary context as women continue to face their "daily" crosses.

Exclusion from the Story

"I know this story already," says one woman of her problems with the Third Week material. Familiarity with the passion narratives and their representations through art, music, poetry, film, and liturgical celebrations may dissuade the one making the Exercises from going deeper in contemplating the passion. Past prejudices, theological misunderstanding, and false expectations could lead us to settle for superficial engagement with the mystery of the passion. Even the selected texts in the Exercises reinforce the assumption that the drama of the passion has an almost exclusively male cast. Yet we can easily reread the passion and balance the actions of the men who dominate the traditional telling with the women who are not represented yet were there and offered care and compassion to Jesus in his suffering. Entering the narrative imaginatively from the perspective of one of the women in the story can be powerfully liberating.

The Exercises begin with the story of a meal: Jesus eating the paschal meal with his apostles. An alternative reading also begins with a meal, this one a supper at the home of Simon the Leper. An unnamed woman (Mark 14:3–9; Matt 26:6–13) anoints Jesus prior to his death. Although a traditional action, she anoints not his feet but his head as a sign of royal commission. Thus, she takes on the "untraditional position of priest and/or prophet" (Levine 1992, 261). Jesus recognized the significance of her action by noting that what she had done would be recounted through the ages "in memory of her." But her name was lost and the pioneering work of biblical scholar Elisabeth Schüssler Fiorenza only recently reclaimed her story. In a similar scene in the Fourth Gospel, Mary of Bethany anoints Jesus's feet, a sign of extravagant love, shortly before he himself washes the feet of the disciples. The scene reminds us of the special friendship among Martha, Mary, Lazarus, and Jesus.

Women's voices can also emerge in the passion story. The maid of the high priest serves as a foil to Peter. Her probing questions demand a truthful answer and stand in sharp contrast to Peter's denial. Pilate's wife, a woman of power through her husband's power, pays attention to the warning in her dream. Yet her warning, spoken on behalf of Jesus, was ignored. The daughters of Jerusalem, weeping and crying out, elicit attention for suffering women and children. The "voiceless" women in the passion narrative communicate eloquently by their faithful presence at the death and burial of Jesus. They remain nameless except for three: Mary Magdalene, Mary the mother of James and Joses, and Salome. Luke also adds Joanna to the list of women present at the cross. The Fourth Gospel vividly portrays Mary, the mother of Jesus, and the beloved disciple standing beneath the cross, exemplifying discipleship as a relationship transcending bloodlines. Jesus's words in death give life to a new community of mutuality and care, which finds its fulfillment in Pentecost.

The women of the passion stand at a distance but share the powerlessness of the one who suffers—Jesus. In contrast, the men engage in a struggle marked by power, domination, fear, dishonesty, cowardice, lying, and physical violence. The grace of the Third Week—to experience sorrow and confusion for the Lord's passion [93]—opens a wider realm of possibility as one prays with Jesus amid his experience with both the men and women who participate in his passion narrative.

Suffering, Guilt, and Compassion

The notion that Jesus suffers because of "my sins," as stated in the text of the *Exercises* ("the Lord is going to his Passion for my sins" [193] and "consider how he suffers all this for my sins" [197]) can block some women from progressing further into the Third Week. The phrase can elicit a pervasive and debilitating guilt over being the cause of Jesus's death. Such guilt has had many centuries to embed itself in the psyche of women. In the third century, Tertullian's treatise *On the Dress of Women* announced this judgment: "God's judgment on this sex lives on in our age: the guilt necessarily lives on as well. *You* are the Devil's gateway... because of *your* punishment, that is, death, even the Son of God had to die" (Clark 1983, 39). Internalizing this kind of guilt can lead to an unhealthy preoccupation: "How am I the cause of Christ's passion? What did I do to him to make him suffer?" Or worse, "Because I did _____, Jesus had to die."

Exercises

This aspect of the Exercises elicits a strong response from women who have been asked and expected to suffer for the wrong reasons, for example, to offer up the actions of an abusive husband "for the sake of the marriage." Certainly, suffering is part of the human condition, but knowing the difference between redemptive suffering and abuse is especially critical for women. Even a sense of meaninglessness and futility can bring us back into the presence of Jesus in his passion and open possibilities for deepening spiritual insight during the Third Week. However, given how problematic much of the pervasive theology of the cross has been for women (and men), it is significant that recent breakthroughs in understanding salvation continue to evolve in ways that are refreshing and life giving.

In his supplementary material, Ignatius suggests contemplating the Seven Last Words of Christ [297]. Contemporary women might listen to these words as the women at the foot of the cross might have heard them. In asking to share the dispositions of Jesus on the cross and allowing his words in death to be words of life, amazing possibilities present themselves. After being with Jesus in his suffering, some experience a breakthrough. They see the passion of Jesus in their experience of suffering. At the same time a poignant question arises: "What needs to die in me in order that I might really live?"

Pain can be a portal leading to a richer life. Occasions of physical, psychological, and spiritual pain are opportunities to discern directions. "What happens as a result of this suffering? How can I learn to suffer for the right reasons and what are they? How can I see meaning in this suffering, leading me to greater faith, hope, and love? How do I identify the value of living with pain and how do I get out of pain that is destructive?" Past interpretations of spirituality and theology uncritically accepted the value of suffering. Today, however, the insights of psychology and liberation theology demand the alleviation of demeaning and unjust suffering and expose the ways people and systems legitimate this kind of oppression.

Yet, a profound and intimate encounter with God can also be called forth as we face our suffering. Discovering personal meaning in suffering brings with it the realization that suffering defies human understanding. The daily deaths we experience can signify Holy Presence in all aspects of human life. No one can ever totally understand the mystery of suffering and death, but being present to God and to those who suffer teaches compassion. These times—when few if any words are needed—remind us that presence alone suffices in the face of inevitable suffering. Suffering, as with other human experiences, moves the seeker into another dimension of the mystery of relationship, compassion, "suffering with."

Set against the backdrop of Christ's suffering, prayer of the Third Week can reveal new understandings of passion and compassion as the seeker connects her passion with that of the larger Body of Christ. Passionate women praying the passion of Jesus Christ can experience deep affective responses: guilt, consolation, fear of her own and Jesus's suffering, love, and intimacy. Sharing in the passion of another leads to communion with them, and praying the passion of Jesus inevitably leads to compassion for those most in need. As we attend to the suffering of another, we cannot force or even predict our own affective response. We simply know that "if one member suffers, all suffer together with it" (1 Cor 12:26).

One of the graces of the Third Week, empathy, or identifying with the thoughts and feelings of another, leads to a self-transcendence that opens up to others. While more than a simple awareness of other persons and their experience, empathy stops short of total absorption in another. Empathy creates transformation through mutuality and fosters a hope for the other's well-being, which paradoxically benefits oneself. "Such a dynamic may well underlie the Christian interpretation of Christ on the Cross identifying with all sin and sinners, and therefore able to redeem all sinners from sin" (Suchocki 1995, 111).

A Theology of Solidarity and Accompaniment

Feminist Theologian Elizabeth Johnson's book *Creation and the Cross: The Mercy of God for a Planet in Peril* examines the way Western theology has grappled with the meaning of the cross and proposes an alternative theological understanding that can undergird the interpretation of the Third Week. In first unpacking Western theology's dominant narrative regarding the cross, she notes that this theological perspective strongly emphasizes the idea of redemption requiring the payment of a penalty. This understanding was linked to the feudal world in which Anselm lived. In this context, if someone broke the law and disturbed the order of the social fabric, they had to pay a penalty to affect the restoration of good order. The argument grounding this perspective claims that because God is infinite, the recompense owed was likewise infinite. Thus, the penalty for sin could only be paid by God in the person of Jesus. The theory was developed into a coherent argument by Anselm in the eleventh century and became the dominant way that that we have understood the meaning of the cross. It was certainly the theology in which Ignatius himself would have been steeped. It is not surprising that he explicitly makes the link of Jesus suffering on the cross "for my sins."

Feminist theologians have long criticized the debilitating psychological effects foisted on women, particularly by this theory's interpretation of the cross. Johnson notes,

> In a strange way, the innocent Christ who suffered willingly on behalf of others has been held up as a model for women in a way different from men. It is women who are supposed to serve silently, obediently, without question, in imitation of the Crucified One. Such glorification of passivity undermines the agency which belongs to women, all the while giving traditional expectations of women and their gendered roles a powerful divine gloss. (2018, 25)

This theology can be very dangerous for women in abusive situations, she emphasizes, whether with a partner or for women (and men) who have experienced abuse as children at the hands of their parents.

Johnson argues that that the time has come for us to retire Anselm's atonement/satisfaction theology. While Anselm's original intent was pastoral, to help people recognize God's goodness and mercy in loving us to the point of substituting his son in reparation for our sins, this flawed theology no longer serves us. It encourages a highly problematic image of God, sadistic and punishing, who requires the death of his son for us to be forgiven. Instead, we need to take back a sense of God's mercy so that "all creation can be included in a theology of salvation" (2018, 158).

In place of Anselm's atonement theory, Johnson proposes a theology of accompaniment based on the notion of a loving merciful God seen throughout the Scriptures and particularly evident in Second Isaiah. This God is always gracious and "accompanies the world with saving grace." Johnson sees a double solidarity: Jesus becomes human and is in solidarity with us in our suffering, and God is in solidarity with Jesus in his suffering. We are accompanied by a God who is in solidarity with all of God's creation.

Johnson also sees the cross as part of what she calls "deep incarnation":

> With the incarnation God's presence abides not only in and for the world but goes deep down to the point of identity as part of the world. An unimaginable act of loving solidarity, it enacts the kind of divine love that not only blesses people benevolently but also enters empathetically into their experience, self-identifying with the glory and the agony of human life from within. (2018, 158)

She further argues that "incarnation places the crucified God on the side of the tortured and the dispossessed, rather than in alliance with the powerful who crush the life out of others in myriad ways" (2018, 179). This idea of deep incarnation also extends beyond humankind to a solidarity with the entire created world.

In this new understanding, the cross is not seen in isolation. The incarnation of Jesus, his life and ministry, his death and resurrection are one movement showing the solidarity and the accompaniment of a loving God. Women resonate with this idea of solidarity and accompaniment far more than to the idea of a God who demands the death of his son as satisfaction for our crimes. For many women who have suffered, the awareness that Jesus enters fully into our experience of human suffering and is in solidarity with them is deeply consoling and liberating.

Wisdom for Those Giving the Exercises

When a woman's theology about the cross creates a block to her experience of the Exercises, it may be helpful to gently introduce a different way of thinking, such as Johnson's theology of accompaniment. It may also be helpful to adjust the language of the grace prayed for in the First Contemplation: "Here it will be to ask for sorrow, regret and confusion, because the Lord is going to his passion for my sins." We could ask for "sorrow, grief, and confusion because the Lord is going to his passion and for the grace to accompany him."

As earlier in the Exercises, Ignatius offers help for the one giving this Week's Exercises. By this point in the Exercises he leaves a good deal of freedom to the woman and her guide. The guide is free to reduce the number of prayer periods each day [205]. The Third Week can also be easily lengthened by dividing each mystery into shorter segments or more aspects of the passion covered by omitting repetitions [209]. Adjusting the second and sixth additions assist in keeping in the mood of sorrow of the Third Week [206], especially useful when a woman is making the Exercises in her daily life. Offering her a small wooden cross to carry with her during the day, for example, can be a powerful reminder of the Week's affective tone. Refraining from attending events such as parties where possible and taking care with the use of television and social media can also help keep the atmosphere of the Week.

Givers of the Exercises need to bear in mind that the Third Week is often a time in which the woman lives into her election, and the likely implications and cost of the living out of that call: a time of seeking confirmation. The guide should watch out for a tendency on the part of the directee to start to doubt the validity of her election or the motivations out of which it was made. In this way, the false spirit can subtly undermine a well-made decision. Many women have often found themselves lacking in confidence in relation to decision-making, and it may be at this point that her confidence in her decision wavers. The guide needs to discern whether the election perhaps needs another look, but often it can simply be that she is not accustomed to trusting her ability to discern God's invitation in her life.

Culturally it can be helpful to ask the woman a bit about her own experience with death and mourning. It can be powerful to invite her on the Tomb Day at the end of the Third Week to spend time being present to Mary or Mary of Magdala as they grieve. In some cultures, grieving is a predominantly individual, private act while in contexts like Africa it is a very communal experience. One woman said, "In my culture people always come to help when someone has died. The dining room is a dining room during the day but at night it becomes the place where those who have come to help the bereaved sleep."

The Third Week presents Scripture's sacred passion stories, releasing ultimate questions and profound feelings. The material often leads to greater personal depth and a deeper level of solidarity in suffering with all human persons and with the earth. The situation of contemporary women around the world, so many of whom are poor or suffer from sexual oppression and gender-based violence, illumine the Third Week through their intimate experience of suffering and death. Perhaps women could begin their contemplations of the Third Week with experiences of

Discovering the Depth of Commitment

passion and compassion for other women. Identifying with the suffering of any part of creation can lead to compassion or a way of being with suffering. One women's experience of the Third Week led to a deeper sense of compassion for the suffering of animals and the destruction of the planet and a decision to change her lifestyle to live in a way that is more compatible with a compassion for the created world.

Ultimately, this week raises questions about who and where God is, and how humans and God are in relationship: "What in my world is suffering? How am I to be compassionate?" Thus, several themes emerge from women's experience of the Third Week.

First, personal experiences of suffering can be helpful bridges to becoming compassionately present to Jesus in imaginative contemplation. Aschenbrenner notes that our "own suffering is the birthplace for compassion" (2004, 122). It may also be that the retreatant has personal experience of journeying with those she loves as they faced suffering or death. Connecting with these memories can be a bridge to help her to become compassionately present to the suffering of Jesus, her friend, or beloved.

Second, the passion narratives are theological statements, not historical accounts, descriptions, or documentary evidence. The Gospel writers were not primarily interested in what happened, but in what the event *meant* in the life of persons and the community. The same perspective has relevance today. In choosing Scripture reflections, the guide can use a single Gospel or weave together various events from different Gospels according to the disposition of the one making the Exercises. Even a single event leaves room for various emphases. The Last Supper, for example, can be experienced as sacrifice, sacrament, sign of a new covenant, a meal with friends, or a table at which one is denied a place.

Third, engaging the whole person in body, mind and will, feelings, ideas, and imagination is crucial to the prayer of this Week. The disposition of the one praying the Exercises is as important as the selection of content. No one can predict what type of experience the seeker will have. Since pain, suffering, and death in the context of love make up the prayer material for this Week, the guide must determine how the one making the Exercises enters into pain, her own and that of her family, society, and world. Discernment is essential. Is the pain redemptive or debilitating? Does pain cause undue self-absorption? What represents authentic grieving? What rhythm and expression lead gradually to a new place of understanding and peace? The Scriptures refer to women weeping, and women making the Exercises may also weep. Let them. Other awkward feelings may arise in difficult moments when she does not know how to respond to suffering or feels unable to connect her suffering with that of others.

Fourth, the guide needs to be alert to signs of unhealthy guilt and grief. Extreme pain, suffering, and guilt can block prayer and increase isolation. One can also get stuck in the pain or develop habits of avoidance or distraction. Dealing with deep affective life makes up part of the process of Third Week contemplations. Unfamiliar or fearful emotions can surface and the temptation to accept superficial responses to the passion can block the grace that leads to the affective depth. Nevertheless, when one has faced and accepted death, life takes on new meaning. One realizes a connection to the larger human community in its vulnerability and finitude. The experience of grief can become an opportunity to care for and connect with others, to reach out instead of withdrawing.

Fifth, if the passion narratives prove problematic, alternative Scripture passages may be used to elicit the graces of the Third Week. These passages include the story of the grain of wheat: "I tell you, unless a grain of wheat falls into the earth and dies, it remains just a single grain; but if it dies, it bears much fruit" (John 12:24); the Suffering Servant Songs from Isaiah; the predictions of the cross at the transfiguration; or situations of death in which Jesus related to women (the stories of the widow of Nain, Jairus's daughter, and Martha, Mary, and Lazarus).

Finally, art, literature, film, music, and even dreams can stimulate and enrich reflection on the passion. Liturgical resources provide prayer, music, Scripture, and gestures that enhance the Third Week exercises. Cultural diversity marks the various observances of Lent and rituals expressing beliefs about death and ancestors. Devotions centered on the passion fill the Christian tradition with many examples of piety, for example, the stations of the cross,[3] the Sorrowful Mysteries of the Rosary, or dramatic representations of the passion.

Death is not final for Jesus, his disciples, or contemporary women praying the Exercises. Who knows the moment when the sorrow and confusion of the Third Week, when "his divinity hides itself" [196], will transform into the gladness and joy of resurrection? But the fruits of the Third Week will manifest themselves in the seeker's deeper identification with Jesus in freedom and gratitude. For the guide, the task continues to recognize and support the movements of the Third Week in the unique experience of the individual seeker.

CHAPTER 9

Mission and Mutuality

Exercises of the Fourth Week

Consider the office of consoler which Christ our
Lord carries out, and compare it with the way friends
console one another.
—*Spiritual Exercises* [224]

I never imagined God could be so real and present
in my life. I will never be the same after making the
Exercises.
—A contemporary woman

Only a few pages of text indicate the direction for the Fourth Week and the conclusion of the Exercises. At this point, the one living the Exercises moves into the fullness of the paschal mystery, the mystery of the resurrection. Just as the Third Week draws the one making the Exercises into the midst of the suffering and death of "Christ the Lord," the Fourth Week inaugurates a time to "be glad and to rejoice intensely because of the great glory and joy of Christ our Lord" [221].

Ignatius encourages the one making the Exercises to "consider how the divinity, which seemed hidden during the Passion, now appears and manifests itself so miraculously in this holy Resurrection" [223]. This Week invites awareness of God's consoling presence in the reality and concrete experience of the one who makes the retreat. Just as the Gospel accounts reveal the risen Christ breaking through physical and psychological barriers in unexpected ways, so God is manifest in daily life—in gifts of joy, love, gratitude, and peace. These moments are marked by pure surprise and giftedness, rejoicing in the resurrection.

Material and Dynamics of the Fourth Week

The Fourth Week, like the Second, begins by inviting the exercitant to enter an imaginative nonbiblical scene. This time, the one making the Exercises is invited to share the intimacy of the reunion of mother and son in imagining the risen Jesus appearing to Mary [218–25].[1] The remainder of the Exercises found in "The Risen Life" [299–312] follow this model of contemplation. Thirteen texts make up the Easter stories. Some, such as those referring to the appearances to the women at the empty tomb, Peter, the disciples on their way to Emmaus, the disciples with and without Thomas, the disciples fishing, and the commissioning on Mount Tabor, are quite familiar. Others are surprising: Jesus appearing to five hundred disciples, to James, and to Paul (see 1 Cor 15:8), as well as an appearance to Joseph of Arimathea taken from the lives of the saints. The final contemplation of the ascension is from the Acts of the Apostles [299–312].

The disposition of the one making the Exercises changes significantly in the Third and Fourth Weeks of the Exercises; her perspective shifts from looking with her own eyes to viewing life through Jesus's eyes. While the process of the Second Week asks the retreatant to consider her own call and response to discipleship, the Third and Fourth Weeks focus the contemplations on the experience of Jesus. Such emphasis presupposes that "being with" means letting go of our personal agenda and taking up God's. This transformation entails intimacy and personal identification with the life, death, and resurrection of Jesus. "Laboring with God" [236] in the world means being with him through contemplation of the paschal mystery in the Gospels and in the contemporary world.

The Fourth Week process notes continue to stress the engagement of the whole person and to emphasize embodiment, so that the total person experiences the prayer of the resurrection. Concrete suggestions include thinking about things that bring pleasure, happiness, and spiritual joy, taking advantage of light and seasonal delights, as well as whatever "will help me to rejoice in Christ my Creator and Redeemer" [229].

Problems and Possibilities for Women

The church's selective memory about the resurrection raises problems for women during the Fourth Week. The tradition has too often forgotten the key role women played as witnesses to the resurrection, and the text of the Exercises reflects this lack. Noticeably absent is Mary Magdalene's encounter with the risen Christ in the garden and her commission to tell the disciples that he is risen (John 20:1–18). Correcting this omission opens up rich ground. Images of women witnessing to the resurrection and being faithfully present to Jesus provide strong models for contemporary women. For example, we might think of Mary Magdalene, reinstated as "apostle to the apostles,"[2] and her active leadership role in the early church. Women played a major role in the paschal mystery. They exemplified faithful presence at the cross and tomb and serve as a bridge to the resurrection. Even when discounted and trivialized (Luke 24:10–11), their voices proclaim truth for the believing community. These reinstated voices provide women with powerful role models of discipleship that can affirm and strengthen their own commitment.

Certain dispositions of contemporary women can raise obstacles to the liberating effect of the Fourth Week. Fear can paralyze women today, just as it did the women in Mark's Gospel (16:8) who fled from the resurrection. Change in their relational world challenges women's self-identity. Commitment can generate fear, for success and joy in our accomplishments demands a response. Becoming an active player in the resurrection drama of daily life promises further engagement with the unknown. Often women desire to cling to the familiar, but the grace of the Fourth Week asks women to move out into the unfamiliar role of witness and public mission. In discovering God at work in the world, women must embrace all aspects of it.

More and more, women are stepping out prophetically in both public life and church life, even when speaking out against injustice may have painful consequences. Many speak from a place of privilege in terms of education and access to opportunity and use their privilege to advocate for those on the margins. We think of women speaking out against the separation of children from their immigrant parents in the United States during the Trump presidency or Sr. Helen Prejean, known for her advocacy on behalf of prisoners on death row. Yet it pains many women that their voices are often unheard, especially within church structures.[3]

While some women living in contexts of advantage have gained more of a voice in the past twenty years, many women around the world still live in situations where there is little or no space for their voices. Some who have meager economic means are caught in situations of violence and abuse from which they cannot easily escape. Some still experience genital mutilation. The voices of these women are rarely heard in society. The experience of women in our time varies dramatically depending on their circumstances. Wherever women find themselves on the continuum of such experiences, praying the Fourth Week can be a liberating and affirming experience of being valued and called as a woman. Of the risen Christ validating the voice of women.

The Fourth Week also calls for a recognition of moments of grace as postresurrection experiences: times when fear is transformed, times when relationships are renewed with God, with our self, with the communities that have been present in prayer and life, and with the risen Christ in the world.

Mary in the Exercises

Despite the general omission of women during this Week, Mary does hold a prominent place in the Fourth Week's first contemplation. Each of her brief but consistent appearances throughout the prior Weeks culminate in her presence here. Ignatius, appropriate to his times and culture, called her "Our Lady." Some women may find this title distancing and may find it more helpful to think of Mary as sister or dear friend.[4]

Mary is initially mentioned in the first prelude or composition of place in the first exercises of the First Week. Ignatius has those making the Exercises imagine a place "where Jesus Christ or Our Lady happen to be" [47]. In the third exercise, she is the initial intercessor in the colloquies: "The first colloquy will be with Our Lady, that she may obtain for me from her Son and Lord three things" [63].

In the Second Week the contemplation on the incarnation asks seekers to visualize "Our Lady and the angel greeting her" [106]. The nativity segment asks those making the Exercises to recall "how our Lady and Joseph left Nazareth to go to Bethlehem.…She was pregnant almost nine months and, as we may piously meditate, seated on a burro; and with her were Joseph and a servant girl, leading an ox" [111].

In the Third Week Mary is present at the removal of the body of Jesus from the cross, and the Exercises refer to "the house where Our Lady went after the burial of her Son" [208]. "Consider, too, Our Lady's loneliness along with her deep grief and fatigue" [208]. In the Fourth Week we contemplate "How Christ Our Lord Appeared to Our Lady" [219].

Additional exercises at the end of the text place Mary in the contemplations of the infancy and hidden life, including the visitation to Elizabeth. In the public life, she appears at the wedding feast of Cana [276] and finally in the passion week, where Jesus speaks from the cross to Mary the sorrowful mother [297–98].

Problems can arise when people uncritically accept images and assumptions about Mary. Clarity about these images and assumptions are both necessary and helpful. First, very little is known about the historical Mary of Nazareth, a first-century Jewish woman and mother of Jesus. Second, contemporary biblical scholars, both Catholic and Protestant, interpret Mary in the Gospels and Paul's singular reference (Gal 4:4) in the context of the faith of the early Christian communities. Third, the Mary of two thousand years of tradition in art and architecture, apocrypha, myth, saints' stories, doctrinal debates, devotions, apparitions, and prayers staggers the mind and imagination in its complexity. The question "Who is the 'real' Mary?" parallels the question posed about Jesus.

Mary's treatment in theological discussions raises a second problem. Until recently, Mary had been primarily interpreted in the dominant European and North American culture by clergymen and male theologians. They have stressed her femininity and unique virginal privilege and idealized maternity. One of the major critiques of Mary today rests on exaggerated attention to her titles of "virgin" and "mother," which emphasize her unique privilege and distances her from women who literally cannot be both at the same time. Such titles equate her value with her sexual role and stress her function more than her person. Others note that her characteristics of docility, humility, and hiddenness often reinforce patriarchal ideals of women's passive and subordinate role. Thus understood, Mary perpetuates the patriarchal family as a model for church and an image of heaven. She reinforces such women's stereotypes as the "Eve-Mary syndrome," where one woman is demeaned as source of sin, the other idolized as without sin. Eve is rejected because she lived too close to the earth, Mary is inaccessible because she is too close to heaven.

However, today's climate offers opportunities to renew our understanding of Mary and her place in the spiritual lives of all believers. She hears the word of God and acts on it. The stages of her life reflect the recurring yes of the annunciation. Some women have found rich prayer by reflecting on the many phases of Mary's life and how each reveals a special relationship with God. She is girl, child, daughter, woman, wife, mother, cousin, friend, teacher, middle-aged woman, widow. In her relationship to Jesus, Mary provides a model for discipleship. Modern biblical scholarship, Vatican II's theological renewal, and greater ecumenical awareness have provided more accurate information about her, while liberation theology and feminist theology critique and reclaim Mary from the perspectives of culture and gender. For example, the Magnificat (Luke 1:46–55), so long a part of the church's spiritual tradition, has been reinterpreted in the light of women's and oppressed peoples' experience.

Today, as a result of women's spirituality, Mary emerges with new vitality as friend, mentor, and sister, thus making her more accessible to all. One important consequence is the openness many Protestants making the Exercises now have to engaging with Mary and how many describe their encounters with her as key moments in their experience of the Exercises. Annemarie Paulin-Campbell relates how a Methodist woman with a conservative evangelical upbringing experienced a significant shift in her understanding and experience of Mary through the Exercises:

> "I resisted the Triple Colloquy hugely. Maybe it was the way it was presented to me. What I heard my director say was this is the Triple Colloquy and in this first prayer you are going to pray to Mary and my Protestant evangelical red lights went flashing." Her director encouraged her to just try and have a conversation with Mary. "I found that very hard at first. I sat in my prayer space for ages trying to decide what she looked like and where could we best meet. But I am glad I persevered, because she actually became very significant throughout the rest of the journey. She was my friend, and I grew to really love her—and I still do. For me she did play a very significant role in the life of Jesus and one of the most powerful prayer experiences I had was at the Resurrection when she was the first person Jesus came to see. That contemplation will be special

forever. And now I do use her in my own Methodist context. I talk about her but very carefully, so I don't offend anyone. But Mary and I are really good friends." (Paulin-Campbell, 2021)

Wisdom for the One Giving the Exercises

As with the other Weeks, the last Week demands that the one giving the Exercises be attuned to its particular dynamics. Here simplicity, quiet, confidence, wholeness, and a sense of centered grounding in God continue to grow in the one living the Exercises. The recognizing, affirming, and challenging role of the guide conforms to the desired graces of the Fourth Week. This guide, like the disciples after the resurrection, needs to recognize and name the resurrection moments present in the life of the one making the Exercises.

The guide also recognizes the signs of the resurrection in the retreatant, who knows the risen Christ in his gifts and in the manifestations of his presence through peace, joy, and consolation. She also has new eyes to see God's presence and action in different ways in her own life and in others and rejoices in the joy of resurrection. She realizes that all is gift and responds with gratitude, confident in relationship with the risen Christ who moves her to mission.

Yet the retreatant may allow uncertainty to pull her back into the "old," forgetting that Christ is "new." She must resist whatever pulls her back into her former and familiar self. It is key that she recognize the postresurrection experiences in her life. The risen Christ encounters her in her own experiences and their many, even contradictory, manifestations (so similar to the gospel appearances to the disciples): feelings of fear and doubt, lack of recognizing God's presence, anxiety combined with joy, a sense of losing and finding, and a pervasive, consoling presence. Dealing with joy and peace does not always occur in the way a woman expects it, so she should be aware of "romance novel syndrome," which glamorizes emotions and expects us to live "happily ever after." Postresurrection appearances are not necessarily ecstatic, dramatic, or highly emotional. Consolation has many, frequently subtle, manifestations. A seeker often needs a companion's assistance to recognize them.

Besides being sensitive to postresurrection appearances, the guide needs to remember and highlight the importance of women in the postresurrection communities. Praying over Pentecost and the events of the early church in the Acts of the Apostles can connect contemporary women to living out the resurrection event in the context of church communities today.

It is important to be aware that at this point in the journey the one making the Exercises may struggle with fatigue and to remember the helps that Ignatius offers in his notes on the Fourth Week. A woman making the retreat in daily life over many months may have been getting up an hour earlier to fit her prayer time into a busy day. In his second note Ignatius counsels a lightening of the retreat load [227] to four periods of prayer in the enclosed retreat, rather than five. In the retreat in daily life, we might also suggest fewer formal prayer periods over a week.

Ignatius also counsels that not all the prayer points must be used: "The person who is contemplating may prepare more or fewer points, according to what is found better" [228]. This directive affirms how the woman herself has learned to pray and her freedom to be aware of what helps her most.

Significantly the fourth note offers important modifications to some of the Additions. Most notably Ignatius encourages the one making the Exercises to make use of the light "or the pleasant features of the seasons, such as the refreshing coolness in summer or the sun or heat in winter, as far as I think or conjecture that this will help me to rejoice in Christ my Creator and Redeemer" [229]. This guidance invites us into a way of living that is life affirming, which might be unfamiliar to many women. We could add other ideas like the use of creativity that brings delight; the quiet savoring of an early morning cup of tea or coffee as I enter into the joy of Christ. In addition, there is a movement from penance to "temperance and moderation" [229, 5] that connects with the idea of living a balanced life of neither overindulgence nor deprivation—something many women struggle with.

Finally, the Exercises can provide a significant opportunity to rediscover the richness of Mary as model disciple and God bearer who crosses the threshold of mystery. She can be a positive role model, showing how God desires all persons to be God bearers, hearing the word of God, receiving it, and allowing it to become fruitful in their lives. Knowing Mary, not only theologically and spiritually, but also with religious imagination and affectivity, becomes vitally important. The meaning of Mary for the life of the Christian community needs renewal in every generation, for Mary stands as model for all believers, women and men.[5]

Contemplation to Attain Love[6]

The culminating prayer of the Spiritual Exercises, the Contemplation to Attain Love, intimates Ignatius's own mystical awareness. Only here does he speak freely of love and the beloved.[7] Through contemplation we look back at the graces of the Exercises and at God's gracious gifting in our own life, savoring this intimate knowledge in gratitude and love. The wider vision gained at this point in the Exercises fosters "finding God in all things." Thus, the prayer of daily living impels us to desire God in every aspect of life. It forms those who pray and live it to become more and more contemplative in action.

This contemplation is also significant as a way of staying connected to God and of arousing hope amid the challenges and difficulties of everyday life. Peter Schineller, writing from his experience in Nigeria, says that as we continue into everyday life, we may start to wonder, "What is the meaning of our sweat and toil, our successes and failures. Is there any meaning in suffering? If one has AIDS or knows someone who does, how does one react? Does one give up in despair or live on in hope? If one is poor and troubled, insecure, where does one turn? Can one find God, keep in union with God even in the midst of difficulties?" (Schineller 2005, 169). He suggests that amid adversity, this contemplation is a source of hope because of the assurance it gives of God's constant presence. This anchoring is especially important when women find themselves doubly oppressed by virtue of their gender/race/sexual orientation and by situations of injustice in their own contexts.

The Contemplation on Love is also significant because it challenges the one making it to look beyond herself and her own situation. If love expresses itself less in words than deeds, and if I desire to offer what I have to the Beloved, I cannot but be impelled by the desire to share my gifts for the benefit of others, especially those who are most vulnerable.

This orientation toward receiving and sharing this gift of God's love appears in Ignatius's two important pre-notes or observations. The first [230] highlights the necessity of deeds rather than words for expressing active love. This wise observation militates against any religious "high" and points to the criterion of authentic love, human or divine (Matt 7:21). The second pre-note [231] underscores mutuality. The lover and the beloved seek to share whatever they have or are. Experience uncovers the enormous difference between gifts given with little thought and those expressing wholehearted love, the very self of the giver.

The first prelude [232] or composition of place asks the one making the Exercises to see herself standing before God with the angels and saints who intercede. The sense that God and all these witnesses are loving and praying for the retreatant conveys the sense that she is "ringed-round with love" that then allows her to extend this love to others (Fleming 2004, 126). The second prelude ("what I desire" [233]) is a threefold plea for interior knowledge of the great good received, profound gratitude, and an ability to love and serve God in *all* things. Finding God in all things means finding God's presence in rejection, betrayal, illness—the general craziness of life—as well as in great joy, faithful friends, or good health. The "more" of the Second, Third, and Fourth Weeks becomes the "all" of total self-gift (Conroy 1995, 17).

The first point [234] offers the seeker an opportunity to reflect on all gifts received, pondering with "deep affection" not only the gifts, but the Giver who offers Self as well. The second [235] emphasizes God's immanence, in all of creation and specifically within the one making the Exercises. The third point [236] focuses on God laboring in all things, continually creating the universe. The fourth point highlights the source of all gifts as goodness itself. This Being empowers and shares divine life with the seeker, allowing her to find God not only in all things, but also to *be* God's presence toward all things.

Although much of the commentary suggests that each of these four points synthesize the corresponding week of the Exercises, the interrelationship of the points and graces is far more dynamic. Contemplation, repetition, application of the senses, colloquies, and discernment lead the one making the Exercises to reflect on herself and respond to God's gifting in mutual love and deep affection. An implied "Take and Receive" [234] concludes each period of prayer, although Ignatius simply calls for a colloquy and recitation of the Our Father. The Exercises seem to have no real conclusion, but the Contemplation propels us forward into daily life.[8] Empowered by the experience of God's engulfing love, the retreatant can depart confident that similar graces continue beyond the retreat proper (Fleming 2004, 25).

Problems and Possibilities of the Contemplation

The Contemplation exemplifies the profound heights possible in the relationship between a person and God. The value of this culminating prayer of the Exercises, however, may be lost for some seekers. Sometimes the Spiritual Exercises are rushed toward the end, and either the retreatant is unaware or afraid to ask for the guidance needed to probe the potential of the Contemplation. Some women mistakenly consider the Contemplation the climax or high point of the Exercise and suffer a letdown at the conclusion of the retreat; they have not understood the Contemplation as a transition into daily life. Some women find it difficult to recognize, name, accept, and take responsibility for their gifts. But gratitude constitutes the prerequisite for the Contemplation and serves as the foundation for the service flowing from the Exercises.

Communicating to God who one is and what one has is a woman's dream, but the seeker might easily exclaim, "How can I give anything to God? I'm not worthy." Yielding in love to the action of the Spirit empowers God. This conscious awareness of God's mutual love and gift can nourish a woman through a lifetime of service and fidelity.

The admonition that love ought to manifest itself more in deeds than words can raise a problem with overgenerosity. Fear of intimacy may motivate some to unceasing action; overemphasized zeal can lead others to pour out their resources for others so that they have nothing left for themselves. They succumb to the cultural temptation that equates personal value with work and productivity.

Although problems with false expectations, feelings of unworthiness, and overgenerosity may arise, the Contemplation to Attain Love offers many possibilities for women. In some ways it is the most appealing exercise of the four Weeks. In response to the Contemplation, women will often exclaim, "This is the God I know!" The relational context, mutuality of love, and tender intimacy create a climate in which women thrive.

The relational context of the Exercises also highlights the God who is ultimately relational. Within the contemplation, the Trinity is imagined as blessing the seeker, presenting God's own Self to her, laboring for her, and energizing and empowering her. Contemporary feminist theology helps us reconceive a trinitarian theology that emphasizes relationship and mutuality among equals. God exists as the mystery of persons in communion. Only in communion can God be what God is and only in communion can God exist at all. In addition, the relational image of Trinity evokes the image of dance (LaCugna 1991, 270). No one "leads" in the divine dance: there exists only the eternal moment of giving and receiving. The ecstatic, relational actions of the persons of the Trinity toward one another constitute the unity.

The awareness of the Trinity then frames the reflection on the nature of human persons in themselves, the relationship between persons and between humankind and all other creatures as well as relationship with God. In the Contemplation to Attain Love, Ignatius notes that reverence, gratitude, and self-gift must mark each relationship.

What is true regarding the human community rings true also of all of creation, the household of God. The doctrine of the Trinity does not abstractly teach about God apart from the world, but about God's love in and with the world and each human being. Living trinitarian life means reverencing the earth, caring for it, and seeing it as companion. "Living trinitarian faith means living together in harmony and communion with every other creature in the common household of God" (LaCugna 1991, 401).

The Contemplation underlines the value of the person created in God's image, another significantly liberating aspect for women. "God makes a temple of me, as I have been created in the likeness and image of his Divine Majesty" [235]. To contemplate the dignity this valuing bestows can profoundly shift the way the one making the Exercises sees herself. Not only does she see in others the image and likeness of God, she is invited to contemplate *herself* as good and beautiful because she is made in God's image.[9] In praying the *Contemplatio* there is also the affirming sense of invitation to partnership and mutuality. The exercitant's gifts are needed in this mission, this working together with the Trinity, for the bringing about of transformation in society.

Wisdom about the Contemplation for the Director

Sometimes the one giving the Exercises minimizes this final exercise, giving it as a handout for use in the days that follow. Often the seeker expends so much time and energy in moving through the first three Weeks that time runs out. Regardless of how far a seeker has progressed, the Contemplation to Attain Love should be offered as the concluding exercise. Here women especially connect with Ignatius's language and perception. While it is important that it is given as part of the retreat, it is so rich that the one who made the Exercises can be encouraged to continue to stay with it for days, weeks, or even months following the retreat.

Many women find the first prelude of the composition of place extremely powerful, and it can fruitfully be offered as a prayer time of its own [232]: "Here it is to see myself standing before God our Lord, and also before the angels and Saints who are interceding for me." The woman can be encouraged to include in her imagination, not only those canonized as saints, but all those people she has loved and who have loved her who have died and are united with Christ praying for her. This helps to deepen the sense of how loved she is.[10]

Because this is contemplation and not meditation, repetition and application of the senses are extremely important in savoring each point. Some seekers may profit by writing their own "Take and Receive." This may be a way of making their self-offering in words that have deep resonance with their own particular experience of the Exercises. In addition, in a kind of retroactive discernment, the one giving the Exercises can use the images for God-self-world of the Contemplation as a sort of touchstone determining the authenticity and wholeness of the retreatant's images from the beginning (English 1995, 252ff.).

Some women might use the Contemplation to Attain Love as a framework for examen. For example, the first point, which highlights continual gifting (including God's own Self), might suggest some of the following questions: "What is the lived depth of my gratitude? Love or obligation? How have I used these gifts for others? Have I been aware of myself as a temple of the Holy Spirit today? Do I see these gifts as signs of God's gratuitous love or as a measure of how effective I am? To what extent do I really believe in God's gift of Self to me? How does this impact my life, my self-identity, my ability to risk?"

The expressed progression of the dynamic of the Exercises develops in terms of relationship. The one making the Exercises begins by seeing her place in the universe, becoming a fallible but faithful follower of Jesus, rejoicing in Jesus's resurrection, and only after that, hearing the *language* of invitation to profound intimacy and mutuality with this God-in-Jesus. This progression moves from transcendence to immanence to intimacy. Since women usually develop by way of intimacy and relationship, the process of the Exercises can be deeply transformational for them, provided relationship is continually stressed throughout the dynamic and the relationship with the one giving the Exercises is sensitive and freeing.

Formation of Contemplatives in Action

The formation of contemplatives in action builds on the experience of the Exercises, culminating in the Contemplation to Attain Love.

Exercises

Contemplation in action invites seekers to discover new meanings in current reality, for God will transform and empower them to be with God and to act with God in the world. When desiring to live out the Ignatian Contemplation to Attain Love, love becomes the basis of all a seeker does and is, love expressed not only in words but also in deeds.

Attention to God's desires for humankind revealed in the desires and worlds of women is crucial: striving for personal integrity, autonomy, and responsible relationships; developing opportunities for leadership and influence; and always sustaining concern for those most abandoned and vulnerable. Women expect to meet and labor with God as they express a deeper interiority and a global consciousness. They will develop a new faith-filled understanding and contemplative stance toward the mystery of God's presence in the world.

God's image, the world's image, and personal image are transformed. God is revealed as God-with-us: God became human, dwelt with people, and still labors on behalf of all creation. This trinitarian God is a God-in-relationship at work in the world. In turn, the world emerges as a place where God dwells and sustains life. This world, which humans can now view from the perspective of space, is seen as beautiful yet vulnerable, rich in resources and linked by a common destiny with all life on the planet.

All these things evoke an image of a contemporary contemplative in action. She welcomes the opportunity to be schooled in the ways of prayer and life. She manifests awareness, imagination, reflection, and the ability to utilize "repetition," going deeper into the sources of God's reality in the world. She expresses the security of a contemplative stance that allows her to respect diversity and acknowledge various spiritual paths to God. She is aware of the bounty of spiritual gifts, faith, trust, and love, and their various manifestations through confirmation, challenge, and courage. She is attentive, free, responsive, participative, relational, and a person of great desires. She taps into life's rhythms of work and rest, giving and receiving, knowing and loving, sinning and being graced. She manifests the fruits of contemplation: integration, wholeness, peace, gratitude, desire for communion with God, with God's people, and all creation. Finally, she gathers with others to create contemplative communities for transforming action in the world, realizing that personal growth flourishes amid relationships.

This dynamic does not just refer to a "peak" experience, but to a passionate life spent growing toward the closeness of God in the continuity of each day. The contemplative in action sees with reverence, awe, and appreciation. She desires to be in touch with the holiness of each moment and encounter.

Jesus as a contemplative in action models a way of life achieved through animation of the Spirit, not just through "the imitation of Christ." Jesus is the one who sees from God's perspective, acts in union with God and God's desires, and is sensitized to all of life received in mystery and love. The contemplative in action desires God and, like Jesus, desires what God desires.

Part IV
DECISION

CHAPTER 10

Developing a Single Eye
Rules for Discernment of Spirits

In every good election insofar as it depends on us, the eye of our intention ought to be single....In the case of those going from good to better, the good angel touches the soul gently, lightly, and sweetly, like a drop of water going into a sponge. The evil spirit touches it sharply, with noise and disturbance, like a drop of water falling onto a stone.
—*Spiritual Exercises* [169, 335]

I just don't know what to do. One day I think I am clear. I should go ahead with the divorce. I feel stuck and dead in the relationship, and I don't want to live the rest of my life this way. The next day I say to myself, "What we had was so good; if only I could get Robert to go to counseling, perhaps we could get to the bottom of it. If I just worked a little harder at it, it could happen." Another day I get overwhelmed with fear: How will I live? I'm nearly sixty and haven't worked outside our home for years.
—A contemporary woman

Angels and evil spirits, sponges, rocks, and single eyes—strange images from Ignatius's material on discernment of spirits and election. Discernment, the art of distinguishing what leads to God from what does not, plays an essential role in our choices; it also holds a central place in the interdependent content and process of the Spiritual Exercises.¹ Discernment also charts the way toward increasing spiritual freedom, the goal of the Spiritual Exercises. A practice of discernment engenders continual self-reflection, which, in turn, helps women grow toward the fullness of their call. The significance of discernment can scarcely be overstated.

The Spiritual Exercises assume three levels to discernment. The most basic consists in a habitual discernment that flows from relationship with the Creative Holy One and comes to fruition in putting on the mind of Christ (Phil 2:2). One learns and practices it continuously in all the contemplations and meditations and reinforces it through the particular examination. The second meaning appears in the Rules for Discernment of Spirits [313–36]. Here, the focus shifts to inner feelings and inclinations, as the one making the Exercises learns to assess them in light of this deepening relationship to God. The third meaning, found in the section on Making an Election [169–89], focuses on choices and actions. The seeker learns how to embody that relationship with the Holy in decisions and actions. These three senses of the term *discernment* are interrelated and cyclic. Each depends on the others.

Ignatius clearly intends that all three levels of discernment, especially discernment of spirits, be used both inside and outside the Spiritual Exercises. Since inner movements continually ebb and flow in response to all aspects of human life, discerning these movements and their causes has potentially unlimited usefulness. If discernment becomes a habitual skill for all of life, it will significantly affect one's relationship with God, oneself, others, and the various structures in which one lives.

The Spiritual Exercises provide a training ground par excellence for learning discernment and growing into its use. The full range of exercises, if entered into wholeheartedly, will evoke inner movements, frequently quite strong ones. In working with this flux, the one making the Exercises quite literally exercises her skills in noticing and interpreting her inner life and its exterior manifestations. The Rules for Discernment of Spirits make up the "how to" of discernment, its grammar, so to speak. Just as speaking is far more important than studying rules of grammar, discerning is far more important than studying the Rules for Discernment of Spirits. But grammar has its place in crafting careful speech, as understanding the Rules has in living a discerned life. Discernment understood in the third level functions most explicitly in the material presented within the Second Week for choosing or "electing" a state in life or making any other major decision [169–89]. To engage these exercises fully, one must have a working knowledge of the Rules for Discernment of Spirits.

The Rules for Discernment of Spirits themselves are useful at varying levels. They can describe the large sweeping movements of one's interior life, a relatively stable condition lasting months or years (e.g., "Those early years were financially hard, but I was never so happy and focused"). The vocabulary and the wisdom of the Rules, however, are even more useful for tracking the day-to-day fluctuations in one's interior movements—here is where the Examen and journaling help trace the ebb and flow. Finally, the Rules for Discernment of Spirits help notice and respond to moment-by-moment states of being ("When I read that Scripture passage, I was flooded with a sense of God's love for me") and situational responses ("I realized how angry I was only after I hung up the phone"). Furthermore, if we extend this notion of states of being to organizations, groups, and interpersonal relationship systems, the wisdom of the Rules for Discernment of Spirits can assist us in assessing the quality of that *organization*'s response, as well as its progress in becoming more attuned to its role in contributing to the actualization of God's reign in the world (Thibodeaux 2020, 7–14).

Women and Discernment

Before embarking on a treatment of the Rules for Discernment of Spirits, some observations about the general situation of women can frame this interpretation. Without intending to make universal statements, how might contemporary women approach discernment?

Central to all discernment is identity, who one is before God. Identity is not a fixed reality handed to a person at birth but is created moment by moment as one responds to the choices presented in one's life. The most basic component of discernment, then, concerns listening to oneself, distinguishing the wisdom of the deepest self, through which God speaks, from other voices and learning to trust this deep inner wisdom. The one estranged from her own wisdom will have a difficult time with discernment. In this sense, identity and discernment act as partners, each reinforcing and clarifying the other.

Inner wisdom often reveals itself through one's body, intuition, and feelings. They provide essential data for assessing choices. Learning to value and "read" them will greatly enhance discernment. The closer one comes to the real, including insights about one's inner self, the closer one comes to God.

Many contemporary women struggle to balance the needs of others with their own needs. This issue may especially challenge those women who habitually interpret selflessness as a virtue and attending to one's own needs as a vice. In some contexts, this struggle may not be as marked as it was twenty years ago, but in many parts of the world, women are still strongly socialized to ignore their own needs. Some women may also need to distinguish passivity from "conformity to God's will." Learning these differences can free these women for appropriate, confident, focused action.

The Rules for Discernment of Spirits primarily concern inner movements, yet important data also comes from the social and cultural forces influencing a situation. What systems and dynamics are present in social arrangements? When one's inner call conflicts with prevailing social structures, might it be that the social arrangements themselves contain unhealthy or sinful dynamics that require challenging and changing? Women may also need to interpret their affective experience in the light of social conditioning. Perhaps what seems "right," "proper," and "good" are social constructions concerning the role and "nature" of women. These social arrangements can exert enormous force, even dictating what one sees and what remains unconscious.[2] Conflict, anger, and sexual feelings may all be internalized as unacceptable and thus carefully censored from consciousness. Important tools for living are thereby ruled out of bounds.[3]

Women may need encouragement to generate alternatives when they feel trapped. Real choices, if only in relation to the attitude with which one approaches the givens in one's life, do exist. Generating possibilities enhances the exercise of genuine inner freedom.

Finally, women will need to consider the price of change. Enduring and substantive change, such as the Exercises encourage, comes gradually and frequently at considerable cost, especially when it involves structures. Mobilizing support systems and companions who help sustain hope during the time of "already but not yet" that makes up most of our days can make the difference between moving ahead and falling back into outworn patterns.

Theologian Kathleen Fischer (1988, 128), whose work is reflected in the points above, proposes an underlying principle: "Whatever promotes the full humanity of women as well as men is redemptive and holy; that is, it is of God. What denies and distorts that full humanity does not bear the power and authority of divine revelation." While this strong statement cannot be applied automatically to every concrete situation, it does state the goal of the Spiritual Exercises. We even need to discern the norms for discernment.

Rules for Discernment of Spirits

Explicating Ignatius's Rules for Discernment of Spirits resembles storytelling. Both ask for a suspension of disbelief and require analogical leaps from one reality to another. Ignatius clothes the dynamic forces that must be discerned with personalities of mythic proportions: God, God's angel, and the bad angel. Ignatius portrays a cosmic struggle between the forces of good and the forces of evil and their increasingly subtle strategies. Surprisingly, this mythic literary form—here "mythic" refers to cosmic scope, not falsity—suits this subject matter. But those who insist either on demythologizing the cosmic drama or on interpreting it literally find it loaded with potential stumbling blocks. Perhaps, in a manner parallel to the way one would read C. S. Lewis's *Screwtape Letters*, the seeker would do best to allow the literary form to carry her beyond either interpretive extreme.

On the other hand, Ignatius Jesudasan (2004, 74, 77) argues that only when angels and demons are carefully interpreted does the use of these metaphors help rather than hinder the interpretation of Ignatius's underlying message. An unnuanced or unconsciously literal understanding of angels and demons masks the prevailing social norms, reinforcing its assumptions, patterns of order, power and control, without any of this becoming explicit to the advantaged members of society. We ourselves, each one of us, are both the angels of good and evil simultaneously, he insists. "Good" and "evil" also function as ideological constructs, serving the ruling powers, disguising as moral the theological codes of honor and dishonor, and must similarly be demythologized to serve helpfully in discernment.

For some persons, a psychological perspective on good and evil provides a more fruitful approach to the Rules, viewing the "enemy" as intrapsychic rather than external. Gerald May, psychiatrist and spiritual director, posits four forces in human spirituality that need recognition:

spiritual longing for God, God's reciprocated longing, internal fears of and resistances to spiritual realization, and evil (1982a, 20–21). The psyche can literally engage in intrapsychic warfare, as one aspect of the total personality longs for God while another longs for control. One need not look for principalities and powers to account for such interior movements. Although this psychological interpretation does not rule out the presence of evil or the demonic, it recognizes the capacity for this kind of drama within the self.[4]

Theologian Walter Wink (1998) employs the concept of angel at an entirely different level. He uses *angel* to refer to the inner organizing personality or dynamic of a whole system or community. He uses the term *powers* to refer to an intricate fabric of dominating power relationships that institutions and systems weave throughout society. Corporations and governments function like "creatures" with ambiguous and conflicted interests subject to discernment and action.[5] Taking a cue from Wink, a structural perspective on discernment greatly extends the power and usefulness of Ignatian discernment given our complex societies. Adding an understanding of the systems in which we all inevitably participate can shift one's perspective from that of an individual standing alone to that of an individual embedded in multiple systems simultaneously. This changed perspective, not available to Ignatius, nuances the experience of spiritual freedom and shifts the flow of consolation and desolation. This perspective will be especially useful when considering election.[6]

Granting Ignatius the prerogative of his mythic literary form, some of his terminology still bears clarification. This section of the Spiritual Exercises speaks of *rules, mortal sin, consolation, desolation, good spirits, evil spirits,* and *angels*.

Ignatian Discernment Terminology

The term *motions*, explained earlier in the book, is shorthand for the processes of thinking, feeling, and imagining. It also covers the contents brought up by memory and the internal aspects of decision-making. The dynamism implied by this term especially interested Ignatius and will likewise interest those giving and making the Exercises, because the origin, orientation, and fruit of this flux will provide the material for discernment. These motions go on continually,[7] but frequently not consciously. Noticing them, naming them, assessing their origin and their direction,

Developing a Single Eye

and finally encouraging some and discouraging others is precisely the goal of the Rules for Discernment of Spirits.

The points that Ignatius calls *rules* actually mix descriptions of spiritual experience with norms for discriminating among them. These descriptions discuss only a relatively small range of possible activities that might be called *discernment*. He covers only inner events, prior to the actions that flow from them (Toner 1982, 11). *Rules*, therefore, is a rather imprecise term as Ignatius uses it.

Furthermore, neither the title "Rules for Discernment of Spirits" nor references such as "Rules for the First and Second Weeks" are Ignatian. His much longer titles [313, 328] suggest at least two quite distinct kinds of discernment situations, each requiring different approaches and therefore different strategies. Note, however, that individual persons making the Exercises may not simply use the first set of Rules in the First Week and the second set in the Second and following Weeks; the determination about which set applies comes from the kinds of temptations occurring in the one making the Exercises, not the content of the Exercises themselves [9, 10]. Ignoring these distinctions risks misinterpreting Ignatius's wisdom on discernment of spirits.

Mortal sin [314] means something close to "capital sin," or a sinful tendency that increasingly hinders relationship with God (Toner 1982, 50). It functions like an Achilles's heel, expressing one's primary weakness and vulnerability to sin. It may not appear significant at first: working overly long hours for the security of a substantial income, immersing one's identity in that of spouse or children, compulsive eating or shopping or other addictive behaviors, nursing a grudge for months. Yet each reflects a sense that one does not need God. Here, Ignatius describes the person who, without much thought or resistance, becomes more and more estranged from God and her authentic self. The distinction is important because Ignatius excludes this person from further consideration in the subsequent Rules. Only the experience of one "advancing from good to better in the service of God" [315], even though she may have only recently set out on this journey, is under consideration in the subsequent comments. What this situation looks like concretely Ignatius does not say. Today's spiritual guide, as yesterday's, must assess this primary orientation in each discerner. What is it that each one most deeply desires?

The next terms, *consolation* and *desolation*, have been the subject of extended discussion. As Ignatius describes them, each consists of three related parts. Consolation includes (1) the consolation proper (affective feelings such as peace or gladness); (2) the causes or sources of consolation ("the soul sheds tears which move it to love for its Lord" [316]); and (3) the consequences of consolation properly speaking ("every increase in hope, faith and charity and every interior joy which calls and attracts one toward heavenly things…by bringing it tranquility and peace in its Creator and Lord" [316]) (Toner 1982, 86). That is, consolation comprises a rich complex of feelings, acts, and consequences that have their origin in God and encourage and intensify the experience of moving Godward. Desolation, the opposite of consolation [317], demonstrates the same three related aspects.

Describing what consolation and desolation are not proves easier than describing exactly what they are. They are neither simply happiness and sadness, nor an "up" or "down" mood, though these feelings may play a role in spiritual consolation and desolation. Rather, consolation is the affective reverberation of the work of the Holy Spirit that draws toward God, and desolation is the affective reverberation of the antispiritual that pulls in the opposite direction. That is, consolation and desolation are *spiritual* realities. Discernment of spirits involves not only the feeling but also its origin and direction.

Consolation encourages and intensifies experiences of relationship to God. Pleasant feelings alone do not necessarily qualify as spiritual consolation, a mistake beginning discerners often make. A feeling of euphoria after two martinis does not make up a spiritual consolation. The Holy Spirit may use many means to promote spiritual growth, even difficult or painful feelings, the so-called painful or difficult consolations. Consider, for example, the anger and frustration arising from injustice to others, or pain and sadness around areas in one's life that need healing. If such feelings draw one deeper into relationship with God, they are truly consolations, albeit painful ones (Lonsdale 1992, 81). Nor should one confuse desolation with the experience of the various dark nights that John of the Cross describes. In this situation, God is at work, not antispiritual forces, gradually stripping away reliance on positive experiences to draw the seeker more deeply into God's own life.[8] Jesuit Mark Thibodeau (2020, 87–89) believes that the experience of difficult consolation is common in the spiritual life and so needs to be named for what it is, and clear strategies developed for responding in these spiritual situations.

Finally, what did Ignatius mean when he referred to *evil spirits*, *good spirits*, and *angels*? In line with the cosmology and theology of his time, Ignatius assumed personal good and evil beings existed and acted on behalf of or against God. Ignatius thought of angels as God's messengers, and in the case of good angels, their activity need not be distinguished from God's—with one exception treated at the end of the second set of Rules. Not all angels, however, are good, and these evil spirits work continually and often subtly to deflect us from our true end (Toner 1982, 32–33). Mark Thibodeaux suggests that the "false spirit," which he defines as "any movement within myself that leads me away from God and away from faith hope and love," not only can serve as an appropriate substitute for *evil spirit*, it is a much more accessible term for contemporary seekers. It functions exactly as Ignatius describes but avoids the interpretive pitfalls that *evil spirit* can connote (2020, 3).

One could dispense with a belief in angels, good or evil, and still profit from Ignatius's wisdom. It would be sufficient, as Toner notes (1982, 35–36), simply to recognize how the Holy Spirit works in one's life, how the opposite dynamic tendency toward evil functions within and around us, and the difference, if any, between promptings arising solely from oneself and those arising from God working within.[9] This latter point, however, brings the discussion immediately back to discernment. How does one determine what voice is speaking? Not infrequently do guides hear, "Is this from me or is this from God?" This question is itself further complicated if one holds that God speaks through our deepest desires, as did Ignatius.

Trusting God to work in and through one's own feelings comes harder for those women raised in theological systems that emphasize God's otherness and the total depravity of the human person; they tend to suspect anything arising from within themselves. The Ignatian wisdom on this question holds that good or evil spirits prompt good or evil interior motions, which issue in good or evil fruits. These fruits, in turn, give clues about which spirit is acting. One may, however, interpret the motions through their fruits without assigning the same ontological status to their origin as did Ignatius.

Ignatian "Contraries"

Ignatius exhibits a penchant for dialectical opposites, especially in his treatment of discernment. Consolation and desolation act as mirror images of each other. Good and evil spirits also act contrary to each other. How does Ignatius develop this dialectical tension?

First, the orientation of the discerner's life plays a role. Is it habitually directed toward increasing intimacy with God or increasing estrangement

Decision

from God? For those persons whose habitual disposition is increasingly *estranged* from God, the evil spirit will encourage more of the same, while the good spirit will oppose that tendency. The evil spirit will appeal to the *imagination*, while the good spirit will appeal to the *judgment* of conscience, causing remorse [314].

In the reverse situation, the players and their actions also reverse. For persons habitually growing in intimacy with God, the good spirit encourages this development by inspiring *feelings* of courage, strength, consolations, tears, inspirations, and tranquility, but the evil spirit upsets the Godward tendency through false *reasonings*, causing anxiety, confusion, and sadness [315]. The spirit that matches the disposition encourages that disposition, while the opposite spirit resists it.

Ignatius continues "working the opposites" in the second set of Rules. In the seventh rule [335], Ignatius offers an image for his principle of contrariety: in the one advancing from good to better, the good angel works gently and lightly, like a drop of water going into a sponge, but the evil spirit touches it sharply like a drop of water falling onto a stone. Reverse the situation of the discerner, that is, the discerner going from bad to worse, and the effects reverse as well. Thus, once the seeker and her guide get their bearings about basic orientation, they can begin to piece together what is going on and by the action of which spirit. But the metaphor works even more subtly. In the person going from good to better, the evil spirit will still try to weaken the resolve and deflect from the better option to one less good. In this frequently subtle situation, the "feel" of the spirit's action still has these qualities, either harmonious or jarring. Noticing this difference, however delicate, helps the discerner and the guide sort out this more subtle case.

Wisdom of the First Set of Rules

Knowing which spirit is operating requires a response. Ignatius concentrates the first set of Rules on the most difficult issue for those recently embarked on the spiritual life—how to survive the inevitable desolations that arise.

Since the evil spirit distracts one from God by any means possible, the seeker will want to act contrary to that spirit whenever it appears. Yet, experiencing desolation does not call for reversing decisions already made [318], but rather in increasing resistance to the evil spirit by, for example, more prayer or penance [319]. Note, however, that "acting against" may mean relaxing, taking more leisure, or doing less, especially for those women who have internalized the belief that they can make things better by working harder. Furthermore, the one experiencing desolation can remember that God will always supply the necessary grace, even when it does not feel like it at the moment [320]. Eventually, consolation will return. Meanwhile, waiting in patience is the counterattack against the present vexations [321].

As one would expect, Ignatius's suggestions for the time of consolation mirror his advice for the time of desolation, though more briefly: consolation provides an opportunity to consider how to act when the desolation returns, to store up new strength against that time [323], and to remain humble about consolation, for, after all, it came as God's gift [324].

Ignatius includes three theological rationales for the existence of desolation [322]; these points are suggestive rather than exhaustive. First, desolation may result from laziness or tepidity—not taking the relationship with God seriously will show up in one's spirit. Second, desolation may serve to strengthen spirituality, causing it to mature beyond the need for constant consolation. Finally, desolation nurtures humility: only God initiates and sustains consolation.

Holding these three possible reasons in dialectical tension will help avoid a potential pitfall for women who may say to themselves, "If I am not experiencing consolation, I must have not worked hard enough or haven't done something right." Ignatius points out that individuals are not primarily responsible for consolation or desolation, but neither are they totally devoid of responsibility, puppets in the control either of inner movements or of their causal forces. The reality allows both for God's sovereignty and human agency.

Ignatius closes the first set of Rules with three metaphors, each describing an aspect of the dynamic treated by this first set of Rules [325–27]. First, at times the enemy acts like a woman, attacking at signs of weakness but fleeing at signs of strength. Unfortunately, Ignatius puts no qualifier on "woman" here. The enemy also acts like a false lover, who threatens the one seduced if she "tells." Finally, the enemy is like a superior military strategist who ferrets out the weakest point in the defenses in order to attack there. These metaphors teach three important things: face temptation boldly and unyieldingly; break the power of secrecy that perpetuates a negative dynamic; know one's weakest point and concentrate vigilance there.

These stark metaphors also invite examination of the negative repercussions Ignatius's formulation can cause among women. In choosing "woman" as a metaphor for the way the enemy works, Ignatius unwittingly employs a deadly stereotype of women, implying that they are vacillating, seductive, cowardly or, at best, weak. Against strong men they wilt, but they turn on weak men. A metaphor must work not only for the teller; it must also function for the receiver. Such a metaphor, reinforcing as it does the worst gender stereotypes, serves neither men nor women.

The second metaphor, that of the seducer, is easier to disassociate from women as a class, perhaps because the evil one is not so directly and baldly associated with the entire sex. Yet this, too, portrays women in an unfortunate light as victims of an attempted seduction who, when they speak to their "heads," either father or husband, are freed from the power of the seducer. Again, the subliminal negative effects compromise the usefulness of this metaphor.

Since these metaphors carry negative baggage, a more useful pastoral alternative suggests either changing the metaphor to one more gender inclusive—"bully" in the place of "woman" in the first metaphor preserves Ignatius's dynamic but avoids the gender stereotype—or not employing them at all. The Sisters of Providence offer a simple approach to this second alternative:

> These points will help you *act against the bad spirits* which foster desolation:
>
> 12. Stand firm. Bad spirits attack where you show fear and flee when you demonstrate courage.
> 13. Be open with your director or another trustworthy person about what you are experiencing, since evil spirits flourish in secrecy and disappear in openness.
> 14. Do all you can to gain self-knowledge regarding your strengths and weaknesses, knowing that bad spirits attack where you are weakest. (1990, 233)[10]

This rewrite sacrifices metaphor in favor of simple imperatives. Others will develop alternative solutions appropriate for their contexts.

If not appropriately interpreted, Ignatius's counsel to not change one's circumstances when in desolation [318] poses a potential danger for women. Consider the following scenario illustrating one such misunderstanding: As a fruit of the Spiritual Exercises, Janet begins to pay more careful attention to what gives her life. She gradually becomes aware that her marriage is slowly strangling her. She realizes she has no separate existence as her husband increasingly demands total availability, acquiescence, and loyalty. Cautiously she begins to assert herself, only to find her husband increasingly violent. Upon voicing her desire to complete her training as an early childhood educator, he explodes and hits her. She identifies this painful situation as desolation and remembers Ignatius's counsel not to change a decision made in consolation during a subsequent time of desolation.

What about this situation, where a difficult and painful situation is facilely equated with desolation? Should a woman like Janet make no move on her own behalf until she experiences consolation? Is physical or psychological danger, in fact, desolation? A surface reading of Ignatius might suggest this interpretation. Jules Toner (1982, 109–212, 283–90), however, clarifies just such a situation by distinguishing spiritual consolation and desolation from natural consolation and desolation. Discernment of spirits applies only at the level of spiritual consolation and desolation. Janet's situation is, by this criterion, a crisis and a natural desolation, even if its effects are felt spiritually. Hence, Ignatius's counsel does not apply. Janet's guide will need to help her understand the actual meaning of this discernment counsel and further reassure her that to act for her own safety does not require discernment and that she should, indeed, move in that direction.

When a person is in actual danger, either physical or psychological, one must *never* wait passively for circumstances to change. Not only should one generate alternatives when feeling trapped (Fischer 1988, 126), but one must actually remove oneself from danger—or in the situation of the woman unable to do that for herself, those who accompany her must help her marshal the resources to act for her own safety. Janet may take some time to come to that realization, as indicated by statistics on battered women, but greater life for her is highly unlikely to occur amidst battering. The conditions for further discernment do not exist until she can calmly and safely consider alternatives. Within such physically and psychologically neutral spaces, such as a shelter, safe house, or foster home, discernment may eventually occur. But even arriving at the conditions for discernment may take weeks or months of painful struggle. Companions to such women have a moral responsibility to accompany them to safety.

The Wisdom of the Second Set of Rules

This set of Rules assumes increasing sensitivity to one's own experience of the spiritual life and increasing skill in noticing, naming, judging,

Decision

and choosing. The more skillful one becomes in noticing the workings of the evil spirit, the more skillful the evil one must become in order to continue confusing the advancing person. In fact, the evil one is quite capable of counterfeiting authentic consolation [331].

In addition to greater sensitivity to spiritual experience, one's understanding of how God works also becomes more nuanced. Only God our Lord can give consolation without a preceding cause [330]. That is, God may directly touch any creature without relying on any mediating reality. Nothing causes such a consolation but God alone, no prayer, no beautiful sunset, no experience of being loved by another person, no victory over struggle, no success, no virtue. When it occurs, this consolation can be trusted. Ignatius here preserves God's sovereignty within a cosmology that believes in a realm of mediating forces and beings. Both good and evil angels, on the other hand, being themselves mediated created beings, can only work in a mediated fashion.

Two Rules will help here. One sketches out the modus operandi of the evil spirit [332], and the second suggests a tactic. The evil one will take on the appearance of the angel of light, and so clothed, will gain admission through "specious reasonings." With the unsuspecting or inattentive discerner, the evil one begins to subvert the consolation little by little. A little less vigor, a little diversion from the mark, a bit of an extreme, a hiding of one reality within its look-alike: these subtleties now confront the discerner. Is this patience or passivity? Is this pride really a sin or an invitation to true self-possession? Is this acting on one's own behalf selfish or virtuous? This alternative feels really freeing, but is it authentic liberty or just a disguised form of license? How can one know?

Second, Ignatius advises seekers to pay attention to the whole progress of one's thought [333]. Is it, from beginning to end, consoling? What is its fruit? Does it end up in something less good? Does it weaken or somehow disquiet? These distinctions are subtle, as vividly suggested by Ignatius's comparison between the drop of water on the sponge and the drop of water on the stone [335]. But just as one can, with attention, notice the difference between these two qualities, one can always—eventually—distinguish the difference between the work of the evil one and the work of God's angel. And even what appears to be a mistake in discernment at a particular moment in time can be turned toward good [334]. Such struggles, paradoxically, can increase one's future ability to discern, another occasion for God's love and mercy. In the pedagogy of discernment, nothing need be wasted.

There is one last subtlety. God acting directly, which can be trusted, and the reverberations that echo in us after God's touch are different realities. Be careful, says Ignatius, not to confuse the two, as the latter reverberations are not always dependable. These look-alikes need to be discerned just like any consolation with cause [336]. How many persons have launched enthusiastically on a course of action at the end of a particularly consoling retreat, assuming it to arise from God, only to have it turn sour?[11]

Problems and Possibilities for Women

Several problems inherent in the Rules for Discernment of Spirits, including aspects of the language of the text and the danger of too facilely invoking Ignatius's caution against making a change in time of desolation, have already been explored. A potentially serious pastoral issue, distinguishing between depression and desolation, remains to be examined. Despite these problem areas, though, the Ignatian material on discernment of spirits also holds significant possibilities for women. Two stand out for consideration. First, the Rules for Discernment of Spirits provide a pattern and discipline for continually appropriating one's life as it unfolds. Second, discernment of spirits helps rehabilitate the role of feelings in discriminating what is from God, a role many women have found ambiguous. Structural theories of women's psychological development prove helpful in illuminating these problems and possibilities for women's discernment by clarifying some aspects of the human ability to discern.

Women's Sense of Self: A Developmental Perspective

The structural developmental perspective of such theorists as Carol Gilligan, Robert Kegan, James Fowler, and Susanne Cook-Greuter[12] sketch the successive patterns of meaning that govern one's life. These theories have proved especially helpful in illuminating women's development. Rather than concentrating on the tasks of each era of life, as did Erik Erikson, the structural developmental perspective focuses on the successive patterns in these underlying and largely unconscious meaning systems and their very gradual shifts over the course of a lifetime. These underlying structures change only when they no longer offer a worldview complex enough to deal with life's challenges. Thus, an adult may go for lengthy periods in the same meaning structure. But when a structural change does occur, it revolutionizes the way a person conceives the whole of reality, transforming one's view of self, friends and associates, culture, creation, and God.

Structural change is not directly tied to age. However, it requires sufficient life experience at each stage for deconstructing one's assumptions of "the way things are." Paradoxically, fully living one's present stage opens the possibly of a new stage. In the structural view of development, stage change is not inevitable. When it does occur, it truly represents a *metanoia*. Once a transition begins, the only course open lies in deconstructing the present meaning structure and more or less painfully constructing a new and more complex view of "the way things are."

One transition in particular—if it occurs—is crucial for discernment of spirits: the transition from a conformist or conventional perspective to a conscientious or postconventional perspective. This shift may happen to some women in their young adulthood and to many by midlife, but others may never experience it. What difference does it make for discernment of spirits?

The key organizing principle of the conformist stage comes from the groups to which one belongs: conforming to the expectations of these groups defines one's identity. The conformist person usually thinks concretely and stereotypically, orders life around external norms, allows few exceptions to the categories of right and wrong, focuses on external behavior with little perception of internal motive or ability to introspect, experiences global and undifferentiated feelings, values external appearances and group status symbols, employs concrete forms of prayer such as rote recitation, follows rules faithfully, denies "negative" feelings such as anger, hatred, or sexual attraction, and lives in a personal world comprising close-in and face-to-face groups.

The great development marking the conscientious stage is the critical appropriation of one's formerly tacit value system. Because one can now create self-evaluated long-term goals and values, a sense of responsibility for living up to goals also appears. One no longer leaves external authorities unquestioned; authority for one's life moves "inside." A person is truly reflexive with a rich and differentiated inner life.

This stage also includes greater conceptual complexity that allows one to see alternatives and contingencies, systems thinking, awareness of psychological causation and motive, a wider range of emotional experience and expression, awareness of relativity and contingency, a focus on self and self-identity, a sense of being the author of one's own destiny, increased objectivity with respect to other persons now seen as selves in their own right, and increased potential for interpersonal relationships, including the relationship with God (Liebert 1992, 84–91, 102–11).

The importance of this shift for discernment of spirits cannot be underestimated. Prior to it, one has little access to the inner life, little sense of self as an actor responsible for one's own life, little sense of the real identity and autonomy of other persons, and a concrete sense of human community comprised of the groups one belongs to personally. Once the momentous developmental shift occurs—if it does—"I" becomes rich and nuanced, but so do other persons, as they become more differentiated and less projected in one's own image. Mature conscience develops because one's motive is now accessible to self-reflection along with long-range plans and goals. Discernment of spirits becomes a real developmental possibility when the locus of authority moves from outside to inside oneself and access to one's inner life becomes habitual. This developmental stage is, in fact, a prerequisite to entering the Spiritual Exercises with the self-reflection they require.

This perspective highlights some of the discernment issues for women raised in this chapter. The certitudes held at the Conformist stage give way to ambiguities as one enters the transition. New questions appear in the place of former certainties: Who am I now that I am not defined by the groups I belong to? Who is God, whom I now can recognize working within me? What do I do with the range of feelings and thoughts cascading around within me? Which voices can I listen to? What do I do when they conflict with my old authorities? Is this new desire for self-fulfillment just selfish? How can I take care of myself and others?

The world is much bigger, not only because one's inner world has come alive, but also because one's social world now includes people whom one might not see face-to-face. New questions appear here, too: What is my obligation to these people, and they to me? What do I do with the complexity that they inject into life? The Rules for Discernment of Spirits offer a pattern for paying attention to this immense range of new data facing the person in the conscientious stage, particularly concerning her inner life.

As with each developmental stage, however, the conscientious stage has an inbuilt limitation that increasing focus on discernment of spirits may unwittingly exacerbate. Regularly turning attention to one's inner movements in discerning may enhance the conscientious tendency to overvalue the "I." "I have discerned" can prevent one from listening to persons with needed wisdom. Such is the pitfall of the overvalued self, one not (yet) balanced by a sense of interdependence. Having both discernment of spirits and the discerner framed by a community of accountability helps prevent this potential overbalance. At the same time, women's sense of self, often gained at the price of great struggle, needs to be honored and affirmed. The balance may be delicate.

Desolation or Depression?

The incidence of depression among women, already at epidemic levels, continues to rise. Depression occurs two to six times more often in women than in men. This reality affects many women making the Spiritual Exercises, begging the questions, Are depression and desolation related? If so, how?

Our understanding of the relationship of desolation and depression runs as follows: all depression has desolating reverberations, but depression and desolation may not be simply equated.

Comparing the phenomenological experiences of desolation and depression highlights striking similarities. Ignatius describes desolation as darkness and turmoil of soul, an impulsive movement toward base and earthly things, disquiet from various agitations and temptations, listlessness, tepidity, and unhappiness. Symptoms of depression include a sense of moving in slow motion, fatigue, sad feelings, numbness, inability to concentrate, sleep disturbances, digestive difficulties, a lack of enjoyment in things that once brought pleasure, loss of interest in sexual activity, a sense of emptiness, guilt, self-blame, pessimism or hopelessness, a sense of hopelessness about ever feeling any different, isolation, and inability to connect with God or one's true self or life-giving relationships (Neuger 1991, 156). Depression can be diffuse, paralyzing most or all aspects of a person's life, or it may be clearly connected to a particular trauma or loss that is consciously known, such as divorce, job loss, or terminal illness. To the extent that depression interferes with one's growth in faith, hope, and love, it could be considered desolation.

From the point of view of their causes, depression and desolation may also be related. Ignatius believes that the evil or antispiritual forces cause desolation and that God might permit short-term desolation for some remedial or pedagogical purpose [322]. Much discussion surrounds the causes of depression. Theories include chemical imbalance, anger turned inward, a learned response to a frustrating environment, negative thinking or "self-critical tapes," and living out roles in the family system. It is only a small step from desolation as caused by the antispiritual to depression as caused by antiholistic forces, especially if one's understanding of *spiritual* contains within it the notion of wholeness and completeness. Both desolation and depression dampen a vigorous, hopeful, generous, and enthusiastic yes to God's call.

Some of Ignatius's wisdom about responding to desolation proves useful in responding to depression as well. His admonition not to change the circumstances of one's life when in desolation [318], for example, parallels the common wisdom that it is unwise to make major changes while depressed. The caveat about always acting for the safety of women also applies in the case of depression. Severe or long-lasting depression needs professional treatment, and guides must be alert to its symptoms and make referrals to appropriate professionals.

Ignatius does encourage making changes in *oneself* designed to act against the desolation. Given his understanding of the nature of the antispiritual, he suggests increased prayer and penance. The therapeutic community suggests analogous ways to "act against" depression: physical examination and appropriate treatment of physical conditions, chemical treatment of bipolar disorder, therapy, body work, meditation and guided imagery, and sustained and direct action to change systems. These help one take control of one's life, and not feel so much like a victim. Of course, such sustained actions may require assistance from others.

The one guiding the Spiritual Exercises, however, should not become the primary caregiver for any serious depression. Those giving the Spiritual Exercises should remain in the role of spiritual guide, recognize their limits, and act within them. But guides may well need to assess the situation in collaboration with the one making the Exercises. Is this desolation or depression? If depression, how debilitating and longstanding is it? If serious, postponing the Spiritual Exercises is probably recommended. Thus, the seeker could focus all her energy on healing from the depression. The Spiritual Exercises can resume later.

Many depressions, though, are much milder and, though painful, are less seriously debilitating. For women experiencing such depressions, discovering the truth about themselves as valuable and loved in God's eyes, exposing the secrets that have burdened them, having their experience validated before God, letting go of destructive images, rigid spirituality, and constricting relationships with the church—all these fruits of the Spiritual Exercises can serve as healing balm.

However, one should not draw too close a connection between desolation and depression. Hence the second part of our understanding states that depression and desolation cannot be equated. First, not all depression can be simply and completely subsumed under the rubric of desolation. For example, a woman, Patrice, who has been clinically depressed for many years, finds her relationship with God the one thing that keeps her going in the face of the "deep black hole." She clearly recognizes that her depression has been a vehicle for forging this hard-won deep relationship. Her depression, stubbornly unyielding to any treatment, has impelled her into deep and continual reliance upon God for the resources to face each day.

Furthermore, desolation may not have any relation to depression. Sometimes experiences of God just "dry up." Other aspects of one's life may be free of signs of depression, yet the old zest for the spiritual has vanished. The favorite images of God leave one cold and spiritual exercises seem distasteful or a waste of time. Similarly, prayer that had been easy and enjoyable is now dull and difficult. All these signs suggest classic experiences of desolation.[13]

From a developmental perspective, a transition from one stage to another shares many phenomenological characteristics of desolation, such as disorientation, loss of familiar images and certitudes, loss of the identity that locates one in the world and disruption of a sense of the future: "I don't know who I am anymore, or who God is." In a developmental transition, initial disorientation yields to a long time "between dreams," as William Bridges puts it. The experience is often marked by an emptiness in which "the old reality looks transparent and nothing feels solid any more" (Bridges 1980, 112, 117). In the structural view of development, such a transition is a lengthy affair.

Many persons seek out the Spiritual Exercises when amid transition; indeed, deconstructing old certitudes may motivate some persons to make the Spiritual Exercises. These transitions are yet another cause of certain desolation-like inner experiences, and the one who gives the Spiritual Exercises is well advised to hold open this latter possibility. The chief ramification appears around election. Making a significant choice such as envisioned in election amid a lengthy transition may not be best. The person making the Exercises will most likely signal this situation by her inability to move ahead with a major decision in the light of her shifting perspective. She may intuitively know that this is not the time for a major life decision.

Feminist researchers also offer theories that suggest refraining from a tight equation of depression and desolation. They propose that depression may stem from deep societal causes. In the wake of the societal changes concerning women's role and status, their optimistic perceptions about the options available to them and about their power to make choices concerning these options never match the reality. Having rising expectations without the means to fulfill them contribute to the frequency and severity of depression in women (Neuger 1993, 201; Liebert 1996, 260). Author Dana Crowley Jack (1991, 5, 16, 21) concludes that understanding depression requires an examination of systemic and interpersonal relationships that result in "loss of self." Depression, then, is frequently more than an individual woman's personal problem; it has a structural and societal foundation in patriarchal institutional oppression. In this system, women never catch up no matter how their situation improves. It may be that the woman experiencing depression is well attuned to the psychological and social environment. Consequently, viewing and treating depression as *purely* intrapsychic while ignoring the overarching system that breeds the power differential does women a disservice.

Everyone has ups and downs, some severe, some transient. The "downs" have different etiologies requiring different responses, and it is not always immediately evident what is at issue. Yet, with appropriate ethical attention to the safety of those coming to the Spiritual Exercises, Ignatius's wisdom about desolations offers a way to remain steadfast during the inevitable discernment about the nature, cause, and response to each individual's lived experience, even those times when God seems distant and unresponsive.

Affirming and Grounding Women's Experience

For the woman just launching herself tentatively into a conscientious developmental stage, consistent and disciplined attention to her inner movements provides one of the best means for consolidating this developmental transition. If the one giving the Exercises encourages her, the seeker will gradually learn to distinguish finer and finer nuances in her inner dispositions. Meanwhile the guide remains a consistent, encouraging, and honest anchor with the external world, balancing the increasing sense of self with a loving community of accountability. Thus, discernment of spirits can provide a pattern and discipline in the service of appropriating one's own life at increasingly deeper levels.

The overview of women's discernment issues alluded to the ambiguous position in which women may find themselves when they employ feelings to assess their surroundings and choices. Many people perceive feelings as "soft," "feminine," "fickle," "unreliable," "fuzzy," and "sentimental," and the person who relies on them, by extension, also takes on all these characteristics. Contemporary culture assesses feelings negatively, stereotypically attributes them to women as a class, though perhaps not to an individual woman, who appears as an exception to the rule. Our culture connects the opposite characteristics, "tough," "masculine," "steadfast," "reliable," "clear," and "unromantic" with the thinking function and stereotypically attributes them to men. Thus, when women pay attention to and make choices by means of their affections, they unwittingly strengthen this feminine stereotype. But the next chapter will show that Ignatius also encourages thinking and imagining in making choices. Women do not have to choose one to the exclusion of the other. Meanwhile, the Rules for Discernment of Spirits provide a pattern for making increasingly subtle distinctions about affectivity and assessing its significant role in responding with ever greater integrity to the circumstances and choices of life.

Wisdom for the One Giving the Exercises

Turning the focus to the person who guides the Exercises highlights some of the perspectives presented above. The key question: How might the one giving the Exercises tailor discernment of spirits to the experiences of women in our culture? As always, the individual woman and her desires and circumstances suggest the manner of proceeding. However, those giving the Exercises might consider the following.

The guide can be sensitive to the underlying structural bases for the situation in which women find themselves. Here "structural" means the systemic, nonpersonal patterns that continue despite individuals coming or going. Thus, structural foundations exist for women's relative economic insecurity, incidence of single parenting, lack of advancement in employment, and high incidence of depression. Abuse and violence directed against women in general, to say nothing of the abuse and violence perpetrated on individual women, as well as a pervading sense that one's environment is dangerous, have a definite deleterious effect. Each of these situations has variations and complexities by race and culture as well as by gender. Attempts to vindicate individual women when they have been violated often get lost in these larger systemic dynamics. Black women, for example, typically get submerged within the definition of Blackness, which is normed on Black men in each culture. All these are among the "spirits" that need to be attended to in discernment.

"Structural" can also apply to a way of looking at development. It can point to the transitional anomie and disintegration that must occur for stage change to take place. Desolation-like manifestations have different causes and different responses; most should be resisted, but one, namely the deconstruction that occurs in developmental transition, should be encouraged. The one giving the Exercises, then, is invited to careful discernment of desolation-like symptoms.

Guides can also help women not blame themselves for inevitable spiritual desolations. They have done nothing wrong. They are certainly not, somehow, "bad" or a failure. Spiritual desolations come and go, an inevitable manifestation of living a spiritual life. They serve, for one aware of them, as indicators of growing edges and what needs attention. The giver of the Exercises also needs to help women understand that "acting against" must also include self-care.

The one giving the Exercises should also pay careful attention to power arrangements, encouraging the autonomy and self-appropriation and personal naming of experience by each person making the Exercises. The seeker should literally make the Exercises her own; in particular, she should appropriate the Rules for Discernment of Spirits to help her notice, name, and choose the direction of her growing integrity.

Finally, the one giving the Exercises might consider ways to expand the community within which discernment occurs. These ways include group sharing within the context of an at-home version of the Spiritual Exercises, a regular liturgical and sacramental community, or through group ministries of direct service. All these communities make their way into each woman's discernment of spirits.

CHAPTER II

Dancing toward the Light

Election

Friday, February 8, 1544
  In the afternoon for an hour and a half or more, I went through the elections in the same way. I made the election to have no fixed income and found myself experiencing devotion and a certain elevation of spirit, with great tranquility and without any contradictory thought of possessing anything. I no longer desired to continue the deliberations for as long as I had thought of doing a few days before.
—Spiritual Diary [10]

You know what is so interesting? I learned a decision-making process in one of my management courses where you line up all the pros and cons and weigh the lists to come to a decision. Now I find that Ignatius suggested just such a process more than four hundred years ago. But it makes such a difference to set everything into a prayer context.
—A contemporary woman

Ignatius's spiritual diary records his decision-making process about the degree of poverty the new Society should hold. It was one of many decisions that affected not only Ignatius, but the whole group. What has he to say to contemporary women regarding their own decisions?

Election (choosing in a faith context) is surely one of the most useful aspects of the Spiritual Exercises. Everyone makes decisions every day. Many are of little consequence, some have more obvious implications for self and others, but all reflect and hone the person one is always becoming. Election offers accessible spiritual practices to bring decision-making to the heart of life. For women, this spiritual practice can be pure gift, but choosing can also offer challenges, as revealed by contemporary research on decision-making.

What, When, Where, and Why?

The most focused and intense application of discernment within the Spiritual Exercises appears toward the conclusion of the Second Week. Here, Ignatius proposes that the person who has not yet chosen a state of life make this choice and offers a systematic process to do so. The Spiritual Exercises provide a privileged context for decisions so basic that they literally form one's deepest identity, one's personal vocation. But these same processes work for many other decisions as well, readily transcending their setting in the Spiritual Exercises.

One specialized term appears in this section, *election*. This word summarizes the process by which one chooses a state of life, the judgment about what that should be, and the actual choice itself (Toner 1991, 103). As long as one understands all the nuances involved in election, one might substitute *choice* as a reasonably acceptable synonym.

Although Ignatius generally uses the term *election* for a particular choice, one's state of life, he also uses both the word and the method for other significant choices [189]. Following Ignatius's lead in his Spiritual Diary, this material has become widely used at other times than the Spiritual Exercises.

Election weaves throughout the Second Week and forms its climax. The Week opens with the meditation on the kingdom and the contemplations on the early life of Christ from the incarnation through the presentation in the temple. At this point, Ignatius introduces the notion of choosing a state in life [135]. The one making the Exercises begins reflecting on her call amid her contemplation of the public life of Jesus, whose disciple she is becoming. To prepare for this journey, Ignatius proposes two more dialectical meditations: the Two Standards [136–48] and the Three Classes of Persons [149–57]. Several days of intense contemplation later, the one making the Exercises has arrived with Jesus at the events of Palm Sunday. One last preparation for the election material remains: the Three Ways (Degrees) of Being Humble [165–68]. All these exercises have been discussed in chapter 7, but it is worth recalling the conditions for election envisioned by Ignatius. We need to be willing to have our assumptions and attachments challenged, to put God's call to the better at the head of our election, and to have a heart centered on deepening our discipleship.[1]

The placement of election within the Exercises, then, is no accident. As the one making the Exercises begins the process, she not only becomes more intimately acquainted with the person of Jesus, but also more acquainted with the workings of her own spirit. She has experienced the dynamics of consolation and desolation and become more skillful in distinguishing the subtle ways the evil one might deflect her from her deepest call. Now she takes time to consider that call.

The first consideration [169] involves setting priorities: Why, ultimately, am I here? Ignatius, speaking from within the worldview of the Spiritual Exercises, summarizes: "the praise of God our Lord and the salvation of my soul." But each person making the Exercises will have to frame her ultimate purpose: How do I understand myself before God? How can I live that call most deeply? Developing this "single eye" is crucial; otherwise, one readily confuses the means (one's state in life) with the end (one's very reason for being). Ignatius's example remains relevant. How often does someone choose marriage (a means) but only long after the fact consider how life as a married person can help fulfill her final purpose. Ignatius wants to put first things first—clarity about means and ends is the "hinge" around which election turns (Ganss 1991, 412n83).

Confusing the means with the end easily happens. One woman, after a concentrated and successful struggle with cancer, realized that, in order to marshal her energy to fight the cancer, she had blocked out everything else, including her husband's expressions of affection and love. She had unwittingly let the cancer create a breach between them. Election for her became a reaffirmation of the centrality of her marriage, and she began searching for new behaviors to replace the old habits that no longer served her healing.

Without clarity of intention about means and end, does Ignatian election exist? The whole point of both discernment of spirits and election consists of the gradual ordering of all aspects of life to one's ultimate identity and purpose. Ultimate purpose as a dynamic reality and integrity is both the product of decisions and the basis for decision-making. This realization grounds our reading of Ignatius's wisdom on election. Election is not simply an expedient method for making an important choice; it is nothing less than seeking our ultimate call from God. Each of Ignatius's suggested methods for making a good election begins and concludes with this central focus.

About what might an election be made? Ignatius proposes several points. First, the moral status of the choice matters: it must be either indifferent or good.[2] Anything clearly involving evil lies outside the realm of appropriate matter for election because it could never lead to the greater glory of God. The difficulty lies in ascertaining whether a specific decision is morally evil, indifferent, or positively good.[3] Ignatius determined what was either indifferent or good by whether it functioned constructively within the institutional church [170]. What might that mean for contemporary women? How does it function for persons not in union with the Roman Catholic Church, Ignatius's context?[4] For example, what about a woman in a psychologically or emotionally abusive marriage? Or the woman who feels so deeply called to ordination that she struggles with whether she should leave the Catholic Church and join another denomination in which she can live out this sense of call. This point connects the election material with the Rules for Thinking with the Church, the subject of the next chapter.

Dermot Mansfield (2008, 158) deals with this question by expanding the concept of church beyond Ignatius's institutional understanding: "I would understand the Church to incorporate all of Christ's disciples, all lovers of the Gospels, all who value the Eucharist and who have allowed their own lives to become eucharistic in some meaningful sense—blessed, broken and shared out. So, in discernment I listen to the Church in this sense and try to hear what the Lord is saying today among his people." Such an expansive understanding of church makes sense to many contemporary women.

Even if one were to accept Ignatius's counsel at face value, it would still not necessarily offer sufficient guidance in deciding about what an election can be made. In significant decisions, the mature moral agent may not totally abrogate, even to the church, the responsibility for decision-making. The person is morally obliged to follow a well-informed conscience. Ignatius assumes that the conscience is formed within a faith community.

Decision

Second, Ignatius assumes that some choices, once made, cannot be undone. In this situation, the only option he sees is "the full-hearted gift of self to this state in life" (Fleming 1978, 105). But what should be done if one later recognizes that, in making this major decision, she confused the ends and the means? One could express sorrow and try to amend by putting efforts into living now as fully as possible within this choice. Today's dynamic understanding of the human person recognizes that one's experience or lack of it, one's knowledge or ignorance, one's options or lack of them, and one's history of prior decisions all play a part in decision-making. Decisions may be flawed according to Ignatius's abstract criteria and yet still occasion great grace, growth, and insight and serve as steps toward greater personal integrity. One can also respond to Ignatius's core insight while holding a more developmental sense of divine call. Responding with integrity to the best lights at the time is all God requires, as *Lumen Gentium* 16 notes (Flannery 1996, 21–22).

Ignatius's examples of irreversible elections include ordination and marriage. But even these "unchangeable" elections are sometimes reversed. Many women, for example, find themselves in a position of discerning whether their marriage ever existed, or whether it is wholesome or even safe to remain in a lifeless or abusive situation. Thus, the notion of an "unchangeable election" may itself need discernment.

Most persons making the Spiritual Exercises will have already chosen a state in life. Ignatius addresses their situation under the heading "To Amend and Reform One's Life and State" [189]. Today's women might have to consider a very different palette of options: for example, if or when parents or in-laws should live with the family, the most appropriate values to instill in their children and the best means to do so, or how to use their material resources to bring about greater justice. In other words, many decisions, large and small, are occasions to use the methods offered under the rubric of election. The attitude of discernment brought to decision-making is one of the primary fruits one can take from the Spiritual Exercises into daily life.

The final introductory point concerns looking back at elections made earlier in life from the point of view of the Spiritual Exercises. In reviewing these important life decisions, it may become clear that important yet changeable elections were made with the ends and means in right relationship. If this is so, there is no need to change them now. But if some were made in a "disordered" fashion, one making the Exercises may wish to return to them, renewing them from the perspective of the glory and service of God [173–74]. Remembering a past decision that was not well made in this Ignatian sense might initiate a profound healing process.

The Three Times for Making an Election

Ignatius next considers three appropriate contexts for making an election, which he calls "Times," each defined by a particular spiritual state. The first two are terse almost to the point of ambiguity. Ignatius divides the third into two processes. Examples given below concerning three women, each of whom faces a similar choice, illustrate the Times by their differing inner processes.

The First Time, or spiritual context for making an election, occurs when God attracts us to an option so clearly the uncertainty evaporates [175]. How often God might work this directly Ignatius does not say. Practically speaking, any claim to such an experience would require discernment. One might discern by examining the sense of direction according to either the suggestions for the Second or Third Times, or both. Brian McDermott notes three qualities that should be present for First-Time discernment: the choice is morally good, one has a sense that this choice is indeed God's call, and one is unable to doubt that it is indeed God's call (2018, 30). Ignatius's examples notwithstanding, this First-Time experience need not be extraordinary. For example, one woman announced with certainty,

> I've spent the past twenty years putting my husband through school, and then the kids. I was happy to be taking the kids to Little League, but now it's time for *me*. There is a community college close, and my son just got his driver's license, so there is no need to be carting him to after-school sports. I'm going to school now. It's the right time and the right thing to do. I just know it.

The Second Time for election, which Ignatius thinks is the most typical, concerns the situation in which the discerner experiences consolation and desolation and receives clarity through discerning these various movements [176]. The one making the Exercises has been noticing, naming, discriminating, and choosing with respect to various spirits throughout the First and Second Weeks. She has gained experience even in subtle situations covered in the Rules more appropriate to the Second Week.

Decision

Now she applies these discriminating skills to her own life. This example of another woman's process has quite a different feel from the first:

> I've been having a real strong sense that I need to investigate something new. The kids are all in school. I've thought about going back to school myself. But I'm afraid that I couldn't do it after all the years I've been out of school. Sometimes it seems like it would be selfish, at my age, because we will be having college expenses for the kids in a few years. But it really would be satisfying to focus some time on my own mind after all these years. When I think about it, I get excited—and really scared.

The Second Time raises questions: How certain should one be? How does one proceed in the case of desolation? Does the appearance of any desolation, or a lot of desolation, rule out the option? Fortunately, Ignatius gives a bit more help in the *Autograph Directory*:

> [18] Among the three modes [times] of making an election, if God does not move him in the first he ought to dwell on the second, that of recognizing his vocation by the experience of consolations and desolations. Then, as he continues with his meditations on Christ our Lord, he should examine, when he finds himself in consolation, in which direction God is moving him; similarly in desolation. (Palmer 1996, 9)

In the Second Time, the seeker proceeds indirectly, returning to the contemplations of the Second Week rather than intensively working on the decision to be made. Then, in the context of a growing relationship with Jesus, she examines the decision.[5] From the perspective of the Rules for Discernment of Spirits, the seeker watches for fruits in the Second-Time process: Does the consolation arise from God or is it counterfeit? Does it remain oriented to good from beginning to end? Is there sufficient evidence from accumulated instances of discernment of spirits that this direction ultimately honors one's deepest call? This Time takes time.[6]

The Third Time for making an election is "one of tranquility," by which Ignatius means that no alternating consolations and desolations are present around the choice being considered. If these and other affects are quiet, intellect becomes the means to a decision. A third woman facing a decision about returning to school relates the following:

I am about to begin a new chapter in my life. There are a number of things I can do, all of which have some appeal. I could enroll in the School of Social Work, which I've always been interested in. I could return to early childhood education, which I was doing before we had our kids and really liked at the time. I'd have to go in as an aide, not a lead teacher, until I picked up some more classes, but I could do that in maybe one or two summers. Either one is possible for us financially, so I really am free to do either. By the end of the year I will probably have reached my decision. I'm still checking out a few things.

The first process that Ignatius elaborates in the Third Time looks enough like contemporary strategies for good decision-making that one might miss the critical distinctions between Ignatian election and decision-making strategies taught in management seminars. The first point [178] asks for clarity about the alternatives and what each involves. It may require several attempts to clearly formulate the choice.

The second, third, and sixth points highlight the difference between election and other contemporary decision-making processes. In the second point [170], the crucial "hinge" appears: one places oneself and the whole decision within the ultimate purpose of life. One then seeks the grace of being disposed to either option, so long as it serves this ultimate end. This "indifference" appeared earlier in the Principle and Foundation. Election is, inescapably, a faith process.

As in the First and Second Weeks, the third point [180] concerns asking for the grace desired, that God will work through one's reasoning to accomplish the greater glory of God through this concrete decision. Asking for this grace reinforces the purity of intention sought in the preceding point. The fourth point [181] sets out the reasoning process itself: consideration of the advantages and disadvantages first of one alternative and then of the other, all framed by the goal of election, the greater glory of God. Four questions are posed for each option:

1. What are the positive consequences for God's glory anticipated for choosing?
2. What are the negative consequences for choosing?
3. What are the positive consequences for God's glory anticipated for not choosing this alternative? and

4. What are the negative consequences for not choosing this alternative (McDermott 2018, 32)?

Pondering these four questions, one uses reason to reach the decision.

But election does not end here. The last point also distinguishes election from other kinds of decision-making. One brings the tentative decision arrived at through reasoning to God for confirmation [183]. Ignatius's text is sufficiently ambiguous about what confirmation entails and thus this question has evoked considerable discussion. Fortunately, a vivid example of one of Ignatius's own elections is preserved in a fragment of his Spiritual Diary, covering the period from February 2, 1544, to February 27, 1545 (Ganss 1991, 215–70). A partial entry from February 8, in which Ignatius considers the degree of poverty that will characterize the Society of Jesus, opens this chapter.

Examining this and other instances of election in Ignatius's own experience communicates several things about confirmation. First, seeking confirmation is, in Ignatius's mind, essential. Second, receiving it depends upon the weightiness of the matter for discernment, the time given to the process, the time frame in which the decision must be made, and so on. The faith perspective underlying election holds that God would, one way or another, give some *disconfirmation*. In its absence one might proceed. Third, confirmation might consist in any or all of the following: spiritual consolations such as courage to proceed, increasing energy and enthusiasm, new reasons for the choice, intensification of the reasons already named or of desire for the choice itself, and a sense of having done everything possible to find God's will in the choice at hand. Fourth, seeking confirmation entails waiting, actively reviewing the process and outcome, offering the decision to God, and asking that the outcome be disconfirmed if not in line with one's ultimate call. A final aspect comes after the completed election: appropriate authorities confirm the decision (Toner 1991, 201–32).

Ignatius realized that imagination also offers powerful ways for making an election and included three exercises of imagination [184]. Each, using a slightly different perspective, creates some objective distance from the discerner's situation. The first directs her to imagine what she might say to a stranger who proposes the same alternatives. The second asks her to consider what she would wish to have done from the perspective of her deathbed. The third asks her to consider what she would wish to have done on the final judgment day. Given Ignatius's penchant for imaginal prayer, these scenarios need not be in the least dry or predictable in their outcome. In addition, one need not restrict oneself to these three considerations, though they all have precedents in the tradition.[7]

Not surprisingly, Ignatius begins these considerations with the "hinge" upon which election turns, asking the one making the election to set the deliberations, once again, within the ultimate purpose of her life [184]. In the other critical dimension in Ignatian election [188], the one making the election again brings the results to God for confirmation.

Although some interpreters of the Spiritual Exercises believe that the Second and Third Times treat separate processes and should remain distinct, the Second- and Third-Time processes naturally complement each other. Using one's whole self, reason, affect, body, imagination, and memory, creates a more holistic process and allows for a fuller devotion of oneself in prayerful decision-making.[8]

All this election material can feel terribly heavy, ponderous, or rigid. Yet it need not be. That which gives God greater glory generally brings great satisfaction and fulfillment.[9]

Before leaving the exposition of Ignatius's election processes, it is also important to note the limitations of his process for today. Ignatius lived on the cusp of the Enlightenment and before the scientific revolution. He would not have been able to imagine the complexity of interlocking systems that impinge on decision-making in today's world. His election processes focus on the individual decision maker without taking much account of the community and culture and other systems within which that individual decides.

One way to deal with this structural complexity involves a process based on the Pastoral Cycle. Here, one moves from first describing the situation to using social analysis to uncover both the systems involved and the linkages that sustain them. With the information from these first two steps in hand, and infused with prayer, the Cycle moves to the discernment proper, which can involve any of the processes Ignatius presents, and also includes following Ignatius, a period of confirmation, subsequent implementation, and review (Liebert, 2015). Such a cycle, and particularly the social analysis aspect, embeds the structural complexity into discernment from the beginning. It also lends itself to communal discernment with respect to a shared structure.

But what if the complexity affects decision-making at a level unnoticed by the discerner and not uncovered by the social analysis described above? Our rapidly escalating engagement with social media provides one such instance. Through engagement with Facebook, Twitter, Instagram, and numerous other platforms, people are unwittingly being manipulated by sophisticated algorithms designed to predict and shape their behavior. Every user is presented with a skewed view of reality as their newsfeeds become an echo chamber reinforcing their beliefs and biases, creating greater fragmentation and polarization in society. Without realizing it, decisions are being impacted by forces with a profit motive, so subtly that the users are not even aware of the manipulation (Standaert 2014).

Too much engagement with social media unconsciously impacts freedom with respect to issues of discernment and decision-making. It may now be important to encourage those making the Exercises to disengage as far as practically possible from social media in order to tune into their own authentic deeper desires more easily.

From a perspective honed by living alternately in North America and Central America, Dean Brackley (2004, 161–70) sets out ten "touchstones" to expand the understanding of context and name some of the dynamics that persons today must internalize to be faithful to the potential of election:

1. Reason and Science—to understand reality we are willing to use the tools of both reason and science, as well as philosophy, psychology, and the social sciences, to enrich both our reason and our affectivity;
2. Personal Transformation—we are willing to open to new things, to form new understandings of the world and one's place in it;
3. Experience and Praxis—we are willing to enter new worlds, look at things from points of view different from our own and then act on what we see; that is, we participate in the life we are discovering, allowing that participation to deepen our understanding about our decisions; we engage in a rhythm of contemplation and action;
4. Love and Discipleship—we open ourselves to the value of all life, adopting love as the supreme norm for action;
5. Discerning Interior Movements—set within this wide context, we welcome new images that arise from consolations as well as noticing the direction of our feelings;
6. Conscientization—we awaken to social reality, both to its cruelty, but also to its promise, allowing ourselves to see

injustices, their causes, and logic and how we ourselves are embedded in unjust systems;
7. Utopian Imagination—we allow our imaginations to roam freely in the wide freedom of God's possibilities such as expressed in Isaiah and Jesus;
8. Community—we search with others rather than in isolation, within a moral community rather than a laissez-faire swamp;
9. Tradition—we cherish the deep wisdom that comes to us through wisdom traditions and millennia of reflection, yet we are also aware that traditions carry prejudice as well as truth;
10. (Appropriate) Authority—we are willing to move in alignment with authority toward truth, toward what is right and good.

Such attitudes and commitments bring Ignatian election into direct dialogue with the complex structural realities that mark our era and invite us to enter complex decisions in a spirit of faith, knowing that we can never consider all the complexities of our lives, yet trusting that God walks with us in our desire to respond faithfully with the lights that we have.

Problems and Possibilities for Women

Everyone makes choices daily, and life-changing decisions occasionally. How can this "coming-to-be-who-I-am," whether daily or at turning points, be woman friendly? What attitudes and adaptations would free women to make the best decisions? These questions obviously move beyond the scope of this work. Restricting the discussion to the Spiritual Exercises, however, reveals several potential difficulties in the processes proposed by Ignatius, including the notion of God's will, the action women might take when faced with "disordered" choices or decisions opposed by various authorities, and some of the tensions women might experience when faced with any serious decision.

Election inevitably raises the concept of God's will, even though the phrases *God's will* and *discernment of God's will* never appear in the text of the *Spiritual Exercises*. For persons, a notion of God's will flows from a medieval cosmology; these persons see God's will as an unchanging reality "out there" where God "dwells in unapproachable light." Their task as Christian moral persons entails discovering what that will is and then conforming themselves to it, whether easily or tortuously.

This theological assumption may exist in subtle forms. For example, one woman, experiencing a deep and generous attraction to discipleship with Jesus, found herself praying, "O Lord, just show me your will, and I will do it." When she reported this prayer to the one guiding her through the Exercises, she added, "As soon as I get a sense from Jesus about how he wants me to serve, I will do it." Her guide gently responded, "Did it ever occur to you that perhaps Jesus might be waiting for you to decide what *you* want to do and then he will join you there?" "Oh!" she replied, "I hadn't thought of that." They went on to explore the seeds of her call planted in her heart, recognizing her attractions, desires, and gifts, the possibilities open to her and so on. Her subsequent prayer was no less generous, but she also began to recognize her own freedom and unavoidable responsibility for setting the direction of her life within the scope of God's love and mercy for her and all creation. She began to see *herself* as a creative act of God.

Even though the concept of God's will does not appear in the *Spiritual Exercises*, a statement that the end of the human person is "to praise, reverence and serve God" frequently does. This framing of one's ultimate end leaves open an immense range of possibilities about decisions, actions, and lifestyles that could embody it. No "blueprint in the sky" exists. This insight can be either frightening or freeing—or both at the same time. To be fully herself, each person must take up her own destiny.

That prospect, especially to one who sees herself as innocent and childlike, can evoke great resistance and even terror. Embracing the feelings and accepting the responsibility for one's life eventually leads to the birth of the adult moral person. But this growth in moral personhood does not take place in isolation from others. The mature conscience is formed in dialogue and exercised in community (Gula 1989, 124).

Women often find it difficult to trust their own experience. To the degree that it has either been actively denied and suppressed or, more subtly, left unnoticed and therefore rendered invisible by those whose power names the world—parents, spouses, educational system, church hierarchy, the culture itself—women's own experience can seem strange and even foreign to themselves. And to the degree that their experience and trust have been abused, women may deny what their experience tells them. Humans have such a need for meaning and coherence that if the world does not make sense—for example, if those who should provide safety violate it—they may deny or forget what has happened to them in the interest of maintaining a cohesive worldview. "I must have asked for it," we might hear one say, or another, "God must be punishing me now for having sex with my boyfriend." The methods for election and skillful accompaniment may offer individual women a graced opportunity to commit to their own identity.

Second, what of so-called disordered choices? What of earlier choices that, in hindsight and from the vantage point of the First and Second Weeks of the Exercises, seem to reflect poor discernment? Take, for example, the woman who married her high school sweetheart soon after graduation, realizing later that she chose the only life she could then imagine and the only way she could find to "leave home" in her small town. What does she do in light of the Ignatian election exercises? What about situations where apparently well-made decisions have gone sour? Generous women can feel especially grieved by and feel greatly responsible for such decisions. Has poor or nonexistent discernment led to these bad outcomes?

Such situations do not necessarily indicate faulty discernment. They point to limited discernment, perhaps, or small horizons, inadequate life experience, limited perceived options, or invincible ignorance. But, in keeping with an understanding that one's final "end" is a process rather than a product, these decisions may have been necessary and appropriate steps toward developing personal integrity, subsequently honed in the face of life's inevitable blows and blessings. Freeing someone from negative judgment of early decisions may also free her to face the difficult decision currently before her.

What of those women facing decisions about something opposed by their communities of moral authority? What about the evangelical woman who files for divorce against the teachings of her church, the divorced Roman Catholic woman contemplating remarriage, the woman who gives up custody of her children to attend school and launch herself professionally, the parent of a twelve-year old considering an abortion, or the woman who relinquishes her faith community or her vows? A literal interpretation of Ignatius's qualifying factors in [170–73] would eliminate several of these decisions. But such existential decisions face real women who have definite limits to their supportive communities, economic and educational means, and autonomy. These decisions make an impact beyond the women themselves that will ripple down through the years. Women who face such momentous and complex situations especially need to examine their concrete experience, gather data, and explore the ramifications of their decisions. Sadly, many feel so unsupported or even betrayed by the church community in such circumstances that they walk away. Ideally, any woman facing such complex choices needs the support of a good spiritual guide who can accompany her in developing the greatest possible degree of inner freedom and integrity out of which she can make these difficult choices. The election methods suggested by Ignatius, coupled with skillful accompaniment, provide a privileged context for their prayerful, discerned decision-making.

Decisions and Commitments: Making, Keeping, Changing

Decisions both express identity and provide the vehicle for further developing it. Decisions have religious import too, even when made and executed without adverting to God at all. They constitute a vantage point for understanding both God's commitment to us and the reciprocal desire on God's part for our commitment. In a real sense, decisions express relationship to God. For this reason, decision-making lies at the center of the Spiritual Exercises. This section first summarizes some recent research on decision-making relevant to election and then looks at gendered aspects surrounding election.

Today's cultural contexts are vastly different from Ignatius's and the early interpreters of the Spiritual Exercises. Women today face more and more complex choices, to the degree that many persons are weary of or overwhelmed by making decisions. In the last century, the scope and complexity and the value associated with this breadth of decision-making has propelled humans, to a greater or lesser degree, into a culture of self-determination. Particularly in European and North American cultures, persons usually think that having more options is better, and making decisions oneself is crucial to the success of the decision and to one's personal freedom and autonomy. If someone makes the decision for another, it is usually interpreted negatively by the recipient of the decision. Yet, this cultural assumption hides the fact that not everyone wants to make more decisions or to make them completely autonomously.

Cultural dynamics matter greatly, however. In some cultures—in

Africa, for example—where decision-making is premised culturally on the involvement of the community and the sanction of the elders, deciding or discerning autonomously may be difficult. Much more weight rests on the ramifications of the decisions of one person for the family and community. In this situation, it may be helpful to engage the community as part of the discernment process and the spiritual guide may need to be sensitive to this communal dimension. On the other hand, for such a person, there can also be a sense of liberation in feeling themselves freed to make a decision that rests only between themselves and God.

Not only do guides need to assess the cultural dynamics underpinning decision-making, but they also need to sense what appeals to a retreatant to most effectively help her approach the indifference that Ignatius presumes in election. For one retreatant, the guide might need to challenge the cultural assumption that narrowly autonomous decisions are better than decisions from an autonomy connected to others and for another, or encourage the exercise of autonomy in decision-making even though it may feel risky to step out and take responsibility for her actions (Standaert, 2014, 33–34).

More options do not necessarily lead to better choices. In fact, a growing body of research on decision-making reveals some counterintuitive results, namely that too many options can lead to paralysis and to decreasing satisfaction with the outcome of a decision.[10] The burden of increasing choice can also be linked to increasing depression in present-day society. Even if we escape the paralysis that can arise when confronted with too many options, paradoxically satisfaction decreases in proportion to the number of options. Our expectations also rise when options increase; when expectations go up, satisfaction levels with the results drop.[11]

Suggestions for election include the following: First, find ways to prioritize and simplify the options so that their number allows the differences between them to appear more clearly and enhances the possibility for deeper freedom to move ahead in Christ. Second, remain aware of the possibility of choice fatigue, noticing how it appears in consolation and desolation, and exploring ways to lower it, which could include setting aside election for the time being.

Recent research has also uncovered more nuance on how emotions undergird reasoning. Emotion and reason are enmeshed from the start, with interesting implications for election.[12] First, our ability to use cognitive strategies at all is probably dependent on our ability to experience emotion; in the absence of the ability to feel emotion, a person lacks the ability to make even rather simple decisions. Feelings, it turns out, point out the proper direction and move one to the appropriate "place" for decision-making, where the strategies of logic can be put to good use. Second, the bodily substrate of emotions *causes* certain emotions, not the reverse. Why might this latter finding be important in election? Over time, certain physiological reactions are associated with events and past actions. These past associations will feed certain emotions, causing us to lean toward or away from certain aspects of a given decision depending on whether its somatic marker triggers positive or negative associations. Knowing that this linkage exists, it is possible to attend to it in the process of weighing and deciding.

Third, feelings themselves fall into several types: (1) basic universal emotions (happiness, sadness, anger, fear, and disgust), and (2) other emotions that elaborate these basic emotions. For example, euphoria and ecstasy, melancholia and wistfulness, panic and shyness elaborate the basic universal emotions of happiness, sadness, and fear, respectively. This second type of emotion is tuned by the experience of subtler shades of cognition and subtler variations of emotional body state. To these two types of emotion add a third type: background emotion, arising from bodily background states. These background states function continuously, persisting long after any previous cause is removed. One thinks here of the ongoing struggles of a sufferer of post-traumatic stress disorder, whose underlying background emotion overwhelms and wreaks havoc on more surface emotions and their role in decision-making. Clearly, awareness of background feelings will be crucial in decision-making, as they are the living heart of our connection to the world.

Finally, certain emotions last longer than others, with grief lasting the longest, followed in decreasing order by happiness, anger, and gratitude. Extroverted people enjoy positive emotions longer than introverted people, neurotic people suffer longer from negative emotions than healthier ones. Negative emotions also generally last longer in collectivist cultures. Again, being aware of these variations and how they might show up in an individual can assist in accompanying another through election (Standaert, 2014, 43).[13]

Much of this research points to a paradoxical application to election: remain attentive to the gifts that come precisely when one is not looking for them but test them nonetheless, remain attentive to other things than that which one is looking for, create space for something new to happen. In the end, we may—or may not—make the better decision. But God is with us nonetheless, as we head into the next decision and the next, learning as we go.

Gendered Aspects of Decision-Making

At the beginning of her study of personal commitments, theologian Margaret Farley (1986, 4–8) suggests why women may have difficulty with decision-making:

> Who, overall, have known better than women the deep needs of the human spirit for commitment? Yet who, overall, through the centuries, have experienced more sharply the bitter pain of being deserted in commitments that were believed to be mutual? Who have learned with untimely grace that promises can rise from a personal freedom that transcends purely cultural roles? Who struggle now so desperately to balance multiple commitments, to forestall guilt in compromise, to accept limitations without abandoning trust and hope? Who press now so consistently to distinguish servile fidelity from a fidelity that is both liberated and responsible? (1986, 8)

Some needed perspective comes from examining what constitutes commitment, how commitment is an outgrowth of love, and the basic considerations around release from obligation.

Commitments are certain kinds of decisions in which a person "places" a part of herself or something that belongs to her into another person's "keeping." It gives the other person a claim over her. In making a promise, she does not give *herself* away, except in the sense that another holds her pledge. In that sense, she binds her future freedom. If she betrays her word, she stands to lose a part of herself (Farley 1986, 16–18).

But why make commitments? Commitments and the trust they engender assure others that one will be consistent. But one also assures oneself in the face of personal unpredictability. Commitments facilitate important aspects of human community: personal relationships, political life, and human communication all depend on promise making and keeping. All stand to gain mutual protection, companionship, and love. Furthermore, while commitments do cut off some options, they give freedom to act.

Decision

Without commitments, all things are possible, but nothing is actualized. As the adage says, "It is impossible to run in all directions at once" (Farley 1986, 19–22, 44). No one is so paralyzed as the person who tries to keep all options open indefinitely.

Fundamental to making a commitment or promise is free choice—no free choice, no binding promise. Choice moves toward action, but the difficulty often centers around letting go of other kinds of actions. Reflective decision-making, which occurs in the methods of election, encourages one to weigh and sift the possible actions, trying to understand and evaluate them.

Below the free choice and the action, however, lie several layers of desire, the deepest of which is desire for love. As Farley (1986, 29) puts it, "Every free choice includes a choice of what and how to love." The methods for election and the entire dynamic of the Spiritual Exercises allow seekers to enact the belief that their deepest desire and ultimate good, and that of other persons as well, are the same. God's preferential love grounds all finite expressions of love, making them possible and completing them. In this sense, love wants commitment because it wants to express itself as fully as it can to assure its completion.

Women may need some general guidelines for making loving commitments. They ought, for example, to have reasonable grounds for trusting themselves to another, and for hope that they can fulfill that promise. They ought to have some evidence that the human relationships constituted by this commitment are subject to the norms of justice, such as respect for persons, equality and mutuality and equitable sharing, as well as some means to redress grievances (Farley 1986, 36). With these parameters in place, a woman can turn to the loves of her heart. What does she most deeply desire? These loves require decisions and commitments as their natural completion and expression (Frankl 1959, 157–58).

The often-difficult question about terminating a major commitment remains. Women who have internalized the responsibility for relationships can be particularly distressed when relationships are strained to the point of collapse, because, for example, women care for aging in-laws and parents as well as dependent children much more frequently than do men.

While each situation has its own particulars, several generalizations can help provide the framework for examination. One might begin by seeing if the conditions for a commitment and the capacities for a choice are present and whether the choice is freely entered into. One can ask, is there enough knowledge of the parameters and consequences of the choice so that it can be competently made? Is the commitment desired by the recipient? Is the sacrifice wholly disproportionate to the value to be gained? In a mutual commitment, does the other party also understand and agree to essentially the same commitment? In addition, the limits of the commitment, both in time and terms need exploration.

Margaret Farley proposes three conditions in which commitments, even serious ones, may be released: (1) when it truly becomes impossible for either party to sustain the commitment-relationship; (2) when a specific commitment obligation no longer fulfills the purposes of the larger commitment it was meant to serve; and (3) when another obligation comes into conflict with and supersedes the commitment in question (1986, 75–84). Careful reflection, usually with the assistance of one or more compassionate companions, helps determine if these conditions are present.

These considerations presuppose commitment grounded in relationship. The commitments made within the Spiritual Exercises ideally flow from vision of a certain kind of world and the call to assist its birth. This vision also rests on relationship with the Holy, the Creative One. This relationship, unlike human ones, is unfailingly characterized by truth, justice, and mercy.

Finally, the reality of self-sacrifice can prove very problematic to contemporary women, as developmental theorist Carol Gilligan (1982) so vividly illustrated. While self-sacrifice is required of all parties in all commitments of any substance, are there limits? Farley offers the following ethical guidelines. First, one may not relate to others in a way that ultimately destroys either the other or the self. In essence, one may sacrifice everything one *has* for the sake of the other or the commitment, but not everything one *is*. One may never sacrifice the capability for union with God and other human persons. Thus, demands that violate personhood, or that rest upon false needs in the other, or that envision sacrifice as an end carry no obligation for a truly just love to fulfill. Furthermore, all this must be examined within an analysis of the power arrangements: When a disproportionate burden of sacrifice is laid upon the less powerful person, then the less powerful person's duty to self-sacrifice needs to be critiqued (Farley 1986, 105–7).

But—and here the presence and action of grace often breaks in—restoration may still be possible. Sometimes situations can be restructured, even radically. Sometimes changing one's interpretation of the situation can make all the difference. And sometimes the grace of forgiveness is given to one or both parties. Forgiveness, an act freely offered, can never be rushed. When forgiveness is present, at least the one forgiving, and possibly the one forgiven, is freed to reenter the commitment or to move on.

This matter of decisions and commitments, so essential to election, is complex and often problematic for women. It asks them to take their own experience seriously, to learn to recognize the deep desires of their own hearts, and to accept responsibility for stepping out in loving commitments that grow out of their experiences of being loved and returning love. The methods for election invite each woman to make or reappropriate her identity in the very lifestyle she will embody. That this identity is essentially apostolic and mission oriented is one of the great graces of the Spiritual Exercises.

Wisdom for the One Giving the Exercises

The opportunity to facilitate the seeker bringing together her identity with its lived vocational expression is a privileged one. It may also be difficult, as it requires a delicate balance not only of interest and affirmation but also of objectivity and dispassion. Ignatius thought election so central to the Spiritual Exercises that he dedicates two of fifteen preliminary notes specifically to the director: the one giving the Exercises is to caution against hasty or ill-considered promises and may not influence the seeker toward one or another decision. The Creator alone must be allowed to deal directly with the seeker. Self-knowledge and indifference on the part of the guide are essential.

The one giving the Exercises can especially help the seeker by helping her broaden the options that she can imagine, focusing them on clear discernment questions, facilitating the healing of old wounds so as to be free to move on, and selecting and attending to the outcome of the various methods. The guide may also offer additional methods complementing those Ignatius has suggested, especially ones tapping the wisdom of the body.

It may seem strange to broaden the imagined possibilities when the ultimate task is choosing a life direction, but many women can imagine only a restricted range of options. Unless real options exist and unless women *experience* them as real options, election will not be as free and true as it might.

Enriching the imagination entails a much larger process than is possible during the Spiritual Exercises. Such education of the imagination may involve art, literature, travel, and education. Some kinds of enrichment fit best in a pre-Exercises time of preparation. These could involve encouraging the one making the Exercises to let herself dream about what she really wants to do before the "voices" of reason, economics, and commitments crash in on fragile new images of possibility or helping her name and feel comfortable with her gifts and voice, both literally and figuratively. Other avenues may involve awakening the imagination or learning to pay attention to dreams. The one giving the Exercises can lend authority to taking this enrichment seriously.

One can also find many ways to continue the enrichment appropriately within the scope of the Exercises, especially in strengthening the imagination through the meditations and contemplations and encouraging the seeker to voice the graces she desires. A fully alive person will respond more fully to the Holy Spirit as she approaches important decisions within the Spiritual Exercises and afterward.

At the appropriate time, a carefully framed discernment question can greatly facilitate the election. However, sometimes a question may be too focused or the process too intense. Persons are often encouraged to make the Exercises before important decisions, in part because of the election aspect of the Exercises. In such cases, the question may loom too large over the dynamics of the Exercises, and the one making the Exercises may need to set the decision aside for the time being. Putting "brackets" around the decision and letting it move from the center of one's consciousness over to the margins allows the one making the Exercises to immerse herself in the dynamics of the First and Second Weeks. These dynamics cultivate the necessary dispositions for election. When the time comes to return to the pending decision, the one making the Exercises will be changed.

In contrast to being too focused, sometimes the matter for election will be diffuse and vague. In some cases, simply encouraging the shift from an open question like "What am I going to do?" to a more specific yes or no question such as "Should I go back to school?" will help bring the appropriate matter into focus. The seeker can try out a number of these questions until she comes as close as possible to the real issue for discernment. Noticing what she desires, what gives her energy, and where her gifts point help refine the discernment question.

Decision

For some, the question changes during the course either of the election exercises or the subsequent Weeks. This development should cause neither distress nor discouragement. It is simply a version of confirmation—the first question was not confirmed as the most appropriate one. One simply frames the new question and returns to the election exercises. The guide may need to encourage this movement back and forth, helping to avoid premature closure.

As the one making the Exercises begins to work with the election processes, she may uncover an old wound or blockage that requires attention. This healing work may need to precede the election. If its scope falls within the competence of the one giving the Exercises and its duration seems proportional to the dynamic of the Exercises, it is perfectly appropriate to focus on the healing. But if immense and complex, for example, in surfacing of memories of early sexual abuse, the one giving the Exercises will have to adjust the process accordingly. The greatest grace of the Exercises might be the courage to attend to one's healing through the necessary means outside the context of the Spiritual Exercises.

The primary function of the one giving the Exercises, however, will consist of introducing the methods for election as appropriate and helping the seeker to notice and interpret the data she receives. Ignatius implies a priority of methods: infused clarity, if given; alternating consolation and desolation; and finally, in the absence of the first two, using the rational processes of thinking and imagining. The one giving the Exercises today may wish to work from the strength of the discerner. How has she made important decisions in the past? How, for example, did she decide to make the Spiritual Exercises? Beginning with the woman's own experience of decision-making allows her to claim it as part of discerned decisions in the future. Thus, the graces of the Exercises may more easily spill over into daily life.

If she begins with the processes that employ her natural ways of making decisions and her personality strengths, the seeker can complement this discernment with an alternate process. A highly imaginative person, for example, might look at her decision using the rational means of listing the reasons for and against. The data elicited will differ, and sometimes crucial insights emerge when employing a less dominant personality function.

The one giving the Exercises might also encourage the seeker not to skip over "negative" data, but to stay with it as attentively as one would with "positive" data. The director may also sometimes notice resistances on the part of the seeker of which she is unaware and help her gently but fearlessly face them.

The processes Ignatius offers can also be elaborated and adapted. The "hinge" of Ignatian election does not lie in the processes, but in the indifference with which one approaches election and the confirmation that one receives about the specific decision. Therefore, any decision-making process placed inside these all-important "hinges" may prove useful for election. The imagination-based exercises can expand to include others derived from the woman's own story. She herself may come up with the scenario. Ignatius does not suggest processes based on intuition, though it is quite possible to understand the First Time as God working directly through intuition. A simple guided meditation that facilitates the emergence of a direction may prove invaluable. The Quaker discernment tradition is based on the premise that wisdom and direction is already planted by God deep within the individual, and the task of discernment consists in removing any obstacles that stifle that inner wisdom. Around intuition the Quaker and Ignatian traditions fruitfully meet.[14]

Human beings are embodied creatures, a theological assertion frequently overlooked in discernment. Thus, the body constitutes another entry point for discerning decisions. Eugene Gendlin (1981) has developed a simple process called focusing, based upon the assertion that the body and the brain know far more than is usually available to the conscious mind. The six-step process takes seriously the wisdom of the body. Anyone can learn it.[15]

Focusing can assist with discerning decisions at several levels. The discernment question might take the place of the "problem." Or the "problem" might reveal the things that the body says must be dealt with before one is free enough to consider the discernment question. Focusing can also be a part of the confirmation process: does the body itself say yes to the outcome of discernment?

Of course, many other ways of working with the body enhance discernment: forms of embodied prayer such as Zen walking, prayer based on data of the various senses, massage, and dance, both spontaneous and liturgical. These embodied prayer forms may offer powerful pathways to divine presence, and thus to discernment.

The process of election has immense significance. As women make important decisions, they embody their ever-forming identity with a

Decision

particular way of living it out. In the context of the Spiritual Exercises, the election process elicits a generous response to the call of God in the person of Jesus. The decision gains depth and clarity throughout the remainder of the Exercises and of their lives. An apostolic identity takes concrete form. Discernment and election are truly precious gifts shaping all of life.

CHAPTER 12

Black Appearing White
Rules for Thinking with the Church

Salamanca, August 1527. A small man with a decided limp, dressed in rough, poorly dyed black clothing, emerges from the local prison. As he comes through the low stone door, he shields his eyes from the bright sunlight. A few moments later, he is joined by several companions, also emerging from the door of the prison. Together they walk toward the town plaza, conversing among themselves: "Now what? We can't do what we are called to do. They have not condemned us, but they have silenced us all the same."

A medium-sized city in the United States, Easter Vigil, 2021. A woman sits in the pew, watching the new pastor baptize the adults and children she has catechized. Two weeks later, she is summoned to his office and told her contract will not be renewed. The staff is to be reorganized. She emerges from the office into the bright sunlight, blinks rapidly and sighs to herself: "Now what? Do I have the energy to start again somewhere else?"

Ignatius of Loyola, following his call and using his unique gifts, encounters church authorities who imprison and silence him. A contemporary woman, using her gifts, is dismissed and effectively silenced. Who or what is this church? What characterizes the relationship between the one making the Exercises and the church in which she or he feels called to serve?

Rules for Thinking with the Church

The final and possibly most problematic section in the *Spiritual Exercises* is a set of directives that has come to be called the Rules for Thinking with the Church. More than any other portion of the Spiritual Exercises, this section must be understood considering its historical context, particularly the theological controversies of the time. Much of its specific advice is dated, and its usefulness to contemporary women appears so compromised that many recommend eliminating this section from consideration by retreatants. Understanding the Rules in their historical context, however, opens the possibility that even this difficult section of the Spiritual Exercises may hold something useful for contemporary women.

The fact that the *Spiritual Exercises* do contain a section entitled Rules for Thinking with the Church raises several crucial and inescapable issues for women's participation. First, it highlights several questions about the relationship between the church and the Spiritual Exercises: "Are the *Spiritual Exercises* emphatically institutional or totally individualistic or somewhere in between?" (Buckley 1995, 441). Can one make the Exercises without relationship to any faith community? Or are they, at root, an instrument of evangelization and church renewal? What does it mean that women disenfranchised from the institutional church increasingly present themselves to make the Spiritual Exercises? Whether one resists or assents to including the Rules for Thinking with the Church in materials presented to the one making the Exercises, the mystery of church requires examination, if only because one's personal spirituality is consciously or unconsciously informed by the larger reality called *church*.

Second, what is the significance of *church* for those who make the Spiritual Exercises and for those who give them? Contemporary women approach the Exercises with a variety of passions and emotions toward church, from anger to indifference to appreciation, and with a variety of ecclesiologies, including Roman Catholic, Orthodox, all varieties of Protestant polities from high Anglican to Pentecostal and independent nondenominational, Quaker, and "post-Christian" groups.[1] These experiences, feelings, and ecclesiologies inevitably color the relationship to the Spiritual Exercises. The relationship between the one making the Exercises and the church also creates a dynamic context in which election occurs. It will be impossible to ignore the reality of church as one proceeds through the Spiritual Exercises.

Third, the relationship of those giving the Exercises to the church matters. The one making the Exercises and the one giving the Exercises each relate to a foundational experience, summarized in a text, the Spiritual Exercises, describing a practice, which is, from its origin, inescapably contextualized by the church, not only of Ignatius's time but also our own. It matters how the director represents the church, invites the one making the exercises to engage with the reference to the church, and helps deepen the relationship to the retreatant's own faith community.

Context of the Rules

The sixteenth century held complex and dynamic challenges for the Roman Catholic Church from both the outside and inside. Within the church, some persons practiced a mysticism that ignored dogmatic accuracy and theological precision, such as the Spanish *alumbrados*, with whom Ignatius was several times confused. Others, such as Luther and Calvin, openly split from orthodox Roman Catholic positions. In the sometimes-heated rhetoric of the era, many elements of Catholic piety came under attack. A third group made up of disgruntled or critical Catholics undermined church morale from within with their sarcasm. The ironic and satirical writings of Erasmus come to mind here (Ganss 1973, 73–77). The church today, now split into various denominations more or less suspicious of one another, faces equally challenging issues and sometimes polarization within denominations.[2] To these historic rivalries one must add modern atheism and a pervasive secularism unknown in Ignatius's day. There is also, however, the gift of a growing ecumenical spirit in many places, especially in Ignatian circles of those who give and make the Spiritual Exercises.

Ignatius's own life brought him both happy and unhappy contacts with the church. Soon after his conversion, he sought out a spiritual director, began conversing with whomever would discuss religion, and set about publicly catechizing. He grew to love the Mass and the sacraments, especially the Eucharist, which he received as often as possible. However, these innocent-appearing contacts with the church yielded no fewer than eight legal processes directed at Ignatius by church authorities between 1526 and 1538. They concerned matters ranging from the clothing he and his early companions wore, the education upon which he based his catechizing, his teaching about mortal and venial sin, his relationships with youth, the Spiritual Exercises themselves, the content and fruit of his spiritual conversations, and his orthodoxy and that of his companions. Several of these investigations entailed his arrest and imprisonment, once for as long as twenty-two days (Padberg 1993, 10–17).

In his later years, Ignatius worked directly with various popes over issues related to the Society of Jesus, relationships both profitable and conflicted. On the one hand, his collaboration with Paul III and Julius III established and strengthened the Society in its fledgling years. On the other, he struggled, especially with Paul III and Paul IV, over attempts to make members of the Society bishops or cardinals, which Ignatius adamantly opposed (Padberg 1993, 10–17).[3]

When Cardinal Gian Carafa was elected Pope Paul IV in 1555, Ignatius feared what the new pope might do to the Society. He is said to have quaked in his bones before he could repair to the chapel to regain his composure (Tellechea Idígoras 1994, 558). Yet the dying Ignatius asked that same pope for a blessing, reflecting the traditional Roman Catholic understanding that the grace of God is transmitted regardless of the disposition of the minister. Clearly, Ignatius was no stranger to the process of reflecting on both consolations and desolations arising at the hand of the institutional church and its leaders.

Contemporary women likewise recount enlivening and disillusioning experiences with the church. The circumstances eliciting consolation for many contemporary women include a new affirmation of a rich variety of spiritualities by Vatican II's universal call to holiness; access to theological and biblical studies and to the fruits of a rich theological and biblical heritage; the ordination of women in most Protestant denominations; and the reclaimed memory of interesting, complex, and effective women within the Christian heritage. Women also struggle with experiences of the church and its ministers. Abuse of power, sexual abuse or harassment, job stratification, unjust salary differentials, lack of access to decision-making, exclusive language, and the loss of traditional and cherished images of God wear down even the most determined and focused church women. The experience of the unnamed woman at the beginning of this chapter is far from unique.

Contents of the Rules

Ignatius probably composed the Rules for Thinking with the Church during his student days in Paris, though he may have completed some points after his arrival in Rome. The Rules bear some resemblance to decrees of the Council of Sens (1528), held just after Ignatius arrived in Paris. The highly public profile of Ignatius and his companions compelled him to formulate an approach not only to the private conscience but also to the public conscience (Boyle 1983, 256). He created a series of counsels about a constructive attitude from which to form concrete pastoral responses to the conflicts of his time.

The usual title, "Rules for Thinking with the Church," is not Ignatius's own, but an attempt to summarize his much longer title.[4] *Sentir*, the Spanish word usually summarized by "thinking," includes both affect and praxis. By using *sentido*, Ignatius wished to convey a habitual way of acting that springs from a loving, reverential, yet critical relationship to the church.[5]

Rules, though Ignatian in origin, is also a misnomer. The points represent a collection of guidelines to be used with flexibility. The early directories suggest they be given only to those whose ministries will plunge them publicly into the complex dynamics of the ecclesial situation of the time.

Although the Rules may appear to be a rather haphazard collection of points, Ignatius states his fundamental principle in the first Rule [353], and then he develops this proposition in three groups of directives. The first set, Rules 2 through 9 [354–61], involves suggestions for an attitude about aspects of the devotional life of sixteenth-century Catholics, under attack either from within or from outside the church of Ignatius's time. The third, sixth, and eighth exhortations, culturally and temporally conditioned as they are, need refreshing for today. The second group, Rules 10 through 12 [362–64], builds up a positive attitude toward authority in the church regarding jurisdiction, learning, and holiness. The third group, Rules 13 through 18 [365–70], treats complex doctrinal truths under heated discussion in Ignatius's day, setting out a positive pastoral strategy for dealing with them. The first Rule in each section, namely the first, tenth, and thirteenth, grounds the subsequent points in that section (Ganss 1973, 77–80).[6]

The first Rule [353] asks those making the Exercises to develop a loving and deeply reverent and obedient attitude toward the church, even with its weak and human leaders, and to let that attitude color all dealings with it.[7] In a climate in which both friends and foes of the church make light of its teachings or actively tear down its leadership, organization, and its very spirit, this Rule exhorts all to speak positively of these same realities. In a climate of cynicism about the church, spontaneous and simple affirmations can speak volumes. This reverential love, Ignatius's own life shows, will be more than our own doing; it will spring from God's grace at work in all parties. Blows suffered at the hands of the church will often be quite sufficient, naturally speaking, to change sympathy to bitterness, friendship to enmity, good will to disillusionment. Just as one would give a longtime friend loyalty, so one tries to develop a habitual reverence and loyalty to the church, which is no less mother and friend.

The tenth Rule [362] echoes the basic attitude with which Ignatius began the Spiritual Exercises [22]. It advises one to be more inclined to praise than to blame the personal and public actions of those who hold positions of authority in the church. Even if their actions are blameworthy, dragging down their reputations serves only to tear down the faith of all. On the other hand, one can and should deal directly and privately with those in a position to do something about a person or problem facing the church. However, this avenue presumes access to persons of power, something for which women have had to continually struggle.

In the thirteenth Rule [365], the most controversial from today's perspective, Ignatius proposes a difficult principle. "What I see as white, I will believe to be black if the hierarchical Church thus determines it." In Ignatius's time, the statement simply reiterated the commonly accepted belief that, in certain cases, what the church defined could contradict the senses. For example, the Roman Catholic position toward the Eucharist holds that the consecrated elements, which appear as bread and wine, are actually the body and blood of Christ. Therefore, the strong reaction against the thirteenth Rule quite possibly arises either from misunderstanding what Ignatius really meant or from changing philosophical, theological, and ecclesiastical circumstances. It would have passed as a noncontroversial statement to Roman Catholics of his era.[8]

The thirteenth Rule encourages a suspension of disbelief out of a spirit of faith when perceptions and judgments appear to contradict the church's position. In a sense, Ignatius proposes an attitude that totally reverses the so-called Protestant principle, which holds that the divine transcends any created reality, including the church (Tillich 1957, xvi–xvii).[9] In other words, God's will transcends any church. Both perspectives, without the balance of its opposite, can lead to extremes: Ignatius's exhortation seems to ask for "blind obedience," while the Protestant principle appears to glorify hanging onto one's version of the truth at the expense of unity. If we look more deeply at the Exercises, we do see elements of the intuition behind the Protestant principle in the high role Ignatius gives to individual freedom and his admonition to the director to permit the Creator and Lord to deal directly with the one making the Exercises [15], that is, to let God be God for the retreatant (Clarke 1990, 57–61). The mystery of the church in its fullness requires an integrity that respects both ends of the continuum.

Controversies and debates have existed in the Church from the very beginning, so debate and discussion are not the issue, but rather the attitude with which we engage in these debates and their effect on believers and nonbelievers alike. Ignatius's encouragement in the presupposition [22] gives a clear sense of the way he wanted differences to be engaged. In this spirit, our attitude must be that of realistic reverence, and our strategies ought to diminish as much as possible the possibility of scandal to believers and nonbelievers. The rise of social media greatly complicates this issue for contemporary believers.

Problems and Possibilities for Women

The Rules for Thinking with the Church point to issues that affect the entire experience of the Exercises. First, however, what can be said about the Rules in relation to women's experiences of the Exercises? This topic then leads to a renewed ecclesiology within which to interpret the Exercises.

How Important Are the Rules for Thinking with the Church?

Why not just quietly relegate the Rules for Thinking with the Church to the end of the Exercises and hope that no one notices them? Are they too central to ignore? Well-respected interpreters of the Exercises hold opposite positions on this question.

Some, such as Juan Polanco, believed that because of the lateness of their composition and appendix-like nature, the Rules for Thinking with the Church are peripheral to the integral dynamic of the Exercises. His *Directory*, composed between 1573 and 1575, suggests that the group of Rules, including those for almsgiving, scruples, and the use of food, should "be proposed not to everybody, but only to persons who seem to need them and for whom it is worth the effort" (cited in O'Malley 1993, 50). John Futrell (Cowan and Futrell 1993, 169), however, claims that the Rules for Thinking with the Church provide the criterion of individual discernment. This challenge is somewhat more difficult to address. The thirteenth Rule, Ignatius's stated norm for certainty, allows a test of Futrell's claim. Gill Goulding (2019, 307–30) believes that the Rules for Thinking with the Church can ground an ecclesial disposition that is crucial for all Christians, not simply those engaged in public ministry. This disposition grows out of and deepens one's relationship with Christ in an immediacy of knowledge, leads to spiritual freedom, provides the context for all individual and communal discernment, and is lived out through engaging in Christ's mission in the world. Goulding sees great potential in a contemporary reclaiming of these Rules.

Ignatius believed that every good impulse, whether personal or ecclesial, comes from the same Spirit. Therefore, in submitting one's personal perceptions and discernment to the public discernment of the hierarchical church, there should be no conflict between one's properly discerned experience and institutional faith. Relinquishing final judgment to the hierarchical church, however, avoids a crucial question. Many contemporary women, both Roman Catholic and Protestant, have difficulty accepting such an unequivocal position on the institutional church's role in confirming individual discernment (O'Connell 1990, 117). What if the hierarchical church itself was prompted by an evil spirit, under the appearance of light, that distorted its perception (Boyle 1983, 255)? The feminist hermeneutic—whatever promotes the full humanity of women as well as men is redemptive and holy and is therefore of God, what denies and distorts that full humanity does not bear the power and authority of divine revelation (Fischer 1988, 128)—too often contradicts the institutional church's positions and its treatment of women. This possibility leaves women with a considerably less certain position than Ignatius asserts.

No certain norms for evaluating concrete and specific discernments exist; the best outcome is more or less relative human certitude. As much as one might wish for certitude, discernment does not abrogate the necessity of faith. Thus, neither the position that one can ignore the Rules for

Thinking with the Church nor the position that they serve as the norm for all discernment expresses a sufficiently nuanced perspective. They are, in fact, both more radical and more relative.

Potential Usefulness

Objections to the Rules for Thinking with the Church are varied. Their imagery is distasteful, even repulsive; they seem to demand unthinking obedience; they grow out of and support a narrow and pre–Vatican II ecclesiology; they are so time bound as to be irrelevant to the contemporary context; they only apply to the Jesuits who by vow have placed themselves at the disposal of the pope for mission; they are not, strictly speaking, part of the Spiritual Exercises.

Yet properly understood, the Rules for Thinking with the Church hold possibilities to move seekers toward a new perspective. The first centers around the notion of a profound affective attitude of love for the church, a sense of ecclesial commitment in response to the issues facing it at a given time (Cowan and Futrell 1993, 170).[10] Ignatius calls for a basic existential love for the church that causes one spontaneously to support and defend it out of this heartfelt connection. This felt experience of love for the church is one of the fruits of the Fourth Week; here the church is the primary vehicle through which Christ carries on his work in the world. Imagine what a difference such a felt love could make inside church institutions and within the wider society.[11]

The tenth Rule also strikes this irenic note: one should be more inclined to praise than blame superiors. This rule proposes a basic good will grounding relationships in the Spiritual Exercises and extends it to one of the most neuralgic issues of his day and perhaps ours, the relationship to the persons in church structures who hold legitimate authority. But note that Ignatius also counsels bringing "bad conduct" to the attention of the appropriate authority, a counsel Ignatius himself was not shy about doing.[12]

Ignatius's praxis regarding his ecclesiastical superiors illuminates what otherwise could come across as naive support of unworthy and corrupt leaders. He did not hesitate to pray ceaselessly, convince politically powerful friends to intervene on his behalf, create a paper trail, or visit the pope personally—Ignatius did whatever it took to hold off or reverse a papal decision he felt was wrong. Ignatian scholar John Padberg calls Ignatius's relationships with popes one of "realistic reverence," noting, "Obviously Ignatius supposes that Church authority has the final say, but clearly only when it was really final" (1993, 26, 31–32).

Goulding (2015, 82–83) summarizes her systematic examination of Ignatius's interactions with various popes by noting that he always tried to see the good in the actions of the pontiff, even when he adamantly opposed the direction the pope was heading. Ignatius believed deeply that the will of God is most coherently known through active obedience to superiors, primarily the pope. He trusted that the Spirit would guide the church across the generations despite the shortsightedness of individuals at any given point. While contemporary women may differ in their issues with the church, these ways of proceeding, namely discerning carefully, working actively to bring about the results of a careful discernment, trying to find anything in the other position that might shed light and grace on the present disagreement or tension, and trusting that the Holy Spirit can bring good out of what today appears messy and unresolved, can serve us well today.

The View of the Church in the Spiritual Exercises and Now

The underlying issue has to do with the nature of the church, its relationship to the Spiritual Exercises and consequently to those making and giving them. What did *church* signify to Ignatius? What does the contemporary church look like on these same issues?

Perhaps the most problematic of Ignatius's images is *hierarchical*. The "hierarchical church" points to one aspect of the mystery of the church, that it is an inescapably earthly reality, incarnated in a human community with a human authority structure. This description reminds us of the need to deal with the concrete manifestations of power and authority; one cannot spiritualize these human aspects of the church out of existence (Cowan and Futrell 1993, 175). By speaking of the hierarchical church, Ignatius signaled that he wanted to serve that church through the direction of the pope. He felt convinced that the pope, for all the faults he might have, had the most all-embracing view of the needs of the church. Ignatius's church is always relational, and the relationships are human as well as divine.

However, Peter-Hans Kolvenbach, Superior General of the Society of Jesus between 1983 and 2008, adds an important nuance to the understanding of the term *hierarchical*, counteracting a negative connotation apparent in much of the contemporary world:

> We must take care to avoid misinterpreting Ignatius when he speaks of "the hierarchical church." He does not take it to mean the world of Popes and bishops, ecclesiastics and clergy. It would seem that Ignatius was among the first to appreciate the hierarchical Church as a church of *mediation*. The divine grace that is given to the world is *mediated* by each believer, of high and low estate, according to his or her life and place [189]. Each person, as a member of the Church, exercises a responsibility in the work of salvation. Thus Ignatius's perception of the Church is that of a body with a head and limbs, each part fulfilling its proper role as God wills. (2004)

This understanding of *hierarchical*, rather than referring only to the organizational aspects of the church, invites us to enter the mystery of the church at an entirely different level: namely, the church as the concrete mediator between the Divine and the earthly and the role of each one of us, including the pope, in that mediation.

In Ignatius's time and up to Vatican Council II, the metaphor of "the church militant" signified the living members of the church continually struggling to bring about the kingdom of Christ. Together with the "glorified members," they make up the whole communion of saints. In exploring the church militant, it helps to recall that Ignatius's fundamental worldview was one of conflict. In living out its essential call, the church inevitably participates in this conflict and must struggle actively against evil. The Rules for Discernment of Spirits indicate the cosmic nature of this struggle in Ignatius's mind. He names that against which the church struggles the "enemy of human nature." For Ignatius, anything antihuman or humanly destructive is diabolical. Asking the one making the Exercises to develop a positive attitude toward and act in harmony with the church militant, then, means asking that person to commit herself constructively and consistently—even passionately—to this struggle against the antihuman wherever it is found (Buckley 1995, 444–46). Struggle is part of obedience today, especially for women, who may capitulate too easily in the face of conflict.[13]

But these two metaphors for church do not exhaust Ignatius's repertoire. In an undated catechetical instruction, for example, Ignatius defines the church simply as "a congregation of the Christian faithful illumined and governed by God our Lord" (Heiding 2012, 28); this same understanding is reflected in the Jesuit ministries of preaching, teaching, distributing the sacraments, and giving the Spiritual Exercises as means of gathering and strengthening communities of the faithful. Ignatius also often spoke of the "bosom of the Holy Church." Within the first Rule [352], Ignatius offers two more balancing images, speaking of the church as "Spouse of Christ" and "our Holy Mother." These two metaphors suggest an intimate unity of Christ and the church and provide an antidote to the imagery of the church militant. The images of the church as spouse and mother illumine the immediacy and intensity of the love with which Christ communicates himself to the one making the Exercises (Buckley 1995, 462). The image of the church as mother evokes one totally taken by God, who brings to birth in love. This reciprocal love allows one to follow the guidance of God. Held together, Ignatius's images create a rich and complex view of the church that invites a response of realistic reverence.

Four hundred years later, a renewed ecclesiology brings new ideas to the Rules for Thinking with the Church. The fruits of Vatican II have affected all contemporary persons, Christian and non-Christian alike. In calling the Council, Pope John XXIII hoped to update the church, to renew it interiorly but also to increase its relevance to the contemporary world. If the church were to be a sacrament of unity in the world, it would first have to confront the scandal of division among the Christian denominations. The very notion of church must undergo conversion.

The vision of church projected by Vatican II is rooted in the mystery of God revealed in Jesus Christ, light of nations. The Council used various biblical images to represent the church, offering a wider palette than did Ignatius: sheepfold, farm, building, temple, as well as mother and spouse (*LG* 6). In this church, persons are called not just as individuals, but "all are called to this catholic unity of the people of God....To it belong, or are related in different ways: the catholic faithful, others who believe in Christ, and finally all of humankind, called by God's grace to salvation" (*LG* 13). The universal call to holiness means loving God and neighbor and thereby fostering a more human manner of life on this earth. The church of Vatican II claims the name "pilgrim," identifying a people on the way, in process, and in relationship to the community of saints who have walked this way before us and share humanity's struggles and successes.

However, the church envisioned by Vatican II not only looks within, but also outward to the world, desiring solidarity with all people, particularly the poor and afflicted in their joys and hopes, griefs and anxieties. The church recognizes the profound dignity of human persons, yet it is not blind to the reality of sin. It recognizes the essential reality of human community, the value of human activity in the world, and the significance of dialogue as the means of transforming the world into a more just society. In this outward focus, the church remains faithful to its mission to facilitate the coming of the reign of God.[14]

A renewed ecclesiology sees the church in process, continually trying to live out its mission. For Vatican II, church is mystery, the people of God gifted with charisms of lifestyle and ministries of ordained, lay, and religious. All are called to holiness on their pilgrim way. This church recognizes its past and continuing role in "the theater of human history," and its credibility today depends as much on what it does as what it says.

The church envisioned by Vatican II is also a community of service, both to the world and to the reign of God. This community follows the servant Jesus Christ, whose life calls all to fullness. This servant church must concern itself with every aspect of the human journey toward life in Christ: economic, political, artistic, scientific, as well as moral and spiritual. Jesus told his disciples, "the kingdom of God has come near" (Mark 1:15). Thus the servant church seeks to call attention to this reign of God and to enable its coming into all parts of creation. This reign can be promoted in an infinite number of ways, both far-reaching and down to earth: in the feeding, clothing, and housing of refugees, including the economic refugees in our own inner cities; in teaching young and old and researching all areas of the arts and sciences; in giving care in the most ordinary of human situations to our children and elders; in struggling with the medical, social, political, and environmental causes of lack of well-being; and in caring reverently for life and all that sustains it. Each person has a particular gift to offer on behalf of this reign (Lonsdale 1990, 153–55).

The church is also the ordinary community of support for expressing discipleship and mission—the church sends individuals and groups for apostolic service. This aspect of a Vatican II ecclesiology has particularly strong resonances in the Spiritual Exercises, which conclude with a mission to apostolic service. As God labors on our behalf [236], so we labor on behalf of others. In this context, discernment may be seen as an effective means for continuously putting on the mind and heart of Christ and election as a similarly effective means for choosing a particular embodiment of discipleship. Discernment and election take place in the context of church, and our choices stand in harmony with the history and faith experience of the individual's or group's faith community (Lonsdale 1990, 156). Discernment and church need each other for their completion.

Fredrik Heiding (2012, viii) offers several theses that can ground contemporary interpretations of the Exercises in relation to the church. First, understand the church as a sacrament of Christ in mission for the sake of the kingdom and healed through the wounds of Christ; understood in this way, it is not contained without remainder in the visible structure. Second, grasp the pilgrim nature of the church, that it exists on the frontiers, and that development and change are normal. Third, take seriously underlying attitudes and how they are communicated—they matter. These principles can also assist the one who gives the Exercises in making appropriate adaptations in specific circumstances.

Vatican II has been called the council of the laity, a significant number of whom are women. For this reason, special issues arise concerning the relationships of women and the church. Many women today, Protestant as well as Roman Catholic, recognize that one area of stress and tension in their lives concerns their relationship with a church that professes to hold women in highest esteem while at the same time prohibiting them from full participation. Church tradition and structures have historically been androcentric, patriarchal, and hierarchical. Many see specific changes in current practice as only cosmetic and pragmatic, not transformative. Roman Catholic documents continue to legitimize the exclusion of women from full participation in church life and mission while affirming their dignity, gifts, and the importance of their participation and leadership. Women in other church structures experience their own versions of alienation and marginalization.[15]

Women making the Spiritual Exercises reflect the rich diversity of the church catholic. Some women's church experience leads to discouragement, alienation, and anger; others' experience of church structures and leadership leads them to such despair that they believe they have no alternative but to leave. On the other hand, numerous women commit themselves to stay with the institutional church and work for change from within. Women with theological and ministerial training provide leadership in the church at local, regional, and national levels, in rural and urban settings, and in traditional and new ministries. Many women's religious orders have publicly placed themselves in solidarity with women in ecumenical, interfaith, and justice networks working for development and liberation. Historically, Protestant women's missionary groups have been rich and effective vehicles for addressing the broader needs of the world's people (Bass 1979); new structures today channel this same energy into solidarity with the human community.

Other women find themselves taking a long perspective, noting that in the big picture women have come a long way and have accomplished much in the current situation. These women wait (with varying degrees of patience) while continuing to work for greater change. Others deny that any issues specific to women deserve this much attention in the church, that issues of global scale and widespread moral decline demand priority. Wherever one finds oneself on this broad spectrum, issues of women in the church touch a wide range of the people of God.

Implications for the Spiritual Exercises

The starting point for the Spiritual Exercises is the Principle and Foundation, which asks the one making the Exercises to situate herself in the context formative for her life, to desire to get in touch with areas of unfreedom and to order her life in God. Although this language emphasizes a person's individual experience, the mystery of God and the life and ministry of Jesus are mediated for the Christian through the church in its various expressions. The experience and current attitudes of the one making the Exercises will affect her liturgical participation, her election orientation, and her sense of call to service in context of the community of faith.

The Exercises move from an individual's consciousness of her own relationship with God to her ability to find God in all things. "All things" includes the church, where increasingly she will be able to identify and distinguish movements of divine breakthrough as well as the reality of the sinful human condition. The Rules for Thinking with the Church suggest that, for a contemporary person engaged in the Exercises, the relationship with the church as a community of faith includes critiquing the past, living gracefully in the present with hope, and imagining a future that will more adequately express the mystery of the church in its fullness.

By faith, these relationships are animated by the Spirit promised by Jesus. The Spirit discovered through personal discernment in the Spiritual Exercises is the Spirit active in the daily life of the church and its people. This same Spirit asks for a renunciation of power, understood as "power over," replacing it with "power with." The quality of relationships constituting the church in its many manifestations must also reflect the intricate interdependence that marks all of creation under the power of the Spirit.

Ignatius intended the Rules for Thinking with the Church for use by public church persons, primarily Jesuits, but also influential clergy and laymen. Today, however, women also teach and preach and enjoy other leadership roles in the church. The call to prophetic consciousness and action are inherent in the Exercises, so women making them are bound both to critique the domination and to celebrate the evolving liberation of women's experience of church.

Women making the Exercises may find that their experience leads them to discern and to dissent. Anthropologist Gerald Arbuckle (1993, 9) cautions against a narrow and highly restrictive understanding of the word *dissent* that interprets it only as pejorative, a sign of disrespect and repudiation of authoritative teaching. He understands dissent as "the prophetic move by people who genuinely love the gospel and the church to offer reasonable alternative ways of preaching the good news to the world of our time." When understood in this way, dissent signifies a healthy organization or society. Although women may have been socialized to acquiescence, understanding agreement and approval as more in harmony with "true womanhood," the experience of the Exercises may lead more women to this broad understanding of dissent by raising disagreement, objection, and protest. These women will cause conflict and opposition as well as pose alternatives. They will combine invaluable prophetic critique and loving service.

Wisdom for the One Giving the Exercises

The Rules for Thinking with the Church have not been given to all those completing the Spiritual Exercises, even in its enclosed form. Thus, the decision about whether to use the Rules for Thinking with the Church for reflection and prayer can flow from the same criterion Ignatius apparently used: Will this person be dealing with the church in any public way? If so, some version of Rules for Thinking with the Church may invite and challenge her to a positive, irenic, though still demanding and lovingly critical perspective on the church and its visible manifestations in structure and personnel.

The deeper issue, however, concerns each person's relationship to the mystery of church as the very human and limited persons and structures struggling to make Christ more fully present. This mystery seems essential to the dynamic of the Spiritual Exercises; for each person making the Exercises has some understanding and relationship to church. Questions may help facilitate this exploration of Church: What words, images, and metaphors would she use to express her vision and experience of church? How has the vision of church emerged from her family and community history? How might her vision deepen as she becomes more and more a disciple of Christ Jesus today? How will that mystery unfold within her and be expressed in her life? As always, the Exercises guide takes his or her cue from the one making the Exercises and her dynamic interaction with the Holy Spirit. Discernment and election in their far-reaching effects become instruments in service to this larger mystery of church.

Similarly, what sense of ministry does the one making the Exercises possess? How might this call be deepened? How will election embody the call to ministry offered to her and to each member of the church through baptism? How has she received the fruits of God's labor and extended that labor in response? What ebb and flow of giving and receiving marks her call at this moment?

To achieve the positive end of the Rules for Thinking with the Church, namely a realistic love for the church in all its human frailty and divine call, those who give the Exercises will need to reframe them for today's women. This is no easy task. Ignatius suggested pertinent answers to precise problems. Today's pastoral and theological issues are vastly more diverse and complex and the cultural context much expanded.

Thinking with the church today, theologian Ladislas Orsy believes, must be ecumenical, precisely if it is to be catholic. It must value internal inspiration and the primacy of individual conscience, while at the same time recognizing the importance of participation in a visible manifestation of the church. Contemporary thinking with the church must oppose disintegrating forces within the church and encourage trends that build the community. Finally, thinking with the church today will recognize the Spirit at work in the secular as well as in the sacred (Orsy 1975, 28–31).

Pastorally, seven conclusions follow: (1) The fundamental attitude of a Christian desiring union with the church consists in an interior alertness to the movements of grace that come from the Spirit of God. This Spirit will bear witness about the church. (2) Being one with the church means being one with a mystery, existing in human form in space and in time. "Blessed," says Orsy, "are those who are not shocked by God's unfolding plan and can recognize a divine presence behind a human reality" (1975, 32). (3) Aware of the church, one must proclaim it, but at the same time seek increasing understanding of this mystery. (4) Those who hold authority in the church hold it in trust and *must* use it according to the mind and heart of God; for the rest, the right attitude toward authority entails recognizing it truthfully, giving it neither too little nor too much power. (5) All charisms given by the Holy Spirit for the good of the church must be honored. Likewise, weaknesses in the church call for compassion and healing action. (6) The greater good may sometimes ask one to sacrifice human respect, personal plans, or institutional expressions. (7) To be one with the church is to hear and respond to the cry of the poor, and of those who hunger and thirst for justice, and to work for the healing of the divisions among Christians (Orsy 1975, 31–40).

Shifting perspective to the one giving the Exercises: How, practically, can the director work with the variety of persons, both women and men, who come to the Exercises today? Fredrik Heiding (2012, 221–244) examines the issues that arise when the Catholic director *accompanies* a retreatant who is a nonpracticing Catholic, a devout Catholic at variance with church teaching, or one who belongs to another Christian denomination.[16] His key interpretive principles include the following:

- focusing on the personal spiritual growth of the person making the Exercises,
- adapting the Exercises to the individual person and her needs while still communicating the ecclesial context of the Exercises for consideration in prayer,
- conveying values without forcing them,
- understanding and accepting one's inescapable role as a representative of the church,
- assuming that grace can be active in everyone,
- encouraging commitment and solidarity to whichever church community the retreatant belongs, and
- inviting the retreatant to expand her horizons with respect to the encounter with Jesus Christ, but also the customs, traditions, and language by which that encounter is communicated.

Heiding concludes that ultimately "the task for the spiritual director is to become aware of his or her own convictions and his or her own bias" (242), a principle that holds for all aspects of the director's role.

A Contemporary Reading of the Rules for Thinking with the Church

Considering the contemporary ecclesiology sketched above, the following rereading of the Rules for Thinking with the Church may prove helpful. Alternately, the one making the Exercises may wish to find her own contemporary analogies, metaphors, and images.

The first Rule speaks about putting personal judgment aside and keeping minds disposed and ready to be obedient to the church. A contemporary rereading suggests the indifference of the Principle and Foundation and openness and obedience to a contemporary vision of the church, such as that of Vatican II and of Pope Francis for how the church can be in dialogue with the contemporary world.

The second Rule praises confession and Eucharist. A rereading names the church as sacrament of unity and affirms a wide understanding of liturgical renewal, so that the sacramental life can be accessible to all.

The third Rule praises the prayer of the church for all occasions. A rereading notes the need for church renewal based on faith, individual and communal spirituality, and a holiness that transforms the world.

The fourth Rule praises religious life and marriage in a hierarchical order. A rereading affirms the many charisms in the church where holiness is lived out in a variety of lifestyles, while rejecting the former concepts of higher and lower states of life.

The fifth Rule praises the religious vows as a way to perfection. A rereading would affirm the worth of various states of life to highlight the deeper value of intentional Christian living and discipleship rooted in baptismal commitment.

The sixth Rule praises the saints and devotional practices. A rereading confirms the importance of the community of saints in a pilgrim church and values the diversity of their religious expression.

The seventh Rule praises fasting and interior and exterior penances. A rereading affirms the value of spiritual disciplines as formative for Christian life.

Decision

The eighth Rule praises church architecture and decoration as well as religious signs and symbols that produce prayer and devotion. A rereading values the sacramental and symbolic aspect of worship, recognizing the whole person at prayer.

The ninth Rule praises the teaching of the church and encourages defense rather than attack. A rereading affirms Vatican II and other contemporary statements of faith as human articulations of a search for truth and life in the process of dialogue between the church and the world.

The tenth Rule speaks of approval of superiors and prudence in the manner of criticism. A rereading encourages leadership in the church and reminds all the responsibility to represent their needs and concerns to persons responsible.

The eleventh Rule speaks of theology and its role in understanding the mystery of God's person and work among God's people. A rereading encourages a variety of theological voices from both the center and the margins—all remaining in creative tension with one another and thereby illuminating the dynamic mystery of God, ever at work among us.

The twelfth Rule concerns comparing the living with the saints. A contemporary rereading discourages holding up present-day persons and practices for adulation in such a way as to disparage past peoples and traditions.

The thirteenth Rule concerns the willing suspension of belief in sense data when it conflicts with the mystery of God's revelation. A contemporary rereading stresses the ability of the Holy Spirit to work with even discordant and discrepant perceptions, drawing deeper unity and expressing deeper truth, and trusts that the Holy Spirit works in the church beyond individual perceptions and constructions.

The fourteenth Rule names the tension between God's prevenient grace and human free will. A contemporary rereading encourages speaking and writing of these two mysteries in a way that upholds both.

The fifteenth Rule speaks of the pastoral problems involved in the doctrine of predestination. A contemporary rereading suggests avoiding either pessimism to the point of despair or presumption that one can become transformed purely through personal efforts.

The sixteenth Rule speaks about the paradox of faith and good works. A contemporary rereading stresses that both are gifts of God and one completes the other.

The seventeenth Rule addresses the paradox of grace and free will. A contemporary rereading underscores using freedom of choice to select, from among the various means of development available, those most suitable while recognizing that the Holy Spirit empowers our very desire to choose.

The eighteenth Rule speaks of the motivations involved in serving God. A contemporary rereading encourages the recognition that motives for serving God are always mixed and gratefulness that God brings good out of our confused and conflicted desires.

Conclusion

From this somewhat extensive investigation of the images and dynamic role of the church in Ignatius's life, in the text and in the experience of contemporary women, one may draw some tentative conclusions about the place of church in discernment, election, and ultimately the whole experience of the Spiritual Exercises.

First, plural ecclesiologies suggest that the church is a rich and dynamic mystery that resists being reduced either to one ecclesiology or one metaphor. This variety of images and ecclesiologies itself creates a dynamic tension in which all inescapably live out their spiritual lives.

Second, encountering the mystery of church is inevitable in the one making the Exercises, as church is integrally associated with bringing about the reign of Christ, the apostolic dynamism nourished by the Exercises.

Third, the impulse of contemporary times, and a positive sign in personal discernment, is toward widening the circle of dialogue, attentiveness, and affection. Discernment is deepened and enriched as it includes more persons. In this way, one comes closer to the mystery of church, though how that is embodied in an institutional form may vary widely.

Fourth, the Rules for Thinking with the Church, conditioned by time and particular controversies, challenge women and men today more by the positive, committed, faithful attitude they call for than by any doctrinal or devotional perspectives.

Finally, this dynamic and faithful attitude coexists with a continuing struggle for the integrity of the church in all its manifestations. A critique issuing from love and commitment to the church empowers each person to work for its renewal and transformation. We are the church.

Appendix

AnyWoman: An Imaginative Reappropriation of the Spiritual Exercises

Ignatius says: "Imagine the place." Countless persons following his direction have encountered the holy through sensory imagination: seeing, hearing, smelling, tasting and touching the memory of biblical and personal stories. This application of the senses provides strong and vivid summary contemplations for each week of the Spiritual Exercises.

We say: "Imagine any woman's experience of the Spiritual Exercises." Our feminist consciousness challenged us not only to critique and reclaim the Spiritual Exercises for contemporary women, but also to offer something new and creative for the profit of all. So we explored ways to re-create, reenvision, and reimagine alternative means of sensing the mystery of God contained in the Spiritual Exercises. By imagining a woman, pilgrim and seeker living the dynamics of the Exercises, using her own language and familiar symbols from her world, we discovered AnyWoman. We offer a creative summary, our "application of the senses," a way of repetition and reviewing the Exercises through the lens of women's experience.

AnyWoman is a modern morality play inspired by medieval drama. The medieval style allows us to personify abstract qualities through imagined characters in action and to tighten and condense mythic realities into a simple text and familiar characters. Conflict resides not so much in external action and events as in the interior struggle of making life choices.

The Spiritual Exercises Reclaimed

Although the language and style may appear unfamiliar, even jarring, compared to contemporary conversation, we hope our readers will engage in this dramatic piece as a way to discover the dynamics of the Spiritual Exercises. An imaginative perspective breaks out of the language of the text and uncovers meaning deeper than words; imagination suggests rather than literally describes. What is left unsaid may be far more important than the actual words of the script.

Our drama is best read aloud, in community. We hope that the characters and their qualities, AnyWoman, Wise Woman, Discernment, Senses, Examen, Principle and Foundation, Grace, Eve, Memory, Intellect, Imagination, Will, Election and Joy will enliven contemporary seekers and deepen their spiritual practices. We trust the reader will recognize AnyWoman's journey converging with her own. We have found that to be true already as we share our recent experience.

What We Did and Why

Imagine a group of forty persons (women and men) making or directing the Spiritual Exercises. These persons have been together for nine months as participants in the adaptation of the Spiritual Exercises called Retreat in Daily Life. Both directors and those making the retreat gathered at year's end for a day's retreat to deepen and integrate the experience of the Exercises in a communal context. In previous years the culminating activity of the program included four talks on each of the four weeks followed by personal and group reflection and sharing. This time we offered the play *AnyWoman* to assist retreatants in reviewing and deepening the graces of the year. Each of the four scenes from the play stimulated the "memory" of each week. The actors in this reader's theater presentation were the directors of the Spiritual Exercises. They assumed the roles with scripts in hand and a few significant props strategically placed. They read aloud with feeling and understanding while emphasizing those aspects of the play having special meaning for this particular group of retreatants.

The staging was simple and flexible in a large space with various "stations" for each scene. The journey image came to life as main characters AnyWoman and Wise Woman, moved from one space to another gathering characters, "friends," who joined them along the way.

Appendix

Thus the exterior journey became a metaphor for the interior spiritual journey of each retreatant during the year.

At the beginning of the morning, we prepared the group for the drama as a unique way of experiencing the Spiritual Exercises. First, we introduced the cast of characters and the various settings, encouraging the retreatants to be open to the portrayal of each character. Then they were invited to recall their own personal experience of the Exercises: their journey, their spiritual guide/director, their graces and significant movements, their struggles, their choices and their joys. Thus their own experience of the Spiritual Exercises provided the background and disposition for watching the drama unfold on stage.

The retreatants were then encouraged to activate their imaginations by the following suggestions: "See the characters on their journey, imagine the place and its environment. Hear the variety of sounds in the voices of each character. Smell the odors and fragrances in the air and atmosphere. Taste the foods mentioned in the dialogue. Feel what it would be like to walk in the shoes of each character. Allow yourself to respond as you walk through the Exercises with these characters, utilizing your memory and imagination, letting this moment lead you to prayer, the Ignatian colloquy."

The retreatants gathered in movable chairs that allowed them to follow as the actors progressed to various "stations." After each scene the retreatants were invited to take some personal quiet time to reflect on questions related to each week and draw on the memory of their own prayer, naming their own personal graces of that particular week. This process of repetition through imaginative re-creation culminated in a deeper level of knowing and claiming their own experience.

The final activity of the retreat day was a eucharistic celebration. The Jesuit presider (who read the role of Imagination in the play) reminded us all at the beginning of liturgy that "Imagination is the heart of the Exercises." Symbols from each of the characters and the four weeks provided the environment for the Eucharist as we all circled the altar.

What Happened as a Result

At the conclusion of the day both retreatants and directors were enthusiastic and affirming in their responses. Some said it brought together their whole year's experience in an integrated and deeper way. Another noted that, as a young person coming from a visual culture, it helped her to see the characters in action. Seeing the dynamics of the Exercises enacted made them even more real for the retreatants and directors.

Directors particularly noted the deepening and refreshing values of the drama experience. One noted: "Acting out this very simple but powerful play was more meaningful than any closure dialogue we could have had. *AnyWoman* provided a timely, prayerful and playful way to conclude the retreat." Another noted that her retreatants were able to remember and articulate their own personal prayer experiences: "As they watched and felt along with AnyWoman they were reliving their own experience." Others described their experience as: "Powerful, emotional, spiritual, awesome." Another realized that terms such as "discernment" and "imagination" took on new meaning as well as revealing something missed earlier in the retreat. One director commented afterward: "I saw before me not just the memory of the Four Weeks but I envisioned the Exercises becoming a whole unified tapestry displayed before us. I felt a deep sense of gratitude to be part of the drama, for we (directors and retreatants) can all recognize AnyWoman in ourselves."

Somebody asked us, "What would Ignatius say about all this?" We think Ignatius would approve, for he knew that truth is deeper than words. He was a visionary who knew the power of imagination, a man unafraid to be moved to tears, a man who valued reason, will and imagination, a man who knew the reality of human embodiment for felt knowledge leads to great desires, and a man who desired freedom for people that they might do great things for God.

Now we invite you to cross the threshold into the world of the imagination and *AnyWoman* and see for yourself.

AnyWoman

Scene One

STORYTELLER: Good day and welcome. Here begins a story of God and AnyWoman, who is precious in God's sight. On their journey together, God gifts AnyWoman with many friends, each a messenger and unique reflection of Godself. One day AnyWoman sets out on a quest, following her questions: "How do I name and claim my true

Appendix

self? How and with whom am I in relationship? How deeply can I commit myself? How can I live a life of love and service more fully?"

Carrying her questions, she first followed a sign called "Faith" although she felt waves of strange uncertainty as she became more conscious of the weight of her questions. Before long, she saw a figure walking ahead of her. She ran to catch up, seeking company. She soon discovered her companion was an old woman whose strong, peaceful presence calmed her. They walked in silence for a while.

ANYWOMAN: Who are you? Where are you going?

WISE WOMAN: Why do you ask?

ANYWOMAN: I am seeking someone wise enough to show me how to care for my questions as I carry them.

WISE WOMAN: How far are you willing to walk and how sturdy are your sandals?

ANYWOMAN: I am willing to walk as long and as far as my questions take me to discover the true meaning of my life. My sandals are new; see how sturdy they are. You look as though you have walked many pathways and pondered many of life's questions. I need someone to walk and talk with me. Will you accompany me, guide me, be a friend and mentor, a companion on the way?

WISE WOMAN: I will walk with you, but you must let your own questions and desires direct you. You will also need some other companions for your journey. They will appear when you need them. Each has something special to offer you. None is more important than she who is behind us now. How frequently we forget her and what wisdom she has to offer if we but call upon her and patiently wait for her. Her name is Memory.

MEMORY: Good day, AnyWoman. I will serve you as you call upon me. In my book I hold your story, all the experiences of your life 'til now, the brokenness and the blessings, the happy and the sad, the wise and the foolish, the finished and the incomplete. I also hold the treasured stories of all the people of your family, by blood and faith, the sacred stories told from generation to generation, those remembered and those forgotten. I will walk as your companion and you can call upon me as you need me.

ANYWOMAN: Thank you, Memory. Sometimes I do forget what is important. I must remember to remember.

WISE WOMAN: In order to know what is important in all life experiences past and present, you need another companion to assist you, a precious one, Discernment.

DISCERNMENT: Greetings, AnyWoman! I will walk with you and help you choose pathways leading you to what you most desire. Yet, to walk with me demands that you pay attention. You need to note all that moves you toward joy or sadness and all that draws you toward goodness and light—or the appearance of light. To profit from my companionship you must learn to be attentive to every moment of your life. Here are more companions who will aid you in this task.

SENSES: I can see, I can hear, I can smell, I can taste, I can touch. What a great gift your senses are for you! What a gift your body is for you: a way of life for communicating with all creation, other persons and God. AnyWoman, how can you taste and see the goodness of God if you haven't enjoyed the color and delicious sweetness of strawberries or the mellowness of a fine wine?

EXAMEN: Wait, don't forget me! I'm here to remind you, AnyWoman, of those moments and movements of everyday that have meaning for you, more than you realize. Each day of your life is like a book, to reveal to you the truth of the mystery of your own life, the blessings and challenges of each day, the sources of your own truth and temptations of falsehood, the lies of your life. But most of all I am your reminder of the graciousness of God, sometimes hidden, sometimes revealed, but always present in the dailyness of life.

WISE WOMAN: Now, AnyWoman, with these companions to assist you, you must continue your journey by standing still. You must plant your feet firmly on the ground, feeling the earth between your toes, casting your eyes to the boundless sky above your head. You must claim your own perspective—where you stand determines what you see. An infant crawling on the ground has a different view of the world than a child sitting in the high branches of a tree beside a river. You must place before your mind's eye the questions with which you began your journey. "How do I name and claim my true self, my relationships, my commitment, my future?" Take time to ponder: What does life mean to you? How do you see your life in relationship to creation: to all the earth and its life, including human persons, female and male? How do you see your relationship with God? Who is God for you? And how is all this life interconnected?

Appendix

ANYWOMAN: But how do I begin to do this?

WISE WOMAN: Well, let me introduce you to the twins, Principle and Foundation. They are identical. You can't tell them apart except that one carries a shovel and the other a watering can. You see, wherever they go they are trying to plant and nourish seeds of truth and life, helping the roots to grow strong and deep. They will most often appear when anxiety or doubt or fear plague you. Their job is always to see that you are grounded in the truth of who you are and who God is.

PRINCIPLE AND FOUNDATION: Good travels to you, AnyWoman! Here is a gift for your journey. It is a walking staff called Indifference. This staff will support you as you weigh your decisions and allow you to walk with energy and purpose toward your goal.

WISE WOMAN: Now, AnyWoman, to set out on this journey you must compose yourself with the help of these companions and know clearly what you desire.

ANYWOMAN: Oh, Wise Woman, now I feel confused and uncertain. How can I know what I want?

GRACE: Perhaps I can help you, AnyWoman. My name is Grace and I will help you ask for what you truly need. Here is a bracelet for you to wear with beads of various shapes and colors. You will find that each bead holds a gift for you. Just let me know when you are ready.

ANYWOMAN: Thank you, Grace; all of a sudden I hardly feel like myself. In the company of so much goodness and so many friends to help me, I feel ashamed and confused. This journey seems too hard and asks too much. And I don't find God in any of this. Perhaps I should turn back. I wonder if I really want to set out on this journey, and besides my feet are hurting.

WISE WOMAN: Ah! I feel the movement of the enemy of human nature close by, perhaps in those shadows by the side of the road. And where is God? Pay attention, AnyWoman, to the desires deep in your heart; you will discover God. Now you must trust me. Your journey is already underway. Trust that your questions will lead you. But it is getting dark and it is time to rest. I bless you AnyWoman. Be attentive to God's visitations this evening.

STORYTELLER: The night passes and the day dawns.

ANYWOMAN: Wise one, awake! I must tell you of a dream I had last night. I saw a struggle, a cosmic conflict between the angels, beings of such beauty and power. I watched in awe and felt within myself that I was being drawn right into their struggle. Before the Holy One of such light and love, each had to choose and name its allegiance. I felt a force within me drawn first to one then to the other. At a final moment I found myself surrounded by those whose "No" to light and love thrust them into darkness and a terrible abyss. I too was falling, falling…. Then I awakened. What does this dream mean?

WISE WOMAN: That is for you to discover. Walk a while with Memory and Discernment; perhaps they can help you understand.

STORYTELLER: So AnyWoman walks on ahead, talking, listening, pondering in the company of her new friends. A little later their conversation is interrupted as they pass a fruit stand and a pleasant middle-aged woman calls out.

EVE: Apples, fresh apples for your journey! Red, yellow and green, many colors for many tastes. Stop a while and refresh yourselves! This fruit of the earth captures the sunlight in its shiny skin and delicious taste, while its juice will quench your thirst.

ANYWOMAN: Let's stop here and try some. Where did you come from?

EVE: My name is Eve, and this is Eve's Stand. Now, don't jump to conclusions and run away. Others may have told you about me; but let me speak for myself. I am a woman, mother of the living, created in God's image along with my partner Adam. The two of us were equal in God's eyes, from the beginning. I made a mistake—that's evidence of being human, isn't it? But I am not my mistake. The real mistake, the original sin, is whatever destroys the equal balance of relationships. God's original plan intended partnership: humans with the earth, women with men, persons with God. I am Eve, and the God I know who created and loves me understands that human beings make mistakes. And God is gracious and forgiving. What is most important is God's love, not my mistake. Don't blame me for the whole world's sin.

ANYWOMAN: Sin! Maybe that was what my dream was about. Maybe sin is about struggle for power, dominion and deception. Maybe sin blinds me to who I am really meant to be. There are times in my life when I feel as if all I am doing is playing a role, sometimes to fit another person's expectations of me and other times to take the easy way out: roles of niceness, passivity, silence, helper, manipulator, victim, peacemaker, beauty queen, superwoman. It's painful to remember how the power of these roles can take over my life. It feels like…hell. I used to say I didn't believe in hell. But if I'm honest, there are moments in my life I'd call "hell." These are only tiny glimpses of the "hells" human beings have created for one another. The story of humankind can be read as a cycle of dominating and deceiving one another expressed in all kinds of violence. How can there be a God when life can be such hell?

WISE WOMAN: Look at the sun, it can warm or burn you; taste the water, it can refresh or poison you; breathe the air, it can strengthen or strangle you; feel the earth, it can nurture or starve you. Human freedom, it can liberate or destroy you! AnyWoman, your only choice is how you live your life right now. At this moment you are *here*.

SENSES: Open your eyes to look around at the beauty of creation. Open your ears to sounds and silence. Feel your heartbeat and the air in your lungs…you are ALIVE.

MEMORY: Remember all the people in your life who have cared for you, who are important to you…you are LOVED.

EVE: You are a woman, created, loved and forgiven by God.

WISE WOMAN: All is gift. You can choose how you wish to respond. What is your deepest desire?

ANYWOMAN: Where are you, God, and who are you? An apple falls and the earth's cushion breaks the fall. A small bird's melody is answered from a distant treetop. The stream rushes by filled with glistening fish. A mother gives birth and holds her tiny infant to her breast. All creation praises you for the gift of life, and so do I. I who am AnyWoman. All these gifts of creation are signs of your love and presence to me. O God, who am I to be surrounded by such love? I have ignored you, doubted you and forgotten the stories of your faithful love for all creation. I have looked by myself for answers to my questions and forgotten you, the source of truth and love. You have called me by name, "AnyWoman." I am precious, and you love me—thank you!

Scene Two

STORYTELLER: Scene two—It is midday the next day. AnyWoman and Wise Woman are continuing their journey together and they come to a crossroads.

WISE WOMAN: Well, AnyWoman, now you need to choose what direction to take. The path to the right will return home, and you can conclude your journey. Or you may continue down the road we are on.

ANYWOMAN: I've learned a lot about myself and my questions. It would be easier to return to where I've come from. This might be a good place to conclude our journey. But there is a restlessness within me, an unfinished feeling, a sense that there is more to this journey. (Pause) Look, by the side of the road up ahead. There is something glittering, caught between the stones of that old wall. Let's continue down this road to see what is there. Look, it's an old locket…

WISE WOMAN:…with an inscription of an ancient royal crest still visible. It reminds me of the story from long ago about a mighty king and queen and their royal partnership. This royal couple, so the story goes, were kind and generous, leaders for their people, brave and wise. They called forth those to serve and struggle with them to establish a reign of peace and justice for all people. Among the most courageous and committed of their followers was a woman who defied the customs of her times by leaving her comfortable and secure life to join the royal supporters. She was revered for her intelligence and compassionate heart. She gave all her energy and passion to the struggle to bring about the vision they shared, royalty and commoner together.

ANYWOMAN: Oh, how I too would like to live life like that! I want to live with courage. I want to make a difference. I want to join others bringing it about. I want to give my life to someone or something I really believe in.

STORYTELLER: As they continue, Wise Woman begins to sing a chant under her breath:

WISE WOMAN: Mary, Theotokos, we remember you, be with us
   Miriam, we remember you, be with us
   Mary of Magdala, we remember you, be with us
   Phoebe, we remember you, be with us
   Thecla, we remember you, be with us
   Macrina, we remember you, be with us
   Egeria, we remember you, be with us
   Helena, we remember you, be with us

Appendix

    Lioba, we remember you, be with us
    Hildegard, we remember you, be with us
    Julian, we remember you, be with us
    Elizabeth, we remember you, be with us
    Catherine, we remember you, be with us
    Teresa, we remember you, be with us
    Mary Ward, we remember you, be with us
    Ann Lee, we remember you, be with us
    Kateri Tekakwitha, we remember you, be with us
    Sojourner Truth, we remember you, be with us
    Dorothy Day, we remember you, be with us

ANYWOMAN: What are you mumbling along the way?

WISE WOMAN: It is my litany of courageous women, women who lived and struggled for a vision: I call them our mothers in faith. They all followed a "King," the Messiah, the Prince of Peace, Emmanuel, Jesus, son of Mary of Nazareth.

ANYWOMAN: I know the stories of Jesus, but they seem so long ago, so distant. What could they contribute to my search now?

STORYTELLER: As AnyWoman fingers the beads on her bracelet, Grace appears.

GRACE: All you need to ask for is that the stories of Jesus will lead you to know him more deeply and follow him more closely.

WISE WOMAN: Look ahead, an old church. Let's go inside and sit down. At this time of day the colors of the sun will shine right through the stained glass.

ANYWOMAN: Who are those figures moving about in the front of the church?

WISE WOMAN: Those are the craftspersons and artisans waiting to serve you. Their names are Intellect, Imagination and Will. Their job is to assist you to see and understand the mystery hidden in the stained-glass windows. Then you can choose the part you want to play in the continuing story.

ANYWOMAN: I don't understand. None of this makes sense to me.

INTELLECT: Sit down here by the first window and think about what you see.

ANYWOMAN: It reminds me of a scene on a Christmas card.

The Spiritual Exercises Reclaimed

MEMORY: And when you were a little girl…

ANYWOMAN: I had forgotten; I played a shepherd in the Christmas play. I remember it was just as though I were really there. And what is that next window?…Up there next to you, Imagination.

IMAGINATION: With my eye I see Mary, Elizabeth, Anna, Martha, Mary, Mary of Magdala, Widow of Naim, bent over woman, woman with the hemorrhage, daughter of Jairus, Samaritan woman…

ANYWOMAN: Where do you see them? I've looked all around this church. I didn't see any of those women in the windows. Where are they?

IMAGINATION: They are hidden in the glass. You must imagine them into the scene with Jesus, for they are also his friends and disciples. Their stories are part of your story; you must continue to look for them everywhere.

WILL: And when you discover them, let them speak to you, in ways that touch your heart.

STORYTELLER: So AnyWoman engages Intellect, Imagination and Will in an animated and lengthy conversation. Time passes as the sun begins to set and the color of the windows changes in the shadows.

WISE WOMAN: AnyWoman, it is getting late in the day. We must move on.

ANYWOMAN: Oh! Can't we stay longer? It's so peaceful and quiet here. There are so many untold stories of Jesus: by the lake and walking through the fields, talking with people, healing them. We haven't seen them all. And Intellect, Imagination, Will and I were talking about building a new church with women's windows, too.

WISE WOMAN: But even Jesus had to move on. There came a moment when Jesus needed to decide. When he did, he turned to walk toward Jerusalem.

ANYWOMAN: Oh, how I hate to make decisions. It always means giving up something. It's always risky. Suppose I make a mistake? How can I be sure what God is calling me to? Sometimes I feel I should move in one direction; other times I feel pulled in the opposite direction. It makes me dizzy.

WISE WOMAN: What you need is balance, a way to measure your steps as you learn to walk in God's ways. But now, judging from who is

Appendix

standing at the door of the church, God is calling you to dance. Look who just arrived; it's Election, the dancing teacher.

ELECTION: I am the one who is the interpreter of movement and the teacher of various steps. You will need your staff of Indifference at all times. But I will teach you various steps for each partner: one type for Intellect, another for Will, a specific step for Memory and yet another for Senses and Imagination. Whatever the movement, I, Election, will be there to assist you to learn the steps you need for the dance that will move you toward God who calls you.

WISE WOMAN: You didn't think this journey would just involve walking, did you?

Scene Three

STORYTELLER: Scene three takes place late in the day and AnyWoman and Wise Woman are crossing a bridge.

ANYWOMAN: Can't we rest awhile? I'm tired and it's getting dark.

WISE WOMAN: I, too, would like to pause and let this night pass, but it is the darkness that we must enter. Come walk by my side. Here it is important that we journey together.

ANYWOMAN: Your voice is serious and sad; it makes me feel afraid.

WISE WOMAN: It is a time for fear, the kind of fear that only love can overcome. But listen. I hear the sound of water. Look, there is a stream. Let us pause and let the water refresh us. Here, AnyWoman, drink from this cup, and then take off your sandals and let me wash your feet.

ANYWOMAN: Oh, no, I can't let you do that. I should be washing yours.

WISE WOMAN: Just rest and receive; your time of service will come soon enough.

ANYWOMAN: It's getting so dark. I can hardly see you now. Where are you? Are you still close by?

WISE WOMAN: Yes, don't be afraid. Can you come and pray one hour with me?

ANYWOMAN: Of course, but my eyes are heavy, the night is so dark, I haven't eaten, and the travel today has tired me. Oh, I almost stumbled over this mound of earth. I can't see, but it feels like something is buried underneath. It feels like a mask, only part of it is burned. How curious. I wonder whose masks these were and what they mean?

WISE WOMAN: This discovery of yours, AnyWoman, reminds me that masks invite us to cross a threshold into mystery, for masks reveal a special kind of story. When one puts on a mask, the wearer shares the power of the story it represents, whatever its sentiments. Masks make visible the inner creative spirit of the human mind and heart. Are you ready? Here put this one on.

STORYTELLER: Wise Woman hands her the Jesus mask to put on.

ANYWOMAN: My Father, if it is possible, let this cup pass from me; yet not as I will, but as you will.

STORYTELLER: Immediately she pulls off the mask and places it at her feet.

ANYWOMAN: No, it's too much. You can't ask that of me. Let me try on another.

STORYTELLER: The old woman offers her many masks: Peter, the serving girl, Pilate's wife, Pilate, soldier. Tentatively AnyWoman chooses the mask of the crowd and places it over her face.

ANYWOMAN: Hail King of the Jews! Crucify Him!

STORYTELLER: She quickly takes off the mask and cries aloud:

ANYWOMAN: How could they? He was so good. I don't know what to do. I need the grace to go on, to enter the mystery of this mask.

STORYTELLER: As she fingers a bead on her bracelet, Grace appears again.

GRACE: If you hold the bead of Compassion, AnyWoman, you will have the ability to feel with, to just be with, the pain and the suffering. Here is your mask.

STORYTELLER: She hands AnyWoman the Jesus mask again.

WISE WOMAN: What do you see, AnyWoman, through the eyes of this mask?

ANYWOMAN: I see the homeless, the starving, refugees, abused women and children. I see people killing other people. I see the land dying from drought and the forests burning. The people, the whole planet is suffering and crying out to God in pain: "My God, my God, why have you forsaken me? O God, into your hands I commend my spirit."

STORYTELLER: The wise woman watches and waits at a distance.

Appendix

Scene Four

STORYTELLER: Scene four: The sun is rising. AnyWoman awakens, blinking with the light in her eyes.

ANYWOMAN: Where am I? It's a garden, with stream and rocks and beautiful flowers and trees. There is the sun just coming up over the distant hills. I hear the whir of a hummingbird's wings, I see fresh dew and smell the fragrance of the rose petals. And look! A beautiful butterfly bursting forth from its bindings. This day feels different. Something is new. And there is a new bead on my bracelet; I never noticed it before.

GRACE: Here I am again, but this time to celebrate with you, to be glad and rejoice. I also want you to meet my special friend. She is a musician and her name is Joy.

JOY: (singing) Morning has broken…

How can I keep from singing?…

Jesu Joy of our desiring…

Alleluia! The strife is over, the battle done…

I know my redeemer lives…

WISE WOMAN: I hear singing, so early in the morning. It must be Joy arriving to join us on our journey.

JOY: There is good news in the town. A mother has just been reunited with her son. She thought he was lost and now he is found. People have been arriving from all over telling stories of meeting him along their way. The whole town is rejoicing.

WISE WOMAN: You go along into the town, AnyWoman, for now I must be on my way. Share with the people the treasures of your journey.

STORYTELLER: As AnyWoman continues to the edge of town she is excited but a little apprehensive.

ANYWOMAN: Where am I? This looks strangely familiar, as though I've been here before. Those people *are* my neighbors. I'm home! I've never seen life like this before. My questions have led me home, and yet I know everything in a new way. It's beautiful! Everywhere I look, it is as though God dwells in all things, the rays coming from the sun, the rain falling from the clouds, all as gift. Look there is a rainbow arching over the whole town. I am so grateful. God, take and receive all I have and possess—all the friends and gifts you've given to me: Wise Woman, Memory, Discernment, Senses, Intellect, Imagination, Will, Joy, all the Graces of this journey. Everything I have and possess you've given to me, and now I want to return all to you. Do with these friends as you wish. Share them with others who also journey. All I ask and desire now, O God, is your love and your grace. You are enough for me.

WISE WOMAN: Good-bye—until we meet the next time.

Epilogue

STORYTELLER: Thus concludes the story of AnyWoman. Since you now have met her and her companions, take to heart what you have learned from her questions: "How do I name and claim my true self? How and with whom am I in relationship? How deeply can I commit myself? How can I live a life of love and service more fully?" Think about the difference this journey makes in your life. For AnyWoman now knows that love and mutual sharing happens through both words and deeds. Speak and act faithfully, with wisdom and courage and compassion. May AnyWoman, Wise Woman and all their friends accompany you.

Notes

Preface to the First Edition

1. The text of the Spiritual Exercises and the process it sets out live deeply in the experience of the members of the Society of Jesus (Jesuits). The conversations about legitimate interpretations, appropriate adaptations, and implications of the Spiritual Exercises have been carried on under the auspices of and largely within Jesuit contexts. Yet the experience of women making the Spiritual Exercises rarely appears in this scholarship.

An examination of the recent English-language bibliography on the Spiritual Exercises by Paul Begheyn and Kenneth Bogart, *Studies in the Spirituality of Jesuits* 23 (May 1991), reveals this lack. Only thirty-six of the 750 entries, or slightly under 5 percent (some works are listed in more than one section of the bibliography), were unambiguously authored or coauthored by women. These include one major biography by Mary Purcell, one translation of the Spiritual Exercises by Elisabeth Tetlow, one coauthored "handbook" on giving the Exercises by Marian Cowan and John Futrell, one five-volume series of retreat exercises based on the Spiritual Exercises by Jacqueline Bergan and Marie Schwan, one dissertation, and twenty-five articles. The vast majority of the 714 remaining works are authored by Jesuits. The bibliography contains no section on Ignatius and women or women and the Spiritual Exercises, presumably because the number of works devoted specifically to this focus does not merit its own section; only three titles specifically refer to women.

The literature about the Spiritual Exercises authored by women has increased in recent years. Two-thirds of the woman-authored works in the Begheyn/Bogart bibliography have appeared since 1980. In addition, the summer 1992 edition of *The Way Supplement* and volume 66 of

Manresa were devoted to women and the Spiritual Exercises, and Anne Carr's *Women Religious and Ignatius Loyola* (Chicago: The Jesuit Community Corporation at Loyola University, 1992) has appeared. Lisa Fullam authored an issue of *Studies in the Spirituality of Jesuits* 31 (November 1999) entitled "Juana, SJ: The Past (and Future?) Status of Women in the Society of Jesus." But the impact and influence of women on the contemporary interpretation of the Spiritual Exercises far exceeds this meager published output.

2. Ignatius's autobiography will follow the translation of Parmananda Divarkar contained in *Ignatius of Loyola: Spiritual Exercises and Selected Works*, ed. George E. Ganss, Classics of Western Spirituality (Mahwah, NJ: Paulist, 1991), 68–111. Citations will be noted in the text as [*Autobiog*, #], following the section numbers used in this edition. Ignatius's correspondence will be cited from *Letters of Ignatius of Loyola*, ed. and trans. William J. Young (Chicago: Loyola University Press, 1959) and Hugo Rahner, *Saint Ignatius Loyola: Letters to Women*, trans. Kathleen Pond and S. A. H. Weetman (Freiburg: Herder KG, 1956; second impression, New York: Herder and Herder, 1960).

3. Of the early versions, the three most important are the Autograph text in Spanish, Ignatius's own copy containing some thirty-two handwritten notations; the early Latin translation of 1534, probably translated by Ignatius himself; and a more stylistic classical Latin translation prepared for Pope Paul III's approval. Both the Latin texts were also used by Ignatius.

4. Ganss's translation employs functional equivalence that allows the reader to grasp the thought accurately and with reasonable ease. It is gender-inclusive in reference to human beings but does employ the masculine pronoun in references to God.

Preface to the Second Edition

1. It is heartening to note that, among its 2020 offerings, Spiritual Directors International (SDI) sponsored a webinar on Ignatian Spirituality and Women led by Sr. Anne Arabome from Nigeria currently teaching in the United States.

2. Philip Endean, "'Applying Such Exercises': Early Jesuit Practice," *Review of Ignatian Spirituality*, 32, no. 3 (2001): 41–65, helpfully clarifies the

distinction between "applying" (the original meaning in Ignatius's text in Annotation 18) and "adapting," which has come to cover all adaptations of the Exercises. In Annotation 18, Ignatius uses the verb form rather than the noun, creating a phrase that sounds awkward in English ("applying such exercises") to suggest that a variety of possibilities exist, and one should "apply such exercises" to meet the individual's desires, context, and needs, even if the resulting palette does not resemble the pattern of the full Exercises as elaborated in Annotation 20.

3. Among the plethora of resources that have emerged since 2001 are new presentations aimed at guiding a wide variety of people through the Exercises in the Daily Life format ("19th Annotation"). Online versions of the Exercises, e.g., may be found at the following two sites: http://www.ignatianspirituality.com/ignatian-prayer/the-spiritual-exercises/an-ignatian-prayer-adventure and http://onlineministries.creighton.edu/CollaborativeMinistry/cmo-retreat.html.

See also Kevin O'Brien, SJ, *The Ignatian Adventure: Experiencing the Spiritual Exercises in Daily Life* (Chicago: Loyola Press, 2000). Between online and print versions, O'Brien's text is probably the most frequently used introduction and guide to the Spiritual Exercises in Everyday Life (the "19th Annotation retreat"). Larry Warner, *Journey with Jesus: Discovering the Spiritual Exercises of Saint Ignatius* (Downers Grove, IL: InterVarsity, 2010) introduces and guides the Spiritual Exercises in such a way that evangelically oriented Christians will find approachable, as does James L Wakefield, *Sacred Listening: Discovering the Spiritual Exercises of Ignatius of Loyola* (Grand Rapids: Baker, 2006). Brandon Peck, "A Lutheran Adaptation of the Spiritual Exercises of St. Ignatius," paper prepared for SP 4042 Spiritual Exercises in Context, Jesuit School of Theology of Santa Clara University, Berkeley, CA, December 2018, creates a Lutheran-friendly adaptation of the Spiritual Exercises.

Other recent sources provide commentary and further resources to aid in internalizing the Spiritual Exercises, including the following general introductions: Philip Endean, "The Spiritual Exercises," in *The Cambridge Companion to the Jesuits*, ed. Thomas Worcester (New York: Cambridge University Press, 2008), 52–67; Elizabeth Liebert, "Ignatius of Loyola (1491–1556), The Spiritual Exercises," in *Christian Spirituality: The Classics*, ed. Arthur Holder (New York: Routledge, 2010), 195–208; Ignacio Ellacuría, SJ, "A Latin-American Reading of the *Spiritual Exercises* of St. Ignatius," *Spiritus* 10, no.2 (Fall 2010): 205–42, with an introduction by J. Matthew Ashley, "A Contemplative under the Standard of Christ:

Ignacio Ellacuria's Interpretation of Ignatius of Loyola's Spiritual Exercises," 192–204. Roger Haight's *Christian Spirituality for Seekers: Reflections on the Spiritual Exercises of Ignatius Loyola* (Maryknoll, NY: Orbis, 2012) constructs an anthropology and Christology that take into consideration a widely diversified population of seekers from a thoroughly secularized North American urban context, Christian and beyond, as well as those dropping out of any religious practice because it no longer has meaning for them.

Book-length general introductions include William Barry, *Letting God Come Close: An Approach to the Ignatian Spiritual Exercises* (Chicago: Loyola Press, 2001); George A. Aschenbrenner, *Stretched for Greater Glory: What to Expect from the Spiritual Exercises* (Chicago: Loyola Press, 2004); David Fleming, *Like the Lightning: The Dynamics of the Ignatian Exercises* (St. Louis: Institute of Jesuit Sources, 2004); Willi Lambert, *The Sevenfold Yes: Affirming the Goodness of Our Deepest Desires* (Notre Dame, IN: Ave Maria Press, 2005); and Paul Kiti, ed., *Dynamics of the Spiritual Exercises: African Perspectives* (Nairobi: Paulines Publications, 2005).

Taking seriously the applications that Ignatius suggests in the Annotation 18 [SE 18]: Michael Hansen, *The First Spiritual Exercises: Four Guided Retreats* (Notre Dame, IN: Ave Maria Press, 2013) constructs four eight-week prayer experiences based on the dynamic of the Exercises. See also John Sassani and Mary Ann McLaughlin, *Meeting Christ in Prayer: An 8-Week Life-Enriching Experience Based on the Spiritual Exercises of St. Ignatius* (Chicago: Loyola Press, 2008) and Dan Schutte, *Walking the Sacred Path: Spiritual Exercises for Today* (New London, CT: Twenty-Third Publications, 2009). This latter is based "loosely" on the Spiritual Exercises in simple, prayerful language.

Other adaptations seek to connect persons or movements abroad in the culture, e.g., Louis M. Savary, *The New Spiritual Exercises: In the Spirit of Pierre Teilhard de Chardin* (Mahwah, NJ: Paulist Press, 2010); Neil Vaney, *Christ in a Grain of Sand: An Ecological Journey with the Spiritual Exercises* (Notre Dame, IN: Ave Maria Press, 2004); and John Pungente and Monty Williams, *Finding God in the Dark: Taking the Spiritual Exercises to the Movies* (Ottawa: Novalis, 2004).

4. See also Ali Chavoshian and Jun Eun Sophia Park, who alert us to the deep power of language in "Listening Not in Spiritual Direction: A Lacanian Inkling," *Presence: An International Journal of Spiritual Direction* 25, no. 2 (June 2019): 8: "When a subject speaks, it is impossible for her to be free from the frame of language, embedded as the subject is

Notes

in a culture of family relationships and a society"; and Joohyung Lee, "The Discerned Choice for East Asian Christian Spirituality: Korean Approach" (PhD diss., Claremont School of Theology, 2015), esp. chap. 1, in which Lee clearly illustrates the intersectional connection between culture and gender, though he does not isolate gender as his primary category.

Chapter 1

1. For a discussion of various aspects of this problem, see Elisabeth Schüssler Fiorenza, "Toward a Feminist Biblical Hermeneutic," in *The Challenge of Liberation Theology*, ed. Brian Mahan and L. Dale Richesin (Maryknoll, NY: Orbis Books, 1981); Anne Carr (1988), esp. chap. 8, "Feminism and Christology," and Elizabeth Johnson (1992), esp. chap. 8, "Jesus-Sophia."

2. While women in some parts of the world may be grappling with issues of lack of inclusion in some ministries in the church, for others, especially on the African continent, the struggles may be on the level not only of their church experience but also economically and socially. There is perhaps a wider spectrum of experience than twenty years ago, with women in some cultures now having more freedom and others struggling with basic survival needs. Women in places like Norway and Canada enjoy equal rights and more equitable pay between men and women, while in some parts of the world women are still struggling for the right to be educated. Some who come to make the Exercises are refugees or migrants, further compounding their ability to participate in the Exercises.

3. See Andrew Dreitcer, *Becoming Compassion: Loving Like Jesus* (Nashville: Upper Room Books, 2017) for a series of exercises to grow in the ability to pay attention and honor one's own experience and that of another.

4. This value was also reported by women in our consultations. One person, however, felt that the Spiritual Exercises would be constraining to persons in the habit of what she called contemplative prayer, presumably meaning quiet, imageless prayer. See also Jacqueline Hawkins, "Foreword," *The Way Supplement* 74 (Summer 1992): 3–6.

5. See, e.g., Jean Baker Miller, "Toward a New Psychology of Women," in *Women's Spirituality: Resources for Christian Development*, ed. Joann Wolski Conn (Mahwah, NJ: Paulist, 1986), 116. Baker's analysis

reveals the underlying systemic oppression that contributes to women's collusion in their own oppression in this fashion. She does not intend to blame women for this situation, nor do we.

6. For an accessible overview of the effect of biblical interpretation on women, see Sharon H. Ringe, "When Women Interpret the Bible," in *The Women's Bible Commentary*, ed. Carol A. Newsom and Sharon H. Ringe (Louisville, KY: Westminster John Knox, 1992), 1–9.

7. See Philip Endean, "'Applying Such Exercises': Early Jesuit Practice," *Review of Ignatian Spirituality* 32, no. 3 (2001): 41–64, for a discussion about why *apply* is a more accurate verb than *adapt*.

8. For working with lower socioeconomic backgrounds, see Martha Skinnider, "Who Is the Nineteenth Annotation For?" *The Way Supplement* 49 (Spring 1984): 59–69. On adaptations with Protestants and Jews, see Michael Ivens, "The Eighteenth Annotation and the Early Directories," *The Way Supplement* 46 (Spring 1983): 3–10; Susan Anderson, "Reflections on the Experience of Making and Giving the Exercises," *The Way Supplement* 68 (Summer 1990): 13–21; Linda Mary Evans, "Catholic and Protestant Approaches to the First Week," *The Way Supplement* 68 (Summer 1990): 5–12; Joyce Huggett, "Why Ignatian Spirituality Hooks Protestants," *The Way Supplement* 68 (Summer 1990): 22–33; and Graham Chadwick, "Giving the Exercises and Training Directors in an Ecumenical Context," *The Way Supplement* 68 (Summer 1990): 35–41. On adapting for Buddhists, Confucians, and Taoists, see Aloysius Pieris, "Ignatian Exercises against a Buddhist Background," *The Way Supplement* 68 (Summer 1990): 98–111; Lily Quintos, RC, "Experiences of the Heart: The Spiritual Exercises across Cultures," in *Common Journey, Different Paths: Spiritual Direction in Cross-Cultural Perspective*, ed. Susan Rakoczy, IHM (Maryknoll, NY: Orbis Books, 1992), 89–96; and William Reiser, "The Spiritual Exercises in a Religiously Pluralistic World," in *Spiritus: A Journal of Christian Spirituality* 10, no. 2 (2010): 135–57.

9. For South Africa, see especially Annemarie Paulin-Campbell, "The Impact of the Imaginal and Dialogical (Relational) Processes in the Spiritual Exercises, on Image of Self and Image of God in Women Making the Nineteenth Annotation Retreat" (PhD diss., University of KwaZulu-Natal, Pietermaritzburg, South Africa, 2008), references throughout, but see, in particular, the case study of Nthabiseng, 148–61. See also Chikere Ugwuni, "Adaptations of the Spiritual Exercises: An Example from Africa," *The Way* 53, no. 3 (July 2014): 56–67. Frances Correia, Puleng Matsaneng, and Annemarie Paulin-Campbell, "The Training of Spiritual

Notes

Directors in the South African Context," *Spiritus: A Journal of Christian Spirituality* 16, no. 2 (Fall 2016): 39–54; and M. Mdluli, "An African Perspective on Spiritual Direction," *Grace and Truth* 12, no. 1 (1995): 28–31. For Latin America, see Ignacio Ellacuria, SJ, "A Latin American Reading of the Spiritual Exercises of Saint Ignatius," *Spiritus: A Journal of Christian Spirituality* 10, 2 (Fall 2010): 205–42.

10. Sandra Schneiders (1991b, 150), describes a classic text as "one whose subject matter is somehow universal, whose composition is singularly effective, and whose style is beautiful to such an extent that the work is relevant to the human situation as such."

11. Elsewhere in *The Revelatory Text* (1991b, 164–67), Schneiders articulates other principles of valid interpretation to which we subscribe. First, the interpretation meets the standard, "that which cannot be done or must not be left undone." Some interpretive processes cannot be applied to some texts without destroying the obvious sense of the text; others must not be omitted at the risk of deforming the text's meaning. Second, the interpretation is fruitful. An interpretation that "makes the text speak" without violating the canons of good exegesis ought to be taken seriously. Third, valid interpretation is consistent with itself, free from internal contradictions. Fourth, it successfully (or as successfully as its competitors) explains anomalies within the text. Fifth, it is compatible with what is known from other sources. Finally, a valid interpretation should have used responsibly all the methods appropriate within the framework of interpretation chosen.

12. Feminist thought can also function as a decisive critical category for spirituality in general because, as Ursula King (1993, 15) claims, "it challenges and examines the foundations of our language, thought and institutions, our social and political power structures and their hierarchical divisions. In its most radical form, feminism asks what, if anything, in the past and present experience of religion and spirituality remains usable for women today. Reformist feminism, on the other hand, holds that aspects of religion and spirituality may be life-giving, and seeks a new approach to symbols, myths, and rites capable of better expressing the richness of women's experience of God, self, world and cosmos." Clearly, our work follows this reformist feminism.

13. While not dealing directly with the Spiritual Exercises, in May 2020, Fr. General Arturo Sosa called together a task force to review the place of women in Jesuit institutions. This task force's report led Fr. Sosa to establish the Commission on the Role and Responsibilities of Women in

the Society of Jesus. One of its specific tasks is to examine the appropriation of Decree 14 of the General Congregation (hereafter, GC) 34. Beginning its work on March 8, 2021, this commission is to work under its own direction for three years to complete its mandate.

14. Webster's *New Collegiate Dictionary*, 8th ed. (Springfield, MA: G. C. Merriam, 1973). *Female* carries its own inherited problems with meaning; besides referring to the sex that produces eggs and produces *young*, *female* also connotes a hollow into which a corresponding (male) part fits and the unstressed endings in poetry or in music—females are passive, receptive, gentle, unstressed, weak.

15. But, today, gender itself is a contested category. Is it fixed or fluid? Is one born with gender, or can one choose it later in life? What about those children born with ambiguous genitalia?

16. Susan Faludi, *Backlash: The Undeclared War against American Women* (New York: Crown, 1991) describes in vivid detail how the process of naming the contours of the discussion forms and unforms the understanding of "woman" and literally changes women's consciousness of themselves.

17. More recently, Pope Francis's (2015) encyclical *Laudato Si'* has focused attention on interconnectedness of all created reality. See also Elizabeth Johnson, *Ask the Beasts: Darwin and the God of Love* (London: Bloomsbury, 2014, and *Creation and the Cross: The Mercy of God for a Planet in Peril* (Maryknoll, NY: Orbis, 2018).

18. See, e.g., the following chapters: "No Women Need Apply" in Jean Lacouture's *Jesuits: A Multibiography* (Washington, DC: Counterpoint, 1995), and "Women" in Meissner (1992), 238–71. Also see our earlier analysis of the citations in a commonly accessible Ignatian bibliography in the preface, n.1a. An exception to this generalization is José García de Castro Valdés, "Las Mujeres y los Primeros Jesuitas," in *Iguales y Diferentes: Interrelación entre Mujeres y Varones Cristianos a lo Largo de la Historia*, ed. Fernando Rivas (Madrid: San Pablo, 2012), 219–82.

19. See, e.g., Jerome's account of Paula and Eustocium, Gregory of Nyssa's life of his sister Macrina, Raymond of Capua's life of Catherine of Siena, Thomas of Celano's legend of St. Clare, Rudolfe's life of Leoba, Joseph Dirvin's life of Elizabeth Seton, Robert Coles's life of Dorothy Day, and Pope John Paul II's "On the Dignity of Women."

20. Several papers in this collection are particularly illuminating on women's relational development, especially "The Development of Women's Sense of Self" (11–26) by Jean Baker Miller, "The Self in Relation: A

Notes

Theory of Women's Development" (51–66) by Janet L. Surrey, and "The Meaning of Mutuality" (81–96) by Judith Jordan.

21. Maria Prieto Ursúa, "Feminine Psychological and Spiritual Clues to the Spiritual Exercises," *The Way*, 59, no. 2 (January 2020): 92; and Michael R. Levinson, "Gender and Wisdom: The Role of Compassion and Moral Development," *Research on Human Development* 6, no. 2 (2009): 45–59.

22. For further discussion on these dynamics, see Dana Crowley Jack (1991) and Christie Cozad Neuger, "Women's Depression: Lives at Risk," in Maxine Glaz and Jeanne Stevenson Moessner, eds. (1991), 146–61.

Chapter 2

1. Recent English-language biographies of Ignatius include Candido de Dalmases (1985); José Ignacio Tellechea Idígoras (1994), Harvey Egan (1987), William Meissner (1992), and Hugo Rahner (1968). See also James Broderick, *St. Ignatius Loyola: The Pilgrim Years* (London: Burns and Oates, 1956); Mary Purcell, *The First Jesuit: St. Ignatius Loyola* (Chicago: Loyola University Press, 1981); and Philip Caraman, *Ignatius Loyola: A Biography of the Founder of the Jesuits* (San Francisco: Harper and Row, 1990). The historical novel by Louis De Wohl, *The Golden Thread* (New York: Lippincott, 1952), imaginatively captures the spirit of Ignatius and his times.

2. *St Ignatius Loyola: Letters to Women*, edited by Hugo Rahner, who collected, translated, and wrote commentary throughout, provides a rich historical resource for knowledge about the women associated with Ignatius, their individual personalities and the events that drew them together. Not only do the letters contribute to a greater understanding of the role of women of sixteenth-century Europe, they also reveal more of the nuances of Ignatius's relationships with women and his corresponding concern for the mission of the Society. The commentary provides the context for the letters, but also reflects the bias of the author, who makes assumptions that perpetuate stereotypes of women. Nevertheless, the book provides valuable information and insights into the world of women and Ignatius and the early Society.

3. Historian Joan Kelly suggests that women's experience of the Renaissance was not the liberating and humanizing event that their male

counterparts experienced. Kelly examines the quality of women's historical experience during this time by comparing several aspects of life: the regulation of female sexuality with male sexuality; women's economic and political roles, such as the kind of work they performed as compared with men, and their access to and education for property and political power; the cultural roles of women in shaping the outlook of their society; and ideology about women in the sex-role system displayed or advocated in the symbolic products of the society. See Joan Kelly, "Did Women Have a Renaissance?" in *Women, History and Theory* (Chicago: University of Chicago Press, 1984), 20. See also the following for further development of feminist historical theory: Gerda Lerner, *The Majority Finds Its Past: Placing Women in History* (New York: Oxford University Press, 1979); Berenice Carroll, ed., *Liberating Women's History: Theoretical and Critical Essays* (Urbana: University of Illinois Press, 1976); Joan Wallach Scott, *Gender and the Politics of History* (New York: Columbia University Press, 1988); Mary Margaret Fonow and Judith Cook, *Beyond Methodology: Feminist Scholarship as Lived Research* (Bloomington: Indiana University Press, 1991); and Joan Kelly, *Women, History and Theory: The Essays of Joan Kelly* (Chicago: University of Chicago Press, 1984).

    4. Joan Segarra Pijuan, SJ (1992), lists these "esteemed and respected" ladies of Manresa as Angela Sequi Amigant, Joana Ferrer, Jeronima Claver, Mrs. Canyelles, Catarina Molins (29). He further describes them as "married women who lived honorably with their husbands, and were very devout and charitable, admiring of holy persons and the poor and engaged in works of charity and mercy" (16). An additional group listed as followers of Ignatius and as "women who performed many exercises" included Brianda de Paguera, Eufrosina Roviralta, Agnes Claver, Agnes Vinyes, Jeronima Sala, Joana Dalmau, Agnes Roca, and "others who were well known in the city" (149).

    5. Tellechea Idígoras (1994, 253–57) devotes an enlightening chapter to María de la Flor. He describes her testimony for Ignatius's canonization with insight and compassion into a woman's spiritual journey of conversion; he does not stereotype her words as those of a prostitute.

    6. For further sources on the presence of and impact of women on Ignatius and on the Society of Jesus, see José García de Castro Valdés, "Las Mujeres y los Primeros Jesuitas," in *Iguales y Diferentes: Interrelación entre Mujeres y Varones Cristianos a lo Largo de la Historia*, ed. Fernando Rivas (Madrid: San Pablo Publishing, 2012), 219–82; Santiago Thió, "Ignacio, Padre Spiritual de Mujeres," *Manresa* 66 (1994): 417–36; Julia A. Dowd,

"Gathering the Graces: Women, the *Spiritual Exercises* and Jesuit Education" (DMin diss. Pacific School of Religion, 2018), chap. 3, "Another Ignatian History," esp. 52–53; Elizabeth Dreyer, "Do as I Do, Not as I Say: The Pedagogy of Action," in *Jesuit and Feminist Education: Intersections in Teaching and Learning for the Twenty-first Century*, ed. Jocelyn M. Boryczka and Elizabeth A. Petrino (New York: Fordham University Press, 2012), 21–36; Annemarie Renee Paulin-Campbell, "The Impact of the Imaginal and Dialogical (Relational) Processes in the Spiritual Exercise, on Image of Self and Image of God in Women Making the Nineteenth Annotation Retreat" (PhD diss., University of KwaZula-Natal, Pietermaritzburg, South Africa, 2008); Elizabeth Rhodes, "Ignatius and the Leyenda de los Santos," in *A Companion to Ignatius of Loyola: Life, Writings, Spirituality, Influence*, ed. Robert Aleksander Maryks (Leiden: Brill, 2014), 7–24; and Maria Prieto Ursúa, "Feminine Psychological and Spiritual Clues to the Spiritual Exercises," *The Way*, 59, no. 2 (January 2020): 90–102.

7. Several authors develop this chronology and the details of the financial conflict that erupted among Isabel, her relatives, and the Society. They also include the deliberations and decisions of the political and religious leaders concerning her case. See de Dalmases (1985, 253–55); Meissner (1992, 260–70); and Jean Lacouture, *The Jesuits: A Multibiography* (Washington, DC: Counterpoint, 1995), 150–54.

8. See Lisa Fullam, "Juana, S.J.: The Past (and Future?) Status of Women in the Society of Jesus," in *Studies in the Spirituality of Jesuits* 31 (November 1999).

9. One cannot help but compare the experience of Teresa of Avila and the affirmation of her spirituality and vision received from Jesuits, particularly Francis Borgia. What if Teresa Rejadell had the same level of support from Ignatius and his influential friends as Teresa of Avila for her reform and spiritual renewal?

10. Gemma Simmonds, "Mary Ward: Then and Now," in *Thinking Faith: The Online Journal of the Jesuits in Britain*, January 22, 2010, https://www.thinkingfaith.org/articles/20100122_1.htm.

11. For further discussion of Mary Ward and her impact on the church, see Kevin Burke, SJ, and Eileen Burke-Sullivan, "Mary Ward (1585–1645)," in *The Ignatian Tradition* (Collegeville, MN: Liturgical Press, 2009): 16–23; Lisa McClain, "On a Mission: Priests, Jesuits, 'Jesuitesses,' and Catholic Missionary Efforts in Tudor-Stuart England" *The Catholic Historical Review* 101, no. 3 (Summer 2015): 437–62; and Gemma Simmonds, "Women Jesuits?" in *The Cambridge Companion to the Jesuits*,

ed. Thomas Worcester (Cambridge: Cambridge University Press, 2008), 120–33.

12. Jesuits themselves have wrestled with this problem. In recent times some women who desired as close an affiliation with the Society of Jesus as possible were welcomed as "Jesuit Associates." This initiative began as an experiment after GC 34, held in 1995, as part of Decree 13: "Cooperation with the Laity in Mission" (See GC 34: paragraphs 23 and 24). This decree allows for a juridical bond to extend the missioning process to laity, including women. Some of those who became Associates took vows of obedience with respect to mission. Sadly, in 2008, GC 35 terminated the experiment. This was partly a result of very differing contexts and understandings of the idea of Jesuit Associates, which led to difficulties in some places. However, those who became Jesuit Associates during the experimental period could continue if they so desired, subject to the agreement of their provincial.

Within the lay movement called "Christian Life Communities," which meet regularly in small communities formed by the Spiritual Exercises and called into mission, many women have played significant roles. Christian Life Communities continue to flourish in many parts of the world.

The input of women in the structures of the Society of Jesus is still extremely limited, though there is a growing commitment to working collaboratively, which is lived out with varying degrees of fruitfulness. In many parts of the world, women now play key roles, and some even head up apostolic works of the Society of Jesus. With the establishment of a commission by Fr. General Arturo Sosa on March 8, 2021, to look at the role and responsibilities of women in relation to the Society, there is hope that there may be greater inclusion of women's voices in Jesuit decision-making structures in the future.

Today, in certain parts of the world, women give the Exercises and train and supervise the giving of the Spiritual Exercises. They work alongside Jesuits and some even train Jesuits in the giving of the Spiritual Exercises. Much has changed. Additionally, the Exercises have extended now far beyond the Society of Jesus into different denominations and are being shaped by the experiences of the wider community that now make and give the Spiritual Exercises.

Notes

Chapter 3

1. The first twenty points include the nature and purpose of the Spiritual Exercises [1], the general procedure [2, 3], the division and duration [4], the disposition required of the one making the Exercises [5], directions to the one leading the Exercises concerning the one making them [6–17] and adaptations for various constituencies [18–20]. Some of the notes deal with the disposition of the one making the Exercises [3, 5, 11–13, 16, 20], while others deal with the giver himself or herself [2, 4, 6–10, 12, 14–15, 17, 18–19]; see Ganss (1991, 387–88). Sprinkled throughout the text are further explanations and directions: a "Presupposition" [22], which we treated in chap. 2; various examinations [24–44]; additional directives and notes [73–82, 99–100, 127–34, 148, 159–64, 174, 188, 199, 204–9, and 226–29]. We will also consider here the "Rules to Order Oneself Henceforth in the Taking of Food" [210–17].

2. Ursúa (2020, 90) clarifies the necessary distinction between sex and gender. Gender is "the complex area which covers all those aspects relating to differences and similarities between the sexes which are not strictly 'sexological.'"

3. Frances Correia, "Listening to Your Story: A Narrative Approach to Spiritual Direction in the South African Context," *The Way* 52, no. 3 (July 2013): 115–28.

4. Barton Geger (2018, 37–42) argues for the most straightforward interpretation of the text as being authentically Ignatian. He claims that the interpretation of desires as indicative of one's truest and deepest self and then giving them a key role in discernment is, in fact, a twentieth-century interpretation that owes its origins to the existentialist philosophers Thomas Merton and Henri Nouwen and to several influential Jesuit authors such as Philip Sheldrake, Michael Ivens, Thomas McGrath, William Barry, and Denis Donoghue. See 41n113.

5. See Peters (1967, 79). Peters insists that the Exercises from the Second Week on are trinitarian, recognizes that the Holy Spirit is nowhere mentioned, and points out that the so-called triple colloquies [147, 156, 199] are always addressed to Our Lady, the Son, and the Father. This association suggests that Mary does the work of the Holy Spirit in the Second and subsequent Weeks. However, the triple colloquies follow the meditations introduced in the Second Week, not the contemplations. The first colloquy of the Second Week contemplations [109], the model

for the remaining contemplations, mentions prayer to "the Three Divine Persons, or to the eternal Word made flesh, or to our Mother and Lady."

6. Elizabeth Dreyer (1996, 77) asserts that the most moving expressions of Augustine's treatment of the Holy Spirit are those in which he links the Holy Spirit with desire. Philip Sheldrake, "Befriending our Desires," *The Way* 35 (April 1995): 92–93, points out the role of desires in Catherine of Siena, Meister Eckhart, and Thomas Cranmer; Sheldrake concludes, "The fact that we frequently do not allow ourselves such risks and lack a lively spirituality has close connections with the historical absence of a serious and healthy theology of the Holy Spirit in western Christianity."

7. For a contemporary perspective on eliciting readiness for the Spiritual Exercises, see Joseph Veale, "The First Week: Practical Questions," in *The Way of Ignatius of Loyola: Contemporary Approaches to the Spiritual Exercises*, ed. Philip Sheldrake (St. Louis: Institute of Jesuit Sources, 1991), 53–65.

8. For a fuller discussion of the developmental perspective on readiness for the Spiritual Exercises, see Elizabeth Liebert, "The Eighteenth Annotation in the Spiritual Exercises of St. Ignatius," in *Symposium: Ignatian Spirituality: Summary of Proceedings* (Guelph, ON: Loyola House, 1993), 10–31.

9. Evidence exists for versions of the Spiritual Exercises of various lengths (8, 8–10, 10–12, and 15 or more days) and for various groups of people. The whole spectrum of devotional activity was included. Closed and open forms were recommended. The time given to prayer varied from a period or two of about thirty minutes to three hours per day, to leaving the amount entirely to the retreatant. Instruction was included when necessary, suitably adapted to the needs of the retreatant. See Martin Palmer (1996): 42–45, 87–100, 105–10, 120–22, 154–55, and elsewhere.

10. In a study of the virtue of magnanimity in the Exercises and the Constitutions, William McCormick helps clarify the delicate balance between humility and greatness that Ignatius was trying to strike, recognizing, as he did, that some would indeed perceive either individual Jesuits or the Society as elitist. For Ignatius, magnanimity is not just being great. Nor does it simply mean great-hearted generosity. In Ignatius's hands, magnanimity becomes the great-hearted orientation *toward God*, acting always for and with God. It means seeking the greater good for oneself and one's community expressed in service for others. It means choosing the more universal good. See "'A Continual Sacrifice to the

Notes

Glory of God': Ignatian Magnanimity as Cooperation with the Divine," *Studies in the Spirituality of Jesuits* 50, no. 3 (Autumn 2018): 15–34.

11. Based on this presupposition and the burden it places on each party to try to understand the other, we have chosen not to use the language of director and directee or exercitant, substituting instead "the one who gives the exercises" and the one who "receives them" or "makes them" or, occasionally, the "retreatant." Alternatively, and more concisely, we sometimes speak of "companion" and "seeker." With this language shift away from language of director/exercitant, we intend to follow Ignatius's lead and assert that the difference between the giver of the Spiritual Exercises and the receiver of them is only functional and does not imply any special holiness or privilege. Furthermore, this difference is strictly temporary, confined to the Exercises alone, and even in that context is constantly mitigated by the revelation and enrichment both parties receive as the one making the Exercises narrates her religious experience.

12. See Dario Restrepo, "'Spiritual Conversation' According to Ignatius of Loyola," *Communications* 6 (February 1976): 16–20. Restrepo traces the evolution of spiritual conversation in Ignatius of Loyola from his earliest conversations with the Trinity begun during his recuperation, to seeking spiritual guidance to gain clarity on what was happening interiorly begun at Montserrat and Manresa, to experiencing the desire to converse with spiritual companions as illustrated in conversations, particularly with women, in Manresa, to recognizing spiritual conversation as a means of sharing the gospel, to articulating a method and rationale for spiritual conversation in the Constitutions and letters. The Principle and Foundation represents a distillation of that method and grounds the ministry of the one who gives the Exercises.

13. In recent years the awareness of the importance of the body has grown in popular literature on spirituality. One such resource is that of Christine Valters Painter, *The Wisdom of the Body: A Contemplative Journey of Wholeness for Women* (Notre Dame, IN: Sorin Books, 2017).

14. Ignatius's positive treatment of the body also spilled over into his pastoral practice as suggested in the earliest of his extant letters, to Inéz Pascual, in 1522: "All the more so since the Lord does not require you to do anything exhausting or harmful to your person. He wants you to live taking joy in him and granting the body whatever it needs. Let all your words, thoughts and behavior be in him and attend to your bodily necessities for his sake, always placing the observance of God's commandments first" (Ganss 1991, 327).

15. This negative view of the body occurs when Ignatius asks the seeker to stand outside her body and reflect on it from within the theological anthropology and rhetoric of his time. See Alison Weber, *Teresa of Avila and the Rhetoric of Femininity* (Princeton, NJ: Princeton University Press, 1990). This strategy's positive goal, according to Margaret Miles, *Fullness of Life: Historical Foundations for a New Asceticism* (Philadelphia: Westminster, 1981), 154, is subverting the unconscious balance of pain and joy ordinarily constructed in daily existence for the purpose of reconstructing a life in which all aspects are consciously chosen to foster loving service.

16. See Ursúa (2020, 95–97) for a summary of contemporary psychological research on gender, particularly the feminine gender.

17. For the concept of the culture of the Exercises, see Howard Gray (1993): 72–84. Gray defines culture as "a total composite of religious values designed to reorient how men and women choose to live their lives," and he names three constitutive elements of the Ignatian Exercises as "a context for discovering God's leadership in life, a statement of priority in God's leadership and the establishment of criteria for discerning whether the leadership attributed to God is authentic" (73).

18. For example, in the years between 1983 and 1996, of the nearly six hundred persons who made the Spiritual Exercises in daily life in the Seattle area, 69 percent were women, 31 percent were men, according to Celia Chappell, SP, *Core Team, Spiritual Exercises in Everyday Life*, Seattle, Washington, private communication.

19. For example, Michael Hansen, SJ, *The First Spiritual Exercises: Four Guided Retreats* and *The First Spiritual Exercises: A Manual for Those Who Give the Exercises* (Notre Dame, IN: Ave Maria Press, 2013). Hansen's adaptation has a further advantage in spreading the Exercises: it assumes that once anyone has made the First Spiritual Exercises, he or she can, with little outside help, use the Manual to assist others through any of the four retreats.

20. The terse wording of the Exercises may not make Ignatius's thought clear on this point. But his letter to Francis Borgia of September 20, 1548, sheds light on the issue: "God sees and knows what is best for each one and, as he knows all, he shows each the road to take. On our part we can with his grace seek and test the way forward in many different fashions, so that a person goes forward by that way which for them is the clearest and happiest and most blessed in this life" (Letters, trans. Young,

1959, 181). See also Ian Tomlinson, "Is the 19th Annotation the Full Exercises?" *The Way Supplement* 49 (1984): 13–20.

21. Extremes of clericalism still occur in some contexts. A striking example came from a director who was very disturbed by the fact that a woman religious from a rural context in Africa whose retreat he was directing had come to her first direction session and taken a kneeling position at his feet. She explained, when asked, that her previous retreat director had insisted on this when she saw him for spiritual direction. In some places, parts of Africa and India for example, where clericalism and patriarchy are still very strongly entrenched, women may still be very disempowered in the spiritual direction relationship. In many parts of the world where women now have much more equality, this is much less of an issue now than it was twenty years ago. And in some of those contexts, it is simply no longer an issue.

22. As noted in the next section, in the situation where the one receiving the Exercises has suffered physical or sexual abuse, we recommend that the receiver's gender preference be honored without question.

23. An increasing body of literature treats the effects of physical and sexual abuse, the healing process, and the role of various helping professionals. See, e.g., Marie Fortune, *Sexual Violence: The Unmentionable Sin* (New York: Pilgrim Press, 1983); Pamela Cooper-White, *The Cry of Tamar: Violence against Women and the Church's Response* (Philadelphia: Fortress, 1995); Mary D. Pellauer, Barbara Chester, and Jane Boyajian, eds., *Sexual Assault and Abuse: A Handbook for Clergy and Religious Professionals* (San Francisco: Harper and Row, 1987); Anne L. Horton and Judith A. Williamson, eds., *Abuse and Religion: When Praying Isn't Enough* (Lexington, MA: D. C. Heath and Company, 1988); and James Leehan, *Pastoral Care for Survivors of Family Abuse* (Louisville, KY: Westminster John Knox, 1989).

24. For example, in some contexts, women prefer to make the Exercises in a group because they feel safer.

25. Ignatius's mature thinking on the place of penances can be seen in his letter to Francis Borgia of September 20, 1548 (Ganss 1991, 346–49).

26. See Stephanie Paulsell, *Honoring the Body: Meditations on a Christian Practice* (San Francisco: Jossey-Bass, 2002) for a rich series of meditations and spiritual practices grounded in the body. She touches on such bodily practices as bathing, clothing, nourishing, eating, resting, suffering, and sexuality as grounds for Christian practice.

27. The placement of the rules for eating has been a source of some discussion. Various suggestions have been offered: this kind of awareness ties in well as an embodiment of Third Week prayer; the one receiving the Exercises is learning to carry the Exercises into daily life by becoming reflective even about so ordinary an occupation as eating, and even that there were so many directions and things to internalize earlier in the Exercises that this position is merely a "clear space" for this new practice of intentionality. See Peters (1967), 13–14, 139–41.

28. Two examples of ethical guidelines are "Spiritual Directors International Guidelines for Ethical Conduct" (San Francisco: SDI Coordinating Council, 1999); and Thomas Hedberg and Betsy Caprio, *A Code of Ethics for Spiritual Directors*, rev. ed. (Pecos, NM: Dove Publications, 1992).

Chapter 4

1. At issue in the phrase "dualistic, patriarchically oriented hierarchy" is not, contrary to the way many feminists seem to use the term, hierarchy per se, but a particular type of hierarchy that consistently ranks males above females, philosophically, economically, legally, morally. Hence, in using the term, we specify the particular kind of hierarchy.

2. Today, adding several days before the Exercises begin, often called "disposition days," can serve the purpose of screening as well as allowing the director and the retreatant to get used to each other.

3. Other works unpacking the Principle and Foundation include Michael Ivens, *Understanding the Spiritual Exercises* (Leominster, UK: Gracewing, 1998), 25–31; Kevin O'Brien, *The Ignatian Adventure*, 63–69; Roger Haight, *Christian Spirituality for Seekers: Reflections on the Spiritual Exercises of Ignatius Loyola* (Maryknoll, NY: Orbis, 2012), 48–50; Joseph Tetlow, *Ignatius Loyola: Spiritual Exercises* (New York: Crossroad, 1992), 53–54; John English, *Spiritual Freedom*, 23–42; Tim Muldoon, "Postmodern Spirituality and the Ignatian Fundamentum," *The Way* 44, no. 1 (January 2005): 88–100; and Helen Orchard, "The Creature and the Sovereign Self: The Anthropology of the Spiritual Exercises and Contemporary Spiritual Narcissism," *The Way* 59, no. 1 (January 2020): 11–21.

4. To further explore this issue, see Adrian Bejan and J. Peder Zane (2012), which illustrates this tendency perfectly.

5. A nontechnical, expansive view of the new cosmologies is given in Brian Swimme (1996). See also B. Bertotti et al., *Modern Cosmology in Retrospect* (Cambridge: Cambridge University Press, 1990); Robert John Russell, "Contemplation in the Vibrant Universe: The Natural Context of Christian Spirituality," in *Spirit and Nature: The Study of Christian Spirituality in a Time of Ecological Urgency*, ed. Timothy Hessel-Robinson and Ray Maria McNamara, RSM (Eugene, OR: Pickwick, 2011), 125–47; for a much more rigorous treatment, see Robert John Russell, *Cosmology: From Alpha to Omega* (Minneapolis: Fortress, 2008). For a philosophical perspective, see Beatrice Bruteau, *God's Ecstasy: The Creation of a Self-Creating World* (New York: Crossroad, 1997) and Beatrice Bruteau, *The Grand Option: Personal Transformation and a New Creation* (Notre Dame, IN: University of Notre Dame Press, 2001).

6. For an excellent treatment of patriarchy, see Gerda Lerner, *The Creation of Patriarchy* (New York: Oxford University Press, 1986); and Thomas Berry and Brian Swimme, *The Dream of the Earth* (San Francisco: Sierra Club Books, 1988), 138–62.

7. Tim McEvoy, "Ignatius and the Stars," *The Way* 60, no. 2 (April 2021): 8–17, beautifully illustrates how Ignatius would have balanced this medieval cosmology, which he would have inhabited without qualms, with his deeply incarnational understanding of God at work in the world. He concludes, "The motions of the heavenly bodies and the interior motions he felt in his own body were not unrelated, but macro- and microcosmic levels of the same phenomenon: the drawing of the creature home to its loving Creator" (17).

8. Some helpful books for explaining the evolution of the universe: John Barrow, *The Origin of the Universe* (New York: Basic Books, 1994); Berry and Swimme (1992); Michael Dowd, *Earthspirit: A Handbook for Nurturing an Ecological Christianity* (Mystic, CT: Twenty-third Publications, 1991); John Barrow and Joseph Silk, *The Left Hand of Creation: The Origin and Evolution of the Universe*, 2nd ed. (New York: Oxford University Press, 1994); and Bruteau, *God's Ecstasy*. From a Jewish perspective, see Daniel C. Matt, *God and the Big Bang: Discovering Harmony between Science and Spirituality* (Woodstock: VT: Jewish Lights, 1996).

9. Sources reflecting the new scientific view of the universe and its implications for theology include, in addition to Bejan and Zane, cited above, Ivone Gebarra, *Longing for Running Water: Ecofeminism and Liberation* (Minneapolis: Fortress, 1999); Fritjof Capra and David Steindl-Rast, *Belonging to the Universe: Explorations on the Frontiers of Science and*

Spirituality (San Francisco: Harper, 1991); Kitty Ferguson, *The Fire in the Equations: Science, Religion and the Search for God* (Grand Rapids: Eerdmans, 1994); Paul Davies, *The Mind of God: The Scientific Basis for a Rational World* (New York: Simon and Schuster, 1992); and Charles Birch et al., eds., *Liberating Life: Contemporary Approaches to Ecological Theology* (Maryknoll, NY: Orbis, 1990) and Robert John Russell, *Cosmology: From Alpha to Omega* (Minneapolis: Fortress, 2008).

10. On this point, see Larry L. Rasmussen, *Earth Community, Earth Ethics* (Maryknoll, NY: Orbis, 1996); Elizabeth Johnson, *Creation and the Cross: The Mercy of God for a Planet in Peril* (New York: Orbis, 2018); and Richard Rohr, *Universal Christ: How a Forgotten Reality Can Change Everything We See, Hope for and Believe* (New York: Convergent Books, 2019).

11. See the comprehensive approach of Michael Himes and Kenneth Himes, "The Sacrament of Creation: Toward an Environmental Theology," *Commonweal* 117 (January 26, 1990): 42–49. The entire focus of Mary E. McGann, *The Meal That Reconnects: Eucharistic Eating and the Global Food Crisis* (Collegeville, MN: Liturgical Press, 2020) is to expand our notion of sacrament.

12. "God's Grandeur," in *Gerard Manley Hopkins*, ed. Catherine Phillips (New York: Oxford University Press, 1976): 128. See also the poems of contemporary Pulitzer Prize winner Mary Oliver and the writings of Annie Dillard.

13. See Rosemary Radford Ruether, *Women and Redemption: A Theological History* (Minneapolis: Fortress, 1998).

14. Neil Vaney, *Christ in a Grain of Sand: An Ecological Journey with the Spiritual Exercises* (Notre Dame, IN: Ave Maria, 2004) provides a way to move through the Exercises in connection within creation.

15. See Anne Carr (1988, 1996), esp. chap. 9; Sallie McFague (1993, 179–82); Rosemary Radford Ruether, *Gaia and God: An Ecofeminist Theology of Earth Healing* (San Francisco: HarperSanFrancisco, 1992); and Elizabeth A. Johnson, *Ask the Beasts: Darwin and the God of Love* (New York: Bloomsbury, 2014), especially chap. 10, "The Community of Creation." While *Gaudete et Exsultate: On the Call to Holiness in Today's World* (2018) has been critiqued for its view of women, Pope Francis does strongly insist that the messiness and beauty of the ordinary world is precisely where we live out our call.

16. *Laudato Si': On Care for Our Common Home* (2015) speaks with prophetic urgency on this point. Pope Francis, *Let Us Dream: The Path to*

a Better Future (New York: Simon and Schuster, 2020) offers an extended meditation on the situation of the world in light of COVID-19, inviting all humanity to see, discern, and act together toward a better future.

17. This reframing has a long history. As early a commentator on the Spiritual Exercises as Mary Ward sought a more easily understood term than *indifference* while still being faithful to Ignatius's intention. For example, she notes, "One is free from all, and desires only one thing, which is to love God, and here one remains free and contented." Mary Ward's Spiritual Notes (Spa, July 1616). See Ursula Dirmeier, ed., *Mary Ward und ihre Gründung: die Quellentexte bis 1645*, vol. 1 (Munster: Aschendorff, 2007), 336: "Freedom, that things desired, was still desired, and an efficacy and readines to effect, but without solicitude, things contrary disliked, but without anxiety, the mind equally sattisfied whichsoever of thes contraryes should happen; [a'] the cheef effect, one loves, or is averted, according to the knowledg that is aforesayd, one is ready to do, or not to do, yet indifferently resigned whatsoever hapens, one seeth the danger of avers things, but without fere, anxiety or trouble, a quiet confidenc that God will do his will, in conclusion, one is free from all, and desires onely one which is to love God, and heer one remayns free and contended, onely in this they feel they want, that they canot be certayn that they love him, and so they endever and desires to do some acts gratefull to him, and the more they do, the greater ther uncertaynty whether in his sight they do in deed love him."

18. A fine book on women balancing relationship to self and others is Dana Crowley Jack's *Silencing the Self: Women and Depression* (San Francisco: Harper Collins, 1991). See also her *Behind the Mask* (Cambridge, MA: Harvard University Press, 1999) for a treatment of women and aggression.

19. Tim Muldoon makes this point with particular clarity in "Postmodern Spirituality and the Ignatian *Fundamentum*," *The Way* 44, no. 1 (January 2005): 88–100. After reviewing Joseph Tetlow's use of *Fundamentum* rather than "Foundation," he claims that the Principle and Foundation actually refers to the very objective of the entire spiritual life. Three themes in the *Fundamentum*, imaginative play, fundamental receptivity, and self-transcending love, provide the basic spiritual practices that can open contemporary persons, particularly the younger generation about whom Muldoon is concerned, to a rich and deep spiritual life. The *Fundamentum*, he says, "can be seen as an attentiveness to the God who is

constantly working with us to co-create our lives—a kind of *lectio divina* in which the text is our own experience" (100).

20. See, e.g., Mary Field Belenky, Blythe McVicker Clinchy, Nancy Rule Goldberger, and Jill Mattuck Tarule (1986) and the pioneering work by Carol Gilligan (1982).

21. See the thoughtful book by Carol Lee Flinders, *At the Root of This Longing* (San Francisco: Harper, 1998) for a reconciliation of some aspects of all the great religions (silence, self-naughting, restraint of desire, and enclosure) and contemporary feminism.

22. Loyola Press, the holder of the copyright on this work at the time of this revision, has graciously given permission to use this quotation in altered form. The original text of the prayer begins "Lord God…" and addresses "Lord God" a second time in line 13. These salutations have been altered to read "Gracious God" and "O God," respectively.

Chapter 5

1. Franz Jalics (2002) makes a convincing case that the Three Ways of Praying are an integral part of the Fourth Week. This argument appears later in the chapter.

2. Our assumption remains despite a burst of writing on prayer in the Spiritual Exercises that spurred their contemporary renewal. See, e.g., Thomas Burke, *Methods of Prayer in the Spiritual Exercises* (Jersey City, NJ: Program to Adapt the Spiritual Exercises, n.d.); Joseph Conwell, *Contemplation in Action: A Study in Ignatian Prayer* (Spokane, WA: Gonzaga University, 1957); Joseph de Guibert, *The Jesuits, Their Spiritual Doctrine and Practice: A Historical Study* (St. Louis: Institute of Jesuit Studies, 1964); and Peters (1967). Collections of articles such as those in *The Way Supplement* 16 (1972) and 82 (1995) reach few persons other than specialists in spirituality.

For contemporary adaptations and presentations of prayer forms within the Spiritual Exercises intended for wider readership, see the Take and Receive series by Jacqueline Bergan and Marie Schwan, *Love* (1985), *Forgiveness* (1985), *Birth* (1985), *Surrender* (1986), and *Freedom* (1988) (Winona, MN: St. Mary's Press); Jacqueline Syrup Bergan and Marie Schwan, *Praying with Ignatius of Loyola* (Winona, MN: St. Mary's Press, 1991); Thomas Green, *A Vacation with the Lord* (Notre Dame, IN:

Notes

Ave Maria Press, 1986); R. Huelsman, *Pray: Participant's and Moderator's Manuals* (Mahwah, NJ: Paulist, 1976); Mark Link, *Challenge: A Meditation Program Based on the Spiritual Exercises of St. Ignatius* (Valencia, CA: Tabor Publishing, 1988); de Mello (1978); George Schemel, ed., *Focusing Group Energies: Common Ground for Leadership, Organization, Spirituality* (Scranton, PA: University of Scranton, 1992, formerly titled *Ignatian Spiritual Exercises for the Corporate Person: Structured Resources for Group Development*, 1987); and Joseph Tetlow, *Choosing Christ in the World* (St. Louis: Institute of Jesuit Sources, 1989).

In the years since the first edition, more resources have appeared. For example, see Timothy Gallagher, *An Ignatian Introduction to Prayer: Scriptural Reflections according to the Spiritual Exercises* (New York: Crossroads, 2007), forty scriptural meditations based on the Spiritual Exercises; Michael Hansen, *The First Spiritual Exercises: Four Guided Retreats* and *The First Spiritual Exercises: A Manual for Those Who Give the Exercises* (Notre Dame: IN: Ave Maria Press, 2013), a thoroughly researched presentation of prayer based in the Eighteenth Annotation of the Spiritual Exercises and recapitulated on 301–64; Tim Muldoon, *The Ignatian Workout: Daily Spiritual Exercises for a Healthy Faith* (Chicago: Loyola Press, 2004), presenting the main forms of prayer and dynamics of the Spiritual Exercises in an idiom designed to appeal to for college-age and young adults; John Sassani and Mary Ann McLaughlin, *Meeting Christ in Prayer: An 8-Week Life-Enriching Experience Based on the Spiritual Exercises of St. Ignatius* (Chicago: Loyola Press, 2008), originally developed to help Catholics in the Archdiocese of Boston prepare for the Jubilee Year 2000; and Margaret Silf, *Companions of Christ: Ignatian Spirituality for Everyday Living* (Grand Rapids: Eerdmans, 2004), whose down-to-earth presentation is designed to connect with God in everyday life; Joseph A. Tetlow, *Making Choices in Christ: The Foundations of Ignatian Spirituality* (Chicago: Loyola Press, 2008), a series of brief reflections including the various forms of prayer. Chapter 22 presents the prayer of consideration or turning one's mind to simple facts and letting those facts teach them about the divine, a practice not considered in this chapter. Fr. Tetlow's most recent book, *Handing on the Fire: Making Spiritual Direction Ignatian* (Boston: Institute of Jesuit Sources, 2021), concludes with a discussion of experiences characteristic of Ignatian spirituality and Ignatian Examen (part 3, 127–47).

3. In our experience, Protestants who make the Exercises increasingly take the opportunity, if it is offered to them, to engage in a confession of the sins of their lives and a ritual of forgiveness and reconciliation, either

with their director or with their pastor/minister. Many have expressed how significant an experience this has been for them as part of their Exercises journey.

4. See also Dennis Hamm, "Rummaging for God: Praying Backward through Your Day," *America* 170 (May 14, 1994): 22–23; and Tad Dunne, *Spiritual Exercises for Today* (San Francisco: Harper, 1991), 122–27.

5. Joseph A Tetlow, SJ, "The Most Postmodern Prayer: American Jesuit Identity and the Examen of Conscience, 1920–1990," *Studies in the Spirituality of Jesuits* 26 (January 1994) offers an analysis of the shifts in philosophy, theology, and American culture in this century and chronicles their effects on the examination of conscience.

6. Further contemporary considerations of examen include Timothy Gallagher, *The Examen Prayer: Ignatian Wisdom for Our Lives Today* (New York: Crossroad, 2006); and Jim Manney, *A Simple Life-Changing Prayer: Discovering the Power of St. Ignatius Loyola's Examen* (Chicago: Loyola Press, 2011). Michael Hansen, *The First Spiritual Exercises* presents four variations on the particular examen that thread through the various retreats: an awareness examen, a particular examen, a reconciliation examen, and a healing examen, which he acknowledges move beyond Ignatius, though very much in Ignatius's spirit. Hansen uses "awareness examen" for the reclamation suggested by George Aschenbrenner in which one notices how God has been involved in one's day, and "particular examen" for the process of tracing progress in achieving something one desires. See also Mark Argent, "Reclaiming the Particular Examen," *The Way* 52, no. 3 (October 2013): 57–64; Argent wants to reclaim the notion of particular examen in this original sense. Finally, see Andrew Walker, "Daydreaming Revisited: A Psychology for the Examen Explained," *The Way* 42, no. 3 (July 2003): 95–105, for a perspective based in various schools of psychology. David Fleming, *Like the Lightening: The Dynamics of the Ignatian Exercises* (St. Louis: Institute of Jesuit Sources, 2004), 53, notes that the Exercises contain directions for another kind of examen not explicitly framed as such, namely the examen that the one giving the Exercises prays while guiding another in the Exercises. This examen is rooted in the Annotations, especially Fourteen, Fifteen, and Seventeen. The director is to stay alert to the ways she or he is supporting the retreatant, helping the retreatant balance the day and balance the decision-making process, whether responding in helpful ways, and how well the director is adapting each Week to the retreatant.

Notes

7. The lack of clarity about Application of the Senses dates from the *Official Directory of 1599*, which summarily dismissed Application of the Senses as a method suitable for beginners or those fatigued by earlier prayer periods (Palmer 1996, 321–23). This interpretation gained ascendancy despite Juan de Polanco's own Directory dated 1574. Polanco, who had served as Ignatius's personal secretary from 1547 on and presumably knew his mind on the Exercises, differentiates two understandings of Application of the Senses: a simple use of imagination and a form of infused contemplation (Alexandre Brou, *Ignatian Methods of Prayer* [Milwaukee: Bruce, 1949], 162). For an excellent and detailed analysis of the discussion within the Society of Jesus on Application of the Senses, see also Hugo Rahner (1968), chap. 5; and Philip Endean, "The Ignatian Prayer of the Senses" *Heythrop Journal* 31 (1990): 391–418.

8. For further discussion on imagination and spirituality, see Kathleen Fischer, "The Imagination in Spirituality," *The Way Supplement* 66 (Autumn 1989): 96. For an excellent explication of imagination in general, see Ann and Barry Ulanov, *The Healing Imagination* (Mahwah, NJ: Paulist, 1991).

9. Dreams are especially significant in some cultures. In African cultures, a directee will readily and frequently bring important dreams to the direction space.

10. Two excellent resources on active imagination are Robert Johnson, *Inner Work* (San Francisco: Harper and Row, 1986) and Barbara Hannah, *Encounters with the Soul: Active Imagination* (Santa Monica, CA: Sigo Press, 1981).

11. See Eugene Gendlin (1979); Peter Campbell and Edwin McMahon, *Biospirituality* (Chicago: Loyola University Press, 1985); and Elizabeth Anne Vanek, *Image Guidance* (Mahwah, NJ: Paulist, 1992).

12. Walter Fabri, "Images That Lead to Prayer, *The Way* 56, no. 1 (January 2017): 57–62.

13. On this point, see Judith A Roemer's "Examination of Unconsciousness," *Human Development* 6 (Fall 1985): 50–52.

14. We recommend the following abbreviated form of examen used by the Spiritual Exercises in the Everyday Life Program, Seattle, Washington:

A Daily Check-in
Jesus
you have been present with me

The Spiritual Exercises Reclaimed

> in my life today
> Be near, now.
>
> Let us look together at my day.
> Let me see through your loving
> eyes…
>
> When did I listen to your voice
> today?
> When did I resist listening to you
> today?
>
> Jesus,
> everything is gift from you.
> I give you thanks and praise
> for the gifts of this day…
> I ask your healing in…
> I ask your forgiveness and
> mercy for…
>
> Jesus,
> continue to be present with me
> in my life each day.

We also recommend Dennis Linn, Sheila Fabricant Linn, and Matthew Linn, *Sleeping with Bread: Holding What Gives Us Life* (Mahwah, NJ: Paulist, 1995) for an excellent treatment of examen and adaptations for various individual and group times of prayer.

15. An interesting comparison between contemporary prayer forms and classical contemplation is Ernest E. Larkin, "Today's Contemplative Prayer Forms: Are They Contemplation?" *Review for Religious* 57 (January/February 1998): 77–87.

16. This section is based on Elizabeth Liebert, *Way of Discernment: Spiritual Practices for Decision Making* (Louisville, KY: Westminster John Knox, 2008). For an expanded treatment of desires as they relate to discernment, see 23–28. See also Philip Sheldrake, *Befriending Our Desires* (Ottawa, ON: Novalis, 2001) for a thorough theological and pastoral treatment of desires as the key to our humanity.

Notes

17. Thomas Ryan, *Four Steps to Spiritual Freedom* (Mahwah, NJ: Paulist, 2003), 243.

18. Milton Walsh, "To Always Be Thinking Somehow about Jesus," *Studies in the Spirituality of Jesuits* 43, no. 1 (Spring 2011) demonstrates the dynamics at work in Ludolph of Saxony's *Life of Christ*, which had such a profound effect on the Spiritual Exercises.

19. For further discussion of imaginative contemplation, see John Wickham, "Ignatian Contemplation Today," in *The Way of Ignatius Loyola*, ed. Philip Sheldrake (St. Louis: Institute of Jesuit Sources, 1991), 145–53; and Kathleen Fischer, *Inner Rainbow* (Mahwah, NJ: Paulist, 1983), 70–88.

20. For a concise article on working with a person utilizing the prayer of faith, see Dermot Mansfield, "The Exercises and Contemplative Prayer," in *The Way of Ignatius of Loyola*, ed. Philip Sheldrake (St. Louis: Institute of Jesuit Sources, 1991), 191–202.

21. On the phenomenology of mysticism, see Nelson Pike, *Mystic Union* (Ithaca, NY: Cornell University Press, 1992); and Janet Ruffing, "Encountering Love Mysticism," *Presence* 1 (January 1995): 20–33, and *Spiritual Direction: Beyond the Beginnings* (Mahwah, NJ: Paulist, 2000).

22. A particularly sensitive treatment of these shifts can be found in Mary Sharon Riley, "Women and Contemplation," *The Way Supplement* 82 (Spring 1995): 35–43.

23. The question of what constitutes "Ignatian Prayer" and its relationship to the so-called degrees of prayer appears regularly in the literature on the Exercises. A particularly well-framed articulation of the position held here can be found in Veale (1995).

24. This document was issued in May 1934 by representatives of the Lutheran, Reformed, and United Churches, to define the Christian opposition to National Socialism in Germany. It was a precursor to the formation of the Confessing Church. See Hubert G. Locke, *The Church Confronts the Nazis: Barmen Then and Now* (New York: Edwin Mellen Press, 1984). The text may be found in *The Constitution of the Presbyterian Church (USA)*, part 1: *Book of Confessions* (Louisville, KY: Office of the General Assembly, 1996).

25. Excellent articles on this question include Veale (1995) and Frank Houdek, "The Limitations of Ignatian Prayer" *The Way Supplement* 82 (Spring 1995): 26–43.

Chapter 6

1. Directives are discussed in chap. 3, particularly around issues of embodiment and appropriate use of penances, as well as in chap. 5, which focuses on the forms of prayer that Ignatius proposes in the Exercises.

2. Howard Gray, "Dynamic, Graces, Direction," Dynamics of the Spiritual Exercises Lectures, #3, Georgetown University, November 6, 2012, stresses that this "colloquy of mercy" is pivotal, and that the colloquy itself may take most of the hour. See https://www.youtube.com/watch?v=iifV3b335QU&ab_channel=GeorgetownUniversity.

3. The life of Francis Borgia attests to this kind of conversion experience. Borgia identified the disfigured and decomposing corpse of the empress Isabel, whose beauty and vivacity had been so precious to him, and he exclaimed, "Never more, never more will I serve a master who can die" (de Dalmases 1991, 16).

4. Larry Warner, *Journey with Jesus: Discovering the Spiritual Exercises of St. Ignatius* (Downers Grove, IL: InterVarsity, 2010), 103–42. Warner takes great pains in the exercises leading up to the First Week that the retreatant has internalized God's personal love, cautioning the retreatant to return to these preparatory exercises if that grace has not yet been internalized. Only then is the retreatant to take up the material of the First Week. As would be appropriate to his evangelical audience, Warner offers biblical texts to unfold the dynamic of the first week. Throughout, he encourages connecting with a spiritual director or taking a break from the exercises if necessary. Although not written specifically for women, this care may be essential for some women making the First Week exercises. Tim Muldoon, *The Ignatian Workout: Daily Spiritual Exercises for a Healthy Faith* (Chicago: Loyola Press), 99–101, takes a more radical approach to this problem by rewriting the dynamic of the whole week into a new format. He proposes an eight-stage movement through the Week (which he calls "The First Workout"): Stage One allows the retreatant to recognize how graced one's life has been. The three movements make up stage one: meditating on why you were created, turning your liabilities into strengths, and discovering the richness in your life. Stage Two introduces the notion of sin and personal responsibility for one's sin: learning from the story of the prodigal son, recognizing where you have missed the mark and confronting your sin, speaking to Jesus on

Notes

the cross, facing up to your sin before God, gaining perspective on who you are, understanding the meaning of Hell, and making your confession.

5. See Brian V. Johnstone, "Fundamental Option," in *The New Dictionary of Theology*, ed. Mary Collins, Joseph Komonchak, and Dermot Lane (Wilmington, DE: Michael Glazier, 1987), 407–8. "Fundamental option" is presented as a corrective to a more legalistic approach to moral life. According to Johnstone, fundamental option can best be understood as an orientation to life as a unified dynamic process where one's choices set a direction, which, according to human freedom, can be changed, deepened, or reversed. For example, a person's basic orientation is toward or away from God. Further discussion on fundamental option occurs in chap. 10.

6. Dr. Peggy McIntosh, Wellesley College Center for Research on Women, has explored this dynamic in detail in her paper "White Privilege Male Privilege." Excerpts are taken from *Spotlight*, American Friends Service Committee (Winter 1989): 2–3.

7. Vatican Council II describes this "Universal Call to Holiness" in *Lumen Gentium* (Dogmatic Constitution on the Church), chap. 5. The document stresses that holiness is a vocation, a lifetime "calling" for the believer. All persons, regardless of age, life choices, or work, are called to live a life based on love of God and neighbor, contributing through their gifts to the betterment of society.

8. According to Saiving (1992, 37), women's sins are better suggested by triviality, distractibility, and diffuseness. She notes that women often depend on others for their own self-definition or use tolerance as an excuse for avoiding the demands of excellence. Women's mistrust of reason is another demonstration of the underdevelopment or negation of the self.

9. Also in relation to the first exercise of the First Week and its biblical content, Carr calls for a critique of the literal reading of the story of Adam and Eve and the centuries of preaching and theological interpretation that resulted from it and suggests a feminist reinterpretation of the Genesis story of sin and its meaning in relation to women.

10. Potter Engel (1990, 156–62) offers four ways to think about sin in situations of abuse: sin as distortion of feeling or hardness of heart that denies authentic anger, sin as betrayal of trust or inability to learn and practice trust, sin as lack of care of oneself, and sin as lack of consent to vulnerability or equating honest dependence with subjection.

11. More recently, we note the women in leadership in the #MeToo and Black Lives Matter movements.

12. See Miriam Therese Winter, *WomenWisdom: A Feminist Lectionary and Psalter—Women of the Hebrew Scripture* (New York: Crossroad, 1991), 142–55, as a contemporary example of response to violence against women.

13. Gerard O'Mahony, "A Bridge Too Far: Spiritual Exercises 50 and 52," *The Way* 50, no. 3 (October 2011): 113–20, critiques the meditation on the Fall of the Angels [50] as unbiblical and nonsensical in light of what we know and believe about God. Likewise, in Ex. 53, would God consign a person to hell for one sin without a moment of repentance and mercy?

14. Tony Kushner's Pulitzer Prize–winning drama *Angels in America* (New York: Theatre Communications Group, 1992), demonstrates this interest. Human interaction with angels provides the dramatic elements of this popular contemporary play. Gerard O'Mahony suggests that we need not attribute sin to the action of individual personal spirits; the "fall of the angels" is simply a colorful way of externalizing the urge to give in to evil. Furthermore, we need not concretize God's messages to us through "good angels." There are three basic messages from God—that God cares for each one, God's ultimate strength, and the arrival of the Day of the Lord—but we need not attribute these messages to Raphael, Michael, and Gabriel. Likewise, one's guardian angel is God's personal message to me that I am loved uniquely (2018, 115). On the other hand, spiritual writer Mary DeTurris Proust describes angels as the "ethereal, often-gritty messengers of God," unseen companions on this journey, serving us in big and small ways, reminding us that we are always accompanied in our journey through life in "Always and Everywhere…Angels," *Give Us This Day* (September 2020): 5. Biblical theologian Walter Wink speaks of angels as the spirit of a whole community, taking his cue from Revelation. See, e.g., Henry French, ed., *Walter Wink, Collected Readings* (New York: Abingdon, 2013). This diversity suggests a variety of ways in which individuals might pray about (and with) angels.

15. See Antonia Fraser, *The Weaker Vessel* (New York: Vintage Books, 1984) for an exploration of the specific situation of women in the seventeenth century. Fraser documents the understanding of the phrase "the weaker vessel." She interprets the phrase not only as applied to the realm of physical prowess but, by association, to morality as well.

16. See John A. Phillips, *Eve: The History of an Idea* (San Francisco: Harper and Row, 1984). Phillips examines Eve's treatment in Scripture,

theological treatises, and literary works to illuminate the tradition that blames Eve for the "fall" in both Catholic and Protestant theology. His sources include artistic illustrations covering 2,500 years.

17. Eric Jensen begins his treatment of hell in the Exercises with the conviction that its whole theology must be rethought. He follows the *Catechism of the Catholic Church* in his reimagining: "Hell is now understood as a 'state of definitive self-exclusion from communion with God and the blessed,' rather than a penalty designed by the Creator." While meditating on the prodigal son, he suggests, fear becomes truly a grace: the fear that one could actually choose to turn away from God, willingly and willfully. Fear is transformed from servile fear of God's wrath to filial fear that I have the power to choose to exclude *myself* from relationship. See "Hell and the Image of God in the Spiritual Exercises," *The Way* 57, no. 3 (July 2018): 91–102. Larry Warner, *Journey with Jesus* (Downers Grove, IL: IVP, 2010), 118–42, likewise offers biblical texts to assist the one making the Exercises to move through the dynamic of the First Week, with no particular exercise to substitute for Ignatius's text on hell.

18. Agbonkhianmeghe Orobator, *Theology Brewed in an African Pot* (Maryknoll, NY: Orbis Books, 2008), 63.

19. See Sally Ann McReynolds and Ann O'Hara Graff, "Sin—When Women Are the Context," in *In the Embrace of God: Feminist Approaches to Theological Anthropology* (Maryknoll, NY: Orbis Books, 1995), 161–72, and the discussion of women's experience of sin and grace in Georgia Masters Keightley, "The Challenge of Feminist Theology," in *Horizons on Catholic Feminist Theology*, ed. Joann Wolski Conn and Walter E. Conn (Washington, DC: Georgetown University Press, 1992), 37–60. The specific section is titled "Woman's Experience: The Discussion of Sin and Grace."

20. At least two adaptations exist in which psalms are suggested as the basis for praying the Spiritual Exercises. See Juan Benitz, *Los Ejercicios Espirituales: Meditados con los Salmos* (Bilbao: Mensajero del Corazón de Jesús, 1965) and Luis Alonso Schökel, *Contempladlo y Quedaréis Radiantes: Salmos y Ejercicios* (Santander: Editorial Sal Terrae, 1996). For an English translation of the suggested psalms and Exercises, see John Endres and Elizabeth Liebert's *A Retreat with the Psalms: Resources for Personal and Communal Prayer* (Mahwah, NJ: Paulist Press, 2001), appendix 2.

Chapter 7

1. Ignatius's personal experience of Christ is deeply affected by his convalescence in the Loyola residence, continuing his pilgrim journey to Montserrat, his formation in the basics of what will become the Exercises at Manresa, and his interaction with persons along the way as he told his story and listened to theirs, and his vision at Loyola of Mary and the child Jesus (*Autobiog*, #10). While at prayer in Manresa, he saw with his interior eyes the humanity of Jesus (*Autobiog*, #29) and describes his enlightenment at the river Cardoner that sustained him the rest of his life. His desire to go to Jerusalem and walk in the footsteps of Jesus propelled him into a pilgrim mode.

Many sources formed his religious imagination: the art found in the churches he so often frequented, the preaching he listened to and eventually practiced, the spiritual conversations so important to him, especially in his early spiritual growth, his all too brief travels in the Holy Land. Being conscious of this imaginative religious influence can assist us in interpreting Ignatius's images and references to Jesus Christ; his constant inclusion of Our Lady, reflecting the influence of the Marian piety of his times; and his references to the saints with the kind of familiarity that suggests he considered them part of the family.

2. For a more extensive analysis of the use of Christology and the oppression of women, see Rosemary Radford Ruether's work on Christology and feminism in *To Change the World* (New York: Crossroad, 1990). She examines the Scholasticism of Thomas Aquinas, who argues that male is normative and the fullness of human potential, thus concluding that women are defective. Therefore, the incarnation of the Logos of God into the male is not a historical accident but an ontological necessity (45).

3. In a recent work, *Creation and the Cross: The Mercy of God for a Planet in Peril* (Maryknoll, NY: Orbis Books, 2018), Elizabeth Johnson takes on Anselmian atonement theory that focuses salvation on Jesus's death on the cross, constructing in its place a Christology flowing from creation that is positive not only to women but to all created beings and the planet itself.

4. Anne Carr (1996, 160–61) gives an example of this scholarly search: "Uses of the Christ symbol in theological anthropology, ecclesiology and ministerial theology to support political, social and ecclesiastical patriarchy are in fact a perversion of its positive religious content. These

uses are a sobering reminder that no symbol, no tradition, is entirely pure but rather all are ambiguous, multivalent, open to both positive and negative human use." See also Mary Hembrow Snyder, *The Christology of Rosemary Radford Ruether: A Critical Introduction* (Mystic, CT: Twenty-Third Publications, 1988).

5. See Caroline Walker Bynum, *Jesus as Mother: Studies in the Spirituality of the High Middle Ages* (Berkeley: University of California Press, 1982). Roger Haight extensively explores various holistic interpretations of Jesus in his chapter "Appropriating Jesus in Christology," in *Jesus, Symbol of God* (Maryknoll, NY: Orbis, 1999).

6. The ideal set forth in Crusader spirituality bears a strong resemblance to the kingdom meditation in the Spiritual Exercises. Hans Wolter, "Elements of Crusade Spirituality in St. Ignatius," in *Ignatius of Loyola: His Personality and Spiritual Heritage*, ed. Friedrich Wulf (St. Louis: Institute of Jesuit Sources, 1977), 101, notes, "In Christ he saw the true leader whom one must follow....The Crusader considered the exertions, deprivations and sufferings of the journey into foreign lands—he wished to be homeless with the homeless Lord—and especially the constant threat of death, to be a spiritual participation in the suffering and death of Christ. Beyond that, victory—granted but seldom—was experienced as a participation in the victory of Christ."

7. Jaroslav Pelikan devotes a chapter in *Jesus through the Centuries* (New Haven, CT: Yale University Press, 1985) to illustrating various interpretations and emphases given to the image of King of Kings. Early Christian martyrs claimed Christ as their king, threatening the political stability of Caesar by refusing to acknowledge the emperor as divine. Constantine attributed his military success to Christ the "victor King," guaranteeing the title permanence and honor in the tradition. The cross became a kingly symbol, emblazoned on the royal crowns and banners of European monarchs. The eternal kingship of Christ evolved into the divine right of kings who waged holy wars justifying political sovereignty. All these images reinforced the belief that political authority was linked to ecclesiastical authority. "Christ was King, the Church was a monarchy, the Pope was a monarch, and it was by his authority that earthly monarchs exercised their authority" (56). Some today still claim this leadership model.

8. The discovery of personally meaningful images and metaphors throughout the Exercises process is extremely important, notes Marion Aggeler, "Women's Metaphors for Freedom," *The Way Supplement* 74

(1992): 20–29. She suggests that the images and metaphors that emerge for women may reflect differences in the way they come to freedom. For example, freedom and healing can come when women identify and live out personally meaningful metaphors.

John Veltri (1998, 352–53) offers some questions that may help a retreatant to get in touch with her personal myth: "If you could take your deepest desire, your vision for yourself in the world and express it in a story what would it be? If you were to die five years from now, for what concrete things or ways of behaving would you like to be remembered in an honest obituary about you? What would you really need in order to survive with energy and meaningful enthusiasm? What images give you life? What stories of the recent past capture your dreams for yourself in the next decade? If you could take your deepest desire and vision for the world and express it in a personal myth or story what would it be? What type of person would embody this vision? What would be an appropriate and expected response to this person? Since Jesus is the embodiment of all our deepest desires, what prayer or offering do you desire to make now?"

9. See Sallie McFague's groundbreaking and scholarly *The Body of God: An Ecological Theology* (1993) as well as *Models of God: Theology for an Ecological, Nuclear Age* (Philadelphia: Fortress, 1987).

10. Additional sources related to humility include the following: G. Gilleman, "Humility," in the *New Catholic Encyclopedia*, vol. 7 (New York: McGraw-Hill, 1967), 234–36, defines *humility* as the "virtue by which a [person] attributes to God all the good he possesses" (234). The article explores the development of humility in the Bible, theological thought, and human practice. A different approach is found in William J. Bennett, *The Book of Virtues* (New York: Simon and Schuster, 1993). This book is intended to aid the moral education of the young. Ten virtues are considered: self-discipline, compassion, responsibility, friendship, work, courage, perseverance, honesty, loyalty, and faith. There is no mention of humility.

11. Barbara Bedolla (1984, 30) offers a down-to-earth reframing of the "Three Classes of Persons" with the example of the various possible responses of a person who is asked to help with an important project. The first kind of response is to say, "I want to help but I can't commit now." The second is to agree to help but by doing what they wish to do to help (even if it isn't what is actually needed). The third response is an open-hearted generous "What do you need? I'll do whatever you ask."

12. Updated historical information and spiritual writing can be found in Paulist Press's Classics of Western Spirituality series. We also recommend biographies of well-known saints of the tradition as well as accounts of modern saints. A recent collection by Robert Ellsberg, *All Saints: Daily Reflections on Saints, Prophets and Witnesses for Our Time* (New York: Crossroad, 1997) could provide a rich resource for directors from Agnes and Anthony of Egypt to Pedro Arrupe and Thea Bowman. Ellsberg also suggests further resources. See also Elizabeth Johnson, *Friends of God and Prophets: A Feminist Theological Reading of the Communion of Saints* (New York: Continuum, 1998).

Chapter 8

1. See Raymond Brown, *A Crucified Christ in Holy Week* (Collegeville, MN: Liturgical Press, 1986). This small, insightful book of essays on the gospel passion narratives provides an invaluable resource for anyone pondering the passion.

2. Elizabeth Johnson describes this event in greater detail in "Redeeming the Name of Christ," in *Freeing Theology: The Essentials of Theology in Feminist Perspective*, ed. Catherine Mowry LaCugna (San Francisco: Harper San Francisco, 1993), 115–16.

3. Readers may be interested in a publication of the Intercommunity Peace and Justice Center in Seattle, Washington. Their 1999 "Stations of the Cross in the Lives of Women" illustrates an effective adaptation of a traditional religious practice by incorporating the experience of women's lives in their prayers and reflection.

Chapter 9

1. This contemplation is titled "First contemplation: How Christ Our Lord Appeared to Our Lady."

2. See Pheme Perkins, "I Have Seen the Lord (John 20:18): Women Witnesses to the Resurrection," *Interpretation* 46, no. 1 (January 1992): 31–61. Her thesis suggests that women were the first to hear the Easter message and played a crucial role in the founding of the earliest Christian community. She also cites the importance of the role of Mary of Magdala.

The Spiritual Exercises Reclaimed

Recent years have yielded significant movement in the reclaiming of Mary Magdalene. Throughout much of Christian history following Pope Gregory (who, in 591, called her a sinful woman), Mary Magdalene was misrepresented as a fallen woman, prostitute, and penitent. She is now being reclaimed as a leading figure among those who followed Jesus and as the one who first witnessed to and proclaimed Christ risen. In 2016 Pope Francis elevated the memorial of St. Mary Magdalene to a feast day on a par with other major apostles like St. Peter. Much recent research has been done on Mary Magdalene and the significance of her role in the early church. Still controversial but widely read works, such as Cynthia Bourgeault's *The Meaning of Mary Magdalene: Discovering the Woman at the Heart of Christianity*, raise important questions in light of recently discovered texts, such as the *Gospel of Mary Magdalene*, which have given scholars new material to work with. Even if one disregards such emerging scholarship and looks only at those Gospel texts included in the traditional canon of Scripture, the role of Mary Magdalene as the first called to preach the good news of the resurrection is indisputable and as such a liberating gift for women making the Exercises.

3. Some women have found the title of Pope Francis's encyclical *Fratelli Tutti*, which literally translates into English as "all brothers," alienating. Furthermore, women's voices are absent from the text despite the fact that the vitally important message of the encyclical is one of inclusion, love, and solidarity—values that women connect with deeply.

4. Elizabeth Johnson, *Truly Our Sister: A Theology of Mary in the Communion of Saints* (2003) does a superb job of reclaiming the "real" Mary and can be helpful for directors in presenting Mary in a way that a retreatant can relate to. See also Julia Dowd, "Gathering the Graces: Women, the Spiritual Exercises, and Jesuit Education" (DMin diss., Pacific School of Religion, 2018) for some touching testimonies about Mary's importance in some of her retreatant's prayer.

5. Some of the significant scholarship on Mary includes R. E. Brown, K. P. Donfried, J. A. Fitzmyer, J. Reumann, eds., *Mary in the New Testament* (Philadelphia: Fortress Press, 1978); Ivone Gebara and Maria C. Bingemer, *Mary, Mother of God, Mother of the Poor* (Maryknoll, NY: Orbis Books, 1989); Hilda Graef, *Mary: A History of Doctrine and Devotion*, 2 vols. (New York: Sheed and Ward, 1965); Carol Frances Jegen, ed., *Mary according to Women* (Kansas City, MO: Leaven Press, 1985); Elizabeth Johnson, "Blessed Virgin Mary," in *Encyclopedia of Catholicism*, ed. Richard McBrien (San Francisco: HarperSanFrancisco, 1995), 832–38;

Notes

Michael O'Carroll, *Theotokos: A Theological Encyclopedia of the Blessed Virgin Mary*, rev. ed. (Dublin: Dominican Publications, 1983); Rosemary Radford Ruether, *Mary, the Feminine Face of the Church* (Philadelphia: Westminster Press, 1977); Marina Warner, *Alone of All Her Sex* (New York: Vintage Books, 1983); and Elizabeth Johnson *Truly Our Sister: A Theology of Mary in the Communion of Saints* (New York: Continuum, 2003).

6. The title of this Contemplation is often translated in English as "The Contemplation to Attain Love" or "The Contemplation to Attain Divine Love." David Fleming, *Like the Lightning: The Dynamics of the Ignatian Exercises* (St. Louis: Institute of Jesuit Sources, 2004), 125, suggests that English translations "usually do not identify clearly the Ignatian movement" and proposes that "a clearer translation, not literal or succinct, but more accurately describing the dynamics of this exercise would be: 'Contemplation on the Ways that God Loves So That We Might Be Graced to Love Similarly.'" If we use the traditional English translation, it is important to explain the word *attain* as meaning "to come to" or "to arrive at" rather than "to earn or achieve."

7. See Michael Buckley's classic article, "The Contemplation to Attain Love," *The Way Supplement* 24 (Spring 1975): 92–104, for discussion of placement and content. See also Ian Tomlinson, "The Contemplation to Attain Love," *The Way* 50, no. 3 (October 2011): 65–76. This article includes useful discussion of living the Contemplation in daily life after the retreat.

8. Franz Jalics, "The Contemplative Phase of the Ignatian Exercises," *The Way Supplement* 103 (2002): 25–42, esp. 33–34, reminds us that the Three Methods of Praying [238–260] follow immediately after the "Our Father" that concludes the Contemplation to Attain Love. This placement strongly suggests that these three Methods, and particularly the third, "Praying According to Rhythmic Methods" [258–260], are especially suited for life following the Exercises. Here, Ignatius is showing those who have completed the full dynamic of the Exercises a whole new way of praying that is simple, direct, and provides the most opportunity for God's grace to continue working.

9. Ian Tomlinson's "The Contemplation to Attain Love" highlights the value of the human person as seen in the contemplation but develops it in relation to how the exercitant comes to see others, which can be extended to how a woman sees herself.

10. George Aschenbrenner, "A Consoling Companion: Faithful Beyond Any Doubts," *The Way* 45, no. 3 (July 2007): 67–83, is very explicit about this reality: "Our beloved friends who have died, who lived and died in [Christ], share in his intercessory love and mission. Thus, they are related to us in a new way, a way that makes them newly present, loving and caring. We have not utterly lost them. Their former friendly and familiar presence we will surely miss, maybe in some cases till we die. But as we stay close to the risen Jesus, we also grow into a sense of their new presence and relationship with us" (71–72).

Chapter 10

1. Discernment of Spirits, central as it is both within and outside the context of the Spiritual Exercises, appears in many recent works on the Spiritual Exercises or Ignatian Spirituality. See, e.g., William Barry, *Letting God Come Close: An Approach to the Ignatian Spiritual Exercises* (Chicago: Loyola Press, 2001), chaps. 8—10; William Barry, *Spiritual Direction and the Encounter with God: A Theological Inquiry*, rev. ed. (Mahwah, NJ: Paulist Press, 2004), chap. 6; Dean Brackley, *The Call to Discernment in Troubled Times: New Perspectives on the Transformative Wisdom of Ignatius of Loyola* (New York: Crossroad, 2004), chaps. 6 and 15; David Fleming, *Like the Lightening: The Dynamics of the Ignatian Exercises* (St. Louis: Institute of Jesuit Sources, 2004), chaps. 15 and 16; George A. Aschenbrenner, *Stretched for Greater Glory: What to Expect from the Spiritual Exercises* (Chicago: Loyola Press, 2004), chaps. 12 and 13; Joseph Tetlow, *Making Choices in Christ: The Foundations of Ignatian Spirituality* (Chicago: Loyola Press, 2008), chaps. 29—32; Brian O'Leary, *God Ever Greater: Exploring Ignatian Spirituality* (Collegeville, MN: Liturgical Press, 2019), pt. 1, chap. 5.

Recent volumes dedicated to Discernment of Spirits or discernment understood more widely include two volumes by Mark E. Thibodeaux, *Ignatian Discernment of Spirits for Spiritual Direction and Pastoral Care: Going Deeper* (Chicago: Loyola Press, 2020) and *God's Voice Within: The Ignatian Way to Discover God's Will* (Chicago: Loyola Press, 2010); Timothy Gallagher's two volumes, *The Discernment of Spirits: An Ignatian Guide for Everyday Living* (New York: Crossroad, 2005) and *Spiritual Consolation: An Ignatian Guide to the Greater Discernment of Spirits* (New York: Crossroad, 2007); and Ladislas Orsy, *Discernment: Theology and Practice,*

Notes

Communal and Personal (Collegeville, MN: Liturgical Press, 2020, first published in 1973).

Recent articles on Discernment of Spirits include Jesús Corella, "Spiritual Desolation in Today's World," *The Way* 43, no. 1 (January 2004): 97–108; Antonio Guillén, "What We Learn From Desolation," *The Way* 43, no. 3 (July 2004): 19–34, and "Deceptions in Discernment," *The Way*, 49, no.3 (July 2010): 81–93; Ignacio Iglesias, "Spiritual Consolation and Envy," *The Way* 43, no. 3 (July 2004): 57–69; Ignatius Jesudasan, "Angels of Light and Darkness," *The Way* 43, no. 3 (July 2004): 71–79; William Barry, "Discernment of Spirits as an Act of Faith" in *An Ignatian Spirituality Reader*, ed. George W. Traub (Chicago: Loyola Press, 2008), 159–70; Timothy Gallagher, "When Do the Second Week Rules Apply?" *The Way* 47, no. 1–2 (January/April 2008): 125–42; Robert R. Marsh, "Discernment of Spirits: A Cosmological View, *The Way* 48, no. 1 (January 2009): 9–24; Gerard O'Mahony, "'From Good to Better' or 'From Bad to Worse': Exercise 335 with Diagram," *The Way* 49, no. 3 (July 2010): 45–51; Mark Rotsaert, "Spiritual Discernment: The Horizon That Is God," *The Way* 58, no. 4 (October 2019): 99–110; and Roger Dawson, "Psychological Understandings of Interior Movements," *The Way* 59, no. 3 (July 2020): 7–14.

2. Ignatius Jesudasan, "Angel of Light and Darkness, *The Way* 43, no. 3 (July 2004): 71–73, 77.

3. See Kathleen Fischer, *Transforming Fire: Women Using Anger Constructively* (Mahwah, NJ: Paulist, 1999) for excellent treatment of the constructive uses of women's anger.

4. Mark Rotsaert, "Spiritual Discernment: The Horizon That Is God," *The Way* 58, no. 4 (October 2019): 101, takes this approach. Thoughts that seem to come from one knows not where need not be attributed to evil spirits, but simply to our own unconscious.

5. Wink's 1998 work, *The Powers That Be: Theology for a New Millennium*, summarizes his trilogy on the Powers. For further detail, see the third volume, *Engaging the Powers: Discernment and Resistance in a World of Domination* (Minneapolis: Fortress, 1992).

6. For a treatment of structural discernment that is based on Ignatian Discernment of Spirits and Election, see Elizabeth Liebert, *The Soul of Discernment: A Spiritual Practice for Communities and Institutions* (Louisville, KY: Westminster John Knox, 2015).

7. We will prescind from the mental activity that occurs when we sleep, although such an investigation could yield interesting implications for discernment of spirits.

8. For a thorough discussion of this distinction, see Jules Toner (1982), app. 2, 271–79. For the relationship between depression and desolation, see Mary Jo Meadow, "The Dark Side of Mysticism: Depression and 'The Dark Night,'" *Pastoral Psychology* 33 (Winter 1984): 105–25; Joann Wolski Conn, *Spirituality and Personal Maturity* (Mahwah, NJ: Paulist, 1989), chap. 6; and Gerald May (1982a), 84–92. For a treatment of the dark night from the perspective of contemporary women's experience, see Constance FitzGerald, "Impasse and Dark Night," in *Living with Apocalypse: Spiritual Resources for Social Compassion*, ed. Tilden Edwards, reprinted in *Women's Spirituality: Resources for Development*, 2nd ed., ed. Joann Wolski Conn (Mahwah, NJ: Paulist, 1996), 410–35.

9. Jules Toner (1982, 260–70) presents theological and scriptural arguments for and against the existence of Satan and evil spirits and concludes that it is wiser to assume their existence as long as they are suitably demythologized.

10. This retreat in daily life developed by the Sisters of Providence contains a rewriting of the first set of rules for discernment that is strikingly simple. It provides another pastoral option for those giving the Exercises; however, its very simplicity may need elaboration.

1. If I'm stuck in a sinful pattern, I GO WITH thoughts of change and GO WITH feelings of remorse; and I LET GO of imaginary satisfactions that keep me stuck in what feels good but isn't.
2. If I'm breaking loose from a sinful pattern, I GO WITH inspiring ideas and GO WITH feelings of courage, strength, and hope; and I LET GO of imaginary obstacles and feelings of discouragement.
3. I know I am in desolation when I sink into feelings that are hopeless, lukewarm, and separated or into thoughts that are despairing, selfish, or put-downs.
4. When I am in desolation, I make no decisions.
5. When I am in desolation, I act against my feelings by prayer, self-knowledge, and penance.
6. When I am in desolation, I put myself in God's care.
7. When I am in desolation, I persevere by thinking of future consolation.
8. When I am in desolation, I look for the cause.
9. When I am in desolation, I pray my own "Psalm 63."

10. I know I am in consolation when I rejoice in feelings of union with God and thoughts of giving myself to God.
11. When I am in consolation, I gather strength for future challenges.
12. When I am in consolation, I'll pray my own "Magnificat."
13. When I sense an evil spirit, I act with courage.
14. When I sense an evil spirit, I am open about my experience.
15. To avoid an evil spirit, I learn my own strengths and weaknesses. (1990, 246–47)

11. Again, the Sisters of Providence have created an elegantly simple rendition of the second set of rules:

1. I expect joy and spiritual gladness from the good spirit.
2. I reject sadness and turmoil from the evil spirit.
3. I recognize the creative power and Providence of God in surprise consolations.
4. I am aware that I may be consoled by good spirits leading me toward action that is better or by bad spirits leading me toward action that is worse.
5. I am alert to recognize a deceitful train of thought which starts out good but ends up less good.
6. I observe the direction of my thoughts; where they begin, continue, and end.
7. I recognize a good spirit when the whole process is good.
8. I recognize an evil spirit when I end up where I didn't intend to go or lose my peace.
9. By reviewing how I got where I did in my thought or action, I avoid repeating the pattern.
10. I expect a gentle touch from a good spirit but a harsh touch from an evil spirit when I am going from good to better.
11. I experience a strong touch from a good spirit and a soft one from the evil spirit when I am going from good to less good.
12. I trust the consolation which comes as a surprise from God; but I discern carefully before I act on what follows. (1990, 248–49)

12. James Fowler's major works include *Stages of Faith: The Psychology of Human Development and the Quest for Meaning* (New York:

Harper and Row, 1981); *Faith Development and Pastoral Care* (Philadelphia: Fortress Press, 1987); *Weaving the New Creation: Stages of Faith and the Public Church* (San Francisco: Harper, 1991); and *Faithful Change: The Personal and Public Challenges of Postmodern Life* (Nashville: Abingdon, 1996). Robert Kegan's two seminal works are *The Evolving Self: Problem and Process in Human Development* (Cambridge, MA: Harvard University Press, 1982) and *In Over Our Heads: The Mental Demands of Modern Life* (Cambridge, MA: Harvard University Press, 1994). See also Gilligan (1982); Jane Loevinger, *Ego Development: Conceptions and Theories* (San Francisco: Jossey-Bass, 1976); and Susanne Cook-Greuter, "Postautonomous Ego Development: A Study of Its Nature and Development" (Integral Publishers Dissertation Series, 1999).

13. Relevant here, as noted earlier, John of the Cross examines a similar phenomenological experience from a different set of presuppositions. For a comparison of John's Dark Night and Ignatius's desolation, see Jules Toner (1982), 271–82. The key ontological difference: desolation is caused by the evil one or permitted by God for a period for purposes of strengthening the seeker, while passive dark nights are caused only by God for purposes of drawing the seeker ever closer—the darkness is the *apparent* absence of God. One of the key phenomenological markers of a passive dark night: despite the absence of positive affect and any sense of God's presence, one still esteems and desires God all the more, painful because the yearning is never satisfied.

Chapter 11

1. George Aschenbrenner offers a thoughtful meditation on the ideal conditions for election in *Stretched for Greater Glory: What to Expect from the Spiritual Exercises* (Chicago: Loyola Press, 2004), 101–16.

2. Joseph Tetlow, *Making Choices in Christ: The Foundations of Ignatian Spirituality* (Chicago: Loyola Press, 2008), 106, points out that any decision among good things necessarily comes back to the question: What do I most authentically desire? Authentic desire is only cultivated through a moral life based on prayer and spiritual companionship by others.

3. Dean Brackley (2004, 126–32) discusses this point in some detail; making this determination can be complex in today's world.

Notes

4. From a biblically oriented perspective such as that held by many mainline Protestants, David A. Brondos, *The Letter and the Spirit: Discerning God's Will in a Complex World* (Minneapolis: Augsburg, 2005), 59–71, works through the exegetical and ethical aspects of some of the complex situations women find themselves in today, including divorce, homosexuality, the position of women in home and church, and abortion. Two principles transcend the different issues he considers: do not separate the letter and the spirit of biblical texts, and seek the ultimate concern of the biblical writers, namely, to bring wholeness, justice, peace, and well-being into the lives of human beings. To accomplish this goal, we must hold fast to our freedom in Christ, becoming a servant to justice despite the difficulties and risks of this path. Brondos does not advert to Ignatius or to election, but his bottom line does seem to be in harmony with Ignatius's insistence on spiritual freedom as the foundational grace of all discerned decision-making and careful conscience formation within a faith community.

5. If using the election processes outside the Spiritual Exercises, prayerfully connecting the decision-making process to this call to discipleship is key.

6. For a discussion on consolation as a criterion for recognizing God's will, see Karl Rahner, "The Ignatian Process for Discovering the Will of God in an Existential Situation," in *Ignatius of Loyola: His Personality and Spiritual Heritage, 1556–1956*, ed. Friedrich Wulf (St. Louis: Institute of Jesuit Sources, 1977), 288. Jules Toner (1982, 301–13) engages in an extended critique of and dialogue with Rahner, taking exception with his interpretation in several places. Finally, Brian McDermott (2018, 34–39) argues carefully for a precise interpretation of the role of Spiritual Consolation in the Second Time and summarizes English language authors on this point (39–50).

For a simple process based on the Second Time, see Sisters of Providence, *The Love of Christ Impels Us* (Spokane: Sisters of Providence Provincial Administration, 1991), 237–38.

7. Nicholas Standaert (2014, 39) offers a slightly different perspective on the relationship of the two processes in the Third Time by focusing on refining the reasoning process: the first process weighs the advantages and disadvantages carefully and the second attempts to filter out any subjective bias by striving toward greater objectivity.

8. Standaert (2014, 40–55) explores recent research on the relationship of thinking to feeling that provides helpful nuance to these various modes of decision-making. He sees the relationship as a circular, though

asymmetrical, movement. When we draw up a list of advantages and disadvantages, we already experience them, and we do so colored by our past experiences. Becoming aware of this linkage can allow us to adjust our judgment to become more able to place God in the center of the decision-making process.

9. Both Mark Thibodeaux, *God's Voice Within: The Ignatian Way to Discover God's Will* (Chicago: Loyola Press, 2010), 158–76; and Elizabeth Liebert, *Way of Discernment: Spiritual Practices for Decision Making* (Louisville, KY: Westminster John Knox, 2008), 19–21, frame Ignatius's election materials into a series of general steps to assist in discerned decision-making. Thibodeaux suggests four basic steps: (1) Becoming quiet, including a regular habit of prayer; (2) Gathering data; (3) Dreaming dreams to unleash deep desires; (4) Pondering the dreams and tracing the movement of consolation and desolation. Liebert stresses (1) Praying for indifference; (2) Framing the matter carefully; (3) Gathering appropriate data; (4) Weighing, using several of Ignatius's processes; (5) Making a tentative decision based on the pondering; and (5) Engaging in a prayerful time of confirmation prior to implementing the decision. For a simple method for making a personal election based on the Spiritual Exercises [178–83] but free from Ignatian jargon, see Sisters of Providence, *The Love of Christ Impels Us* (Spokane: Sisters of Providence Provincial Administration, 1991), 241–45. For another straightforward process, likewise based on Ignatian election, see Wilkie Au and Noreen Cannon Au, "Refining the Acoustics of the Heart," in *Ignatian Spirituality Reader: Contemporary Writings on St. Ignatius of Loyola, the Spiritual Exercises, Discernment, and More*, ed. George W. Traub (Chicago: Loyola Press, 2008), 192–219, esp. 204–7.

10. The optimal number of options is between four and six, and within this range, people feel more satisfied with their decision after the fact. Standaert (2014, 37), citing Sheena Iyengar, *The Art of Choosing* (New York: Twelve, 2010), 48–49, 183ff.

11. Standaert (2014, 38), citing Barry Schwartz, *The Paradox of Choice: Why Less Is More* (New York: HarperCollins, 2004), 29–33.

12. Standaert (2014, 40ff), citing Antonio Damasio, *Descartes' Error: Emotion, Reason and the Human Brain* (New York: Avon, 1995), multiple places.

13. For more insight into and an accessible look at the neuropsychology of how the brain works and how this influences the way we make

decisions, see Jonah Lehrer, *The Decisive Moment: How the Brain Makes Up Its Mind* (Edinburgh: Canongate, 2009).

14. Helpful resources on the Quaker Clearness Committee include Suzanne Farnham, Joseph P. Gill, and Taylor McLean, *Listening Hearts: Discerning Call in Community* (Harrisburg, PA: Morehouse, 1991); Parker Palmer, "The Clearness Committee," *Weavings* 3 (July/August 1988): 37–40; and Parker J. Palmer, *The Courage to Teach* (San Francisco: Jossey-Bass, 1998).

15. Focusing, as developed by Eugene Gendlin, can be summarized in six steps. Of course, much more can be said about each step, but even this outline can provide sufficient structure for experiencing profound inner wisdom.

    Focusing: A Short Form

1. Clear a space (inside of you)

   How are you? What's between you and feeling fine? Don't answer; let what comes in your body do the answering. Don't go into anything. Greet each concern that comes. Put each aside for a while, next to you. Except for that, are you fine?

2. Felt sense

   Pick one problem to focus on. Don't go into the problem. What do you sense in your body when you recall the whole of that problem? Sense all of that, the sense of the whole thing, the murky discomfort or the unclear body-sense of it.

3. Get a handle

   What is the quality of the felt sense? What one word, phrase, or image comes out of this felt sense? What quality word would fit it best?

4. Resonate

   Go back and forth between word (or image) and the felt sense. Is that right? If they match, have the sensation of matching several times. If the felt sense changes, follow it with your attention.

5. Ask

   "What is it about the whole problem, that makes me so_____?"

When stuck, ask questions: What is the worst of this feeling? What's so bad about this? What does it need? What should happen? Don't answer; wait for the feeling to stir and give you an answer.

What would it feel like if it was all OK? Let the body answer: What is in the way of that?

6. Receive

Welcome what came. Be glad it spoke. It is only one step on this problem, not the last. Now that you know where it is, you can leave it and come back to it later. Protect it from critical voices that interrupt.

Does your body want another round of focusing, or is this a good stopping place? (1981, 177–78).

Chapter 12

1. Erin M. Cline (2018) not only raises the possibility that the Spiritual Exercises might be offered to adherents of traditions other than Christianity, but she also carefully articulates principles for adapting in a variety of interreligious contexts while carefully maintaining the integrity of the Exercises.

2. This polarization is currently very evident in the Roman Catholic Church in the United States.

3. Gill Goulding (2015, 9–80) summarizes Ignatius's response to the possibility that Claude Jay might be made a bishop of Trieste, showing clearly how Ignatius, as a result of his own discernment, actively lobbied personally and used all his high-ranking connections to get the pope and the king to withdraw the nomination. See also Ignatius of Loyola, *Letters and Instructions* (St. Louis: Institute of Jesuit Sources), 159–64. Ignatius's letter to Francis Borgia dated June 5, 1552, reveals his personal discernment in response to a proposal from Charles V to Pope Julius III to confer the cardinalate on Francis Borgia. After three days of intense discernment, Ignatius came to peace about opposing this move directly to the pope. However, Ignatius also recognized the possibility that the Holy Spirit could move one person to favor something for a particular reason while moving another person to oppose it for a different reason. When Ignatius shared his discernment with Borgia, Borgia hesitated for two

years, until finally he himself decided not to accept such an honor. See *Letters and Instructions*, 376–77.

4. The literal translation, according to Michael Buckley (1995, 452n39), is "For the true sense of things which we should maintain in the Church militant, the following rules are to be observed." George Ganss (1991, 211) tries to capture the polysemic nature of *sentir* by his translation of the title as "Rules for thinking judging and feeling with the Church to have the genuine attitude which we ought to maintain in the Church militant, we should observe the Following Rules."

5. Ganss (1991, 431n153) explains his translation decision as follows: "*Sentido*, sense, reason, feeling and many other meanings, is often used by Ignatius with nuances of his own. Frequently, as here, it means cognition which is basically intellectual but is savored so repeatedly that it becomes also deeply emotional and 'satisfies the soul.' Thus it becomes a habitual attitude of mind, a frame of reference instinctively used to guide one's life."

6. For a systematic discussion of each rule, see Jesús Corella, *Sentir la Iglesia: Comentario a las Reglas Ingacianas para el Sentido Verdadero de Iglesia* (Bilbao, Spain: Mensajero, 1996): chaps. 5—7; and Gill Goulding (2015, 19–51).

7. Vatican Council II calls for this same attitude in *Gaudium et Spes* 92.

8. According to O'Malley (1993, 49–50), the Rule most likely to cause controversy in Ignatius's time was the fourteenth [366], which advised great caution in preaching about predestination.

9. The principle of justification by faith alone is tied to the Protestant principle because, in our relation to God, it holds that we are dependent on God alone, and in no way on ourselves. We are thus grasped by grace, which is another way of saying that we have faith. The Protestant principle was frequently at work in the theological struggles of Ignatius's time. The 1999 document "Joint Declaration on the Doctrine of Justification by Faith," signed by the Roman Catholic Church and the Lutheran World Federation, marked a historic moment in the reunion of Christian churches and a striking reversal of earlier entrenched positions about the meaning of church.

10. Douglas Marcoullier, "Archbishop with an Attitude: Oscar Romero's Sentir con la Iglesia," *Studies in the Spirituality of Jesuits* 35, no. 3 (May 2003) provides a stunning example of this kind of love for the church that led Romero, over time, to such radical clarity and consistency in identifying with and speaking about the concrete circumstances of the poor in his archdiocese that it ultimately cost him his life. Romero's conflicts

were with a range of persons: members of the hierarchy who understood church teachings differently than he did, Vatican officials who were often misinformed, oligarchs who absolutized their wealth, soldiers who absolutized their military power, and politicians who absolutized their governmental power (51). Yet his love for the church was deeper than any of these conflicts.

11. Joseph Tetlow (2008, 116–18) makes just this point.

12. John W. Padberg (1993, 3–9) gives an overview of the eleven popes during Ignatius's lifetime. Even such a brief sketch reveals the substance of the saying of the time: "Everything is for sale in Rome" (8).

13. The doctrinal assessment of the Leadership Conference of Women Religious (a hierarchically approved entity representing most of the Women's Religious Congregations in the United States) conducted 2012–15 by the Congregation for the Doctrine of the Faith provides a current example of such realistic reverence in the face of struggle with the Catholic Church. The Major Superiors quietly but insistently and prayerfully stood their ground concerning the accusations leveled against their recent decisions and actions. See Leadership Conference of Women Religious, *However Long the Night: Making Meaning in a Time of Crisis* (2018). The authors, all of whom took part in the process, describe how their own spiritual groundings helped them make the journey and how it led to their own spiritual growth. They describe methods, processes, and practices that can transfer to other situations of conflict with or in the church.

14. Pope Francis, *Fratelli Tutti* (2020), contains numerous passages that make this point, as is indicated by the chapter titles "Envisaging and Engendering an Open World" (chap. 3), "A Heart Open to the Whole World" (chap. 4), and "Dialogue and Friendship in Society" (chap. 6).

15. See Elizabeth Johnson, *The Quest for the Living God: Mapping Frontiers in the Theology of God* (New York: Continuum, 2007), 90–100, for the role of the church in women's images of God and of themselves in relation to God.

16. By design, Heiding only very briefly addresses the situation of a director who is not Catholic presenting the Exercises to Catholics or to other Christians, but the principles he sets out could serve by analogy in this situation. Erin Cline (2018) develops interpretive strategies to assist a Christian in faithfully presenting the Spiritual Exercises to persons who belong to Hindu (chap. 3), Buddhist (chap. 4), and Confucian-oriented traditions (chap. 5).

Works Cited

Aggeler, Maureen. 1992. "Women's Metaphors for Freedom." *The Way Supplement* 74: 20–29.

Arbuckle, Gerald A. 1993. *Refounding the Church: Dissent for Leadership*. Maryknoll, NY: Orbis Books.

Aschenbrenner, George. 1972. "Consciousness Examen." *Review for Religious* 31 (January): 14–21.

———. 2004. *Stretched for Greater Glory: What to Expect from the Spiritual Exercises*. Chicago: Loyola Press.

Augustine. 1961. *Confessions*. Translated by R. S. Pine-Coffin. New York: Penguin Books.

Barnes, Michael. 1989. "The Body in the Spiritual Exercises of Ignatius of Loyola." *Religion* 19: 263–73.

Barry, William. 1994. *Allowing the Creator to Deal with the Creature*. Mahwah, NJ: Paulist.

———. 2001. *Letting God Come Close: An Approach to the Ignatian Spiritual Exercises*. Chicago: Loyola Press.

Barry, William, and William Connolly. 1982. *The Practice of Spiritual Direction*. New York: Seabury Press.

Bass, Dorothy. 1979. "Their Prodigious Influence: Women, Religion and Reform in Antebellum America." In *Women of Spirit: Female Leadership in the Jewish and Christian Traditions*, edited by Rosemary Ruether and Eleanor McLaughlin, 279–300. New York: Simon and Schuster.

Bedolla, Barbara. 1984. "Presenting the Key Meditations." *The Way Supplement* 49: *The Spiritual Exercises in Daily Life*, 25–32.

Bejan, Adrian, and J. Peder Zane. 2012. *Design in Nature: How the Constructal Law Governs Evolution in Biology, Physics, Technology and Social Organization*. New York: Anchor Books.

Belenky, Mary Field, Blythe McVicker Clinchy, Nancy Rule Goldberger, and Jill Mattuck Tarule. 1986. *Women's Ways of Knowing: The Development of Self, Voice and Mind.* New York: Basic Books.
Bergan, Jacqueline, and S. Marie Schwan. 1985. *Love: A Guide for Prayer.* Winona, MN: St. Mary's Press.
Berry, Thomas, and Brian Swimme. 1992. *The Universe Story: An Autobiography of Planet Earth.* New York: Harper and Row.
Blaisdell, Charmarie J. 1988. "Calvin's and Loyola's Letters to Women: Politics and Spiritual Counsel in the Sixteenth Century." In *Calviniana: Ideas and Influence of John Calvin*, vol. 10, *Sixteenth-Century Essays & Studies*, edited by Robert Schnucher, 235–53. Kirksville, MO: Sixteenth-Century Journal Publishers.
Boyle, Marjorie O'Rourke. 1983. "Angels Black and White: Loyola's Spiritual Discernment in Historical Perspective." *Theological Studies* 44 (June): 241–57.
Brackley, Dean. 2004. *The Call to Discernment in Troubled Times: New Perspectives on the Transformative Wisdom of Ignatius of Loyola.* New York: Crossroad.
Bridges, William. 1980. *Transitions: Making Sense of Life's Changes.* Reading, MA: Addison-Wesley.
Bryant, Christopher. 1984. "Images and the Psyche." *The Way* 24 (April): 83–91.
Buckley, Michael. 1995. "Ecclesial Mysticism in the Spiritual Exercises of Ignatius." *Theological Studies* 56 (September): 441–63.
Buechner, Frederick. 1973. *Wishful Thinking: A Theological ABC.* New York: Harper & Row.
Burke, Kevin, and Eileen Burke-Sullivan. 2009. *The Ignatian Tradition.* Collegeville, MN: Liturgical Press.
Burrows, Ruth. 1980. *Guidelines for Mystical Prayer.* Denville, NJ: Dimension Books.
Capps, Donald. 1984. *Pastoral Care and Hermeneutics.* Philadelphia: Fortress Press.
Carr, Anne. 1988, 1996. *Transforming Grace: Christian Tradition and Women's Experience.* San Francisco: Harper and Row. 2nd ed., New York: Continuum.
Christ, Carol. 1980. *Diving Deep and Surfacing: Women Writers on the Spiritual Quest.* Boston: Beacon Press.
Clancy, Thomas. 1978. *The Conversational Word of God.* St. Louis: Institute of Jesuit Sources.

Works Cited

Clark, Elizabeth A. 1983. *Women in the Early Church*. Wilmington, DE: Michael Glazier.

Clarke, Thomas. 1990. "Ignatian Spirituality and the Protestant Principle." *The Way Supplement* 68 (Summer): 52–61.

Cline, Erin. 2018. *A World on Fire: Sharing the Ignatian Spiritual Exercises with Other Religions*. Washington, DC: Catholic University of America Press.

Colledge, Edmund, and James Walsh, trans. 1983. *Julian of Norwich: Showings*. Classics of Western Spirituality. Mahwah, NJ: Paulist.

Conroy, Maureen. 1995. "Prayer and Life: Experiencing the Fullness of God's Love." *The Way Supplement* 82 (Spring): 15–26.

Correia, Frances, Puleng Matsaneng, and Annemarie Paulin-Campbell. 2016. "The Training of Spiritual Directors in the South African Context." *Spiritus: A Journal of Christian Spirituality* 16 (2a): 39–54.

Cowan, Marian, and John Futrell. 1981. *Companions in Grace: A Handbook for Directors of the Spiritual Exercises of St. Ignatius of Loyola*. Kansas City, MO: Sheed and Ward, 1993. Reprint of *The Spiritual Exercises of St. Ignatius of Loyola: A Handbook for Directors*. Ministry Training Services.

Cusson, Gilles, SJ. 1988. *Biblical Theology and the Spiritual Exercises*. St. Louis: Institute of Jesuit Sources.

Daley, Brian E. 1995. "To Be More Like Christ: The Background and Implications of 'The Three Kinds of Humility.'" *Studies in the Spirituality of Jesuits* 27 (January): 6–39.

de Dalmases, Candido, SJ. 1985. *Ignatius of Loyola, Founder of the Jesuits: His Life and Work*. Translated by Jerome Aixalá, SJ. St. Louis: Institute of Jesuit Sources.

———. 1991. *Francis Borgia: Grande of Spain, Jesuit, Saint*. Translated by Cornelius Michael Buckley, SJ. St. Louis: Institute of Jesuit Sources, 1991.

de Mello, Anthony. 1978. *Sadhana: A Way to God*. St. Louis: Institute of Jesuit Sources.

Demoustier, Adrien. 2002. "Ignatian Contemplation and the Contemplative Way. *The Way Supplement* 103: 16–24.

Dowd, Julia A. 2018. "Gathering the Graces: Women, the Spiritual Exercises, and Jesuit Education." DMin dissertation, Pacific School of Religion.

Dreyer, Elizabeth A. 1989. *Passionate Women: Two Medieval Mystics*. Mahwah, NJ: Paulist.

———. 1996. "Narratives of the Spirit." In *Proceedings of the Fifty-First Annual Convention of the Catholic Theological Society of America*, 45–90. San Diego.

Dyke, Doris Jean. 1991. *Crucified Women*. Toronto: United Church Publishing.

Economic Justice for All: Pastoral Letter on Catholic Social Teaching and the U.S. Economy. 1986. Washington DC: National Conference of Catholic Bishops.

Egan, Harvey. 1978. *Ignatius the Mystic*. Wilmington, DE: Michael Glazier.

Endean, Philip. 2001. "'Applying Such Exercises': Early Jesuit Practice." *Review of Ignatian Spirituality* 32 (3): 41–64.

English, John. 1995. *Spiritual Freedom*. 2nd ed. Chicago: Loyola University Press.

Fabella, Virginia. 1989. "A Common Methodology for Diverse Christologies." In *With Passion and Compassion: Third-World Women Doing Theology*, edited by Virginia Fabella and Mercy Amba Oduyoye, 108–17. Maryknoll, NY: Orbis.

Farganis, Sondra. 1986. *Social Construction of the Feminine Character*. Totowa, NJ: Rowman and Littlefield.

Farley, Margaret A. 1986. *Personal Commitments: Making, Keeping, Changing*. San Francisco: Harper.

Fischer, Kathleen. 1988. *Women at the Well: Feminist Perspectives on Spiritual Direction*. Mahwah, NJ: Paulist.

———. 1989. "The Imagination in Spirituality." *The Way Supplement* 66 (Autumn): 96–105.

Fischer, Kathleen, and Thomas Hart. 1995. *Christian Foundations: An Introduction to Faith in Our Time*. Mahwah, NJ: Paulist.

Flannery, Austin, OP, ed. 1996. *Vatican Council II: Constitutions, Decrees, Declarations*. Northport, NY: Costello Publishing Company.

Fleming, David, SJ. 1978. *The Spiritual Exercises of St. Ignatius: A Literal Translation and a Contemporary Reading*. St. Louis: Institute of Jesuit Sources.

———. 2004. *Like the Lightening: The Dynamics of the Ignatian Exercises*. St. Louis: Institute of Jesuit Sources.

Francis. 2015. *Laudato Si': On Care for Our Common Home*. Huntington, IN: Our Sunday Visitor.

———. 2020. *Fratelli Tutti: On Fraternity and Social Friendship*. Washington DC: U. S. Conference of Catholic Bishops.

Frankl, Viktor. 1959. *Man's Search for Meaning: An Introduction to Logotherapy*. Pocket Book Edition. New York: Simon and Schuster.
Freedman, David. 1983. "Woman, a Power Equal to Man." *Biblical Archeology Review* 9 (January/February): 56–58.
Ganss, George E. 1973. "Thinking with the Church: The Spirit of St. Ignatius's Rules." *The Way Supplement* 20 (Autumn): 72–82.
———, ed. 1991. *Ignatius of Loyola: "Spiritual Exercises" and Selected Works*. Classics of Western Spirituality. Mahwah, NJ: Paulist.
García de Castro Valdés, Jose. 2012. "Las mujeres y los primeros Jesuitas." In *Iguales y diferentes: Interrelación entre mujeres y varones Cristianos a lo largo de la historia*, edited by Fernando Rivas, 219–82. Madrid: San Pablo Publishing.
Gateley, Edwina. 1990. *I Hear a Seed Growing*. Trabuco Canyon, CA: Source Books.
Geger, Barton, SJ. 2018. "Ten Things That St. Ignatius Never Said or Did." *Studies in the Spirituality of Jesuits*. Jesuit Assistancy Seminar 50, no. 1 (Spring).
Gendlin, Eugene. 1981. *Focusing*. 2nd ed. New York: Bantam.
Gilligan, Carol. 1982. *In a Different Voice: Psychological Theory and Women's Development*. Cambridge: Harvard University Press.
Goulding, Gill. 2015. *A Church of Passion and Hope: The Formation of Ecclesial Disposition from Ignatius Loyola to Pope Francis and the New Evangelization*. New York: Bloomsbury.
Grant, Jacquelyn. 1993. "Come to My Help, Lord, for I'm in Trouble: Womanist Jesus and the Mutual Struggle for Liberation." In *Reconstructing the Christ Symbol: Essays in Feminist Christology*, edited by Maryanne Stevens. Mahwah, NJ: Paulist.
Gray, Howard. 1993. "Changing Structures." *The Way Supplement* 76 (Spring): 72–84.
Gula, Richard. 1989. *Reason Informed by Faith: Foundations of Catholic Morality*. Mahwah, NJ: Paulist.
Hart, Ray. 1968. *Unfinished Man and the Imagination*. New York: Herder and Herder.
Heiding, Fredrik. 2012. *Ignatian Spirituality at Ecclesial Frontiers*. Oxford: University of Oxford Faculty of Theology.
Herrera, Marina. 1993. "Who Do You Say Jesus Is? Christological Reflections from a Hispanic Woman's Perspective." In *Reconstructing the Christ Symbol: Essays in Feminist Christology*, edited by Maryanne Stevens. Mahwah, NJ: Paulist.

Houdek, Frank. 1995. "The Limitation of Ignatian Prayer." *The Way Supplement* 82 (Spring): 26–34.
Ignatius of Loyola. 1970. *The Constitutions of the Society of Jesus*. Translated by George Ganss. St. Louis: The Institute of Jesuit Sources.
———. 1991a. "The Autobiography." In *Ignatius of Loyola: Spiritual Exercises and Selected Works*, translated by Parmananda R. Divarkar, edited by George Ganss, 66–111. Mahwah, NJ: Paulist.
———. 1991b. "The Spiritual Exercises." In *Ignatius of Loyola: Spiritual Exercises and Selected Works*, edited and translated by George Ganss, 113–214. Mahwah, NJ: Paulist.
Ivens, Michael. 1983. "The Eighteenth Annotation and the Early Directories. *The Way Supplement* 46 (Spring): 3–10.
Jack, Dana Crowley. 1991. *Silencing the Self: Women and Depression*. New York: HarperCollins.
Jalics, Franz. 2002. "The Contemplative Phase of the Ignatian Exercises." *The Way Supplement* 103: 25–42.
Jesudasan, Ignatius. 2004. "Angels of Light and Darkness." *The Way* 43 (3): 71–79.
"Jesuits and the Situation of Women." 1995. 34th General Congregation, Rome. *Origins* 24 (April 13): 740–42.
Johnson, Elizabeth A. 1991. "The Maleness of Christ." In *The Special Nature of Women?* edited by Anne Carr and Elisabeth Schüssler Fiorenza, 108–16. Philadelphia: Trinity Press International.
———. 1992. *She Who Is: The Mystery of God in Feminist Theological Discourse*. New York: Crossroad.
———. 1993. *Women, Earth, and Creator Spirit*. Mahwah, NJ: Paulist.
———. 1996. "Turn to the Heavens and the Earth: Retrieval of the Cosmos in Theology." In *Proceedings of the Fifty-First Annual Convention of the Catholic Theological Society of America*, 11–14. San Diego.
———. 2007. *Quest for the Living God: Mapping Frontiers in the Theology of God*. New York: Continuum.
———. 2014. *Ask the Beasts: Darwin and the God of Love*. New York: Bloomsbury.
———. 2018. *Creation and the Cross: The Mercy of God for a Planet in Peril*. Maryknoll, NY: Orbis Books.
Johnston, William. 1995. *Mystical Theology: The Science of Love*. London: Harper Collins.

Jordan, Judith, Alexandra Kaplan, Jean Baker Miller, Irene Stiver, and Janet L Surrey. 1991. *Women's Growth in Connection: Writings from the Stone Center*. New York: Guilford Press.

Kaschak, Ellyn. 1992. *Engendered Lives: A New Psychology of Women's Experience*. New York: Basic Books.

Kavanaugh, Kieran, and Otillo Rodriguez, trans. 1976. *The Collected Works of St. Teresa of Avila*. Washington, DC: Institute of Carmelite Studies.

Kelly, Justin. 1991. *Absence into Presence: A Theology of Imagination*. Warren Lecture Series 16. University of Tulsa, September 8, 12–16.

Kim, Grace, and Susan Shaw. 2018. *Intersectional Theology: An Introductory Guide*. Minneapolis: Fortress Press.

King, Ursula. 1993. *Women and Spirituality: Voices of Protest and Promise*. 2nd ed. University Park: Pennsylvania State University Press.

Kolvenbach, Peter-Hans. 2004. "The Rules for Thinking, Judging, Feeling in the Post-conciliar Church." Rome, *CIS*, March 22.

LaCugna, Catherine. 1991. *God for Us*. San Francisco: Harper.

Levine, Amy-Jill. 1992. "Matthew." In *The Women's Bible Commentary*, edited by Carol A. Newsom and Sharon H. Ringe, 261. Louisville, KY: Westminster John Knox.

Liebert, Elizabeth. 1992. *Changing Life Patterns: Adult Development in Spiritual Direction*. Mahwah, NJ: Paulist.

———. 1996. "Coming Home to Themselves: Spiritual Care of Women." In *Through the Eyes of Women: Insights for Pastoral Care*, edited by Jeanne Stevenson Moessner, 257–84. Minneapolis: Fortress.

———. 2008. *The Way of Discernment: Spiritual Practices for Decision Making*. Louisville, KY: Westminster John Knox.

———. 2015. *The Soul of Discernment: A Spiritual Practice for Communities and Institutions*. Louisville: Westminster John Knox.

———. 2019a. "Interior Motions from a Female Perspective." Paper delivered at the Symposium on Psychology and the Spiritual Exercises, Loyola, Spain and published in *Sentir y conocer: Psycología y Ejercicios Espirituales*, ed. José García de Castro and Maria Prieto Ursúa, 539–56. Madrid: Mensajero/Sal Terrae/Comillas University, Manresa Collection, n. 80, May/June 2021. English language version published as "Interior Motions from a Female Perspective: Their Role in Guiding the Spiritual Exercises." *Studies in Spirituality* 31 (2021): 71–84.

———. 2019b. "Memory as an Entry Point for Discernment." Workshop presented to the Atlantic Association of Spiritual Exercises Apostolate, September 29.

Lonsdale, David. 1990. *Eyes to See, Ears to Hear: An Introduction to Ignatian Spirituality*. Chicago: Loyola University Press.

———. 1992. *Listening to the Music of the Spirit: The Art of Discernment*. Notre Dame, IN: Ave Maria Press.

Mansfield, Dermot. 2008. "Spiritual Accompaniment and Discernment. *The Way* 47, nos. 1–2 (January–April): 155–64.

Marsh, Robert. 2006. "Id quod volo: The Erotic Grace of the Second Week." *The Way* 45, no. 4 (October): 7–19.

May, Gerald. 1982a. *Care of Mind, Care of Spirit: A Psychiatrist Explores Spiritual Direction*. San Francisco: Harper and Row.

———. 1982b. *Will and Spirit: A Contemplative Psychology*. San Francisco: Harper and Row.

———. 1988. *Addiction and Grace*. San Francisco: Harper and Row.

McClain, Lisa. 2015. "On a Mission: Priests, Jesuits, 'Jesuitesses,' and Catholic Missionary Efforts in Tudor-Stuart England." In *The Catholic Historical Review* 101, no. 3 (Summer): 437–62.

McDermott, Brian. 2018. "Spiritual Consolation and Its Role in the Second Time of Election." *Studies in the Spirituality of Jesuits* 50, no. 4 (Winter).

McFague, Sallie. 1993. *The Body of God: An Ecological Theology*. Minneapolis: Fortress Press.

McGrath, Thomas. 1993. "The Place of Desires in the Ignatian Exercises." *The Way Supplement* 76 (Spring): 25–31.

Meissner, W. W. 1992. *Ignatius of Loyola: The Psychology of a Saint*. New Haven, CT: Yale University Press.

Merchant, Carolyn. 1983. *The Death of Nature: Women, Ecology, and the Scientific Revolution*. San Francisco: Harper.

Miles, Margaret. 1981. *Fullness of Life: Historical Foundations for a New Asceticism*. Philadelphia: Westminster.

———. 1992. *Desire and Delight: A New Reading of Augustine's Confessions*. New York: Crossroad.

Morton, Nelle. 1985. *The Journey Is Home*. Boston: Beacon Press.

Muldoon, Tim. 2004. *The Ignatian Workout: Daily Spiritual Exercises for a Healthy Faith*. Chicago: Loyola Press, 2004.

Nelson, James. 1983. *Between Two Gardens: Reflections on Sexuality and Religious Experience*. New York: Pilgrim Press.

Works Cited

Neuger, Christie Cozad. 1991. "Women's Depression: Lives at Risk." In *Women in Travail and Transition: A New Pastoral Care*, edited by Maxine Glaz and Jeanne Stevenson Moessner, 146–61. Minneapolis: Fortress Press.

———. 1993. "A Feminist Perspective on Pastoral Counseling." In *Clinical Handbook of Pastoral Counseling*, edited by Robert J. Wicks and Richard D. Parsons, vol. 2, 195–209. Mahwah, NJ: Paulist.

Noffke, Suzanne, ed. and trans. 1980. *Catherine of Siena: The Dialogue*. Classics of Western Spirituality. Mahwah, NJ: Paulist.

Norris, Kathleen. 1993. *Dakota: A Spiritual Geography*. New York: Houghton-Mifflin.

O'Connell, Timothy E. 1990. *Principles for a Catholic Morality*. San Francisco: HarperCollins.

Oduyoye, Mercy Amba. 2001. *Introducing African Women's Theology*. Sheffield Academic Press.

O'Malley, John. 1991. "Early Jesuit Spirituality: Spain and Italy." In *Christian Spirituality: Post-Reformation and Modern*, edited by Louis Dupré and Don E. Saliers, 3–27. New York: Crossroad.

———. *The First Jesuits*. 1993. Cambridge, MA: Harvard University Press.

O'Murchu, Diarmuid. 1997. *Quantum Theology: Spiritual Implications of the New Physics*. New York: Crossroad.

Orchard, Gillian, ed. 1985. *Till God Will: Mary Ward through Her Writings*. London: Darton, Longman and Todd.

Orobator, Agbonkhianmeghe. 2008. *Theology Brewed in an African Pot*. Maryknoll, NY: Orbis Books.

Orsy, Ladislas. 1975. "On Being One with the Church Today." *Studies in the Spirituality of Jesuits* 8 (January): 21–41.

Padberg, John W. 1993. "Ignatius, the Popes, and Realistic Reverence." *Studies in the Spirituality of Jesuits* 25 (May): 2–38.

Palmer, Martin E., trans. and ed. 1996. *On Giving the Spiritual Exercises: The Early Jesuit Manuscript Directories and the Official Directory of 1599*. St. Louis: Institute of Jesuit Sources.

Paulin-Campbell, Annemarie. 2008. "The Impact of the Imaginal and Dialogical (Relational) Processes in the Spiritual Exercises on Image of Self and Image of God in Women Making the Nineteenth Annotation Retreat." PhD dissertation, University of KwaZulu-Natal, South Africa.

———. 2021. "Ecumenical Engagement with the Spiritual Exercises in South Africa." In *Catholics and Protestants in Africa*, edited by Peter Knox, 229–56. Nairobi: Jesuit Historical Institute in Africa.

Pelikan, Jaroslav. 1985. *Jesus through the Centuries: His Place in the History of Culture*. New Haven, CT: Yale University Press.

Peters, William A. M. 1967. *The Spiritual Exercises of St. Ignatius: Exposition and Interpretation*. Jersey City, NJ: Program to Adapt the Spiritual Exercises.

Piercy, Marge. 1996. *City of Darkness, City of Light*. New York: Fawcett.

Plaskow, Judith. 1980. *Sex, Sin and Grace*. Lanham, MD: University Press of America.

Potter Engel, Mary. 1990. "Evil, Sin and Violation of the Vulnerable." In *Lift Every Voice: Constructing Christian Theologies from the Underside*, edited by Susan Brooks Thistlethwaite and Mary Potter Engel, 152–64. San Francisco: Harper and Row.

Rahner, Hugo. 1968a. *Ignatius the Theologian*. Translated by Michael Barry. New York: Herder and Herder.

———. 1968b. *Saint Ignatius Loyola: Letters to Women*. Translated by Kathleen Pond and S. A. H. Weetman. Freiburg: Herder KG; New York: Herder and Herder, 1960.

Rahner, Karl. 1979a. "The Doctrine of the 'Spiritual Senses' in the Middle Ages." In *The Experience of the Spirit: Source of Theology*. Vol. 16 of *Theological Investigations*, 104–34. Translated by David Moreland. New York: Crossroad/Seabury.

———. 1979b. "The 'Spiritual Senses' according to Origen." In *The Experience of the Spirit: Source of Theology*. Vol. 16 of *Theological Investigations*, 81–103. Translated by David Moreland. New York: Crossroad/Seabury.

———. 1986. *The Practice of Faith*. New York: Crossroad.

Ranft, Patricia. 1996. *Women and the Religious Life in Premodern Europe*. New York: St. Martin's Press.

Roszak, Theodore. 1992. *The Voice of the Earth*. New York: Simon and Schuster.

Ruether, Rosemary Radford. 1983. *Sexism and God-talk: Toward a Feminist Theology*. Boston: Beacon Press.

———. 1990. *To Change the World: Christology and Cultural Criticism*, 2nd ed. New York: Crossroad.

Ruffing, Janet. 1995. "You Fill Up My Senses." *The Way* 35 (April): 101–10.

Works Cited

Saiving, Valerie. 1992. "The Human Situation: A Feminine View." In *WomanSpirit Rising: A Feminist Reader in Religion*, edited by Carol P. Christ and Judith Plaskow, 25–42. 2nd ed. San Francisco: Harper.

Schineller, Peter. 2005. "Seeking, Finding and Serving God in All Things: The Fourth Week and the Contemplation to Attain Love." In *Dynamics of the Spiritual Exercises: African Perspectives*, edited by Paul Christian Kiti, 165–73. Nairobi: Paulines Publications Africa.

Schneiders, Sandra. 1991a. *Beyond Patching: Faith and Feminism in the Catholic Church*. Mahwah, NJ: Paulist.

———. 1991b. *The Revelatory Text: Interpreting the New Testament as Sacred Scripture*. San Francisco: Harper, 1991.

Schüssler Fiorenza, Elisabeth. 1984. *Bread Not Stone: The Challenge of Feminist Biblical Interpretation*. Boston: Beacon Press.

Segarra Pijuan, Joan. 1992. *Manresa and Saint Ignatius of Loyola*. Manresa: Ajuntament de Manresa.

Sheldrake, Philip. 1983. "The Principle and Foundation and Images of God." *The Way Supplement* 48 (Autumn): 90–96.

———. 1987. *Images of Holiness*. Notre Dame, IN: Ave Maria Press.

Simmonds, Gemma. 2008. "Women Jesuits?" In *The Cambridge Companion to the Jesuits*, edited by Thomas Worcester, 120–33. Cambridge: Cambridge University Press.

———. 2010. "Mary Ward: Then and Now." *Thinking Faith: The Online Journal of the Jesuits in Britain*. January 22. https://thinkingfaith.org/articles/20100122_1.htm.

———. 2018. "Making Sense of the Application of the Senses." *Thinking Faith: The Online Journal of the Jesuits in Britain*. March 7. https://thinkingfaith.org/articles/making-sense-application-senses.

Sisters of Providence. 1990. *The Love of Christ Impels Us: Providence Retreat in Everyday Life*. Spokane, WA: Sisters of Providence Provincial Administration.

Standaert, Nicolas. 2014. "What Ignatius Did Not Know about Making Decisions." *The Way* 53 (3): 32–55.

Steinke, Johannes Maria. 2013. "The Single Day of the First Week Exercises." *The Way* 49, no. 3 (July): 23–44.

Suchocki, Marjorie Hewitt. 1995. *The Fall to Violence: Original Sin in Relational Theology*. New York: Continuum.

Swimme, Brian. 1996. *The Hidden Heart of the Cosmos*. Maryknoll, NY: Orbis.

Tellechea Idígoras, José Ignacio. 1994. *Ignatius of Loyola: The Pilgrim Saint*. Translated by Cornelius Buckley. Chicago: Loyola University Press.

Teresa of Avila. 1976. "The Book of Her Life." In *The Collected Works of St. Teresa of Avila*, vol. 1:54–365. Translated by Kieran Kavanaugh and Otilio Rodriguez. Washington, DC: ICS Publications.

Teresa of Jesus, Saint. 1950. "Conceptions of the Love of God." In *The Complete Works*, vol. 2. Edited and translated by E. Allison Peers. New York: Sheed and Ward.

Tetlow, Joseph A. 1989. "The Fundamentum." *Studies in the Spirituality of Jesuits* 21 (September).

Thibodeaux, Mark E. 2015. *Reimagining the Ignatian Examen: Fresh Ways to Pray from Your Day*. Chicago: Loyola Press.

———. 2020. *Discernment of Spirits for Spiritual Direction and Pastoral Care: Going Deeper*. Chicago: Loyola Press.

Tillich, Paul. 1957. *The Protestant Era*. Abridged edition. Chicago: University of Chicago Press.

Toner, Jules. 1982. *A Commentary on Saint Ignatius's Rules for the Discernment of Spirits: A Guide to the Principles and Practice*. St. Louis: Institute of Jesuit Sources.

———. 1991. *Discerning God's Will: Ignatius of Loyola's Teaching on Christian Decision Making*. St. Louis: Institute of Jesuit Sources.

Turner, Alice K. 1993. *The History of Hell*. New York: Harcourt Brace.

Ulanov, Ann, and Barry Ulanov. 1982. *Primary Speech: A Psychology of Prayer*. Atlanta: John Knox Press.

Ursúa, Maria Prieto, 2020. "Feminine Psychological and Spiritual Clues to the Spiritual Exercises." *The Way* 59, no. 2 (January): 90–102.

Veale, Joseph. 1995. "Manifold Gifts." *The Way Supplement* 82 (Spring): 44–53.

Veltri, John. 1998. *Orientations*. Vol. 2: part B. Guelph, ON: Loyola House.

Wildiers, N. Max. 1982. *The Theologian and His Universe: Theology and Cosmology from the Middle Ages to the Present*. New York: Seabury.

Wink, Walter. 1998. *The Powers That Be: Theology for a New Millennium*. New York: Doubleday.

Young, William J., ed. and trans. 1959. *Letters of Ignatius of Loyola*. Chicago: Loyola University Press.

Zohar, Danah. 1990. *The Quantum Self: Human Nature and Consciousness Defined by the New Physics*. New York: Quill/William Morrow.

Author Index

Aggeler, M., 325n8, 341
Anderson, S., 398n8
Arbuckle, G., 270, 341
Aschenbrenner, G., 7, 92, 99, 167, 175, 187, 296n3, 316n6, 330n10, 330n1, 334n1, 341
Ashley, M., 295n3

Barnes, M., 98, 341
Barrow, J., 311n8
Barry, M., 350
Barry, W., 73, 96, 106, 296n3, 305n4, 330n1, 331n1, 341
Bass, D., 269, 341
Bedolla, B., 159, 326n11, 341
Begheyn, P., 293n1
Bejan, A., 78, 310n4, 311n9, 341
Belenky, M. F., 17, 314n20, 342
Benitz, J., 323n20
Bennett, W. J., 326n10
Bergan, J., 89, 293n1, 314n2, 342
Berry, T., 78, 311n6, 311n8, 342
Berry, W., 79
Bertotti, B., 311n5
Bingemer, M. C., 328n5
Birch, C., 312n9
Blaisdell, C. J., 28, 342
Bogart, K., 293n1

Boryczka, J., 303n6
Bourgeault, C., 328n2
Boyajian, J., 309n23
Boyle, M. O., 259, 262, 342
Brackley, D., 240, 330n1, 334n3, 342
Bridges, W., 226, 342
Broderick, J., 301n1
Brondos, D., 335n4
Brou, A., 317n7
Brown, R. E., 327n1, 328n5
Bruteau, B., 311n 5, 311n8
Bryant, C., 100, 342
Buckley, M., 256, 265, 266, 329n7, 339n4, 342
Buechner, F., 106, 342
Burke, K., 303n11, 342
Burke, T., 314n2
Burke-Sullivan, E., 303n11, 342
Burrows, R., 122, 342
Bynum, C. W., 325n5

Campbell, P., 317n11
Capps, D., 11, 342
Capra, F., 311n9
Caprio, B., 310n28
Caraman, P., 301n1

Carr, A., 15, 87, 136, 179, 294n1, 297n1, 312n15, 321n9, 324n4, 342, 346
Carroll, B., 302n3
Chadwick, G., 298n8
Chappell, C., 308n18
Chavoshian, A., 296n4
Chester, B., 309n23
Christ, C., 5, 6, 342, 351
Clancy, T., 46, 342
Clark, E. A., 140, 181, 343
Clarke, T., 5, 261, 343
Clinchy, B., 314n20, 342
Cline, E., xxii, xxiii, 338n1, 340n16, 343
Coles, R., 300n19
Colledge, E., 134, 155, 343
Collins, M., 321n5
Conn, J. W., 297n5, 323n19, 332n8
Conn, W. E., 323n19
Connolly, W., 96, 341
Conroy, M., 198, 343
Conwell, J., 314n2
Cook, J., 302n3
Cook-Greuter, S., 221, 334
Cooper-White, P., 309n23
Corella, J., 331n1, 339n6
Correia, F., 298n9, 305n3, 343
Cowan, M., 262, 263, 264, 293n1, 343
Cusson, G., 71, 72, 133, 176, 343

Daley, B. E., 168, 343
Damasio, A., 336n12
Davies, P., 312n9
Dawson, R., 331n1
de Dalmases, C., 27, 28, 31, 301n1, 303n7, 320n3, 343

de Guibert, J., 314n2
de Mello, A., 101, 315n2, 343
Demoustier, A., 96, 343
De Wohl, L., 301n1
Dillard, A., 312n12
Dirmeier, U., 313n17
Dirvin, J., 300n19
Divarkar, P., 294n2, 346
Donfried, K. P., 328n5
Donoghue, D., 305n4
Dowd, J., xx, xxi, 302n6, 328n4, 343
Dowd, M., 311n8
Dreitcer, A., 297n3
Dreyer, E. A., 45, 303n6, 306n6, 343
Dunne, T., 316n4
Dyckman, K. M., v, xix
Dyke, D. J., 179, 344

Edwards, T., 332n8
Egan, H., 119, 301n1, 344
Ellacurria, I., 295n3, 296n3, 299n9
Ellsberg, R., 327n12
Endean, P., 294n2, 295n3, 298n7, 317n7, 344
Endres, J., 323n20
English, J., 201, 310n3, 344
Erikson, E., 221
Evans, L. M., 298n8

Fabella, V., 153, 344
Fabri, W., 317n12
Faludi, S., 300n16
Farganis, S., 12, 49, 344
Farley, M., 247, 248, 249, 344
Farnham, S., 337n14
Ferguson, K., 312n9

Author Index

Fischer, K., 104, 110, 133, 210, 219, 262, 317n8, 319n19, 331n3, 344
FitzGerald, C., 332n8
Fitzmyer, J. A., 328n5
Flannery, A., 234, 344
Fleming, D., 98, 155, 156, 159, 198, 234, 296n3, 316n6, 329n6, 330n1, 344
Flinders, C. L., 314n21
Fonow, M. M., 302n3
Fortune, M., 309n23
Fowler, J., 221, 333n12
Francis, Pope, 50, 81, 82, 117, 273, 300n17, 312nn15–16, 328nn2–3, 340n14, 344
Frankl, V., 248, 345
Fraser, A., 322n15
Freedman, D., 139, 345
French, H., 322n14
Fullam, L., 294n1, 303n8
Futrell, J., 262, 263, 264, 293, 343

Gallagher, T., 315n2, 316n6, 331n1
Ganss, G. E., xvi, 26, 43, 45, 70, 71, 81, 92, 93, 118, 163, 165, 166, 169, 232, 238, 257, 259, 294n4, 305n1, 307n14, 309n25, 339nn4–5, 345, 346
García de Castro Valdés, J., 300n18, 302n6, 345, 347
Garvin, M., v, xix
Gateley, E., 158, 345
Gebara, I., 328n5
Geger, B., 305n4, 345
Gendlin, E., 253, 317n11, 337n15, 345
Gill, J. P., 337n14
Gilleman, G., 326n10

Gilligan, C., 17, 221, 249, 314n20, 334n12, 345
Glaz, M., 301n22, 349
Goldberger, N., 314n20, 342
Goulding, G., 262, 264, 338n3, 339n6, 345
Graef, H., 328n5
Graff, A. O., 323n19
Grant, J., 153, 345
Gray, H., 55, 308n17, 320n2, 345
Green, T., 314n2
Guillén A., 331n1
Gula, R., 242, 345

Haight, R., 296n3, 310n3, 325n5
Hamm, D., 316n4
Hannah, B., 317n10
Hansen, M., 296n3, 308n19, 315n2, 316n6
Hart, R., 99, 345
Hart, T., 133, 344
Hawkins, J., 297n4
Hedberg, T., 310n28
Heiding, F., 266, 268, 272, 273, 340n16, 345
Hessel-Robinson, T., 311n5
Himes, K., 312n11
Himes, M., 312n11
Holder, A., 295n3
Hopkins, G. M., 79, 312n12
Horton, A. L., 309n23
Houdek, F., 319n25
Huelsman, R., 315n2
Huggett, J., 298n8

Iglesias, I., 331n1
Intercommunity Peace and Justice Center, 327n3

Ivens, M., 9, 298n8, 305n4, 310n3, 346
Iyengar, S., 336n10

Jack, D. C., 227, 301n22, 313n18, 346
Jalics, F., 114, 116, 117, 314n1, 329n8, 346
Jegen, C. F., 328n5
Jensen, E., 323n17
Jesudasan, I., 211, 331nn1–2, 346
John Paul II, Pope, 300n19
Johnson, E. A., 15, 50, 76, 78, 152, 183, 184, 185, 297n1, 300n17, 312n10, 312n15, 324n3, 327n2, 327n12, 328nn4–5, 329n5, 340n15, 346
Johnson, R., 317n10
Johnston, W., 104, 346
Johnstone, B. V., 321n5
Jordan, J., 17, 301n20, 347
Jung, C., 100

Kaschak, E., 12, 13, 347
Kavanaugh, K., 166, 347
Kegan, R., 221, 334n12
Keightley, G. M. 323n19
Kelly, Joan, 301n3, 302n3
Kelly, Justin, 101, 347
Kim, G., xxi, 347
King, U., 299n12
Kiti, P., 296n3, 351
Kolvenbach, P., 265, 347
Komonchak, J., 321n5
Kushner, T., 322n14

Lacouture, J., 300n18, 303n7
LaCugna, C. M., 199, 200, 327n2, 347

Lambert, W., 296n3
Lane, D., 321n5
Larkin, E. E., 318n15
Lee, J., 297n4
Leehan, J., 309n23
Lehrer, J, 337n13
Lerner, G., 302n3, 311n6
Levine, A., 180, 347
Levinson, M., 301n21
Lewis, C. S., 211
Liebert, E., xx, xxi, 7, 11, 44, 83, 223, 227, 239, 295n3, 306n8, 318n16, 323n20, 331n6, 336n9, 347
Link, M., 315n2
Linn, D., 318n14
Linn, M., 318n14
Linn, S. F., 318n14
Locke, H. G., 319n24
Loevinger, J., 334n12
Lonsdale, D., 214, 267, 268, 348

Mahan, B., 297n1
Manney, J., 316n6
Mansfield, D., 233, 319n20, 348
Marcoullier, D., 339n10
Marietti, xvi
Marsh R., 150, 177, 331n1, 348
Maryks, R., 303n6
Matsaneng, P., 298n9, 343
Matt, D., 311n8
May, G., 165, 211, 332n8, 348
McBrien, R., 328n5
McClain, L., 303n11, 348
McCormick, W., 306n10
McDermott, B., 235, 238. 335n6, 348
McEvoy, T., 311n7

Author Index

McFague, S., 75, 79, 312n15, 326n9, 348
McGann, M., 312n11
McGrath, T., 45, 61, 305n4, 348
McIntosh, P., 321n6
McLaughlin, E., 341
McLaughlin, M., 296n3, 315n2
McLean, T., 337n14
McMahon, E., 317n11
McNamara, R., 311n5
McReynolds, S. A., 323n19
Mdluli, M., 299n9
Meadow, M. J., 332n8
Meissner, W. W., 31, 300n18, 301n1, 303n7, 348
Merchant, C., 75, 348
Miles, M., 13, 59, 308n15, 348
Miller, J. B., 279n5, 300n20, 347
Moessner, J. S., 301n22, 347, 349
Morton, N., 80, 348
Muldoon, T., 93, 310n3, 313n19, 315n2, 320n4, 348

Nelson, J., 86, 348
Neuger, C. C., 224, 227, 301n22, 349
Newman, J. H., 100
Newsom, C. A., 298n6, 347
Noffke, S., 163, 349
Norris, K., 59, 349

O'Brien, K., 295n3, 310n3
O'Carroll, M., 329n5
O'Connell, T. E., 262, 349
Oduyoye, M., 153, 344, 349
O'Leary, B., 330n1
Oliver, M., 312n12
O'Mahony, G., 322n13, 331n1

O'Malley, J., 24, 30, 53, 262, 339n8, 349
O'Murchu, D., 79, 349
Orchard, G., 34, 35, 349
Orchard, H. 310n3
Orobator, A, vii, xi, 142, 323n18, 349
Orsy, L., 271, 272, 330n1, 349

Padberg, J. W., 258, 264, 340n12, 349
Paintner, C., 307n13
Palmer, M. E., 98, 235, 236, 306n9, 307n13, 317n7, 349
Palmer, P., 337n14
Park, J. E., 296n4
Paulin-Campbell, A., iii, iv, xx, 20, 162, 194, 195, 298n9, 303n6, 343, 349
Paulsell, S., 309n26
Peck, B., 295n3
Pelikan, J., 157, 325n7, 350
Pellauer, M. D., 309n23
Perkins, P., 327n2
Peters, W. A. M., 94, 119, 305n5, 310n27, 314n2, 350
Petrino, E., 303n6
Phillips, C., 312n12
Phillips, J. A., 322n16
Piercy, M., 163, 350
Pieris, A., 298n8
Pike, N., 319n21
Plaskow, J., 136, 350, 351
Pond, K., 294n2, 350
Potter Engel, M., 136, 137, 321n10, 350
Presbyterian Church (USA), 319n24
Proust, M., 322n14

Pungente, J., 296n3
Purcell, M., 293n1, 301n1

Quintos, L., 298n8

Rahner, H., 23, 25, 26, 29, 31, 32, 33, 34, 112, 294n2, 301nn1–2, 317n7, 350
Rahner, K., 112, 121, 122, 335n6, 350
Rakoczy, S., 298n8
Ranft, P., 350
Rasmussen, L. L., 312n10
Restrepo, D., 307n12
Reumann, J., 328n5
Rhodes, E., 303n6
Richesin, L. D., 327n1
Ricoeur, P., 10
Riley, M. S., 319n22
Ringe, S. H., 298n6, 347
Rodriguez, O., 166, 347, 352
Roemer, J. A., 317n13
Rohr, R., 312n10
Roszak, T., 350
Rotsaert, M., 331n1, 331n4
Ruether, R. R., 15, 75, 178, 312n13, 312n15, 324n2, 325n4, 329n5, 341, 350
Ruffing, J., 109, 319n21, 350
Russell, R., 311n5, 312n9
Ryan, T., 319n17

Saiving, V., 136, 321n8, 351
Sassani, J., 296n3, 315n2
Savary, L., 296n3
Schemel, G., 315n2
Schineller, P., 197, 351
Schneiders, S., 10, 299nn10–11, 351
Schökel, L. A., 323n20

Schüssler Fiorenza, E., 14, 180, 297n1, 346, 351
Schutte, D., 296n3
Schwan, M., 89, 293n1, 314n2, 342
Schwartz, B., 336n11
Scott, J. W., 302n3
Segarra Pijuan, J., 25, 302n4, 351
Shaw, S., xxi, 347
Sheldrake, P., 87, 107, 305n4, 306nn6–7, 318n16, 319nn19–20, 351
Silf, M., 315n2
Silk, J., 311n8
Simmonds, G., 35, 98, 109, 303nn10–11, 351
Sisters of Providence, 218, 332n10, 333n11, 335n6, 336n9, 351
Skinnider, M., 298n8
Snyder, M. H., 325n4
Sosa, A., 299n13, 304n12
Spiritual Directors International, 294n1, 310n28
Standaert, N., 240, 245, 246, 335nn7–8, 336nn10–12, 351
Steindl-Rast, D., 311n9
Steinke, J., 129, 351
Stiver, I., 347
Suchocki, M., 134, 135, 183, 351
Surrey, J. L., 301n20, 347
Swimme, B., 77, 78, 311nn5–6, 311n8, 342, 351

Tarule, J., 314n20, 342
Tellechea Idígoras, J. I., 23, 26, 27, 32, 258, 301n1, 302n5, 352
Tetlow, E., 293n1
Tetlow, J., 71, 72, 73, 310n3, 313n19, 315n2, 316n5, 330n1, 334n2, 340n11, 352

Author Index

Thibodeaux, M., 93, 209, 215, 330n1, 336n9, 352
Thió, S., 302n6
Tillich, P., 260, 352
Tomlinson, I., 309n20, 329n7, 329n9
Toner, J., 213, 214, 215, 219, 231, 238, 332nn8–9, 334n13, 335n6, 352
Traub, G., 331n1, 336n9
Turner, A. K., 140, 352

Ugwuni, C., 298n9
Ulanov, A., 105, 317n8, 352
Ulanov, B., 105, 317n8, 352
Ursúa, M., 45, 54, 58, 301n21, 303n6, 305n2, 308n16, 347, 352

Vanek, E. A., 317n11
Vaney, N., 296n3, 312n14
Vatican Council II, 321n7, 339n7
Veale, J., 90, 306n7, 319n23, 319n25, 352
Veltri, J., 158, 326n8, 352

Wakefield, J., 395n3
Walker, A., 316n6
Walsh, J., 134, 155, 343
Walsh, M., 319n18
Warner, L., 295n3, 320n4, 323n17
Warner, M., 329n5
Weber, A., 308n15
Weetman, S. A. H., 294n2, 350
Wickham, J., 319n19
Wildiers, N. M., 75, 352
Williams, M., 296n3
Williamson, J. A., 309n23
Wink, W., 212, 322n14, 331n5, 352
Winter, M. T., 322n12
Wolter, H., 325n6
Worcester, T., 295n3, 304n11
Wulf, F., 325n6, 335n6

Young, W. J., 112, 294n2, 308n20, 352

Zane, P., 78, 310n4, 311n9, 341
Zohar, D., 74, 352

www.ingramcontent.com/pod-product-compliance
Lightning Source LLC
Chambersburg PA
CBHW060938230426
43665CB00015B/1991